JN329753

ModalP and Subjunctive Present

Hituzi Linguistics in English

No. 1 Lexical Borrowing and its Impact on English   Makimi Kimura-Kano
No. 2 From a Subordinate Clause to an Independent Clause
                                                      Yuko Higashiizumi
No. 3 ModalP and Subjunctive Present   Tadao Nomura

Hituzi Linguistics in English No. 3

ModalP and Subjunctive Present

Tadao Nomura

Hituzi Syobo Publishing

Copyright © Tadao Nomura 2006
First published 2006

Author: Tadao Nomura

All rights reserved. Except for the quotation of short passages for the purposes of criticism and review, no part of this publication may be reduced, stored in a retrieval system, or transmitted in any form or by any means, electronic, mechanical, photocopying, recording or otherwise, without the written prior permission of the publisher.
In case of photocopying and electronic copying and retrieval from network personally, permission will be given on receipts of payment and making inquiries. For details please contact us through e-mail. Our e-mail address is given below.

Book Design © Hirokazu Mukai (glyph)

Hituzi Syobo Publishing
5-21-5 Koishikawa Bunkyo-ku Tokyo, Japan 112-0002

phone +81-3-5684-6871 fax +81-3-5684-6872
e-mail: toiawase@hituzi.co.jp
http://www.hituzi.co.jp/
postal transfer 00120-8-142852

ISBN4-89476-267-6
Printed in Japan

Acknowledgements

This book is a revised version of my doctoral dissertation, submitted to Aoyama Gakuin University in September 2004 and accepted in March 2005. I am deeply indebted to the four members of my committee, Minoji Akimoto, Shigeo Tonoike, Kazuyoshi Yamanouchi, and Shuji Chiba, for their numerous informative comments.

My foremost and deepest gratitude should go to Minoji Akimoto, chairman of the committee, who has guided me since I entered the graduate course of Aoyama Gakuin University in 1996. He has been appointed head of the English Department of Aoyama several times, which is very time consuming, but he has always taught me both directly and indirectly, and at the same time he himself has been constantly publishing books and papers every year. He often says that the most important education for graduate course students is for the teachers themselves to write as many papers as possible; he actually did so for years despite his hard public service. His research is to establish linguistic theory based not on abstract discussions but on empirical data. In that sense he is both a linguist and a philologist. I believe that I have followed his footsteps.

I would also like to express my deep appreciation to Shigeo Tonoike. We have known each other about ten years; I incidentally attended his class at Gakushuin University in 1994, where he came as a part-time teacher from Meiji Gakuin University, but never did I, nor probably he, dream that I would continue to attend his classes at Gakushuin, Meiji Gakuin, Aoyama Gakuin, or join his personal study group since then up to now, and that he would become Professor at Aoyama Gakuin University and one of my supervisors. His keen observations and surprising ideas helped me many times. And I went drinking with him many times and have had many intense arguments with him about linguistics, education, or whatever topics that would come up, from which I learned much.

Kazuyoshi Yamanouchi, also a member of the committee, and Kazuo Nakazawa encouraged and helped me with writing this thesis as well. Professor

Yamanouchi came to Aoyama from Tokyo Metropolitan University in 2001 and since then he has always thought about what Aoyama ought to be in the future. When I had hard time in writing this thesis, he told me to write a dissertation not so much for myself but for my followers in the graduate course of Aoyama. Professor Nakazawa is always a calm spectator and not upset however heated the discussion became whenever he joined Professor Tonoike and me for an excited discussion over beer. He always studies not only core grammar but also periphery phenomena of language, which standpoint I also take and regard as important.

I am also grateful to Shuji Chiba, Professor at Tsuda College, the outside committee member. I have not taken any of his classes, but it was my honor to submit my thesis to him because he is one of the most important scholars focusing on the subjunctive present in English. Chiba's (1987) *Present Subjunctive in Present-Day English* and his subsequent works are very comprehensive studies about English subjunctives, where every aspect and every problem about English subjunctives is discussed. Were it not for his studies and his critical studies of English subjunctives, I could not have completed my thesis.

I have been interested in the English modals and moods since my high school days. But I came to have my greater interest in English modals in my undergraduate days probably because I took courses by Harumi Sawada at Gakushuin University. I also learned a great deal from his constant smile and constructive way of thinking about life. After graduating from Gakushuin, I decided to go on studying in the graduate course of Aoyama, and one year after that he also left Gakushuin and became Professor at Kansai Gaidai University, but he continued to encourage me even far from Tokyo.

As for the approaches of generative grammar, I am most influenced by Shigeo Tonoike, as I mentioned above, and Kinsuke Hasegawa among others; their approaches to generative syntax are quite different, but they had a good influence upon me. As is well known, Professor Hasegawa taught many students generative grammar at TEC (The Tokyo Institute for Advanced Studies of Language) from 1967 to 2000. I was happy that I was able to attend his TEC classes and get to know his approach in the last two years of his assignment there. Recent generative grammar has been more focused on explanatory adequacy and language universals. But his theory and ideas made me recognize generative grammar also as a linguistic theory for explaining particular languages and meeting descriptive adequacy.

I would also like to express my sincere gratitude to Ken-ichi Takami. I had a chance to attend his class about the various topics on the Unaccusative Hypothesis in English and Japanese in 1997. Since then, though I am not his student, he has kindly offered me valuable and constructive suggestions about my papers, and encouraged me to write a dissertation again and again. I cannot thank him enough for his constant encouragement. I respect him not only as a very excellent theoretical linguist but also as a man of character. I have never forgotten and will not forget that he sent my wife and me an unused ten-thousand-yen-bill for a present the moment we informed him of our marriage.

I also owe a special debt of gratitude to Donald L. Smith. He not only suggested stylistic improvements throughout this thesis but also gave me invaluable comments. His keen insight about language phenomena and native speaker intuitions helped me many times. I want to learn his way of living. He really enjoys both linguistics and life itself every day. His family, friends, students, colleagues, and my family and I—everybody likes him. Before he moved to Notre Dame Seishin University in Okayama from Aoyama Gakuin University in March 2004, I was happy to see the words, "Best Wishes to my good friend, student and teacher, Tadao Nomura", when I asked him to autograph on the copy of a certain English-Japanese dictionary that he helped edit.

I am also indebted to all the colleagues in the Department of Literature at Wako University. I am grateful for and even proud of the fact that I was hired by Wako University even though I had never studied abroad nor did I have a Ph.D.; recently persons like me seem to have much more difficulty in getting full-time jobs in universities than before. But the members of the Literature Department in Wako chose me as a colleague from among a large number of applicants without prejudice, which I appreciate very much. Without their encouragement I could not have done this work.

Here let me mention my family, who live in Hokkaido, where I was born and brought up till I was 19 years old. I would like to express my hearty and sincere appreciation to my parents, Hideo Nomura and Shizuko Nomura, my sister, Koko Mori, my paternal grandparents, Matsuo Nomura and Kimie Nomura, and my late maternal grandmother, Ume Fujita, for their constant encouragement, patience and understanding, financial support, moral support, and love and faith.

I owe what I am today to them all. My deep thanks also go to my parents-in-law, Hisao Fujita and Etsuko Fujita, and my grandparents-in-law, Shigeyuki Mori and Fumiko Mori, both of whom passed away after they saw their great-grandchildren. When I got married in 1999, I was not a graduate course student and did not have full-time work either, but they accepted our marriage warmly and have been supporting my family. And, my lovely children, Yuta and Moeno, always make me happy. Their smiles give me energy when I come home utterly exhausted from work. I want to say to both of them, "Thank you for being born to our family."

Last, but not least, I owe my deepest thanks to my wife, Miyuki Nomura. Ever since I first met her, I have always respected her; I learn many things from her every day. I suppose that the thing that has brought the most happiness to my life, including my past, present, and probably the future, is having her as my wife. Without her smile, understanding, patience, encouragement, moral support and her hard work as homekeeper and caring mother and playmate with Yuta and Moeno, I could never have finished writing this dissertation.

October 2005

Tadao Nomura

Finally, I must express my gratitude to Isao Matsumoto, Ryoko Adachi, and Azusa Matsubara, of Hituzi Syobo, who kindly offered to publish a purely academic book on linguistics and helped me bring this book up to its present shape.

The publication of this book was supported in part by a Grant-in-Aid for publication of Science Research Results (175169, 2005) from the Japan Society for the Promotion of Science.

Table of Contents

Acknowledgements   i

Chapter 1 Introduction and the Theoretical Framework   1

    1.1 Aim of the Book   1
    1.2 Theoretical Background   2
    1.3 Chomsky's (2000, 2001a, b) Case Checking System   2
    1.4 The Status of Head Movement   4
    1.5 EPP Feature   6
    1.6 Case Checking System and V-Movement Theory in This Book   7
    1.7 Evidence for Hybrid Approach   15
    1.8 Comparisons with Chomsky's (2000, 2001a, b) and Lasnik's (1995=1999: Chapter 5) System   19
    1.9 Organization of the Book   21
Notes to Chapter 1   25

Chapter 2 ModalP Hypothesis   35

    2.1 Introduction   35
    2.2 Ouhalla's (1991) and Cinque's (1999) ModP   35
    2.3 Chomsky's (1995, 2000, 2001a, b) Sentence Structure   37
    2.4 ModalP Hypothesis   38
    2.5 Scope between Modal and *Not*   39
        2.5.1 Two Relations between Modals and *Not*   40
        2.5.2 A Problem with Generally Assumed Phrase Structure (4b)   40
        2.5.3 An Alternative Account Based on the ModalP Hypothesis   43

      2.5.4 Absence of Modal Negation or Propositional
            Negation in Modals   45
  2.6 Concluding Remarks   52
Notes to Chapter 2   53

Chapter 3 The Structure of Infinitival Clauses 63

  3.1 Introduction   63
  3.2 Basic Evidence   64
      3.2.1 Basis for Distribution   64
      3.2.2 Syntactic Support   65
  3.3 Case Checking in Infinitival Clauses   68
      3.3.1 The Framework of Case Checking in Infinitival Clauses 68
      3.3.2 Complement Structure of *Try*-type Infinitival Clauses   74
      3.3.3 Case Checking in *Want*-type Infinitival Clauses   78
  3.4 VP-Deletion in Infinitival Clauses   80
  3.5 Concluding Remarks   85
Notes to Chapter 3   87

Chapter 4 On the Position of *Not* in Infinitival Clauses 97

  4.1 Introduction   97
  4.2 Pollock's (1989) Analysis   98
  4.3 Hasegawa's (2003) Analysis   100
  4.4 An Alternative Analysis   104
  4.5 Concluding Remarks   111
Notes to Chapter 4   113

Chapter 5 *Ought to* and *Be to* 123

  5.1 Introduction   123
  5.2 Improper Analyses   124
  5.3 Previous Analyses   128
      5.3.1 Sawada's (1985, 1995) Analysis   128
      5.3.2 Ando's (1996) Analysis   130
      5.3.3 Ando's (2003) Analysis   132

5.4 An Alternative Analysis	134
5.4.1 *Ought to*	134
5.4.2 *Be to*	139
5.5 Concluding Remarks	141
Notes to Chapter 5	143

Chapter 6 The General Properties of the Subjunctive Present   149

6.1 Introduction	149
6.2 Mood, Modal, and Modality	149
6.3 Types of Mood	151
6.4 The Presence of Subjunctive Mood in Present-Day English	153
6.5 The Uses of the Subjunctive Present	156
6.6 Three Formal Characteristics of the Subjunctive Present	161
6.7 Concluding Remarks	162
Notes to Chapter 6	163
Appendix to Chapter 6 On Phonetic *That*-Deletion in Mandative Subjunctive Clauses	169
Appendix 6.1 Studies Assuming That the Subjunctive *That* Cannot Be Deleted	169
Appendix 6.2 Examples Where the Subjunctive *That* Is Deleted	170
Appendix 6.3 The Phonetically Deleted Complementizer *That*	172
Appendix 6.4 The Null Complementizer vs. the Phonetically Deleted Complementizer	175
Appendix 6.5 Concluding Remarks	177

Chapter 7 The Structure of Subjunctive Present Clauses   179

7.1 Introduction	179
7.2 Proposals	179
7.3 Tense and Three Formal Characteristics of Subjunctive Clauses	185
7.4 On the Non-cooccurrence of Modals	186
7.5 The Position of Adverbs	186

7.6 Negative Inversion	188
7.7 Phonological Support	189
7.8 VP-Deletion	191
7.9 Concluding Remarks	191
Notes to Chapter 7	193
Appendix to Chapter 7 The Subjects of Imperative Sentences	196

Chapter 8 On the Modal *Should* in Mandative Subjunctive Clauses — 199

8.1 Introduction	199
8.2 The Obligation Meaning of *Should* in Mandative Subjunctive Clauses	200
8.3 The Syntactic Status of the Quasi-Subjunctive Modals	203
8.4 Dialectal Variations	205
8.5 Quasi-Subjunctive *Should* and Emotional *Should*	207
8.6 *Should*-Deletion	209
8.7 Concluding Remarks	212
Notes to Chapter 8	215

Chapter 9 Tense in Subjunctive Present Clauses — 219

9.1 Introduction	219
9.2 Previous Studies and Issues Raised (I)	219
9.2.1 Studies Where Aux (=Tns (Mod)) is Deleted or Lacking	219
9.2.2 Studies Where INFL Is Lacking	220
9.2.3 Studies Where Subjunctive Is Assumed as a Disjunctive Category with Aux (=Tense and Modal)	220
9.2.4 Problems with the Studies in Sections 9.2.1-9.2.3	222
9.3 Previous Studies and Issues Raised (II)	223
9.3.1 Studies Assuming Empty or Null Modal	223
9.3.2 Studies Assuming Generalized IP Structures	224
9.3.3 Problems with the Studies in Sections 9.3.1-9.3.2	225
9.4 Syntactic Supports for the Assertion That Subjunctive Clauses Have Tense	225
9.5 Tense or Agr?	229

9.6 Concluding Remarks	231
Notes to Chapter 9	233
Appendix to Chapter 9 A Note on Hasegawa's (2003) Tensed-S Condition	241
Appendix 9.1 The Definitions of the TSC	241
Appendix 9.2 Basic Supporting Data	242
Appendix 9.3 Comparison between the TSC and the Extraction from NP	243
Appendix 9.4 Extraction of *Wh*-phrase from Tensed-S vs. Non-tensed-S	244
Appendix 9.5 Reflexive Pronouns as the Subject in Tensed-S	245
Appendix 9.6 Reflexive Pronoun Interpretations in the Picture Nouns	246
Appendix 9.7 Language Universals	247
Appendix 9.8 Concluding Remarks	248

Chapter 10 On Lexical Items Requiring a Subjunctive Present Clause ... 249

10.1 Introduction	249
10.2 Chiba (1991)	250
10.3 Konno (2002)	251
10.4 Problems with Konno (2002)	253
10.5 An Alternative Account	256
10.5.1 Syntactic Condition	256
10.5.2 Semantic Condition	257
10.5.3 Potential Subjunctive-Taking Verbs	259
10.6 Concluding Remarks	262
Notes to Chapter 10	265

Chapter 11 NegP and VP-Deletion in Subjunctive Present Clauses ... 269

11.1 Introduction	269
11.2 The Presence of NegP	269

11.3 Matsubara (1997a, b)   271
11.4 *Not* as a Spec or *Not* as a Head?   273
11.5 VP-Deletion in Subjunctive Present Clauses   281
    11.5.1 Potsdam (1997, 1998)   282
    11.5.2 Problems with Potsdam (1997, 1998) and an Alternative Analysis   285
11.6 Concluding Remarks   292
Notes to Chapter 11   293

Chapter 12 *Have-Be* Raising in Subjunctive Present Clauses   303

12.1 Introduction   303
12.2 A Reconsideration of the Analysis of the Word Order <Have/Be + Not> in Subjunctive Present Clauses   303
    12.2.1 Proposals   303
    12.2.2 Studies Claiming That the <Have/Be + Not> Word Order Is Ungrammatical   304
    12.2.3 Counterexamples   306
    12.2.4 Semantic Condition on the <Have/Be + Not> Word Order in Subjunctive Present Clauses   309
12.3 Historical Overview   314
    12.3.1 The Development of the Negative and the <Not + V> Word Order in Subjunctive Present Clauses   315
    12.3.2 The Development of Modals and the Subjunctive Present   320
12.4 Concluding Remarks   325
Notes to Chapter 12   327

Chapter 13 Conclusion   335

References   343

Index   369

Chapter 1

Introduction and the Theoretical Framework

1.1 Aim of the Book

In this book I mainly discuss (i) the ModalP[1](=Modal Auxiliary Phrase) Hypothesis and related phenomena and (ii) the subjunctive present based on the ModalP Hypothesis.

Modals and the Auxiliary system have been extensively discussed throughout the history of generative grammar since Chomsky (1957), but a decisive analysis has not yet been established in the Minimalist Program. Considering that, for example, Chomsky (1981, 1986a, b, 1995) has not hypothesized a syntactic category ModalP, the ModalP Hypothesis proposed in this book is clearly not taken for granted in the present theory of generative grammar.[2] However, I will show in this book that the syntactic category ModalP is needed to explain various syntactic phenomena in English and that this hypothesis is well motivated.

The subjunctive present is a topic that I have been most interested in for several years. As is well known, since *the Principles and Parameters* (P & P) *approach* was proposed in the 1980's, generative grammar has shown the greater interest in Explanatory Adequacy and Universal Grammar related topics than in Descriptive Adequacy and Particular Language specific topics. In this situation the English subjunctive has been considered to be a marginal construction[3] and has not been studied very much in generative theory[4] except in Chiba (1987), which is the most comprehensive and important study of the subjunctive present in English thus far. Despite the fact, many interesting characteristics are seen in the subjunctive present, which clearly play an important role in linguistic theory and thus deserve our detailed consideration. In this book I will focus on and discuss various aspects of the subjunctive present precisely and formalize its characteristics.

1.2 Theoretical Background

This book is mainly based on the framework of *the Minimalist Program* (cf. Chomsky (1995, 2000, 2001a, b)), but I will assume a *revised model* to approach empirical adequacy. Moreover I will sometimes refer to what is called *GB Theory* and sometimes the pre-P & P framework as well if need be. Indeed, the Minimalist Program attempts to minimize language specific rules and principles as much as possible,[5] but this is still a research objective and must be confirmed and falsified empirically. Thus in this book I will use some rules or principles based on the pre-Minimalist framework if they appear to be appropriate for the general linguistic theory. Moreover, in this book I will try to give *formal syntactic explanations* as much as possible, but when we find what we should regard as non-syntactic phenomena, I will also use a *pragmatic or functional approach* (cf. Kuno and Takami (1993)) because I consider that the formal approach and the functional approach are not incompatible but supplemental to each other.

1.3 Chomsky's (2000, 2001a, b) Case Checking System

As for the mechanism of movement theory, what I think to be the most important difference is that Case checking is completely separated from movement. In GB Theory (e.g. Chomsky (1981)) the driving force for NP-movement was assumed to be Case (assignment or checking). For instance, in (1b) *he* moves to IP-Spec for I to assign Nominative Case and thus derives (1a):

(1) a. He seems to be happy.
  b. [IP [I′ I [VP seem [IP he to be happy]]]].

In Chomsky (1995) (i.e. the early Minimalist Program) it is assumed that *he* moves in order to check off the *strong D feature* (not Nominative Case), but that Nominative Case checking (as a *free rider*) occurs at the same time, as seen in (2). That is, NP-Movement and Case checking occur at the same time and they still relate to each other.

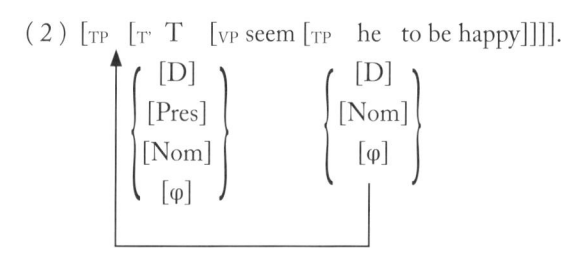

(2) [TP [T' T [VP seem [TP he to be happy]]]].
$$\begin{Bmatrix} [D] \\ [Pres] \\ [Nom] \\ [\varphi] \end{Bmatrix} \qquad \begin{Bmatrix} [D] \\ [Nom] \\ [\varphi] \end{Bmatrix}$$

But in the recent Minimalist approach (Chomsky (2000, 2001a, b)) Chomsky proposes that Case is checked *without movement*, i.e., Case is assigned in situ, by an operation called *Agree*. As an illustration of this, see (3):

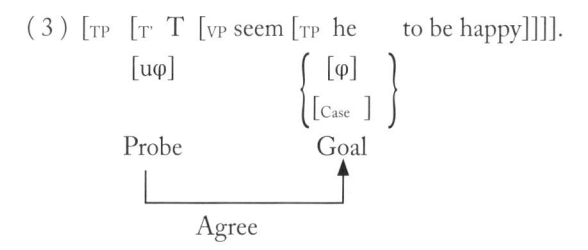

(3) [TP [T' T [VP seem [TP he to be happy]]]].
　　　　　[uφ]　　　　　　　$\begin{Bmatrix} [\varphi] \\ [\text{Case}] \end{Bmatrix}$
　　　　　Probe　　　　　　　Goal
　　　　　　　　　　Agree

This Agree operation is implemented because a *Probe* having an *uninterpretable* feature must search a *Goal* having the same (=identical) interpretable feature, which is the closest in the domain c-commanded by the Probe, and must be checked under *Matching*. Here in (3) T has a φ feature [i.e. person and number] but it is uninterpretable, so that T as a Probe searches for the Goal *he* having the same φ feature and thus [uφ] (=uninterpretable phi feature) is checked *under identity* and deleted. Here the unvalued Case [Case] is assigned Nominative Case as a *reflex* of the uninterpretable φ feature deleted by the probe, i.e. finite T.

After the operation Agree, *he* moves to TP-Spec because of the *EPP feature*:

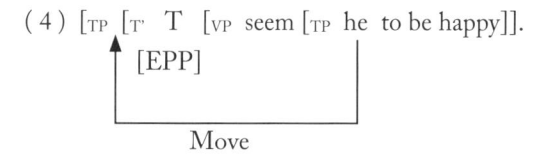

(4) [TP [T' T [VP seem [TP he to be happy]]].
　　　　[EPP]
　　　　　　　　Move

Note here that the movement operation is completely independent of Case checking (valuation). Carefully reviewing the relation between Agree and Move (motivated by the EPP feature), we may safely say that the Agree operation determines what element or what part should move.

1.4 The Status of Head Movement

In generative grammar three types of movement are traditionally assumed, as shown in (5a-c):

(5) a. A-Movement (i.e. NP-Movement)
  b. A'-Movement (i.e. *Wh*-Movement)
  c. Head Movement

As for A-Movement, we have already reviewed the movement mechanism (i.e. *Agree* and attraction by EPP) that Chomsky (2000, 2001a, b) proposed, and it can be said that a similar system is assumed for A'-Movement. But it seems to me that Chomsky's recent thinking is that substantial movement in human language is only XP-Movement and he wants to regard Head Movement as not *real*, i.e., Head Movement is not applied in narrow syntax but only in the *phonological component* (=PF). Consider the following statement of Chomsky (2000b):

(6) The account so far leaves open the possibility that V-raising is comparable to Th/Ex and DISL: not part of the narrow-syntactic computation but rather an operation of the phonological component. Either way, the phonological content of base V is determined prior to Spell-Out at the phase level, so that the effects of the revised HG are determined as well.

There are some reasons to suspect that a substantial core of head-raising processes, excluding incorporation in the sense of Baker (1988), may fall within the phonological component. One reason is the expectation of (near-) uniformity of LF interface representations, a particularly compelling instance of the methodological principle (1) [=In the absence of compelling evidence to the contrary, assume languages to be uniform, with variety restricted to easily detectable properties of utterances.], as in the case of Th/Ex (see (27)

[=Th/Ex is an operation of the phonological component.] and comment). The interpretive burden is reduced if, say, verbs are interpreted the same way whether they remain in situ or raise to T or C, the distinctions that have received much attention since Pollock (1989). As expected under (1), verbs are not interpreted differently in English vs. Romance, or Mainland Scandinavian versus Icelandic, or embedded vs. root structures. More generally, semantic effects of head-raising in the core inflectional system are slight or nonexistent, as contrasted with XP-movement, with effects that are substantial and systematic. That would follow insofar as head-raising is not part of narrow syntax. (Chomsky 2001a: 37)

But is this approach really on the right track, considering that V-to-I Movement (like *Have-Be* Raising in English or the V-movement in French and Older English) or I-to-C movement in *Subject-Aux Inversion* (SAI) have been intensively discussed for many years in generative grammar?

As for this problem, consider the following simple examples:

(7) a. *Anyone didn't come.
　　b. Didn't anyone come? [6]

It goes without saying that a Negative Polarity Item (=NPI) is licensed in narrow syntax, never in the phonological component; (7a) is ungrammatical because the NPI element *anyone* is not c-commanded by the negative *not*. But note here that (7b), where *didn't* is raised to C by SAI to c-command *anyone*, is grammatical. This strongly implies that Head Movement applies in narrow syntax; generally speaking, and no operation in the phonological component can influence core syntax phenomenon.

I will not discuss this problem any further (see, e.g., further Zwart (2001) and Embick and Noyer (2001) for this problem), but most of the phenomena covered in this book involve Head Movement, and I will continue discussion in every chapter on the assumption that Head Movement consistently applies *in narrow syntax*.

1.5 EPP Feature

As I discussed in 1.3, Chomsky claims that NP-Movement is motivated by the EPP feature, not Case.[7] However, the EPP feature is only a *stipulation*.

The same problem has been discussed concerning Head Movement: i.e., what drives overt V-movement. This has been one of the most important problems since generative grammar came into existence. Especially since Pollock (1989) and Chomsky (1995: Chapter 2), this problem has received much attention. Many linguists have engaged in complex discussions about this problem, but the basic intuition is rather simple. Consider the following English and French examples:

(8) a. John often kisses Mary.
　　b. *John kisses often Mary.
(9) a. Jean embrasse souvent Marie.
　　b. *Jean souvent embrasse Marie.
(10) a. John {is not/*not is} happy.
　　b. John {has not/*not has} come.

The questions to consider are as follows:

(11) a. Why do (all the) verbs in French raise to T overtly, and why don't main verbs in (Present-Day) English raise to T overtly?
　　b. Why do only auxiliary verbs (i.e. modals and *have* and *be*) raise to T overtly unlike main verbs in English?

Pollock's and Chomsky's solution is as follows:

(12) French verbs and English auxiliary verbs are *strong*, while English main verbs are *weak*.

After this proposal, various features have been advanced in Chomsky (1995: Chapters 3-4, 2000, 2001a, b): *strong* and *weak* features, *transparent* and *opaque*, *V-* and *D-*features, *interpretable* and *uninterpretable* features, and the *EPP* feature.

But these are only *stipulations* after all, though their putative conceptual necessity is discussed from various viewpoints.[8] Ideally, we should eliminate the EPP feature in V-movement if possible,[9] and I also believe that NP-Movement in English is consistently motivated by Case[10] and at the same time the EPP feature can be abolished under XP-Movement as well. So in this book I will use the theoretical framework where no EPP features are assumed, as shown in the next section.

1.6 Case Checking System and V-Movement Theory in This Book

Here I make the following *hybrid* assumption as to checking V-movement:

(13) a. *Functional Verb Elements* are inserted into Modal^0 in *full* forms, carrying along all the features. Since these features are *uninterpretable* for verbs themselves and thus must be checked off, the functional verbs raise to higher functional heads (e.g. T^0, C^0, etc.) as the last resort in narrow syntax (cf. Chomsky (1995: Chapter 4)).
   b. *Lexical Verb Elements* are inserted into V in *bare* forms, having no features. Since they cannot move in themselves because they have no features, *Affix Hopping* must apply *in PF* (i.e. after Spell-Out) so that features in I can be discharged and the lexical verbal elements be pronounced (cf. Chomsky (1957), Lasnik (1995=1999: Chapter 5, 2000), McCawley (1998^2), Hasegawa (2003), and Radford (2004)).

The definitions of Functional and Lexical Verb Elements are as follows:

(14) a. Functional Verb Elements are basically *modals* (including the infinitival marker *to* and the covert modal of the subjunctive present, as we shall discuss in later chapters) except for the finite forms of *have* and *be*.
   b. Lexical Verb Elements are all *main verbs* in (Present-Day) English.

First of all, consider the case of Functional Verb Elements in (13a). As an illustration of this, consider the following example (15a) and its corresponding underlying structure (15b):

(15) a. He can go.

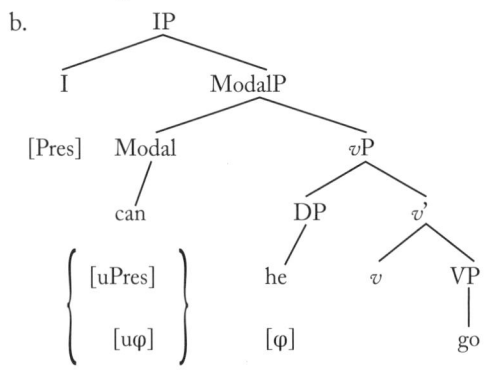

b.
```
                IP
              /    \
             I      ModalP
          /    \   /      \
      [Pres]  Modal        vP
              /           /   \
            can         DP     v'
         ⎧        ⎫    /      /  \
         ⎨ [uPres]⎬   he     v    VP
         ⎪        ⎪                |
         ⎩ [uφ]   ⎭   [φ]          go
```

Here I make the following assumptions about Case in nouns and *Feature Dribbling*:

(16) a. Nouns are base-generated carrying N-features and φ-features (i.e. person, number, and gender features) but not Case.[11] Thus nouns must get Case in order to *be pronounced as full forms in PF*.[12]

b. Case is a reflex of the [φ] features and the (i) T-feature, (ii) V-feature, (iii) P-feature, or (iv) P_ϕ-feature;

  (i) Nominative Case is a *reflex* of [φ] and the finite Tense feature (i.e. [Pres] or [Past]).
  (ii) Accusative Case is a *reflex* of [φ] and [V]. (See also note 12 and (27a, b) in Chapter 3)
  (iii) Oblique Case is a *reflex* of [φ] and [P]. (See also (16a) in Chapter 3)
  (iv) Null Case is a *reflex* of [φ] and [P_ϕ]. (See also (16b) in Chapter 3)

(17) Feature Dribbling[13]

Features are copied to the element within the maximal projection which is (i) dominating, or (ii) being dominated.[14]

Under these assumptions, consider the derivation of (15b). First, *he* raises to IP-Spec to get a Case and become a full form (see (16a)). Second, [Pres] in I is copied to I', IP, the raised DP (=*he*), and [φ] in *he* is copied to IP, I', and I due to Feature Dribbling in (17):[15]

(18)

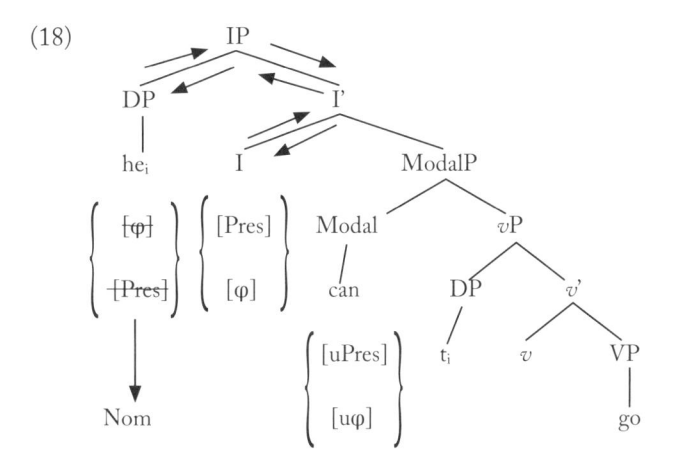

```
         IP
      ╱  ↕  ╲
    DP      I'
    │    ╱ ↕ ╲
   heᵢ  I    ModalP
                ╱    ╲
           Modal      vP
              │      ╱  ╲
             can   DP    v'
                   │    ╱ ╲
                   tᵢ  v   VP
                           │
                           go
```

Under DP heᵢ: { [φ̶], [P̶r̶e̶s̶] } → Nom

Under I: { [Pres], [φ] }

Under Modal can: { [uPres], [uφ] }

Here *he* is assigned Nominative Case as a reflex of [φ] and [Pres] (see (16bi)), following that [φ] and [Pres] are both deleted. Note also that a Case feature is not assumed here. Third, the modal *can* raise to I to check off the uninterpretable features [uPres] and [uφ] as a last resort:

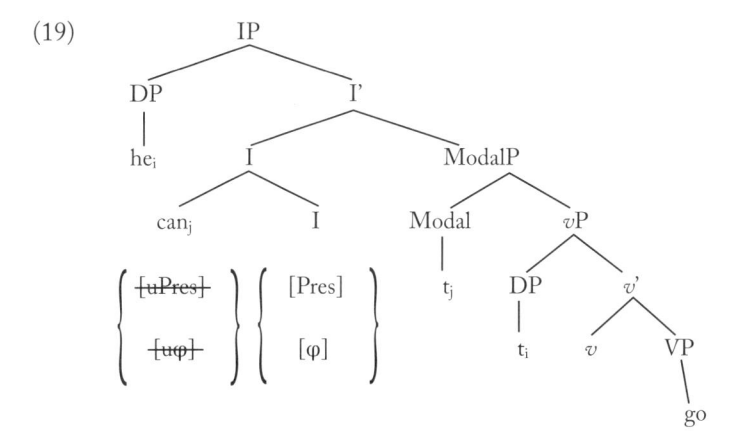

(19)

```
         IP
       ╱    ╲
     DP      I'
     │     ╱   ╲
    heᵢ   I     ModalP
         ╱ ╲       ╱   ╲
      canⱼ  I   Modal   vP
                  │    ╱  ╲
                  tⱼ  DP   v'
                       │   ╱ ╲
                       tᵢ v   VP
                               ╲
                               go
```

Under canⱼ: { [u̶P̶r̶e̶s̶], [u̶φ̶] }

Under I: { [Pres], [φ] }

As shown in (19), [uPres] and [uφ] in *can* are checked by [Pres] and [φ] in I under a *head-head relation*, and thus the derivation converges.

Here I assume that both [Pres] (i.e. Tense feature) and [φ] are interpretable for I. In this book I will not assume AgrP (see Chapter 2), but only assume IP (cf. Chomsky (1981, 1986a, b)).[16] This means that I plays the roles of Agr (i.e. φ-feature complex) in Pollock (1989) and Chomsky (1995: Chapters 2-3) as well as T, that is, I is the feature complex including T, Agr, and sometimes Mood, as I will discuss this topic in this book later. This assumption naturally means that not only T but also φ features are interpretable.

In addition, note that IP also has [Pres] and [φ],[17] which is compatible with the selection of C. Consider (20a-c), assuming that the complementizer *that*, having [Pres] and [φ], is merged with IP:

(20) a. I think that [IP he walks every day].

$$\begin{Bmatrix} [\text{Pres}] \\ [\varphi] \end{Bmatrix} \begin{Bmatrix} [\text{Pres}] \\ [\varphi] \end{Bmatrix}$$

b. *I think that [IP he walk every day].

$$\begin{Bmatrix} [\text{Pres}] \\ [\varphi] \end{Bmatrix} \begin{Bmatrix} [\text{Pres}] \\ \end{Bmatrix}$$

c. *I think that [IP him to walk every day].

$$\begin{Bmatrix} [\text{Pres}] \\ [(\text{complete})\varphi] \end{Bmatrix} \begin{Bmatrix} [\text{Nonfinite T}] \\ [\text{Person}] \end{Bmatrix}$$

Judging from the fact that only (20a) is grammatical, it is appropriate to suppose that IP also has [Pres] and [φ].[18]

Next, let us return to the case of Lexical Verb Elements in (13b). As an illustration of this, consider the following example (21a) and its corresponding underlying structure (21b):

(21) a. He walks.
b.

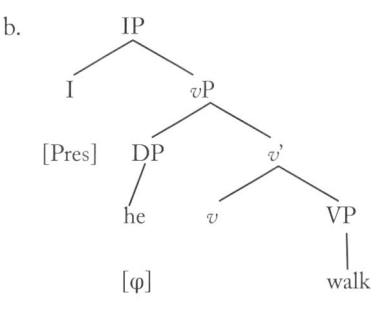

```
            IP
           /  \
          I    vP
       [Pres] /  \
             DP   v'
             |   /  \
             he  v   VP
             |       |
            [φ]     walk
```

First, *he* raises to IP-Spec to get a Case and become a full form (see (16a)), just as in the case of Functional Verb Elements. Second, [Pres] in I is copied to I', IP, the raised DP (=*he*), and [φ] in *he* is copied to IP, I', and I due to feature dribbling in (17):

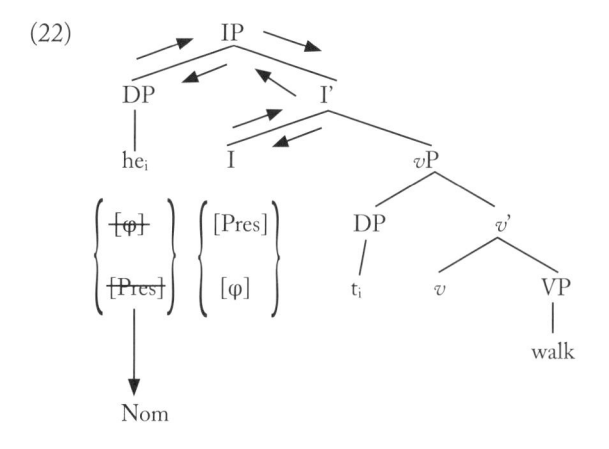

(22)

```
              IP
             /  \
            DP   I'
            |   / \
           he_i I   vP
               {[φ̶]}  {[Pres]}   DP   v'
               {[P̶r̶e̶s̶]} {[φ]}    |   / \
                |              t_i v   VP
                                       |
                                      walk
               Nom
```

Then *he* is assigned Nominative Case as a reflex of [φ] and [Pres] (see (16bi)), and thereby these [φ] and [Pres] features are both deleted. Note that [Pres] and [φ] are interpretable for I, as we discussed above, and thus the derivation should converge in narrow syntax. However, the verb *walk* cannot be pronounced yet, as in the case of *he* before getting Case.[19] Here I assume the proposals in (23) and (24):

(23) Bare form verbs (i.e. Lexical Verb Elements) must get the finite tense feature

(i.e. [Pres] or [Past]) and [φ] feature in order to be pronounced as full forms in PF (cf. (16a)).

(24) Affix Hopping

The Computational System of the English Language can copy the finite tense feature and [φ] in I and use them as a verbal affixes,[20] which are lowered onto and attaches to the nearest bare verb in PF (i.e. after Spell-Out).[21]

Under these assumptions, the derivation in (22) will further be something like (25) which converges in PF as well:

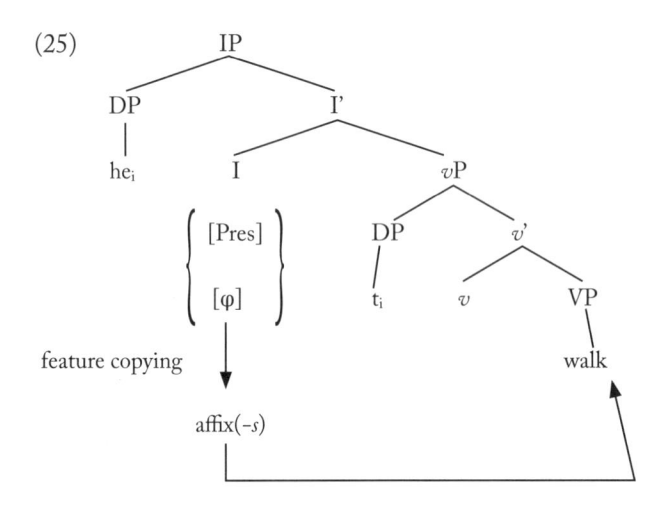

(25)

```
                IP
             /      \
           DP         I'
           |        /    \
          he_i     I       vP
                         /    \
                  {[Pres]}    DP    v'
                  {     }    |    /  \
                  { [φ] }    t_i  v   VP
                                      |
feature copying    ↓                 walk
                 affix(-s)
```

Affix Hopping

Here we should mention *do*-support. Consider the following simple example in (26a) and its underlying structure in (26b):

(26) a. John does not walk.

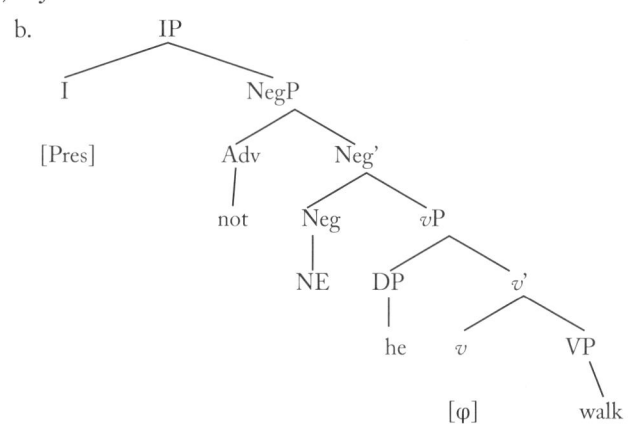

b.
```
            IP
           /  \
          I    NegP
        [Pres] /   \
             Adv   Neg'
              |    /  \
             not Neg   vP
                  |   /  \
                 NE  DP   v'
                     |   / \
                    he  v   VP
                       [φ]   |
                            walk
```

The structure would be as follows after the subject *he* moves to IP-Spec, Feature Dribbling applies, and an affix is made by the feature copying of I:

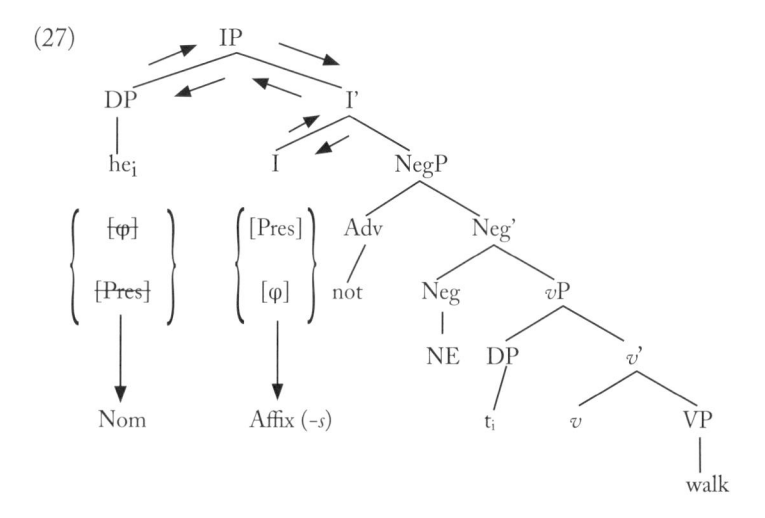

(27)
```
              IP
             /  \
           DP    I'
           |    / \
          heᵢ  I   NegP
               |   / \
         { [φ]    Adv  Neg'
           [Pres] } [Pres]  |   / \
             ↓    { [φ] }  not Neg  vP
            Nom     ↓          |   / \
                 Affix (-s)   NE  DP  v'
                                  |  / \
                                  tᵢ v  VP
                                        |
                                       walk
```

However, note that the negative *not* intervenes between the affix and *walk*. This time Affix Hopping cannot apply because of the PF adjacency condition, as shown in (28), and thus this derivation crashes:

(28) Affix Hopping is a PF operation and thus demands that an affix and V be adjacent.[22)]

Here, as for the periphrastic *do*, I make the following assumption (Nomura (1999b, 2000a, b, d, 2001a, 2002a, 2003)), unlike the traditional generative assumptions that the dummy *do* is automatically inserted to support the stranded Tense:

(29) The periphrastic auxiliary *do* is *a type of modal* and is base-generated in Modal^0, carrying along the necessary features, just as ordinary modals.

This leads us to conclude that the underlying structure of (26a) is not (26b) but the following:

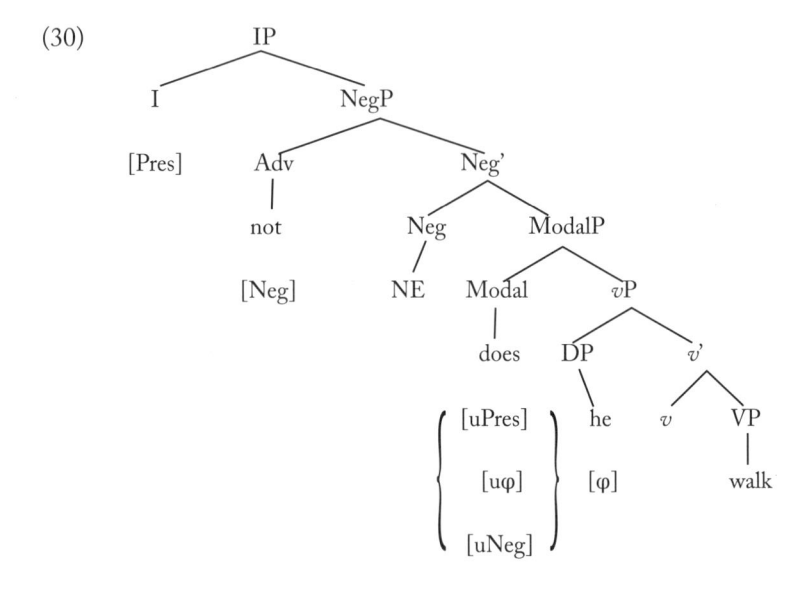

(30)
```
                IP
         ┌──────┴──────┐
         I            NegP
       [Pres]    ┌─────┴─────┐
                Adv         Neg'
                 │      ┌────┴────┐
                not    Neg      ModalP
                      ╱  ╲    ┌────┴────┐
                   [Neg] NE  Modal      vP
                              │    ┌────┴────┐
                            does   DP        v'
                          ⎧[uPres]⎫  ╲   ┌───┴───┐
                          ⎨ [uφ] ⎬   he  v      VP
                          ⎩[uNeg]⎭      [φ]      │
                                                walk
```

The derivation to follow is almost the same as (15b), except that *does* firstly moves to Neg to check off [uNeg]. Note that *does* (and *did*) is fully inflected in the lexicon under (13a), unlike the traditional *do*-support assumption where *does* is produced by the merger of the stranded Tense and the supporting *do*.

As discussed above, I have assumed that *do* is a type of modal from the syntactic point of view, but this assumption is also reasonable from the viewpoint of the formal characteristics of modals under Coates's (1983) definition. She lists the *Seven Formal Characteristics of Modals* in the definition of modals, as shown in (31a-g):[23]

(31) a. Takes Negation directly (*can't, mustn't*)
    b. Takes inversion without DO (*can I?, must I?*)
    c. 'Code' (*John can swim and so can Bill*).
    d. Emphasis (*Ann COULD solve the problem*).
    e. No -*s* form for third person singular (**cans, *musts*)
    f. No non-finite forms (**to can, *musting*)
    g. No co-occurrence (**may can*)   (Coates 1983: 4)

The auxiliary *do* satisfies as many as six of these characteristics, though it does not satisfy (31e), i.e., *do* has the form *does* for the third person singular:

(32) a. Takes Negation directly (*don't*)
    b. Takes inversion without DO (*do I?*)
    c. 'Code' (*John doesn't swim every day but Mary sometimes does*).
    d. Emphasis (*Ann DID solve the problem*).
    e. (*Do* does not satisfy "No -*s* form for third person singular".)
    f. No non-finite forms (**to do, *doing*)
    g. No co-occurrence (**I can do swim*)

In conclusion, although the syntactic status of the auxiliary *do* has long been debated in the history of generative grammar,[24] from the present perspective it would be most reasonable to assume that the auxiliary *do* is a type of modal in most respects.[25],[26]

1.7 Evidence for Hybrid Approach

In the previous section I have discussed the basic framework for V-movement under a hybrid approach. From the viewpoint of the history of generative grammar, (13a) is based on a *lexicalist* perspective while (14b) is a *transformationalist* perspective. Chomsky first took a lexicalist perspective in Chomsky (1970), but we may say that in the Minimalist Program he took a *strict lexicalist hypothesis* about verbal morphology in Chomsky (1995: Chapter 3):

(33) The main verb typically "picks up" the features of T and Agr (in fact, both Agrs and Agro in the general case), adjoining to an inflectional element I to form [V I]. There are two ways to interpret the process, for a lexical element α. One is to take α to be a bare, uninflected form; PF rules are then designed to interpret the abstract complex [α I] as a single inflected phonological word. The other approach is to take α to have inflectional features in the lexicon as an intrinsic property (in the spirit of lexicalist phonology); these features are then checked against the inflectional element I in the complex [α I]. If the features of α and I match, I disappears and α enters into the PF component under Spell-Out; if they conflict, I remains and the derivation crashes at PF. The PF rules, then, are simple rewriting rules of the usual type, not more elaborate rules applying to complexes [α I].

I have been tacitly assuming the second option. Let us now make that choice explicit. (Chomsky 1995: 195)

However, conceptually speaking, the idea that the many forms of *each* verb independently exist in the lexicon seems very uneconomical as redundant, as illustrated in (34), and this will cause the problem of *exponential blowup*:

(34) a. walk (Root), walks (3rd Person, SgNum, Pres), walked (Past), walked (Past Participle), walking (Present Participle), walking (Gerund)
b. go (Root), goes (3rd Person, SgNum, Pres), went (Past), gone (Past Participle), going (Present Participle), going (Gerund)
c. ...

From the viewpoint of economy or simplicity, it is reasonable to assume that the lexicon contains only the *root forms* of the verbs excluding the marked verbs (i.e. modals and the finite forms of *have* and *be*), as I assumed in the previous section. Though, the objection might be raised that our framework wrongly predicts that sentences like (35a, 36a), rather than (35b, 36b), are grammatical:

(35) a. *John *goed* to school yesterday.
   b. John *went* to school yesterday.
(36) a. *John has already *goed* to England.
   b. John has already *gone* to England.

But this would be a technical problem after all, not a problem of narrow syntax (cf. *Morphophonemic Rules* in Chomsky (1957) or *Distributed Morphology* in Halle and Marantz (1993)). In fact, Chomsky himself claims that inflectional morphological properties entering into computational operation are distinct from derivational lexical morphological properties, as shown in (37), though he ironically thinks of this as a premise for assuming the lexicalist hypothesis in Chomsky (1995: Chapter 2):

(37) I am thus assuming a sharp and principled distinction between inflectional morphology, part of syntax proper, and strictly derivational morphology, part of the lexicon, perhaps subject to such principles as right-headedness in the sense of Edwin Williams and others. I am, then, assuming something like the earliest version of the lexicalist hypothesis. (Chomsky 1995: 133)

This assumption is supported by the fact English speaking children commonly apply the past -*ed* forms to all the verbs including irregular ones, such as *goed instead of *went*, *comed instead of *came*, etc., at a particular period of development.[27]

Next, Lasnik (1995=1999: Chapter 5) argues that Chomsky's strict lexicalist approach is empirically problematic. For example, he submits the following examples, which he claims Chomsky (1995: Chapters 3-4) cannot give an account of:[28]

(38) a. *John not likes Mary.
   b. *John likes not Mary.

Lasnik concludes that Chomsky's (1957) classical approach of Affix Hopping is more explanatory and proposes a revised Affix Hopping approach.[29] However, the main reason I adopt the hybrid approach in this book is Lasnik's persuasive discussion about *VP-deletion*. Following his argumentation, I claim that we can explain the following examples, as shown in (40-53), where [ ] stands for an affix, under the assumption in (39):

(39) a. VP-deletion is a *PF operation*[30] and applies *before* Affix Hopping.
    b. All verbs can be deleted *under identity* when they are inserted from the lexicon. (Note that *have* and *be* are inserted *fully inflected* while main verbs are inserted as *bare forms*.)
(40)   John slept, and Mary will too.
(41) a. *John *slept*, and Mary will *slept* too.
    b. John [-ed] *sleep*, and Mary should *sleep* too.
(42)   John sleeps (every after noon), and Mary should too.
(43) a. *John *sleeps*, and Mary should *sleeps* too.
    b. John [-s] *sleep*, and Mary should *sleep* too.
(44)   ?John was sleeping, and Mary will too.
(45) a. *John was *sleeping*, and Mary will *sleeping* too.
    b. John [-ing] *sleep*, and Mary will *sleep* too.
(46)   John has slept, and Mary will too.
(47) a. *John has *slept*, and Mary will *slept* too.
    b. John [-en] *sleep*, and Mary will *sleep* too.
(48)   *John was here, and Mary will too.
(49) a. *John *was here*, and Mary will *was here* too.
    b. John [-ed] *be here*, and Mary will *be here* too.[31]
(50)   *John was being obnoxious, and Mary will too.
(51) a. *John *was being obnoxious*, and Mary will *was being obnoxious* too.
    b. John [-ed] *be* [-ing] *be obnoxious*, and Mary will *be be obnoxious*.
(52)   *The men have left, and women shouldn't.
(53) a. *The men have (3rd, Pl) *left*, and women shouldn't ~~have(root) left~~.
    b. The men [φ=3rd, Pl, Pres] have left, and women shouldn't have left.

(cf. Lasnik (1999: 108-110))

These examples strongly suggest that the present proposal of the hybrid approach is appropriate.[32],[33]

1.8 Comparisons with Chomsky's (2000, 2001a, b) and Lasnik's (1995=1999: Chapter 5) System

Before closing this introduction, I should mention the main differences between our framework and Chomsky's (2000, 2001a, b) *Agree* system and Lasnik's (1995=1999: Chapter 5) Affix Hopping system. First, consider the following summary of Chomsky's system:

(54) Chomsky's System
   a. Uninterpretable features are deleted in situ (i.e. without Movement) under the operation Agree, i.e., Probe searches Goal.
   b. Nominative Case is assigned to the Goal (=the subject DP) after Agree by the Probe (=T) as a reflex of φ features.
   c. EPP (or OCC) features drive Move (=NP-Movement and *Wh*-Movement), and they exist in Probe, not Goal.
   d. Thus Nominative Case assignment is totally independent from the raising of the subject DP to Spec-TP.
   e. Head Movement is not *real* in narrow syntax and considered to be a PF phenomena.
   f. Checking domain and feature checking under a Spec-Head relation assumed in Chomsky (1995) are both eliminated.

Next, as for Lasnik's system, I will show differences from ours, because both he and I take the hybrid approach as to verbal morphology.

(55) Lasnik's System
   a. He does not discuss Nominative Case checking in his paper.
   b. He assumes the following list of pairs of features and affixes, as shown in (56), instead of *strong* and *weak* features about V-movement assumed by Chomsky (1995):

(56) a. ... Infl ...V...   OK. V will overtly raise.
         +F   +F
    b. ... Infl ...V...   OK. PF merger.
         Af   bare
    c. ... Infl ...V...   *at LF. +F of Infl will not be checked;
         +F   bare   *at PF as well, since +F is strong.
    d. ... Infl ...V...   *at LF. +F of V will not be checked.
         Af   +F   *at PF also, if merger fails.

(Lasnik's 1995=1999: 106)

Last of all, the following summarizes our framework:

(57) Our Framework
   a. The operation Agree is not assumed.
   b. NP-Movement is driven for *Case* (assignment).
   c. Nominative Case is a reflex of the [φ] feature and the T-feature.
   d. I assume that Head Movement (i.e. V-movement) is *real* and thus applies *in narrow syntax*.
   e. Move applies to the *attractor* (=Chomsky's Probe) as well as to the *attractee* (=Chomsky's Goal), which assumption is in line with Lasnik's (1999: Chapter 4) *Enlightened Self Interest*.
   f. No EPP features are assumed at all, nor Lasnik's list of pairs of features and affixes in (54), be they XP-Movement or Head Movement.
   g. *Feature Dribbling*,[34] feature checking under a *Head-Head relation* and a *Spec-Head relation*, and *Affix Hopping* as *a last resort* are assumed.
   h. Functional Verb Elements are inserted into Modal^0 in full forms, carrying along all the features, while Lexical Verb Elements are inserted into V in bare forms, having no features. *Do* is also a type of modals and is base-generated fully inflected in Modal^0, unlike the traditional approach with *do*-support or *do*-insertion.
   i. VP-deletion is a *PF operation*; all VPs can be deleted *under identity* when they are inserted from lexicon.

1.9 Organization of the Book

This book is organized as follows: Chapter 1 constitutes introductory remarks in which I have presented the aim of this book and the theoretical framework. After discussing Chomsky's (2000, 2001a, b) Case checking system, the status of Head Movement, and the EPP feature, I proposed a Case checking system without the EPP feature with the assumption that V-movement is visible and thus evidently applies in narrow syntax.

In Chapter 2 I propose the ModalP Hypothesis, which will be the fundamental framework throughout this book. After reviewing Chomsky's (1995, 2000, 2001a, b) sentence structure, which is generally assumed, I will show that it cannot generate the interpretation of Modal Negation in principle. On the other hand, I claim that the ModalP Hypothesis can provide adequate accounts for the scope interpretations between modals and *not*.

Chapters 3-5 are concerned with infinitival clauses. In Chapter 3 I discuss the structure of infinitival clauses, which has been one of the central issues in generative grammar. I propose that the infinitival clause is a type of ModalP in syntactic structure. After reviewing basic evidence for assuming that the infinitival marker *to* is a type of modal, I also propose a framework for Case checking in infinitival clauses and discuss related topics. I also discuss VP-deletion in infinitival clauses and point out similarities to VP-deletion after modals.

In Chapter 4 I discuss the position of the negative *not* in infinitival clauses. As for the two word orders of <not to V> and <to not V> seen in infinitival clauses, Pollock (1989) and Hasegawa (2003) assume that the one word order is derived from the other order, though their concepts are rather different, but I will show that both analyses are empirically problematic, and claim that the two word orders are not identical constructions and thus only the <not to V> word order is negation of the whole infinitival clause and the <to not V> word order is verb phrase negation.

Chapter 5 is concerned with the problems with *ought to* and *be to*. In all appearances, the assumption that the infinitival marker *to* is a type of modal raises a serious problem; the infinitival marker *to* and *ought* or *be* should not co-occur by the general principle that modals do not co-occur. However, I will show that we can explain the exceptional behavior of *ought to* and *be to* assuming two or three types of *ought* or *be* in a non *ad hoc* fashion.

Chapters 6-12 are concerned with the subjunctive present and constitute the main body of this book, covering topics that I have been most interested in for several years. In these chapters I will focus on and discuss various aspects of the subjunctive present precisely and formalize its characteristics.

In Chapter 6, before discussing the subjunctive present in detail in Chapters 7-12, I review the terminology of *mood*, *modal*, and *modality*, the status of the subjunctive mood in Present-Day English, and the general properties of subjunctive present in this chapter. In particular, I discuss the three important formal characteristics seen in the subjunctive present clauses. In the appendix to Chapter 6 I will modify my assumption on *that*-deletion in mandative subjunctive clauses proposed in Nomura (2000b). Though many linguists assume that the subjunctive *that* cannot be deleted, I show that this assumption is empirically wrong by submitting many examples where the subjunctive *that* is deleted.

In Chapter 7 I discuss the syntactic structure of subjunctive present clauses, especially mandative subjunctive clauses. The purpose of Chapter 7 is to explain the three formal characteristics discussed in Chapter 6, which seem to be quite peculiar compared to indicative finite sentences, and to account for various phenomena in subjunctive present clauses. After presenting my proposals, I will examine in detail various behavior in subjunctive present clauses and show that the present proposal is appropriate.

In Chapter 8 I discuss the quasi-subjunctive *should* and related topics. After pointing out that the quasi-subjunctive *should* is semantically empty, I assume that only the quasi-subjunctive modals *should*, *shall*, *may*, and *might* have the [uSubj] feature as a placeholder auxiliary. Then I discuss emotional *should* as well and the possibility of *should*-deletion in subjunctive present clauses.

In Chapter 9 I discuss the role of tense in subjunctive present clauses. Though it is widely accepted in traditional grammar and many previous studies that subjunctive present clauses have no tense in Present-Day English, I claim that subjunctive present clauses do, in fact, have *present tense*, by presenting that there are many linguistic facts that force us to conclude that subjunctive present clauses are tensed. Additionally I will show that Nominative Case checking is based on the presence of *Tense* rather than *Agr*. In connection with the discussion in Chapter 9, I discuss the possibilities and problems with Hasegawa's (2003) *Tensed-S Condition* (TSC) in the appendix to the chapter.

In Chapter 10 I discuss the rather complex problems as to what lexical items can select a subjunctive present clause. After reviewing Chiba (1991) and Konno (2001), I argue that Konno's *Condition of an Underlying Appeal* is rather insufficient. Instead, I propose that both syntactic conditions and a semantic condition are needed. As for the semantic condition, I assume that when the subjunctive *that* is introduced, the sentence must express an *unspecified desirable future* by linguistic elements or contextual meanings.

In Chapter 11 I discuss the problem of the presence of NegP and the controversial problem as to which position *not* occupies, the *Spec* position or the *Head* position. In connection with this problem, I discuss the licensing condition on VP-deletion in subjunctive present clauses. Though Potsdam (1997, 1998) claims that the negative *not* alone licenses VP-deletion in subjunctive present clauses and therefore conclude that *not* is the Head of NegP, I will show that not only the negative *not* but also other elements can license (VP-)deletion in subjunctive present clauses, and thus I conclude that the VP-deletion phenomena in subjunctive present clauses is not decisive evidence for the claim that *not* is the Head of NegP.

In Chapter 12 I discuss the various possibilities of *have-be* raising in subjunctive present clauses. First, I reconsider the word order <have/be + not> as sentential negation seen in subjunctive present clauses. After showing that even in Present-Day English both the word orders of <not + have/be> and <have/be + not> are allowed in subjunctive present clauses as sentential negation, I propose that the latter marginal word order must be subject to the semantic condition (cf. Chapter 10). Next, I briefly discuss the historical overview from the perspective of the word order of negative and verbs. As for the <not + V> word order in subjunctive present clauses, I argue that this word order is a comparatively new usage in American English, by examining the historical development of this word order both in indicative and subjunctive sentences. Last, I argue that until the 19th century the subjunctive verbs raised to I^0 carrying along all the features, but since the 20th century those features were separated from the verbs and raised to Modal0 resulting in the covert subjunctive Modal M_ϕ. This category change is parallel to the development of ordinary modals.

Chapter 13 contains concluding remarks and I mention some residual problems.

Notes to Chapter 1

1. I have been using the term *ModP*, not *ModalP*, since 1999 (e.g. Nomura (1999a, b, 2000a, b, d, 2001a, 2002a, 2003)), but in this book I will use ModalP, since the term ModP is often misunderstood as the projection of *Mood*, not *Modal Auxiliary*. As an example of this, see Chiba (2001):

   (i) The functional category Mood in the structure (31) would be in part Aux or AGR (rather than Mood) discussed above.
   As for studies on subjunctive other than Pollock (1997), where the syntactic category Mood (or the syntactic feature [+Mood]) is used, see Murakami (1995[b], 1999 [i.e. 2000]) and Nomura (1999[b]).
   (Chiba 2001: 17, fn. 7, translations are mine)

   Chiba probably understands the real concept of my term ModP in Nomura (1999a) considering the first paragraph in (i), but nonetheless the ModP could be taken to mean the projection of Modal Auxiliary, so I will use the term ModalP below.
   Note incidentally that Pollock (1997) assumes the structure mentioned by Chiba (=(31) in (i)) is as follows:

   (ii) [$_{MoodP}$ Mood [$_{NegP}$ neg] [$_{TP}$ T [$_{AgrP}$ AGR [$_{VP}$ α]]]]   (Pollock 1997: 262)

   Whether we assume MoodP in clause structure is an important problem, but I will assume only ModalP but not MoodP in this book. I will leave this open and for future study.

2. But as for a few studies mentioning this possibility, see Section 2.1.

3. As for this, see Chomsky (1981):

   (i) For example, I have said nothing about <u>subjunctives, a somewhat marginal construction</u>....   (Chomsky 1981: 230, fn. 73, underlines are mine)

4. In contrast, we can see comparatively many studies about the subjunctives in other languages (e.g. Germanic, Romance, Balkan languages, etc.), where the subjunctive inflections strongly remain and their characteristics are easily seen; see Mailing (1984),

Johnson (1984), Grosu and Horvath (1984), Picallo (1985), Kempchinsky (1986), Sigurðsson (1990), Farkas (1992), Terzi (1992, 1997), Watanabe (1993a, b, 1996a), etc. For the subjunctive complement in Japanese, where the subjunctive inflections are not seen, unlike the European languages above, see Watanabe (1996b) and Uchibori (1997, 2000).

For a comprehensive study in the *semantics* of the English subjunctive, see James (1986). Especially for the semantics in past forms in *if*-clauses, see Nomura (2000e).

5. As for this guideline of Chomsky's, see the following (i) and (ii), which statement I think to be important:

   (i) The P & P approach held that languages have no rules in anything like the familiar sense, and no theoretically significant grammatical constructions except as taxonomic artifacts. There are universal principles and a finite array of options as to how they apply (parameters), but language-particular rules and no grammatical constructions of the traditional sort within or across languages. (Chomsky 1995: 5-6)
   (ii) The minimalist program is the attempt to explore these questions. Its task is to examine every device (principle, idea, ...) that is employed in characterizing languages to determine what extent it can be eliminated in favor of a principled account in terms of general conditions of computational efficiency and the interface condition that the organ must satisfy for it to function at all. Put differently, the goal is to determine just what aspects of the structure and use of language are specific to the language faculty, hence lacking principled explanation at this level.
   (Chomsky 2001b: 3)

   If I summarize (ii) in my understanding, it will be that Chomsky wants to explain language only in terms of *interface conditions* and *computational efficiency* that the organ must satisfy, not seemingly in terms of any unique properties that the language (i.e. *grammar*) itself has.

6. Nobuko Hasegawa raised the same question in respect to Watanabe (2001).

7. We may say almost the same thing as in the case of *Wh*-Movement; Chomsky uses a *p[eriphery]-feature* as well as a wh-feature in explaining the *successive cyclic wh-movement*. (The movement to the initial CP-Spec position is motivated by the *wh*-feature all the same.)

   Chomsky (2001b) uses the term *OCC* feature with almost the same meaning as EPP feature.

8. Pollock (1989) attempts to give an explanation in terms of the *transparency* of the realizations of θ-*roles*. Chomsky (1995: Chapters 2-4) argues that movement is *morphologically* driven. Roberts (1998) also discusses the characteristics of the overt movement peculiar to *have* and *be* in English (see also Arimura (1998)).

Furthermore, Chomsky presumes that parameters in languages can be reduced to *morphological properties* and differences among specific languages come from differences in *PF*, as shown in (i), including *movement* and *word order* (cf. Kayne's (1994) *Linear Correspondence Axiom*; LCA):

(i) Furthermore, parametric differences must be reduced to morphological properties if the Minimalist Program is framed in the terms so far assumed. There are strong reasons to suspect that LF conditions are not relevant. We expect languages to be very similar at the LF level, differing only as a reflex of properties detectable at PF; the reasons basically reduce to considerations of learnability. Thus, we expect that at the LF level there will be no relevant difference between languages with phrases overtly raised or in situ (e.g., *wh*-phrases or verbs). Hence, we are led to seek morphological properties that are reflected at PF.   (Chomsky 1995: 192)

These discussions are interesting, but the matter is not so simple; for example, whether V-to-I movement exists or not in particular languages is discussed in terms of their morphological properties (*Rich Agreement Hypothesis*) in many studies (see Rohrbacher (1999), Vikner (1997), and Bobaljik (2001)), but Murakami (2002) and Nawata (2003) point out empirical problems (see also Chiba (2001: Sections 7-8)).

In this connection, we should also note that Pollock (1997) and Murakami (2002) argue that *mood* is crucially concerned with V-to-I movement.

9. This problem might mean that the existence of the EPP feature (or some kinds of uninterpretable feature) itself is the essence of human language that cannot be reduced from some principle or other. But this will ultimately lead to the following question:

(i) Why does *Displacement* (i.e. *Movement* or *Transformation*) exist in human language?

One of the most important contributions of generative linguistics is showing the necessity of *Phrase Structure Rules* and *Transformations* in describing any language. The theory of generative grammar has been continuously revised and developed since the

1950's, but we may say that this contribution and leading idea has never been changed; as is well known, *PS rules* developed into *X-bar Theory* and is now called *Merge*, and many transformations were reduced into the operation *Movement* alone. Since the P & P approach was proposed in 1980's, Movement has been variously called *Move* α, *Affect* α, and *Attract F*, but the essence is the same. Recently Chomsky (2000, 2001a, b) often uses the term *Displacement*.

We should and may think that *Merge* is the most basic operation and necessary and thus *least costly*. However, Displacement is unnecessary from the viewpoint of the *optimal design* of human language, as is also shown by the fact that computer language has no displacement properties.

Chomsky (2000) argues that there are two *imperfections* in human language: *Displacement* and *Uninterpretable Features*. But Chomsky (2001a) implies that so long as a certain imperfection exits in order to eliminate (other) imperfections, it is not an imperfection in a true sense. Consider (ii):

(ii) The relation Agree and uninterpretable features are prima facie imperfections. In MI and earlier work it is suggested that both may be part of an optimal solution to minimal design specifications by virtue of their role in establishing the property of "displacement," which has (at least plausible) external motivation in terms of distinct kinds of semantic interpretation and perhaps processing. If so, displacement is only an apparent imperfection of natural language, as are the devices that implement it.

(Chomsky 2001a: 3)

Following this idea, I claim the following:

(iii) The only imperfection in the computational system of human language is the existence of Uninterpretable Features, and Displacement (i.e. movement) is not a real imperfection but an apparent one in that it exists (or is driven) for the purpose of eliminating Uninterpretable Features.

But it seems to me that, contra (ii) in Chomsky (2001a), Chomsky (2001b) holds the premise that Displacement, not Uninterpretable Features, *does* exist in human language and thus Displacement is not an imperfection. Moreover he seems to think that Uninterpretable Features are not an imperfection *in that they are used for triggering Displacement*, which he considers is a property of human language. Consider (iv):

(iv) All of this falls into place if uninterpretable features are the mechanism for displacement, perhaps even an optimal mechanism. But displacement comes "free," and its application is determined by IC [=interface conditions]: the duality of semantic interpretation at SEM. If this line of reasoning is tenable, then uninterpretable features and the extra relation Agree move from the unexplained category (2i) [=unexplained element of S_0] to the category of principled explanation (ii [=IC (the principled part of S_0)]-iii [=General properties]), and the discussion so far continues to conform pretty closely to the strong minimalist thesis (3) [=(2i) is empty]. (Chomsky 2001b: 14)

I agree with (ii), not (iv), and would like to claim (iii), but this problem is beyond the scope of this book, so I will leave it for future study.

10. However, Chomsky cannot but assume the EPP feature because he wants to explain the *expletive construction* in Icelandic or other constructions in a generalized way (see Chomsky (2000, 2001a, b)). As for this important problem, note that Tonoike (2002a) attempts to eliminate what Chomsky calls both the obligatory *TH* (=Thematization)/ *EX* (=Extraction) *Rule* (applied *in PF*) specific to English and the EPP feature, which I think is an interesting proposal and in a desirable direction.

11. Thus under the strict notation *he* would be only a feature bundle {D-feature, 3rd-Person, Sg-Num, Mas} because *he* has not become a full form yet due to lacking (Nominative) Case.

12. This idea is in line with Halle and Marantz (1993), whose theory is called *Distributed Morphology*, and Tonoike (1999, 2001).

13. This naming of *Feature Dribbling* is suggested by D. L. Smith (personal communication, 2001). He pointed out that *Feature Percolation*, the term often used, usually refers to an upward movement. (Percolation is upward and dribbling is downward.)

14. Note that (i) and (ii) include the *sister relation*.

15. In recent approaches in the Minimalist Program, the notation of *X-bar Theory* is no longer used. Moreover *trace* and *index* are abolished and only *copy* exists in the derivation. Through this book I will use these terms only for the exposition.

16. I have been using the term *TP* since 1999 (e.g. Nomura (1999a, b, 2000a, b, d, 2001a,

2002a, 2003)), but in this book I will use *IP* for the reasons mentioned in this section.

17. Note that I' level is not visible in the computational system in human language (see Chomsky (1995)).

18. From the perspective of comparative studies, it is considered to be appropriate that IP also has [Tense] and [φ]; in some languages what is called *Switch Reference* and *Complementizer Agreement* is observed, where some or other agreements of [Tense] and [φ] features are seen. For Switch Reference, see Finer (1985) and Watanabe (1996, 2000), and for Complementizer Agreement, see Zwart (1993, 1997) and Watanabe (1996, 2000).

19. Thus, I assume that the *bare* form is in fact different from the *root* form. That is, *go* in (i) is the bare form in the underlying structure but it is given the *root* form by the modal *can* in the derived structure and thus can become a full form and be pronounced.

    (i) He can *go*. (=(15a))

    This assumption is quite natural considering the agreement relations in *have* and the following *-en* form in the perfect or *be* and the following *-ing* form in the progressive. If I were to use Chomsky's (1957) famous formalization in (ii), it would be better expressed in (iii) in my assumption.

    (ii) Aux→C (M) (have+en) (be+ing) (be+en)   (Chomsky 1957: 39)
    (iii) Aux→C (M+*Root*) (have+en) (be+ing) (be+en)

20. The idea of *feature copying* and *recycling the copy* is also seen in Takahashi (2001, 2002) and Tonoike (2001), though the concept is different from mine.

21. Since Affix Hopping is also, needless to say, an operation as the last resort, it does not apply in the derivation of Functional Verb Elements (e.g. modals and *have/be*). On the other hand, the Lexical Verb Elements cannot move to I to get the [Tense] and [φ] features either, because they have no uninterpretable features, to trigger the operation *Move*. This follows the general condition in (i):

    (i) The Move operations cannot apply to verbs having *root forms*.

Note incidentally that the following pairs are often discussed as examples of general locality conditions applying to movement (e.g. Rizzi's (1990) *Relativized Minimality*, Chomsky's (1995) *Minimal Link Condition*; MLC, etc.):

(ii) a. *John$_i$ seems that *it* is certain t$_i$ to fix the car. (Superraising)
 b. *How$_i$ did John wonder *why* we fixed the car t$_i$? (*Wh*-Island Constraint)
 c. *Have$_i$ John *could* t$_i$ been there? (Head Movement Constraint)

However, we may say that the cases in (iia, b) are different from that in (iic); *Have* in (iic) has no possibility of moving due to (i) while *John* in (iia) and *How* in (iib) have the potentiality of moving in that they have some or other uninterpretable features. Though, Chomsky's (2000, 2001a, b) *Defective Intervention Constraint* (DIC) would only deal with (iib, c) not (iia) because he holds that head movement is not real, as we discussed in 1.4.

22. Note that under our assumptions the derivation crashes even if we assume the traditional idea of *do*-support; the verb walk remains *bare* and thus cannot be pronounced. Moreover, since I am assuming that Affix Hopping itself is an operation of the last resort, the general idea that *do*-support is an operation of the last resort (Chomsky (1995: Chapter 2)) would be incompatible; namely, this would require *double* last resort.

    More generally, the traditional idea of *do*-support or *do*-insertion would be dubious from the perspective of the *Inclusiveness Condition* assumed by Chomsky (2000b: 2), "which bars introduction of new elements (features) in the course of computation: indices, traces, syntactic categories, or bar levels, and so on," though one might propose that phonological operations are out of computation.

23. (31a-d) are what Huddleston (1976: 339) calls the *NICE properties* (Negation, Inversion, Code, Emphasis), which are needed to separate main verbs from auxiliaries, and (31e-g) are *Modal Criteria* (Palmer (1990)), which are specifically needed to exclude the auxiliaries *be*, *have* (, and *do* in a sense) from the set of proper modals.

    These formal characteristics are a very important diagnosis in defining English auxiliaries or modals; for example, *have to* (especially in American English) is often called a *quasi-modal auxiliary*, but it is in fact a kind of *main verbs* because it does not satisfy any of the seven characteristics. On the other hand, *ought to*, though selecting not a root form but a *to*-infinitive, should be a modal, as I shall discuss in Chapter 5.

24. As for a good review or study of the history of the formalization of *do* (e.g. *do*-support, *do*-insertion, or *do*-deletion), see Nakao and Amano eds. (1994) and Amano (1999: Chapters 1-2).

25. As is well known, the affirmative and non-stressed *do* does not exist in English:

    (i) *He dŏes walk. (˘ means no stress)

    This will lead us to assume the following condition as to using do:

    (ii) Since *do* is entirely empty in meaning, it must acquire features entering into *semantic interpretation* (e.g. [Q], [Neg], [Affirmative] (=used with Emphasis), etc.).

    That is to say, *do* has *only* a Tense feature and φ-feature in the lexicon.

26. Shiro Wada asked me why the periphrastic *do* is considered to be a type of modals at the presentation of Nomura (2003b). The discussion in this section will be an answer.

27. I will leave it open whether our framework applies to the derivation from category to category; in this book words contain *categorial features* (V, N=D, A, P, etc.) in the lexicon, as I noted in note 11. For example, *decide* and *decision* each exist in the lexicon in following forms:

    (i) a. decide
           Categorial Feature: [V-feature]
           Semantic Feature: [make up one's mind]
        b. decision
           Categorial Feature: [D-feature]
           Semantic Feature: [make up one's mind]

    But, if categorial features were also assigned *in narrow syntax*, we might assume that the lexicon economically contains *only abstract semantic features*. As for this problem, we should also note the claims that all the categories can be reduced into two categories, i.e. *nouns and verbs*, discussed by the generative semantics linguists (Ross (1969, 1972, 1973), McCawley (1970, 1971, 1975, 1977)), or cognitive linguists (Langacker (1987)). As an illustration of this, note Smith (1978):

(ii) There are only two fundamental categories in language. Nouns, clauses, and adverbs are nominal (NP). All other traditional categories are verbal (V). All basic orderings follow according to the primary NP^n-V or V-NP^n conventional ordering of the language. (Smith 1978: 88)

But, at the same time, we should consider Chomsky's (1970) persuasive discussion about *nominalization*, where he supports the *lexicalist hypothesis*. Moreover, each derivative has a different meaning in a sense, as shown in (iii), and has a different phonetic realization, as shown in (iv):

(iii) a. decide: 1. settle (a dispute, an issue or a case); give a judgment on (sth)
                2. consider and come to a conclusion; make up one's mind; resolve
     b. decision: 1. deciding; making up one's mind; conclusion reached; judgment
                2. ability to decide quickly
     c. decisive: 1. having a particular, important or conclusive effect
                2. having or showing the ability to decide quickly
                                                                    (quoted from *OALD*)

(iv) a. decide [disaid]
     b. decision [disiʒn]
     c. decisive [disaisiv]

The latter phonetic problem could perhaps be solved in some technical way or other, as in the cases of the irregular verbs.

28. Hasegawa (2003) also claims that Chomsky (1995: Chapter 4) cannot explain the ungrammaticality in (ib) because he should predict that both of (ia) and (ib) are grammatical:

(i) a.   John has not come.
     b.   *John not comes.   (Hasegawa 2003: 59)

29. Note that Chomsky (1957) assumes that Affix Hopping applies to *all* the verbs including *have* and *be*.

30. Akira Watanabe (TEC lecture in 2000) argues that VP-deletion analyses *under LF copying* are problematic with (i) θ-marking of the subject and its derivational history and (ii) copy intonation.

31. As I defined in (14b), 'finite' *have* and *be* verbs belong to the class of Functional Verb Elements, and thus the *bare* forms of *have* and *be*, needless to say, belong to the class of Lexical Verb Elements, which is compatible with the following examples of VP-deletion.

   (i)   John will be here, and Mary will too.
   (ii) John will [Root] *be here*, and Mary will *be here*.
   (iii) ?John should have left, but Mary shouldn't.
   (iv) John should [Root] *have left*, and Mary should *have left*.

32. Shigeo Tonoike (personal communication, 2004) is exploring the possibility that VP-deletion is accounted for under the *feature copying and recycling approach* (see Tonoike (2001), cf. Takahashi (2001, 2002)). See also note 20.

33. Note incidentally that we might say that Halle and Marantz's (1993) *Distributed Morphology* is in line with a transformationalist approach as to verbal morphology, though the conceptual necessity is very different. So it seems to me that Chomsky (1995), who takes a strict lexicalist approach, does not approve of Distributed Morphology. However, recent Chomsky (2000, 2001a, b) seems to be more favorable to it.

34. Though conceptually different from our framework, Watanabe (2000, 2001) claims that the formal features of the Goal are copied onto the Probe in the Agree operation contra Chomsky (2000), where feature checking and feature movement are abolished, and more in line with Chomsky (1998), where feature checking and feature movement are still assumed.

Chapter 2

ModalP Hypothesis[1]

2.1 Introduction

In this chapter I propose the ModalP Hypothesis, which will be the fundamental framework throughout this book; I claim that modals constitute their own projections and NegP is placed between IP and ModalP. I will show that the phrase structure generally assumed by Chomsky (1995, 2000, 2001a, b) and others cannot properly account for the scope ambiguities of modals and negation, that is, cannot generate the interpretation of Modal Negation in principle, while the ModalP Hypothesis can generate both interpretations of Modal Negation and Propositional Negation in a principled way. Lastly, I observe that though the ModalP Hypothesis predicts that negated modals always have the two interpretations shown above, this is not empirically true. However, I claim that this fact is not a counterexample to the present proposal, but that the accidental gaps for some modals are subject to the functional system that English modals themselves have and thus is compatible with the ModalP Hypothesis.

2.2 Ouhalla's (1991) and Cinque's (1999) ModP

There have been other, but not many, studies where ModP is used or its possibility is discussed; for example, see Ouhalla (1991) and Cinque (1999). But we should point out differences between the ModalP Hypothesis in this book and their ModP.

First, Cinque (1999) hypothesizes many functional categories (including Mood and Modal) toward a universal hierarchy of clausal functional projections based on various typological facts, and especially the positions where adverbs occur (*AdvP-in-Spec-Hypothesis*), as shown in (1):

(1) [*frankly* Mood_speech act [*fortunately* Mood_evaluative [*allegedly* Mood_evidential [*probably* Mood_epistemic [*once* T(Past) [*then* T(Future) [*perhaps* Mood_irrealis [*necessarily* Mood_necessity [*possibly* Asp_possibility [*usually* Asp_habitual [*again* Asp_repetitive(I) [*often* Asp_frequentative(I) [*intentionally* Mood_volitional [*quickly* Asp_celerative(I) [*already* T(Anterior) [*no longer* Asp_terminative [*still* Asp_continuative [*always* Asp_perfect(?) [*just* Asp_retrospective [*soon* Asp_proximative [*briefly* Asp_durative [*characteristically*(?) Asp_generic/progressive [*almost* Asp_prospective [*completely* Asp_SgCompletive(I) [*tutto* Asp_PlCompletive [*well* Voice [*fast/early* Asp_celerative(II) [*again* Asp_repetitive(II) [*often* Asp_frequentative(II) [*completely* Asp_SgCompletive(II)]]]]]]]]]]]]]]]]]]]]]]]]]]]]]]] (Cinque 1999: 106)

This seems to be one of the interesting directions of study, but at the same time we should be very careful in hypothesizing so many new functional categories. Moreover, Amano (1999: Chapters 13-14) argues that the licensing of adverbs strongly depends on *semantic* conditions and that it will not suffice to account for the licensing of adverbs by (functional) heads alone (e.g. Travis (1988), Bowers (1993), Cinque (1999)). In these respects my proposal is different from Cinque's in that I argue that ModalP is needed in English grammar *as a minimum* requirement.

Second, Ouhalla (1991) gives the following structure:

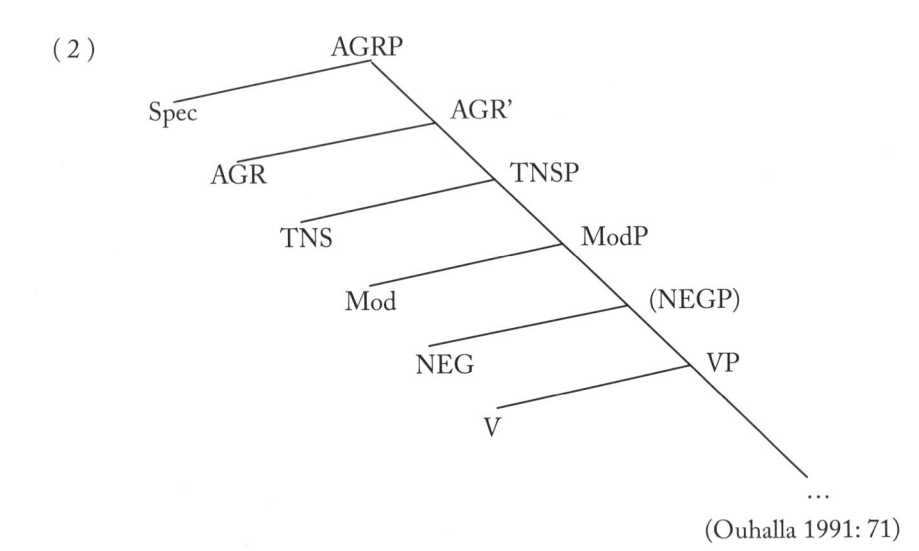

(2)

```
              AGRP
             /    \
          Spec    AGR'
                 /    \
              AGR    TNSP
                    /    \
                 TNS    ModP
                       /    \
                    Mod    (NEGP)
                          /    \
                       NEG    VP
                             /  \
                            V   ...
```

(Ouhalla 1991: 71)

This structure is different from mine in two points: first, Ouhalla assumes AGRP (note that Chomsky abolished AgrP in Chomsky (1995: Chapter 4)). Second, he assumes *ModP over NEGP*, but I assume *NegP over ModalP*, which will be discussed later (see Chapter 11).

2.3 Chomsky's (1995, 2000, 2001a, b) Sentence Structure

For the discussion below, it would be useful to review Chomsky's standard sentence structure. Chomsky has developed the Minimalist Program since 1995 (Chomsky (1995, 2000, 2001a, b)), but we may say that sentence structure has not been changed, as far as *Modals are concerned*.[2] As an illustration of this, observe the following structure (3):

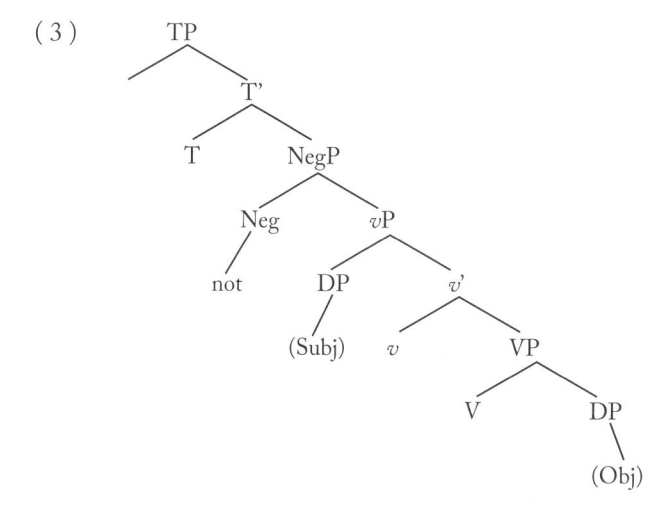

(3)
```
         TP
          \
           T"
          /  \
         T    NegP
             /    \
           Neg     vP
           /      /  \
         not    DP    v'
               /     /  \
            (Subj)  v    VP
                       /    \
                      V      DP
                              \
                             (Obj)
```

Compared with Chomsky (1995: Chapters 2-3), there are two important changes: (i) Chomsky (1995: Chapter 4) eliminates the syntactic nodes *Agr* (i.e. AGRsP and AGRoP), which Chomsky (1995: Chapters 2-3) assumed following Pollock's (1989) AgrP (*Split-I Hypothesis*), for *conceptual* or *theory internal reasons*.[3] (ii) Instead, Chomsky (1995: Chapter 4, and his subsequent work) assumes *the Split VP Hypothesis*, where the verb phrase is divided into a main verb phrase VP and a functional verb projection *v*P.[4), 5)]

Based on (i) and (ii) (i.e. the tree diagram (3)), the structure of a simple sentence including a modal auxiliary in (4a) must be as shown in (4b):

(4) a. You must not go.
b.
```
              TP
              |
              T'
             /  \
            T   NegP
            |   /  \
         must Neg   vP
              |    /  \
             not  DP   v'
                  |   /  \
                 you v    VP
                          |
                         go
```

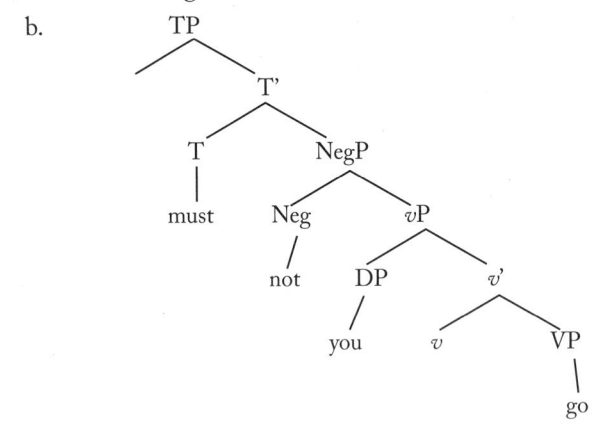

2.4 ModalP Hypothesis

In this section I will propose *the ModalP Hypothesis*, which will be assumed throughout this book:

(5) a. AgrP or AGRsP and AGRoP are all eliminated just as in Chomsky (1995: Chapter 4) and in his subsequent work.
b. I hypothesize *IP* rather than *TP* for the reasons discussed in Chapter 1 (see especially Section 1.6), though I assumed TP in Nomura (1999a, b, 2000a, b, d, 2001a, 2002a).
c. Modals constitute their own projections, i.e. *ModalP*.
e. I hypothesize NegP, which I assume to be between IP and ModalP. However, unlike Pollock (1989), Zanuttini (1990), or Chomsky (1995), I assume that *not* is not in the Head but in the Spec of NegP, as discussed in Rizzi (1990). Thus, in this book I also assume that the covert element [NE] occupies the head of NegP.[6] (cf. *ne...pas* in French or *ne...noht* in Old English.)

Based on these assumptions, the structure of a simple sentence including a modal auxiliary in (6a) will be shown in (6b) (cf. (4b)):[7]

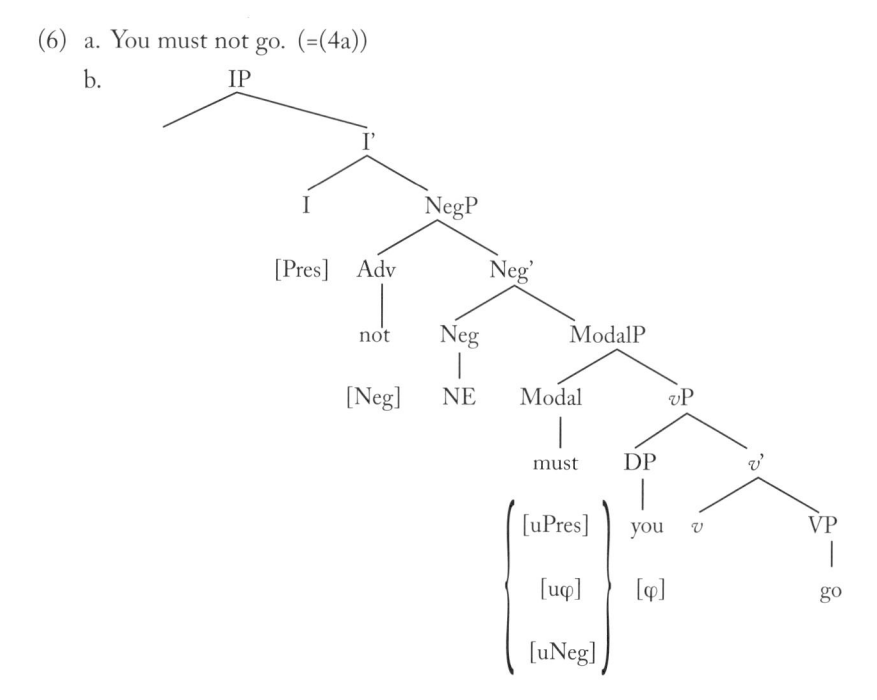

(6) a. You must not go. (=(4a))
    b.
```
                IP
               /  \
              I'
             / \
            I   NegP
         [Pres]  /  \
               Adv   Neg'
                |   /  \
               not Neg  ModalP
                   |    /   \
                [Neg] NE  Modal    vP
                          |       /  \
                         must    DP   v'
                                 |   /  \
                       [uPres]  you v    VP
                                              |
                         [uφ]    [φ]         go

                       [uNeg]
```

As I discussed in Chapter 1, the modal *must*, having the feature [uPres], raises to I[0] for checking off [uPres]. Before raising to I, *must* raises to Neg[0] to check off [uNeg] under the Spec-Head configuration in NegP.

Note also that I hypothesize *NegP over ModalP* unlike Ouhalla (1991). Syntactically, it seems most reasonable to assume this structure, at least in *English*, which will be supported by various discussions in this book.

2.5 Scope between Modal and *Not*

In this section I discuss two relations between modal auxiliaries and the negative word *not*, which will be an important basis for assuming the ModalP Hypothesis.

2.5.1 Two Relations between Modals and *Not*

As is well known, there are two relations between modals and *not*; namely, *Propositional Negation* (Main Verb Negation) and *Modal Negation* (Auxiliary Negation).[8] As an illustration of this, consider the following examples of the root uses of *must* (=obligation) and *may* (=permission):

(7) a. Propositional Negation (Main Verb Negation)=NOT > MUST
   You must [not go to the party].
   =I oblige you [not to go].
 b. Modal Negation (Auxiliary Negation)=MAY > NOT
   You [may not] go to the party.
   =I do [not permit] you to go.

How can we express these two patterns of negation structurally? We shall consider this problem in the next sections.

2.5.2 A Problem with Generally Assumed Phrase Structure (4b)

Let us begin with Main Verb Negation. The following root modals in (8a-e) can have the interpretation of Propositional Negation:

(8) a. You must[n't go/not go]. (MUST > NOT)
   =I oblige you [not to go].
 b. You should[n't go/not go]. (SHOULD > NOT)
 c. You ought[n't to go/not to go]. (OUGHT > NOT)
   =I advise you [not to go].
 d. You may [not go]. (MAY > NOT)
   =I permit you [not to go].
 e. You can [not go]. (CAN > NOT)
   =You are permitted [not to go].

However, we need not consider the cases in (8d, e); they surely have the interpretation of Propositional Negation, but we should regard them not as instances of *sentential negation* but as *verb phrase negation*. First, neither *may not* nor *can not* can be contracted in Propositional Negation:[9]

(9) a. *You *mayn't* go. (=I permit you not to go.)
   b. *You *can't* go. (=You are permitted not to go.)

If they were sentential negations, *contraction* could apply just as does in sentential negation of the *root* use, as shown in (10):

(10) a. You [may not] go. (I do [not permit] you to go.)
      =You *mayn't* go. (BrE, but seems to be almost obsolescent[10])
   b. You [cannot] go. (I do [not permit] you to go.)
      =You *can't* go.

Second, the tag question will be negative, not affirmative:[11]

(11) You can not go to the party, *can't you?/*can you?*

If (11) were a case of sentential negation, *can you* should be grammatical. Considering the result of the two tests, the structure of (8d, e) can be shown as in (12), given the structure (4b):

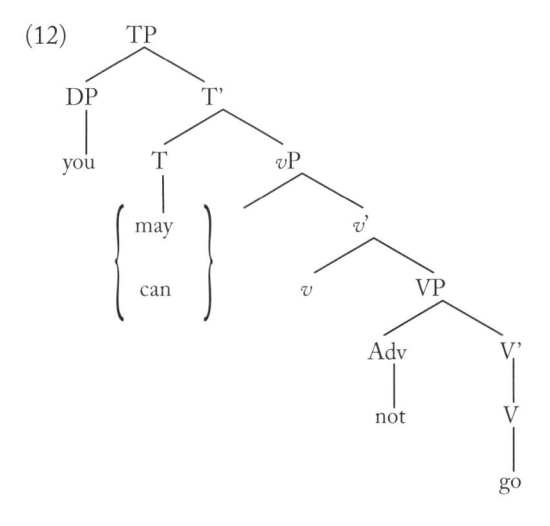

(12)
```
        TP
       /  \
      DP   T'
      |   /  \
     you T    vP
         |   /  \
       {may} v'
       {can}  /  \
             v   VP
                /  \
              Adv   V'
              |     |
             not    V
                    |
                    go
```

Under this structure, the interpretation will be, needless to say, not Modal Negation but Propositional Negation, since the VP-adverb *not* is always *under the modal* and thus cannot c-command it.

Let us turn to (8a-c), which are without doubt instances of sentential negation;[12] first, contraction is possible:

(13) a. You *mustn't* go. (=I oblige you [not to go]).
   b. You *shouldn't* go. (=I advise you [not to go]).
   c. You *oughtn't* to go. (=I advise you [not to go]).

Second, the tag question is affirmative:[13]

(14) You shouldn't go to the party, *should you*?

Now, how could we express this pattern of negation? In the cases of Propositional Negation, there would be no problem if we assumed the generally assumed phrase structure (4b); these modals are base-generated in T and are structurally placed *over NegP*, so that they properly c-command *not*, as shown in (15):[14]

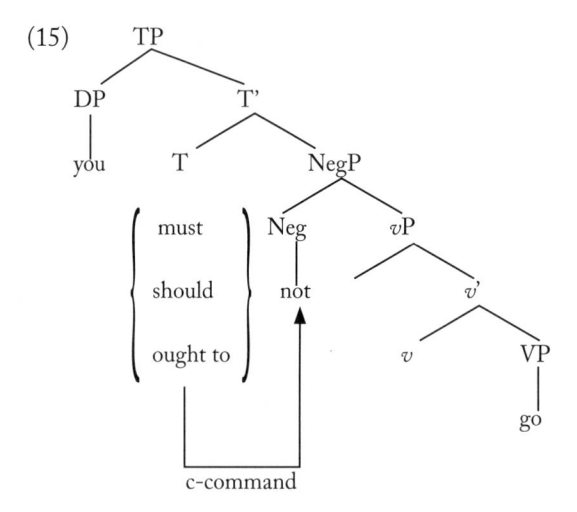

Next let us consider the case of Modal Negation. Consider the following examples:

(16) a. You [may not] go. (NOT > MAY)
    =I do [not permit] you to go.
  b. You [can't/cannot] go. (NOT > CAN)
    =You are [not permitted] to go.
  c. You [needn't/need not] go. (NOT > NEED)
    =You are [not obliged] to go.

In this case, we could not have the interpretation of Modal Negation in (16a-c) even if we assumed (4b); the negative *not* cannot c-command T^0, where the above modals are base-generated:

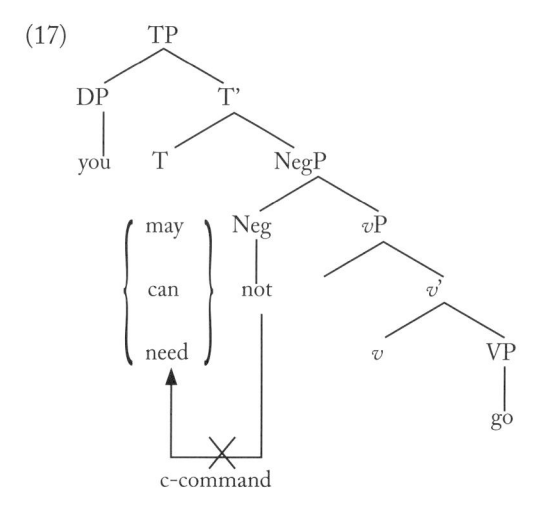

(17) [tree diagram: TP dominating DP (you) and T'; T' dominating T and NegP; T containing {may, can, need}; NegP dominating Neg (not) and vP; vP dominating v'; v' dominating v and VP; VP dominating go. Arrow from T to below with "c-command" crossed out.]

In conclusion, the generally assumed phrase structure (4b) cannot account for the interpretation of Modal Negation.[15]

2.5.3 An Alternative Account Based on the ModalP Hypothesis

Now, let us examine whether the present proposal, i.e. the ModalP Hypothesis, can properly explain the two interpretations. Here I assume only the following hypothesis (18):

(18) Scope relations between the negative word *not* and the modal obtain *optionally* either (i) in the Modal-underlying structure (i.e., where the modal is in Modal^0 position) or (ii) in the Modal-derived structure (i.e., where the modal is in I^0 position):

As an illustration of this, let us consider the above example of the root use of *may* (=permission) in (7b) again. First, the case (18i) generates the interpretation of Modal Negation, as shown in (19b):

(19) a. Modal Negation=MAY > NOT
   You [may not] go to the party.
   =I do [not permit] you to go.
 b. the Modal-underlying structure before moving the modal to T

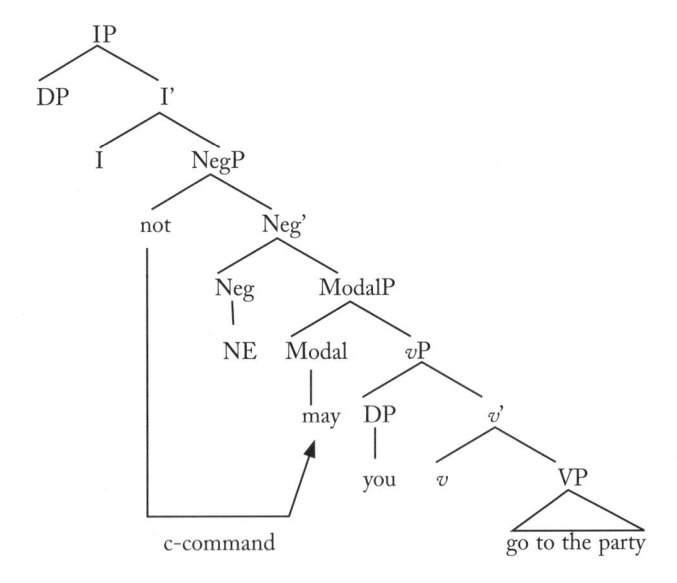

```
              IP
             /  \
           DP    I'
                /  \
               I    NegP
                   /    \
                 not    Neg'
                        /  \
                      Neg   ModalP
                       |    /    \
                      NE  Modal   vP
                           |     /  \
                          may   DP   v'
                                |   /  \
                               you v    VP
                                       /\
                                      go to the party
          c-command
```

On the other hand, the case (18ii) generates the interpretation of Propositional Negation, as shown in (20b), just as the generally assumed structure (4b) does:

(20) a. Propositional Negation=MUST > NOT

You must [not go to the party]. (=(7b))
=I oblige you [not to go].[16)]

b. the Modal-derived structure after moving to T

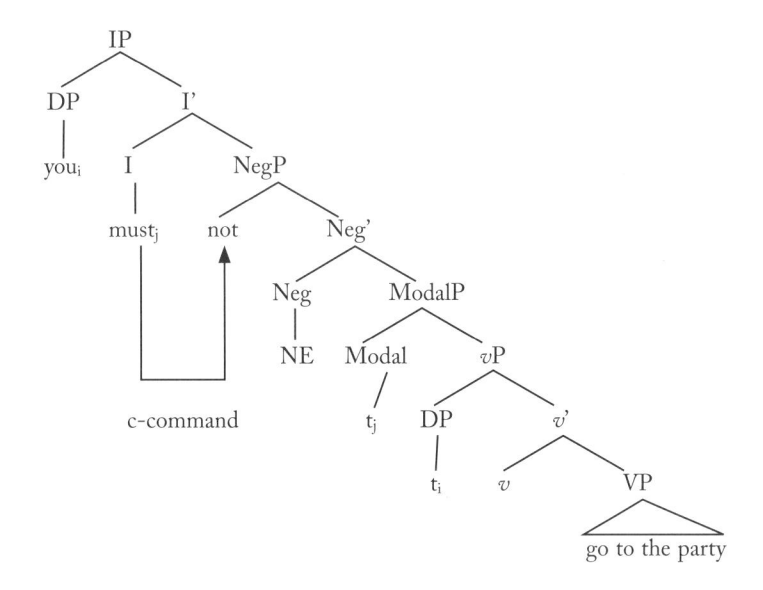

```
              IP
             /  \
           DP    I'
           |    /  \
         youᵢ  I    NegP
              |    /    \
           mustⱼ  not    Neg'
                        /    \
                      Neg    ModalP
                       |     /    \
                       NE  Modal   vP
                            |     /  \
                            tⱼ   DP   v'
                                 |   / \
                                 tᵢ v   VP
                                        /\
                                   go to the party
```
c-command

In sum, I have shown that the generally assumed phrase structure (4b) is inadequate in that it cannot generate the interpretation of Propositional Negation, while the ModalP Hypothesis can naturally generate both the interpretations of Modal Negation and Propositional Negation.[17), 18)]

2.5.4 Absence of Modal Negation or Propositional Negation in Modals

Here the objection might be raised that the present proposal wrongly predicts the following (21):

(21) As for the interpretations in the negative sentences including modals, both the interpretations of Modal Negation and Propositional Negation *always* hold.

Needless to say, (21) is empirically wrong. Consider the following examples of epistemic uses of *may*:

(22) You may not go to the party. (=epistemic use)
   a. Propositional Negation=MAY>NOT
      You may [not go to the party].
      =It is possible [that you will not go to the party].
   b. *Modal Negation=MAY>NOT
      *You [may not] go to the party.
      =It is [not possible] that you will go to the party.[19)]

That is to say, the epistemic *may* does not have the Modal Negation interpretation unlike the root use of *may* in (19a). The same thing applies to many epistemic modals, as shown in (23):

(23) a. He should [n't/not be at home now]. (SHOULD>NOT)
   b. He wo[n't be at home now]. (WILL>NOT)
      He will [not at home now].

Moreover, as I discussed in the previous section, the root use of *must* also has only the interpretation of Propositional Negation, as shown in (24):

(24) You must not go to the party. (=root use)
   a. Propositional Negation=MUST>NOT
      You must [not go to the party].
      =It is essential [that you not go to the party].
   b. *Modal Negation=MUST>NOT
      *You [must not] go to the party.
      =It is [not essential] that you go to the party.

The same thing applies to other root modals expressing obligation, as shown in (25):

(25) a. You should[n't go/not go]. (SHOULD>NOT)
   b. You ought[n't to go/not to go]. (OUGHT>NOT)

However, in this section I claim that these are not counterexamples to our framework under the following hypothesis in (26):

(26) All the modals *can* have both interpretations of Modal Negation and Propositional Negation *in syntax*, but *accidental gaps* exist, each of which is consistent with the harmonic system that English modals themselves exhibit.[20]

First of all, let us consider Coates's (1983) *Principle of the Inviolability of Epistemic Modality*, as shown in (27), and a tentative assumption about the negation of the root modals expressing obligation tentatively made, as shown in (28):

(27) Principle of the Inviolability of Epistemic Modality
    a. Negation affects the main prediction.
    b. Hypothetical meaning affects the main prediction.
    c. Past time marking affects the main prediction.   (Coates 1983: 244)
(28) The negation of the root modals expressing *obligation* affects the main prediction.

As for Coates's principle, we are now concerned with only (27a). She submits (27a-c) as a summary based on examining many examples from linguistic corpora, but we should say that at least (27a) is empirically wrong, because some epistemic modals can generate the interpretation of *Modal Negation*. Consider the following examples and statements:

(29) a. He [can't/cannot] be at home now. (NOT>CAN)[21]
      =It is [not possible] that he is at home now.
    b. He [needn't/need not] be at home now. (NOT>NEED)
      =It is [not necessary/necessarily the case] that he is at home now.
    c. He [mustn't/must not] be at home now. (NOT>MUST) (AmE)
      =It is [not certain] that he is at home now.
(30) There must have been hundreds of people waiting, *mustn't there*?

(Leech 1987²: 93)

(31) However, *must not/mustn't* is occasionally used in this sense [i.e. epistemic modality], especially in American English.

> I haven't heard Molly moving about. She *mustn't* be awake. Her alarm *mustn't* have gone off. (OR ... She *can't* be awake. Her alarm *can't* have gone off.)

And *mustn't* is normal in this sense in British English in question tags after *must*, in negative questions.

> It must be nice to be a cat, *mustn't it?* (NOT ... *can't it?*)
> *Mustn't it* have been strange to live in the Middle Ages?

(Swan 1995²: 342)

(32) a. He must be quite exhausted, *mustn't he?*　　　(Declerck 1991a: 408)
　　b. *Mustn't there* be a rational explanation for these psychic phenomena?

(Ibid.: 407)

The implication is that (27a) might be a *necessary* condition but cannot be a *sufficient* condition at all.

Next, let us consider the assumption in (28). First of all, (28) is a mere stipulation. Second, (28) literally applies to the root modals expressing *obligation* only and cannot apply to other root modals; on the contrary, root modals generally have the interpretation of Modal Negation, as shown in (33). Note especially that *need*, which express *necessity* similar to *obligation* in meanings, has the interpretation of Modal Negation, not Propositional Negation:

(33) a. You [may not] go to the party. (NOT > MAY)
　　　 =I do [not permit] you to go to the party.
　　b. You [can't/cannot] go to the party. (NOT > CAN)
　　　 =You are [not permitted] to go to the party.
　　c. You [needn't/need not] go to the party. (NOT > NEED)
　　　 =You are [not obliged] to go to the party.

That is, (28) cannot be generalized to the properties of other English root modals. Third, from the comparative linguistic perspective (28) does not necessarily apply to other languages. Consider the following example from German:

(34) Du mußt nicht gehen, wenn du nicht willst.[22)]
    you must not go if you not will
    'You don't have to go if you don't want to.'

This means that even if (28) were right in English it could not be a universal principle. Furthermore, the following example (35) shows that even in English the root modals expressing *obligation* can be negated as Modal Negation:

(35) You must not go home now to look after the children, *mustn't you*?
$$\text{(Declerck 1991a: 375)}$$

In conclusion, neither (27a) nor (28) can be on the right track in many respects.[23), 24)]

Here we can turn to our hypothesis (26). Consider the following tables (*means verb phrase negation, and p means proposition):

(36) Root Modals

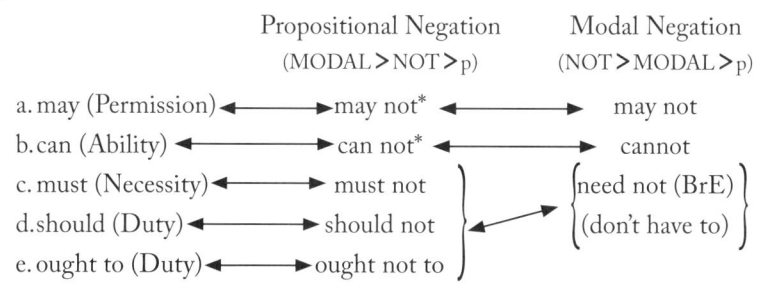

	Propositional Negation (MODAL>NOT>p)	Modal Negation (NOT>MODAL>p)
a. may (Permission)	⟷ may not* ⟷	may not
b. can (Ability)	⟷ can not* ⟷	cannot
c. must (Necessity)	⟷ must not	need not (BrE)
d. should (Duty)	⟷ should not	(don't have to)
e. ought to (Duty)	⟷ ought not to	

(37) Epistemic Modals

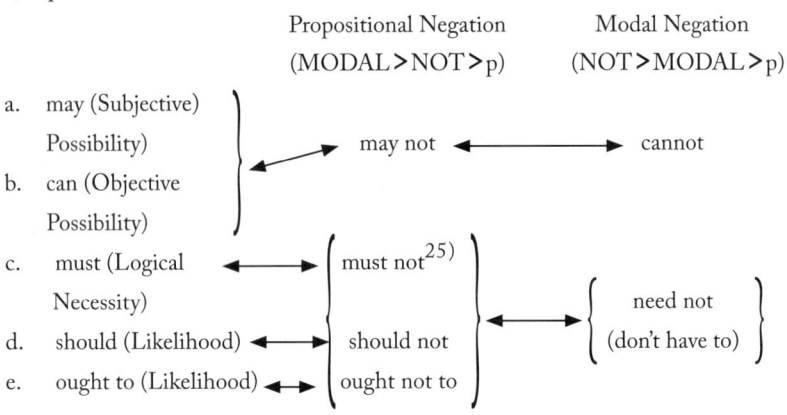

		Propositional Negation (MODAL > NOT > p)	Modal Negation (NOT > MODAL > p)
a.	may (Subjective Possibility)	may not	cannot
b.	can (Objective Possibility)		
c.	must (Logical Necessity)	must not[25]	need not (don't have to)
d.	should (Likelihood)	should not	
e.	ought to (Likelihood)	ought not to	

Note that the affirmative use of the modal *need does not exist in (36) or (37). If we dare to include the main verb use of *need to*, it would be as in (38) be it a root use or an epistemic use:

(38) need to ⟷ { must not / should not / ought not to } ⟷ need not

Here I will explain what I mean by this. We can best regard the *accidental gaps* of modals as depending *functionally* on what I describe as the *harmonic system of the English modals*.[26] The main points are as follows: first, as for (36a, b), the gaps of Propositional Negation of the root *may* and *can* are occupied by the verb phrase negation *may not* and *cannot*. Second, as for (36c-e), the gaps of Modal Negation of the root *must*, *should*, and *ought to* are all substituted for by *need not* or (the quasi-modal) *don't have to*. This is because it is meaningful for us to mention the degree of the obligation but it is meaningless to mention the degree of obligation if we negate the obligation itself, as shown in (39):

(39) must
　　(have to)
　　(need to)
　　ought to
　　should　　　　　　　　↑　　Degree of Obligation

------------------------------------+------------------------------------
　　need not (don't have to)　↓　　Negation of Obligation

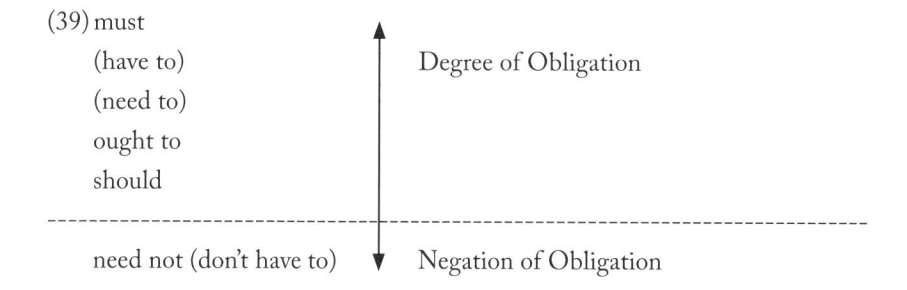

To put it in other words, the negation of the root modality of *must*, *should*, and *ought to* would be logically equal to the negation of the root modality *need*, as shown in (40):

(40) It is not { imperative (i.e. *must*) } that you go.
　　　　　　　 { advisable (i.e. *should* or *ought to*) }
　　=It is not necessary (i.e. *need*) that you go.

The same is true of (37c-e). Consider (41) and (42):

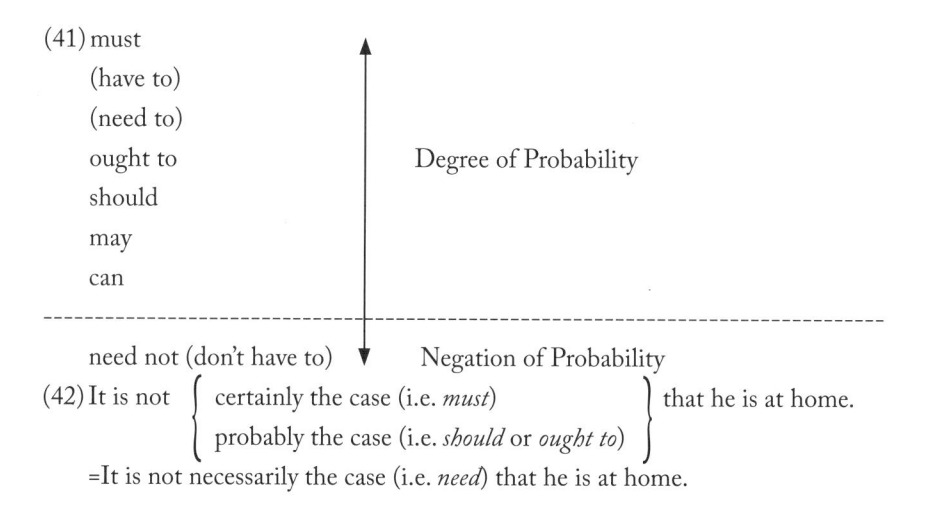

(41) must
　　(have to)
　　(need to)
　　ought to
　　should
　　may
　　can　　　　　　　　↑　　Degree of Probability

------------------------------------+------------------------------------
　　need not (don't have to)　↓　　Negation of Probability

(42) It is not { certainly the case (i.e. *must*) } that he is at home.
　　　　　　　 { probably the case (i.e. *should* or *ought to*) }
　　=It is not necessarily the case (i.e. *need*) that he is at home.

Third, as for (37a), the gap of Modal Negation for the epistemic *may* is filled by *cannot*. On the other hand, the gap of Propositional Negation for the epistemic *can* is filled by *may not*, as shown in (43):

(43) In the negative, *can't* only express the idea of 'never'. To express 'sometimes ... not' we have to use *may not*.
   a. Such people *can* be spiteful. (Such people are sometimes spiteful.)
   b. Such people *cannot* be spiteful. (=They are never spiteful.)
   c. Such people *may not* be spiteful. (Sometimes they are not spiteful.)
(Declerck 1991a: 415-416)

Note here that each modal appears only once both in (34) and in (35) and thus is consistent with the system

In sum, in this section I have argued that some modals indeed lack the interpretation of Modal Negation or Propositional Negation, but the accidental gaps are subject to the functional system that English modals themselves have and thus is compatible with the ModalP Hypothesis.

2.6 Concluding Remarks

In this chapter I proposed the ModalP Hypothesis, where modals constitute their own projections and NegP is between IP and ModalP. Then I showed that the phrase structure generally assumed by Chomsky (1995, 2000, 2001a, b) and others cannot account for the scope relations of modals and negation properly, i.e., they cannot generate the interpretation of Modal Negation in principle, while the ModalP Hypothesis can generate both interpretations, i.e. Modal Negation and Propositional Negation, in a principled way. Lastly, modals do not always have the two interpretations, but I claim that these are not counterexamples to the present proposal but that the gaps can be fully explained under the English modals system itself.

Notes to Chapter 2

1. As I mentioned in note 1 in Chapter 1, I have already used the ModP Hypothesis in Nomura (1999a, b, 2000a, b, d, 2001a), but I discussed the ModP Hypothesis extensively in Nomura (2002a), on which this chapter is partly based.

2. Strictly speaking, it seems to me, Chomsky's interest is not in the syntactic structure of the modals (in English) but in the structural refinement of the shape of VP *under ModalP*. In this sense, I stated that *the sentence structure has not been changed*. But note that the problems pointed out in this book persist under whatever framework proposed by Chomsky (1995, 2000, 2001a, b) we adopt.

3. *Conceptual or theory internal reasons* means that Agr has no support from any interface (i.e. LF or PF) relations, that is, one should not assume any functional categories such as Agr, whose existence do not have any semantic effect.

    For the *empirical* critique on the node Agr or AGRP, see Iatridou (1990), Tonoike (1993), Ando (1996), Matsubara (1997a, b), Hasegawa (2003), etc. Iatridou and Hasegawa criticize assuming functional categories easily and at the same time argue that most of Pollock's data are not *real* evidence for assuming Agr and thus we need not assume Agr empirically. Tonoike argues that if we assumed the syntactic node Agr and the notion of *equidistance* it would paradoxically follow that we cannot account for many linguistic data. Ando and Matsubara argue that since there are many agreement phenomena other than subject and object agreement, it would not appropriate if functional categories were confined to only the two agreement relations.

4. For the Split VP Hypothesis, see Koizumi (1999). Note that Koizumi (2002) proposes a *Partial Interpretation Hypothesis*, where the adequacy of the Split VP Hypothesis is discussed from the viewpoint of language acquisition.

5. We can also say that Chomsky uses vP as *a substitute for AgrP* even if he eliminates Agr. For this matter and the status of the EPP feature, see also Hasegawa (2002=2003: Chapter 3 in Part II), where he claims that both the EPP feature and covert feature movement in *wh*-movement be abolished.

6. This assumption on NegP will be discussed in detail in Chapter 11.

7. Here I would like to point out that to the best of my knowledge, Chomsky himself has not dealt with the syntactic category of Modal and the base-generated position of modals strictly since the 1980's. This means that we do not know whether or not Chomsky himself assumes the structure as in (4b), where modals are base-generated in the position I^0 or T^0.

   However, many linguists *tacitly* assume that modals are base-generated in the position I^0 or T^0. I suppose that this tacit assumption is based on Chomsky's (1981) following note:

   (i) Perhaps the Modals also appear within INFL. I will omit any discussion of their status, as well as other questions relating to the auxiliary system which have been the topic of much study and debate. (Chomsky 1981: 140, fn. 28)

   But we should pay attention to the word *perhaps* and the statement *I will omit any discussion of their status* in (i).

8. For studies of modals and negation, see particularly Ota (1980), Leech (1987^2), Coates (1983), Sawada (1993, 1995), Declerck (1991a), Nakano (1994), and Haan (1997).

9. Note also that *not* is stressed in (8d, e):

   (i) a. You may NOT go. (=I permit you not to go.)
       b. You can NOT go. (=You are permitted not to go.)

10. Leech (1971) notes the rare BrE form *mayn't* is used only in the use of permission, but the statement disappears in Leech (1987^2). See also Swan's (1995^2) comment:

    (i) *Might* has a contracted negative *mightn't*. <u>*Mayn't* is very unusual</u>.
    (Swan 1995^2: 323, underlines are mine)

    However, according to D. L. Smith (personal communication, 2004), contracted *mayn't* is also found in some American Dialects, e.g., in South Dakota.

11. I am grateful to Harumi Sawada (personal communication, 2001) for pointing out this fact.

12. Tonoike (2002b) notes two possibilities of treating interactions between modals and

negation, as shown in (i), but our discussion suggests that the first possibility should be discounted:

(i) The notorious and recalcitrant cases involve interaction between negation and modal auxiliaries. See Ernst (1992) for a treatment based on a chain c-command relationship. I cannot offer any illuminating alternative, but I suspect that one of the following two possibilities will turn out to be the correct analysis. One possibility is that problematic cases like *must not* involve VP negation while normal cases like *need not* involve sentence negation. The other possibility is that modals that take scope over negation like the quantifier *some* in "I didn't buy something" and are lexically specified as taking wide scope over negation. (Tonoike 2002b: 146, fn. 19)

13. In the cases of *mustn't* and *oughtn't to* we do not make tag questions easily, as shown in (i), for other reasons:

(i) a. ? We mustn't go to the party, *must we?*
 b. ? We oughtn't (to) go to the party, *ought we?*

But the contraction test crucially shows that (8a-c) are sentential negation. Additionally, Ando (2003) shows that *mustn't* is sentential negation since the connecting of *neither* proves it, which judgment is Lawrence Horn's, as shown in (ii):

(ii) "You mustn't tell lies." "*Neither* must you." (Ando 2003: 35)

14. There is a problem with base-generating *ought to* in T^0, as shown in (15), as we shall discuss in later in Chapter 5, but we tentatively assume this for the purpose of discussion.

15. Note that Mori (1995b) points out the same problem with Pollock's (1989) and Ouhalla's (1990) analyses of NegP; that is, their assumed structure can generate only the interpretation of Propositional Negation.

16. Note interestingly that auxiliary *beki* in modern Japanese or *beshi* in classical Japanese has the interpretation of Propositional Negation just as English modals *must, should,* and *ought to*. Consider the following examples:

(i) a. Kimi-wa paatii-e iku-beki-de-nai.
    you-Top party-to go-should-copula-not
    'You should [not go to the party].'
  b. Kore-wa nanji-no-motodori-to omoo-bekara-zu. (*Heekemonogatari*)
    This-Top you-Gen-hair-Comp think-must-not
    'You must [not think of this as your hair].'

It is often claimed that the phrase structures of Japanese and English form a *mirror image* (e.g. Smith (1978), Tonoike (1991, 1995)), and (ia, b) furthermore implies that the present hypothesis (18i, ii) can also apply to Japanese, considering that *zu* (=not) c-commands *beshi* (=must) in surface structure just as in the case of English *must*, *should*, or *ought to*. I will leave it open for now whether or not ModalP exits in Japanese as well.

17. Incidentally, it seems that examples such as in (ia, b), where the subject including negative elements (e.g. nothing, nobody, etc.) is linearly to the *left* to the modal and whose scope of the modal is over that of the negative subject are counterexamples to our system:

  (i) a. *Nothing may* be more controversial than modern art and architecture, ...
      (MAY>NOTHING) (*Times*, Jan. 1995, quoted from Sawada (2001: 70))
      =It may be [that nothing is more controversial than modern art and architecture],
      ....
    b. Nobody may be serious. (MAY>NOBODY)   (Kasai 2000: 275)
      =It may be [that nobody is serious].

But in this case as well, (18i) works and thus (ia, b) are not counterexamples; under the *VP Internal Subject Hypothesis*, the negative subject originally generated in *v*P-Spec is c-commanded by the modal *may*. Consider the following structures (iia,b):

(ii) a. [IP [ModalP may [*v*P nothing be more...]]] (the Modal-underlying structure)
  b. [IP [ModalP may [*v*P nobody be serious]]] (the Modal-underlying structure)

Moreover, we can, of course, find examples where the scope shows the same relation as the surface linear order. Consider the following examples:

(iii) *Nobody may* eat the cake. (NOBODY > MAY) (Sawada 2001: 69)
   =Nobody is permitted to eat the cake.

This time the scope relation follows from (18ii), as is seen in the structure (iv):

(iv) [IP Nobody_i [I' may_j [ModalP t_j [vP t_i eat the cake]]]
   (the Modal-derived structure)

18. Note incidentally that Tonoike (1999, 2002b, 2003) claims that in A-Movement only the phonetic features raise but that the semantic features stay in situ. For example, the underlying structure of (ia) can be shown in (ib) given his claim, where <he> stands for the phonetic feature and {he} the semantic feature and <{he}> stands for a combination of the phonetic feature <he> and the semantic feature {he}:

(i) a. He may go.
   b. [TP [Nom] may [vP <{he}> go]]

Under his discussion, <he> raises to Spec-TP to receive [Nom], as shown in (iia), and thus is replaced by the phonetic form of *he* represented as /he/ but the semantic feature {he} remains in VP-Spec, as shown in (iib):

(ii) a. [TP <he> [Nom] may [vP {he} go]]
    b. [TP /he/ may [vP {he} go]]

However, formal features other than phonetic ones can raise, considering the example in (iiia) and its structure in (iiib):

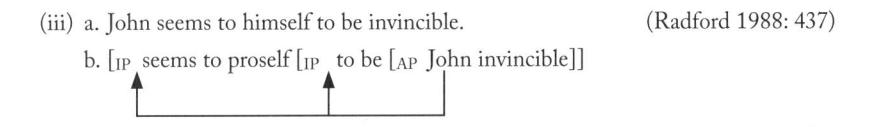

(iii) a. John seems to himself to be invincible. (Radford 1988: 437)
     b. [IP seems to proself [IP to be [AP John invincible]]

We cannot but think that not only phonetic features but also φ-features (i.e. [3rd-Person], [Sg-Num], and [Mas]) raise to IP-Spec because the subject *John* should bind the reflexive pronoun. (Tonoike (2003) provides a similar discussion in explaining *Quantifier Scope*.) This will support the following assumption in (iv), which is in line with Chomsky (2001) in (v):

(iv) Other features may raise only when they contribute to semantic interpretation.
(v) Optimally, OCC should be available only when necessary: that is, when it contributes to an outcome at SEM that is not otherwise expressive, the basic Fox-Reinhart intuition about optionality. (Chomsky 2001b: 10)

Here, if we applied his theory about A-Movement to Head Movement as well, the following analyses could also hold:

(vi) a. When only the phonetic features of modals raise to I^0 and the semantic features of modals stay in $Modal^0$, Propositional Negation will be produced in semantic interpretation. (cf. (18ii))
b. When both the phonetic features and the semantic features of modals raise to I^0, Modal Negation will be produced in semantic interpretation. (cf. (18i))

Given (via), the structure of (viia) can be shown in (viib), and given (vib), the structure of (viiia) can be shown in (viiib):

(vii) a. You must [not go to the party]. (=(20a))
b. [$_{IP}$ [$_{I'}$ <must> [$_{NegP}$ not [$_{Neg'}$ NE [$_{ModalP}$ {must} [$_{vP}$ you go]]

c-command

(viii) a. You [may not] go to the party. (=(19a))
b. [$_{IP}$ [$_{I'}$ <may>{may} [$_{NegP}$ not [$_{Neg'}$ NE [$_{ModalP}$ [$_{vP}$ you go]]

c-command

This account is an interesting direction to pursue, but we should mention contrasts between Tonoike's theory and Chomsky's: Tonoike assumes a kind of feature movements in A-Movement in his system, but Chomsky (1995: Chapter 4) claims that not only *formal features* but the *word* itself must move in overt movement in order to converge in PF:

(ix) (26) F carries along just enough material for convergence.
The operation Move, we now assume, seeks to raise just F. Whatever "extra baggage" is required for convergence involves a kind of "generalized pied-piping."

In an optimal theory, nothing more should be said about the matter; bare output conditions should determine just what is carried along, if anything, when F is raised.

For the most part — perhaps completely — it is properties of the phonological component that require such pied-piping. Isolated features and other scattered parts of words may be not subject to its rules, in which case the derivation is canceled; or the derivation might proceed to PF with elements that are "unpronounceable," violating FI. (Chomsky 1995: 262-263)

Moreover, Chomsky attempts to eliminate feature movements themselves in Chomsky (2000: fn. 35). But Tonoike might claim that the feature movements which he assumes are in fact *feature copying* and thus are different from the ones that Chomsky attempts to eliminate.

19. Note incidentally that several studies take the *monosemy approach* of the meanings of modals, especially based on *Relevance Theory* (see Groefsema (1995), Papafragou (1998, 2000), etc.). But Sawada (2001) argues that their approaches should wrongly generate the Modal Negation reading in (22b) (=epistemic use) for just the same reason they generate the Modal Negation reading in (19a) (=root use), and that they would have much difficulty ruling out (22b) in a principled way. I will leave this problem for future study, but I agree with him at present.

20. As for this problem, Shigeo Tonoike (personal communication, 2005) suggested the following idea (see also (i) in note 12):

   (i) Positive Polarity Items (PPI) (see, e.g., *something* in (ii)) exist in modals as well.
   (ii) I saw many things but I didn't see *something*. (SOME > NOT)

21. Sawada (1993) proposes the following constraint, just as Coates submits the Principle of the Inviolability of Epistemic Modality:

   (i) Constraint A on Subjective Modals
       Subjective Modals (and Epistemic Adverbs) are not in the scope of negation.
       (Sawada 1993: 197, translations are mine)

He accepts the case of epistemic *can't* to be *exceptional* (Ibid.: 196), but note that he uses the term *subjective* modals, not *epistemic* modals. According to him, most of the epistemic modals, e.g. *may* (=possibility), *must* (=certainty), *will* (=probability), and *should* (=probability), are classified as subjective modals, but the affirmative form of epistemic *can* (=possibility) is classified as an *objective* modal. Furthermore, he claims that it is only when *can* is used in interrogative or negative sentences that it will become a subjective modal (the *Objective-Subjective Transfer Model*, cf. Tokieda (1941)).

22. The formalization of the phrase structure of German (i.e. a kind of V2 language) is no easy problem, but it would be certain that *nicht* (=not) c-commands *müssen* (=must) somewhere during the derivation under whatever assumption we may take.

23. Note that the following principle which Coates puts forth is not an absolute *principle* but a *tendency*:

(i) Epistemic modals are not found in the interrogative (apart from WILL, SHALL and WOULD which may be considered only marginally Epistemic).

(Coates 1983: 244)

Indeed, (i) is generally right, as shown in (iia-b), but we can easily find the following counterexamples, as shown in (iiia-h):

(ii) a. A: *{May/Must/Can't/Should} John have left?
B: *Yes, he {may/must/can't/should} have. (Sawada 1993: 199)
b. A: *{Can/Might/Could} they be lost?
B: *Yes, he {might/could} be. (Ibid.)
(iii) a. There must have been hundreds of people waiting, *mustn't there*? (=(28))
b. It must be nice to be a cat, *mustn't it*? (NOT ...*can't it*?) (=(29a))
c. *Mustn't it* have been strange to live in the Middle Ages? (=(29b))
d. He must be quite exhausted, *mustn't he*? (=(30a))
e. *Mustn't there* be a rational explanation for these psychic phenomena? (=(30b))
f. *May* the news be true? (Hornby 1975: 202)
g. *May* John be in his office? (Palmer 1987[2]: 108)
h. *May* we not be making a big mistake? (very formal) (Swan 1995[2]: 324)

As for dialectal differences between American and British English, see Kashino (2002: Chapter 10). Sawada (1993, 1995) gives an account for this problem by assuming *the Objective-Subjective Transfer Model*, as I mentioned in note 22, and *Constraint B on Subjective Modals* (=Subjective Modals (and Epistemic Adverbs) cannot be interrogative sentences)(see Sawada (1993: 200)).

Interestingly, the marginal interrogative uses of *may* in Present-Day English, as shown in (iiif-h), were normally seen in Shakespearean Days:

(iv) a. What *may* you be? (*Othello*, V. i. 65)
 b. *May* one be pardon'd and retain th' offense? (*Hamlet*, III, iii. 56)
 c. *May* it be possible? (*Henry V*, II. ii, 100) (Abbot 1870^2: 219)
 d. *May* this be possible? *may* this be true? (*John V*, V. iv. 21) (Franz 1934^4: §604)
 (All quoted from Nomura (2001b: 8))

In sum, even if we could assume (27a) or (i) as some kind of *semantic* tendency, we should think that *all* the modals *can* have both the interpretations of Modal Negation and Propositional Negation, and that they *can* be interrogated *syntactically*.

24. So far we have taken it for granted that the epistemic use of *cannot* is Modal Negation, as shown in (ii):

(i) He can't/cannot be at home now.
(ii) It is [not possible] that he is at home now. (NOT > CAN)

However, Halliday (1970: 333) claims that (i) has in fact the interpretation of Propositional Negation, as shown in (iii):

(iii) It is *possible* [that he is *not* at home now]. (CAN > NOT)

This paraphrase is based on the assumption that epistemic modality is the degree to which a proposition is true or false and thus the degree cannot be minus. However, I claim that (iii) is caused by the confusion of *modal logic* and *syntax*. As for this problem, Yasui (2004) claims that if we attempted to solve this problem by resorting to the *reduction to absurdity*, we should say that *can't* should be interpreted as external negation (i.e. Modal Negation), and concludes that *can't* is not *negative modality* but *the negation of modality*. I agree with him.

25. As I quoted in (31), it is often claimed that *must not/mustn't* is used as a substitute of the epistemic *cannot/can't* especially in American English. But Kashino (2002: Chapter 6) discusses this problem precisely and comes to the following conclusion:

(i) a. *Must not/mustn't* is not used only in AmE, but used in both in AmE and in BrE.
   b. *Must not* is a basic form, but reanalysis has produced the contracted form *mustn't*.
   c. Generally speaking, *must not* is used in AmE, and *mustn't* is used in (part of) BrE.
   d. Each of *can't*, *must not*, and *mustn't* is used in a different context, and the use is different between AmE and BrE.

Furthermore, he claims the following:

(ii) a. must not/mustn't: (AmE)(BrE) It seems certain that ... not
   b. can't: (AmE)(BrE) It is not possible that ...
      (BrE) It seems certain that ... not   (Kashino 2002: 82)

(iia) means that *must not/mustn't* is in fact Propositional Negation, not Modal Negation. (Note that this is compatible with the table (37).) (iib) means that *can't* is always Modal Negation in AmE (see also note 25) and, on the other hand, *can't* generates both interpretations of Modal Negation and Propositional Negation in BrE. All the same, these facts could not be explained if our ModalP Hypothesis were not assumed.

26. We can often observe the tendency where morphologically or syntactically expected forms do not exist because of the presence of *other corresponding forms* (cf. *blocking* in the study of morphology). Consider the following examples:

   (i) a. John would much prefer PRO going to the movie.
      b. John would much prefer his going to the movie.

Binding Condition (B) should predict that *his* in (ib) can refer to *John* or other person, but in fact Chomsky (1981) argues that there is at least a strong preference for taking it to be someone other than *John*. This would be caused by *the presence of PRO* in (ia). Chomsky (1981: 65) calls this *conversational* principle *Avoid Pronoun*.

Chapter 3

The Structure of Infinitival Clauses[1]

3.1 Introduction

In this chapter I consider the structure of infinitival clauses. Though this problem has been one of the central topics of generative grammar, a decisive conclusion has not been reached as yet.

First of all, I will present my proposal on the infinitival clause:

(1) a. The infinitival clause is a type of ModalP in syntactic structure, i.e., the infinitival marker *to* is generated in Modal^0. Unlike other modals (cf. (13a) in Chapter 1), the infinitival marker *to* has no formal features except the Root affix [φ] (see note 19 in Chapter 1).
   b. Infinitival clauses include the [Nonfinite Tense] feature (cf. Chomsky's (2000, 2001a, b) *Defective T* and Martin's (1992, 2001) *Unrealized Tense*) and the [*Unspecified Person*] feature (following Chomsky (2000, 2001a, b) in this point). However, unlike the generalized assumptions, *to* itself does not have these features, but they are base-generated in I, and thus *to* does not raise at all because it does not check any Tense or Person features.
   c. Furthermore, I do not assume two kinds of [Nonfinite Tense], i.e. Control type tense and Raising type tense, unlike Chomsky and Lasnik (1993)=Chomsky (1995: Chapter 1) and his subsequent work, Stowell (1982), Bošković (1996), Martin (1992, 2001), etc. Namely, I assume only one type of *to* and one type of [Nonfinite T].

Here I will examine the adequacy of (1a-c) from various aspects. This chapter is organized as follows: in Section 3.2 I review basic evidence for assuming that the infinitival marker *to* is a type of modal. In Section 3.3 I propose the framework of Case checking in infinitival clauses and discuss related topics. In Section 3.4 I discuss VP-deletion in infinitival clauses and point out some similarities to VP-deletion after ModalP. Section 3.5 is a conclusion.

3.2 Basic Evidence

First of all, I will examine the adequacy of the hypothesis that the infinitival marker *to* is a type of modal by reviewing the characteristics of infinitival clauses.

3.2.1 Basis for Distribution

First, both Modals and infinitival clauses come after the subject DP and Tense in IP:

(2) a. John expects that [$_{IP}$ the bus [$_{I'}$ [Pres]   [$_{ModalP}$ *will be late*]]].
b. John expects   [$_{IP}$ the bus [$_{I'}$ [nonfinite T] [$_{ModalP}$ *to be late*]]].

Second, both can contain perfect aspect:

(3) a. John   [$_{ModalP}$ must   [$_{PerfP}$ *have finished the work*]].
b. John seems [$_{ModalP}$ to   [$_{PerfP}$ *have finished the work*]].

Third, both can contain progressive aspect:

(4) a. John   [$_{ModalP}$ may   [$_{ProgP}$ *be sleeping*]].
b. John seems [$_{ModalP}$ to   [$_{PerfP}$ *be sleeping*]].

Fourth, modals have no infinitive forms, and modals do not co-occur in Standard English.[2]

(5) a. *It is not easy for me *to can* swim fast.
b. *You *will can* swim fast by next year.

Assuming that the infinitival clause is a type of ModalP, this fact is naturally explained by a general principle such as the following:

(6) Modals do not co-occur. (Coates 1983: 5) (See (31) in Chapter 1)

Fifth, many of the verbs or adjectives taking subjunctive equivalent *should* (the no obligation meaning) also take infinitival clauses as complements, as shown in (7):

(7) a. Is it really necessary that [$_{\text{IP}}$ there [$_{\text{ModalP}}$ *should* be a showdown]]?
b. Is it really necessary for [$_{\text{IP}}$ there [$_{\text{ModalP}}$ *to* be a showdown]]?

With regard to *syntactic uniformity*, infinitival clauses and ModalPs behave like the same syntactic category.

3.2.2 Syntactic Support

Here I will give syntactic support for my analysis. First, the present proposal can explain the position of negative *not*, just as in the case of modals and *not* in Chapter 2. Consider the following example:

(8) Be careful *not to* catch a cold.

If we took the generally assumed phrase structure in (4b) in Chapter 2 (Chomsky (1995 and his subsequent work) etc.), the sentence structure (8) would be shown as in (9):

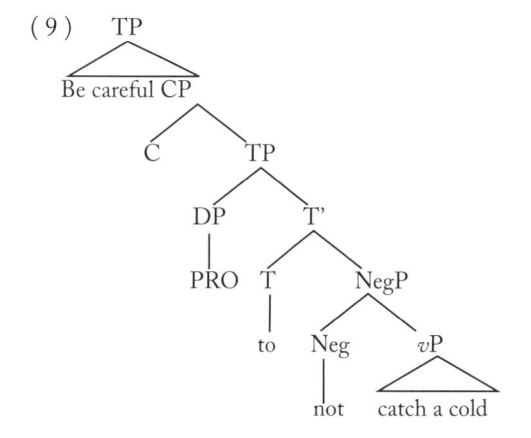

(9)
```
        TP
       /  \
Be careful  CP
           /  \
          C    TP
              /  \
             DP   T'
             |   /  \
            PRO T    NegP
                |   /   \
                to Neg   vP
                   |    /  \
                  not  catch a cold
```

Clearly, this structure cannot explain the <not to VP> word order since there is no motivation and no position to which *not* can raise over T.[3]

On the other hand, based on the ModalP Hypothesis the structure in (8) can be shown as in (10):

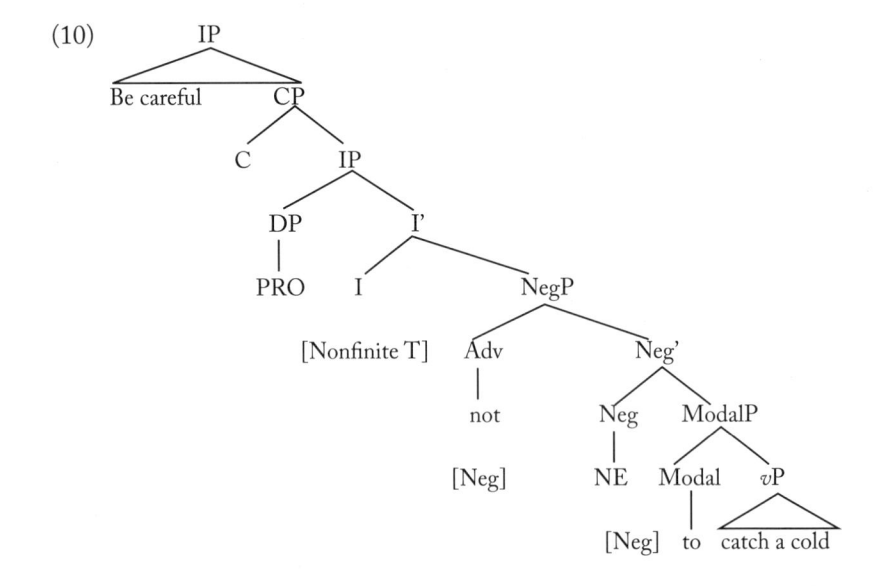

(10)

```
                    IP
           ┌─────────┴─────────┐
       Be careful              CP
                        ┌───────┴───────┐
                        C               IP
                                ┌───────┴───────┐
                                DP              I'
                                │       ┌───────┴───────┐
                               PRO      I              NegP
                                                ┌───────┴───────┐
                                          [Nonfinite T]   Adv       Neg'
                                                          │     ┌────┴────┐
                                                         not    Neg     ModalP
                                                          │     │    ┌────┴────┐
                                                        [Neg]   NE  Modal     vP
                                                                    │
                                                                  [Neg]  to  catch a cold
```

Given this structure, we can naturally account for the <not to V> word order since the infinitival marker *to* does not raise to I (see (1b)).

Second, the VP-deletion phenomena (see (11a-e)) and the VP-preposing phenomena (see (11f-h)) show that modal auxiliaries and the infinitival marker *to* behave like elements in the same syntactic category:[4]

(11) a. I don't really want to go to the dentist's, but I know I *should*.
   b. I know I should go to the dentist's, but I just don't want *to*.
   c. *I know I should go to the dentist's, but I just don't *want*.

   (Radford 1997: 54)

   d. John promised to [vp fix the car], but he didn't α.
   e. Though he wanted to α, John couldn't [vp speak to Mary].

   (Tonoike 1989c: 227)

   f. They say that I couldn't solve the problem, but [vp solve it] I will α.

g. ... and fix the car, he tried [PRO to t]. (Rizzi 1990: 33)
h. ?John said he cannot solve this problem easily, but [vp solve it] I want him to α.

Third, in connection with (11a-e), consider VP-deletion including *be* after modals (see Shumaker and Kuno (1980) and Asakawa and Kamata (1986)). Shumaker and Kuno (1980) argue that VP-deletion can apply when the predicate VP including *be* is *self-controllable*, but that when the predicate is not self-controllable VP-deletion cannot apply. Consider the following examples:

(12) John must be *tall* and Mary { a. must be ϕ }, too.
{ b. *must ϕ }
(13) Peter must be *polite* to his parents, and you { a. must be ϕ }, too
{ b. must ϕ }
(Asakawa and Kamata 1986: 32-33)

Note here that both (12) and (13) are structures where *be* can be deleted *syntactically*. The adjective *tall* in (12) is not self-controllable, so that the interpretation is that "It is certain that John is tall, and so is Mary" (epistemic use). Thus (12a) is grammatical since *be* remains, but (12b) is ungrammatical since non-self-controllable *be* is deleted. On the other hand, (13a, b) are both grammatical, which difference comes from the fact that the adjective *polite* is self-controllable. (13a) has two interpretations; one is (i) "Peter has an obligation to be polite to his parents, and you also have an obligation to be polite to your parents" (root use), and the other is (ii) "It is certain that Peter is polite to his parents, and so are you" (epistemic use). But, interestingly, (13b), where *be* is deleted, has only one interpretation of (i) (=root use), just as (12b) is ungrammatical.

In reality, the same principle works in infinitival clauses as well. Consider the following examples:

(14) He didn't want to be *frank*, but I finally succeeded in persuading him to ϕ.
(Shumaker and Kuno 1980: 359)
(15) I believe John to be *a genius*, but Mary believes him { a. to be ϕ. }
{ b. *to ϕ. }

(Ibid.: 358)

In (14) *be* can be deleted since the predicate is self-controllable. But in (15b) *be* cannot be deleted since the predicate is not self-controllable. In conclusion, we must say this contrast supports our claim that modals and the infinitival clause are the same syntactic category.[5]

3.3 Case Checking in Infinitival Clauses
3.3.1 The Framework of Case Checking in Infinitival Clauses

Next, I will discuss Case checking in infinitival clauses. Based on the above assumptions in (1a-c), I submit the following framework for Case checking in infinitival clauses:

(16) a. Lexical subjects are assigned *Oblique Case* always by the prepositional complementizer *for*.[6]
 b. PRO is assigned *Null Case* by the null prepositional complementizer ϕ, not by [Nonfinite Tense] (cf. the above studies in (1c)).[7]

This framework is based on the following premise:

(17) Infinitival clauses are basically CPs from the viewpoint of *syntactic uniformity*. Raising infinitivals are exceptionally IPs, whose structures are marked in syntax.[8]

Let us take examples in each pattern. First of all, consider the following example (18a) and its underlying structure (18b):

(18) a. John longed for Mary to come back.

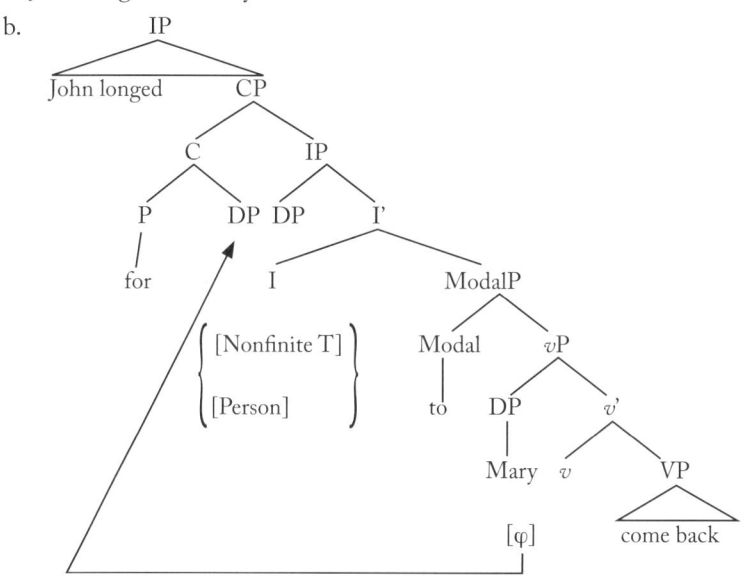

b. [Tree diagram:
- IP
  - John longed
  - CP
    - C: P (for)
    - IP
      - DP
      - DP
      - I'
        - I: {[Nonfinite T], [Person]}
        - ModalP
          - Modal: to
          - vP
            - DP: Mary [φ]
            - v'
              - v
              - VP: come back]

First, since the [Person] feature in I is specified, *Mary* is raised to IP-Spec and thus the [3rd Person] feature is assigned to the unspecified [Person] by Feature Dribbling (see (17) in Chapter 1)), as shown in (19):

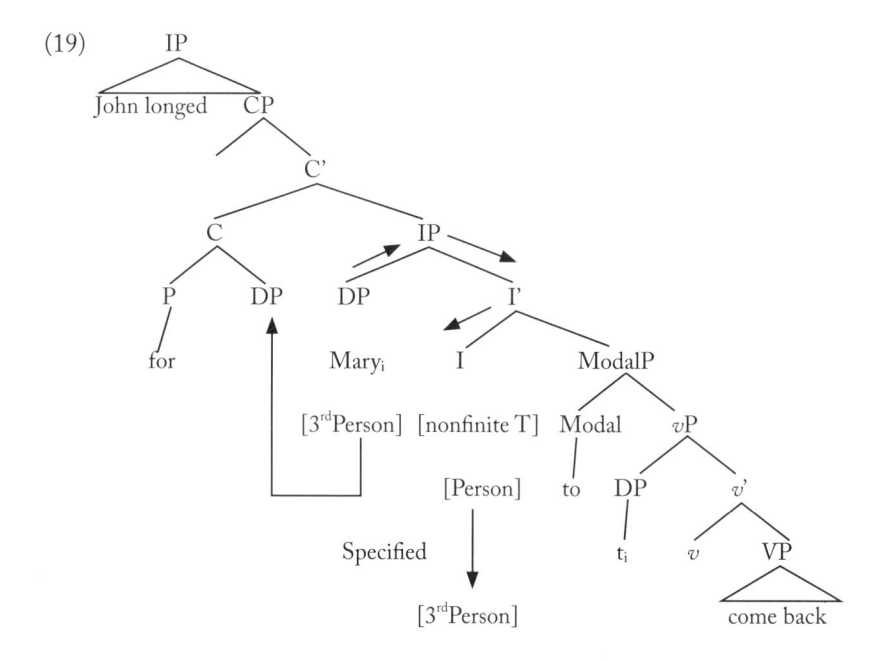

(19) [Tree diagram:
- IP
  - John longed
  - CP
    - C'
      - C
        - P: for
        - DP
      - IP
        - DP: Mary_i [3rd Person]
        - I'
          - I: [nonfinite T], [Person] → Specified → [3rd Person]
          - ModalP
            - Modal: to
            - vP
              - DP: t_i
              - v'
                - v
                - VP: come back]

Then *Mary* further raises to C to get a Case and becomes a full form in Spell-Out (see (16a) in Chapter 1):

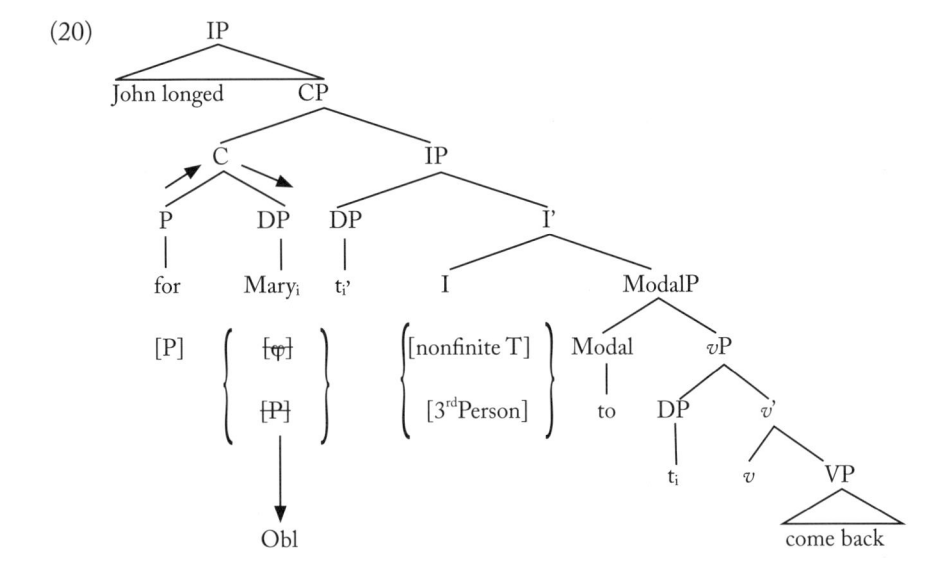

(20)

```
                    IP
         ┌──────────┴──────────┐
    John longed                CP
                     ┌──────────┴──────────┐
                     C                     IP
              ┌──────┴──────┐       ┌──────┴──────┐
              P    DP    DP         I'
              │    │     │     ┌────┴────┐
             for  Maryᵢ  tᵢ'   I       ModalP
                                   ┌────┴────┐
             [P]   {[φ]}  {[nonfinite T]}  Modal   vP
                   {[P]}  {[3ʳᵈPerson]}      │  ┌──┴──┐
                                            to  DP    v'
                    ↓                            │  ┌──┴──┐
                   Obl                           tᵢ  v   VP
                                                        come back
```

Last, *Mary* is assigned Oblique Case as a reflex of [φ] and [P] (see (16biii) in Chapter 1). Subsequently, [φ] and [P] are both deleted, and thus the derivation converges.

Next, consider the example of Control structure (21a) and its underlying structure (21b):

(21) a. John tried to solve the problem.

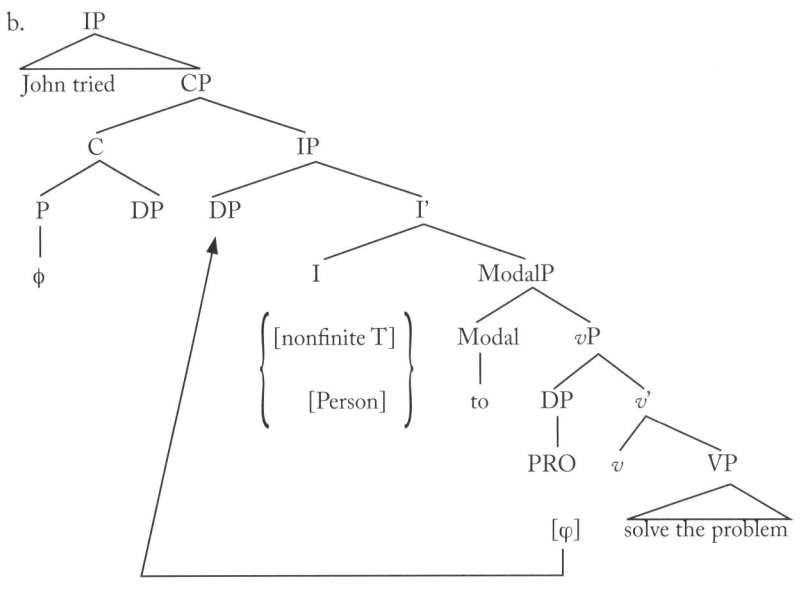

b.
```
              IP
         ╱────────╲
    John tried     CP
               ╱────────╲
              C          IP
           ╱────╲    ╱────────╲
          P     DP  DP         I'
          │             ╱──────────╲
          φ            I            ModalP
                  ⎧[nonfinite T]⎫  ╱────────╲
                  ⎨             ⎬ Modal      vP
                  ⎩  [Person]   ⎭  │     ╱────────╲
                                   to   DP         v'
                                        │      ╱───────╲
                                       PRO    v        VP
                                        │         ╱─────────╲
                                       [φ]       solve the problem
```

First, I assume that PRO has the same φ-features of the controller *John*, i.e. [3rdPerson], [SgNum], and [Mas].[9] Here, just as in the case of (18a), since the [Person] feature in I is specified, PRO is raised to IP-Spec and thus the [Unspecified Person] is specified as the [3rdPerson] feature by Feature Dribbling, as shown in (22):

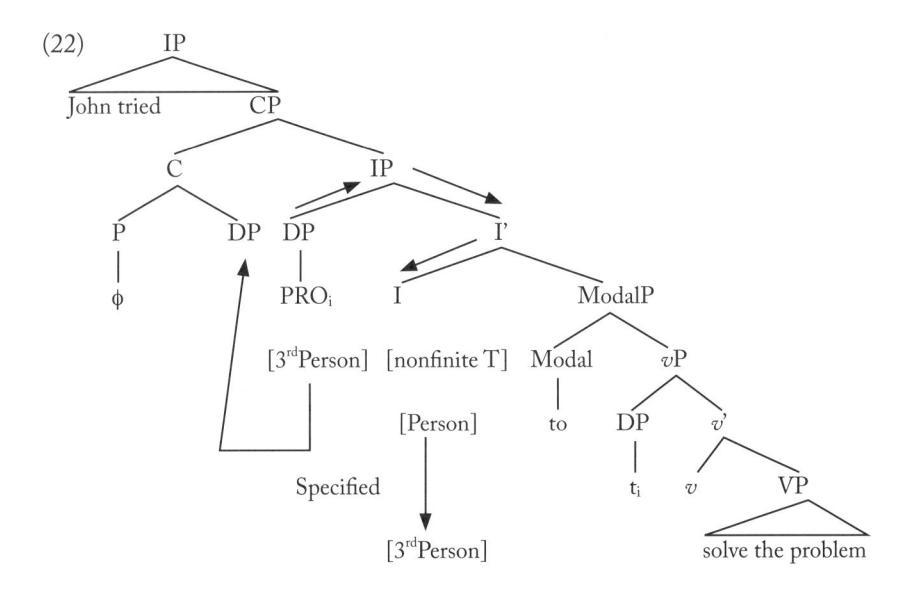

(22)
```
              IP
         ╱────────╲
    John tried     CP
               ╱────────────╲
              C              IP
           ╱────╲      ╱──────────╲
          P    DP  DP              I'
          │         │         ╱──────────╲
          φ        PROᵢ       I           ModalP
              [3rdPerson] [nonfinite T]  ╱────────╲
                                Modal    vP
                             [Person]    │    ╱────────╲
                                          to  DP        v'
                             Specified    │        ╱───────╲
                                          tᵢ      v        VP
                           [3rdPerson]                ╱─────────╲
                                                      solve the problem
```

Then PRO further raises to C to get a Case and becomes a full form in Spell-Out:

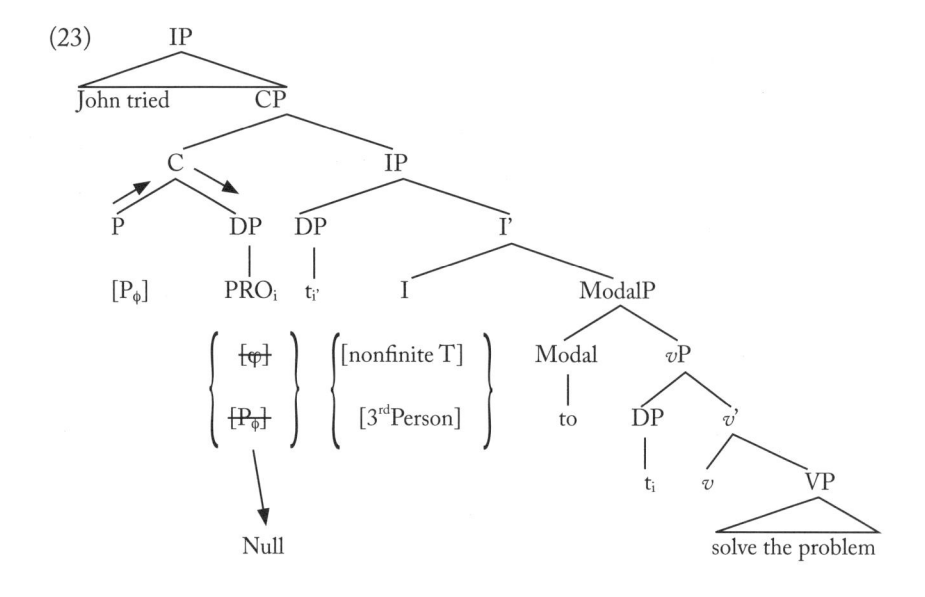

(23)

```
                IP
        ┌───────┴───────┐
    John tried         CP
                ┌───────┴───────┐
                C               IP
            ┌───┴───┐     ┌─────┴─────┐
            P       DP   DP           I'
            │       │    │      ┌─────┴─────┐
          [P_φ]   PRO_i  t_i'   I         ModalP
                                      ┌─────┴─────┐
                                    Modal         vP
                                      │      ┌────┴────┐
                                      to     DP        v'
                                             │     ┌───┴───┐
                                             t_i   v       VP
                                                       solve the problem
```

Under DP/I node: { [φ̶], [P̶_φ̶] } { [nonfinite T], [3rd Person] } → Null

Last, PRO is assigned Null Case as a reflex of [φ] and [P_φ] (see (16biv) in Chapter 1). Subsequently, [φ] and [P_φ] are both deleted, and thus the derivation converges.

Here we should consider the ungrammaticality of (24a) and (25a):

(24) a. *John longs Mary to come back. (cf. (18a))
 b. John longs [CP φ [IP Mary to come back]]
(25) a. *John tried for to solve the problem. (cf. (21a))[10), 11)]
 b. John tried [CP for [IP PRO to solve the problem]]

These are explained straightforwardly by (16a, b): the covert complementizer φ can check only PRO, not lexical NPs, while the overt complementizer *for* can check lexical NPs, not PRO. Then the question will be raised about the case of *want*, as is shown in (26a, b), but we shall discuss this in detail in the next section.

(26) a. I want him to solve this problem.
 b. I want very much *for* him to solve the problem.

Third, consider the example of the Raising-to-Object (or ECM) structure (27a) and its structure (27b):

(27) a. I believe him to be honest.

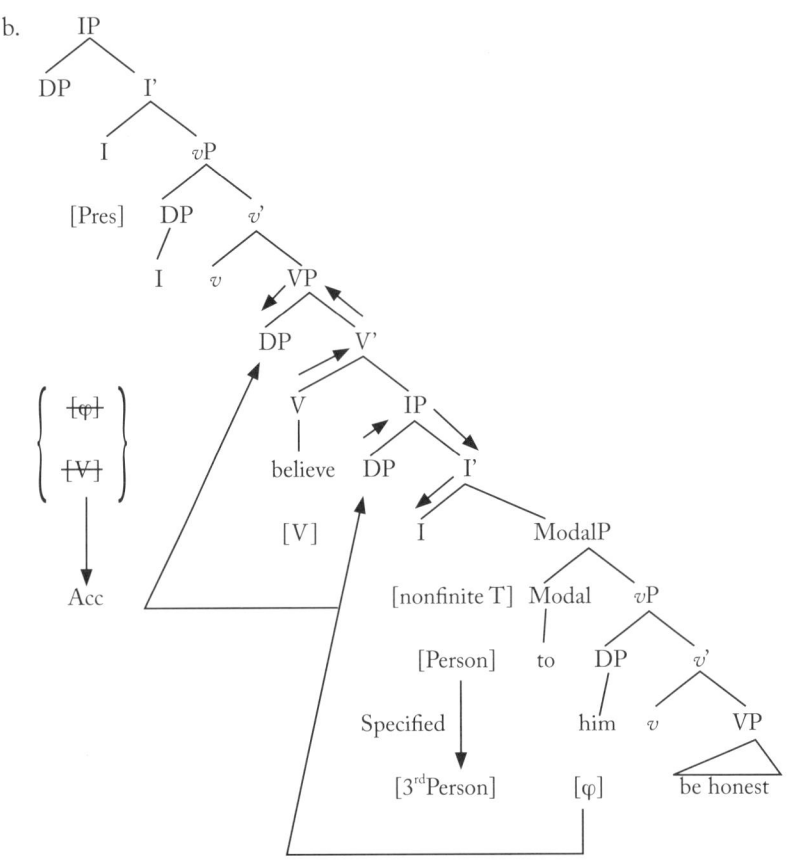

b.

[Tree diagram:
IP
├── DP
└── I'
    ├── I [Pres]
    └── vP
        ├── DP
        │   └── I
        └── v'
            ├── v
            └── VP
                ├── DP
                └── V'
                    ├── V believe [V]
                    └── IP
                        ├── DP
                        └── I'
                            ├── I [nonfinite T]
                            │   [Person] Specified → [3rd Person]
                            └── ModalP
                                ├── Modal to
                                └── vP
                                    ├── DP him [φ]
                                    └── v'
                                        ├── v
                                        └── VP be honest

{ [φ], [V] } → Acc]

First, the subject *him* of the complement clause raises to IP-Spec for just the same reason as in (7a), but this time the prepositional complementizer *for* having the potentiality of Case assignment is not present, so *him* further raise to VP-Spec in main clause as *the last resort*. Next, the [V] feature of *believe* is copied to VP-Spec by Feature Dribbling, then, *him* is assigned Accusative Case as a reflex of [φ] and [V] (see (16bii) in Chapter 1), after which [φ] and [V] are both deleted, and thus the derivation converges.[12], [13]

Note here that I am assuming the same [Nonfinite T] (or *to*) as in the case of the Control structures like in (21a). Consider the following further examples:

(28) a. *I believe for him to be honest.
 b. *I believe PRO to be honest.

Under our assumptions, the ungrammaticality of (28a, b) results from the general lexical property of ECM predicates, as is shown in (29):

(29) Raising predicates select only IP in the lexicon. Thus they cannot select CP as the lexical property.

Neither *him* nor PRO can be assigned Case because the Case assigner, i.e. the prepositional Complementizer *for* or ϕ, are not present. Note that it is not necessary to stipulate that the Raising Tense or the Raising *to* cannot check Null Case.

(29) is not *ad hoc* at all; the *stipulation* that Raising predicates *exceptionally* select IP not CP (see (17) and note 8) must be written in the lexical entry *as a minimum* (see especially Hasegawa (2003)).[14] (Control structures are *unmarked*, which need not be written in the lexical entry.)

In sum, we can deal with the three patterns of Case checking of infinitival clauses under the same system assumed here.[15]

3.3.2 Complement Structure of *Try*-type Infinitival Clauses

Here I would like to mention Bošković's (1996) analysis of *try*-type infinitival clauses. First, consider the following examples:

(30) a. I tried two days ago [CP [c *e*] [IP PRO to leave]].
 b. [CP [c *e*] [IP PRO To buy a car]] was desirable at that time.
 c. *It was believed at that time [CP [c *e*] [IP John would fail Mary]].
 d. *[CP [c *e*] [IP John would fail Mary]] was believed t.

(cf. Bošković (1996: 281))

(31) a. What the terrorists tried was [CP [c *e*] [IP PRO to hijack an airplane]].

    b. They demanded and we tried [CP [C *e*] [IP PRO to visit St. John's hospital]].
    c. *What I believe is [CP [C *e*] [IP they will hijack an airplane]].
    d. *John believed and we claimed [CP [C *e*] [IP they would hijack an airplane]].
(cf. (ibid.: 282))

Bošković claims that the complements of *try*-type infinitival clauses is not CP but IP judging from the contrasts between (30a, b), (31a, b) and (30c, d), (31c, d) each, since (30a, b) and (31a, b) should be also ungrammatical just as (30c, d) and (31c, d) are due to violation of the *Empty Category Principle* (ECP) (see note 3 in Chapter 4), based on Stowell's (1981) assumption that the empty complementizers are properly governed by the verb. Thus Bošković concludes that the complements of *try*-type infinitival clauses are IPs and thus the structures of (30a, b) and (31a, b) will be such as the following:

(32) a. I tried two days ago [IP PRO to leave]].
    b. [IP PRO To buy a car] was desirable at that time.
(33) a. What the terrorists tried was [IP PRO to hijack an airplane].
    b. They demanded and we tried [IP PRO to visit St. John's hospital].

Under this hypothesis, he attempts to explain the grammaticality in (34a-c):

(34) a. John tried [IP PRO to solve the problem]. (=(21a))
    b. *John tried [IP Mary to solve the problem].
    c. *John$_i$ was tried [IP t$_i$ to solve the problem].

Following Chomsky and Lasnik (1993) and Martin (1992), he claims that (34a) is grammatical because PRO is assigned Null Case by the Control-type infinitive I^0(=*to*), and (34b, c) are ungrammatical because Null Case cannot be charged by *to* and remains unchecked.

    However, his discussion is very dubious; first, now that *government* has been abolished all in the Minimalist Program, the explanations by ECP cannot hold at all. Second, even if we accepted Stowell's explanation by ECP, we can easily find the following counterexamples:

(35) a. *The committee may insist [he resign].   (Radford 1988: 308)
   b. *I suggested to John [α he should leave early].   (Nakajima 1996: 154)

Though in (35a, b) the empty complementizer is properly governed by the matrix verb, both sentences are ungrammatical.[16] This means that the deletion of the complementizer *that* including the cases in (30c, d) and (31c, d) should be explained by other ways, e.g., by using functional explanations (cf. Kuno and Takami (1993)) or *perceptual strategies*.[17]

Third, his IP analysis in (32a, b) and (33a, b) means that the argument positions, especially subject positions, can be occupied by IP. However, generally speaking, this is not the case, as is shown in (36):

(36) *[IP John died last year] is obvious.

As is well known, not only DP but also PP marginally can appear in subject positions, as shown in (37a-c), and we can express characteristically that none of these two categories contain the [V]-features, as shown in (39a, b). On the other hand, VP and AP, which cannot appear in subject positions, as shown in (38a, b), both contain the [N]-feature, as shown in (39c, d).

(37) a. *John* hit Mary. (DP)
   b. *Under the chair* is a nice place for the cat to sleep. (PP)
                                           (Stowell 1981: 268)
   c. John considers *under the bed* a good hiding place. (PP)
(38) a. **Get up early* is good for the health. (VP) (cf. Getting)
   b. **Beautiful* is but skin-deep. (AP) (cf. Beauty)
(39)   [V] feature
   a. N   –
   b. P   –
   c. V   +
   d. A   +

The [−V] feature in N and P is characterized by the fact that such categories can appear in the focus position of the cleft sentences. Consider the following examples:

(40) a. It was *John* that hit Mary. (DP)
　b. It was *in July* that John met Mary. (PP)
　c. *It was *hit Mary* that John. (VP)
　d. *It was *happy* that John was at that time. (AP)

Applying this diagnosis to CP and IP, we will conclude that CP has the [−V] feature, not IP.

(41) a. It was [CP that he would say such a thing] that surprised me.[18]
(cf. Prince (1978: 884))
　b. *It was [IP he would say such a thing] that surprised me.

It follows that CP, not IP, can appear in the subject position, contra Bošković's assumption. Furthermore, CP has many *noun features*, as Ross (1973) discusses with the concept of *nouniness*.[19] Moreover, many linguists discuss the similarities between *noun phrases* and *sentences* (i.e. DP and CP) (see Chomsky (1970), Abney (1987), Tonoike (1989a, 1991), etc.), including the basic property that both express *propositions*. As discussed above, we can conclude that the CP analysis based on our framework, as shown in (30a, b) and (31a, b), is more appropriate than Bošković's IP analysis, as shown in (32a, b) and (33a, b).

It goes without saying that our framework can give an adequate account of (34a-c): as for (34a), see the explanation of (21a) above. As for (34b), since infinitival clauses are always CPs except for Raising infinitivals under our framework, the structure of (34b) cannot be generated. Moreover, even if we assume the structure of the infinitival clause in (34b) to be CP, as shown in (42), ungrammaticality will result all the same because the lexical NP cannot be assigned Case by the prepositional complementizer ϕ (see (16a, b)).

(42) *John tried [CP ϕ [IP Mary to solve the problem]]

As for (34c), its underlying structure cannot be generated, but even if we could assume the underlying structure (43a), ungrammaticality would result, as shown in (43b), because of the general condition that *NP-Movement cannot move across CP* under any theory.

(43) a. *__ was tried [CP ϕ [IP John to solve the problem].
   b. *John_i was tried [CP ϕ [IP t_i to solve the problem].

3.3.3 Case Checking in *Want*- type Infinitival Clauses

As I mentioned in section 3.3.1, questions might be raised as to *want*-type infinitival clauses (cf. Bošković (1997: 2.2.3), Martin (2001: Section 5)). I will repeat (26a, b) as (43a, b) again:

(44) a. I want him to solve this problem.
   b. I want very much *for* him to solve the problem.

There exist no problems with (44b), assuming (16a). However, apparently (44a) is an apparent counterexample to (16a), because *him* seems to be assigned Case by the empty prepositional complementizer ϕ. Here I will discuss this problem.

One might assume that (44a) is a type of ECM and thus *him* is assigned Accusative Case by the matrix verb *want*. However, this hypothesis cannot hold: first, the coordination test in (45) shows that XP in question now is in fact CP:

(45) I want [XP Mary to come to Japan], and [CP for her to see my parents].
(cf. Sawada (1995: 406, fn. 5))

Second, Lasnik and Saito (1991) argues that the ECM subject is raised to a position which can c-command into adjuncts in the higher clause, based on the contrast between (46a) and (46b) (cf. Postal (1974)), while the *want*-type subject is not raised to such a position, i.e., stays at the subject position of the complement clause, based on the contrast between (47) and (46a, b), and (48a) and (48b):

(46) a. Joan believes he_i is a genius even more fervently than Bob's_i mother does.
   b. ?Joan believes him_i to be a genius even more fervently than Bob's_i mother does.   (Lasnik and Saito (1991)=Lasnik (1999: Chapter 1: 11))
(47) ?Joan wants him_i to be a genius even more fervently than Bob's_i mother does.
(Ibid.: 20)

(48) a. ??*I wanted [those men to be fired] because of each other's statements.
   b. ?I believed [those men to be fired] because of each other's statements.
   (Ibid.)

It follows that *want*-type infinitival clauses are not IPs but CPs regardless of the presence of *for*.

Considering the discussion above, I submit the following assumption:

(49) a. The structure of [want (for) NP to VP] is always CP regardless of the presence of *for*.
   b. In the [want (for) NP to VP] construction the lexical complementizer *for* is generated in the underlying structure, and this complementizer *for* can be *phonetically deleted* under the *perceptual condition* in the surface structure. (I also assume that the complementizer *that* can also be deleted under the same perceptual condition.)
   c. The phonetically deleted *for* in the surface structure is different from the null prepositional complementizer ϕ base-generated in the underlying structure assumed in (16b).

I am assuming that the lexical complementizer *for* is generated in the underlying structure regardless of the presence of *for* for the following reasons: first, the coordination test in (45) discussed above also shows that (49c) is on the right track. Second, some people (or the dialects) allow the following (50) instead of (44a):

(50) %I want *for* Mary to solve this problem.

Third, the pseudo-cleft sentence test also supports (49c):

(51) What I want is *(for) Mary to solve this problem.

In (51) *for* cannot be deleted despite the fact that (44a) is grammatical.

Furthermore, we can assume that both the complementizers *that* and the prepositional complementizer *for* can also be deleted under the same perceptual condition (e.g. *parsing*, avoiding *ambiguity*, etc.) (cf. Bolinger (1972), Chiba (1995), etc.), judging from the following similarities of grammaticality between (52a-c) and (53a-c):

(52) a. I want (for) Mary to solve this problem.[20]
   b. He wants very much *(for) his team to win.
   c. What I want is *(for) Mary to solve this problem. (=(51))
(53) a. I believe (that) Mary will solve this problem.
   b. *I believe very strongly *(that) Mary will solve this problem.
   c. *What I believe is *(that) Mary will solve this problem.

In this section I conclude that [want (for) NP to VP] type constructions are not counterexamples to our framework.

3.4 VP-Deletion in Infinitival Clauses

One of the strong pieces of evidence that leads Martin (2001) to assume two types of infinitival marker *to*, i.e. the Control *to* and the Raising type *to*, is based on the differences in deletability of VP after *to* (cf. Saito and Murasugi (1990) and Takahashi (1994)). Consider his examples:

(54) a.*I consider Pam to [VP like soccer], and I believe [Rebecca [T to] [VP e]] as well.
   b.*Bill believes Sarah to be [AP honest], and he believes [Kim [T to] [VP e]] as well. (Martin 2001: 154)
(55) a. Kim isn't sure she can [VP solve the problem], but she will try [PRO [T to] [VP e]].
   b. Rebecca wanted Jill to [VP join the team], so Pam persuaded her [PRO [T to] [VP e]].

However, in this section I argue that his discussion is empirically problematic and that VP-deletion *can* apply after the infinitival marker *to syntactically* be it the Control type of *to* or the Raising type of *to*. (Note that I am assuming only one type of *to* in this chapter. See (1c).) Furthermore, I claim that both the infinitival *to* and modals are subject to the same functional condition on VP-deletion since both belong to the same category.

First of all, we can find not a few counterexamples to Martin's claim that VP-deletion is not possible in Raising Predicates.[21)] Consider the following examples:

(56) a. I don't really like to talk about my work with my friends. They don't really *seem to* ϕ either. (Zwicky 1982: 9)
 b. Bob says that he doesn't know if he will succeed, but I think he is *certain to* ϕ.[22)] (Amanuma 1987: 77)
 c. John seems to have been working hard, but Bill doesn't seem {to have been ϕ/to have ϕ ϕ/to ϕ ϕ ϕ}. (Schachter 1978: 219)

Moreover, even his examples (54a, b) would be much better or almost acceptable if we added *not* to them, as shown in (57a, b):

(57) a. I consider Pam to like soccer, but I believe Rebecca *not* [т to] ϕ. (cf. (53a))
 b. Bill believes Sarah to be honest, and he believes Kim *not* to ϕ. (cf. (53b))

Note that for Martin's theory the presence of *not* is irrelevant to whether the infinitival marker *to* in (57a, b) is the Raising *to* or the Control *to*. In sum, we should consider that VP-deletion is possible in Raising infinitivals as well as Control infinitivals.

Next, interestingly, an observation similar to what Martin makes is also seen in VP-deletion after modals. Consider the following examples:

(58) Root Modals
 a. I'll try the soup if I must ϕ.
 b. John should go to the party and Mary should ϕ.
(59) Epistemic Modals
 a. *John must be tall and Mary must ϕ. (=(12))
 b. *Mary may be stupid, but you may ϕ.

Many linguists have discussed the possibility of VP-deletion in the clauses containing several auxiliaries after epistemic modals. Consider the following examples:

(60) a. Sam might have been at the scene of the murder, but Bill couldn't have been ϕ.
b. Sam might have been at the scene of the murder, but Bill couldn't have ϕ ϕ.
c. *Sam might have been at the scene of the murder, but Bill couldn't ϕ ϕ ϕ.
(Akmajian and Wasow 1975: 236)
(61) a. If Bill had been using drugs, then his brother Sam must have been ϕ.
b. ?If Bill had been using drugs, then his brother Sam must have ϕ ϕ.
c. *If Bill had been using drugs, then his brother Sam must ϕ ϕ ϕ. (Ibid.)
(62) a. John must have eaten, and Bill must have ϕ.
b. *John must have eaten, and Bill must ϕ ϕ. (Sag 1980: 28)

However, in these cases as well we can find not a few grammatical sentences or judgments. Consider the following examples:

(63) a. My baby may be crying, and yours may be ϕ, too.
b. My baby may be crying, and yours may ϕ ϕ, too.
(Asakawa and Kamata 1986: 29)
(64) a. She doesn't think he would have come, but I think he would have ϕ.
b. She doesn't think he would have come, but I think he would ϕ ϕ.
(Terazu 1980: 201)
(65) a. John couldn't have been studying Spanish, but Bill could have been ϕ.
b. John couldn't have been studying Spanish, but Bill could have ϕ ϕ.
c. John couldn't have been studying Spanish, but Bill could ϕ ϕ ϕ.
(Akmajian, Steel, and Wasow 1979: 15)[23)]
(66) a. Fred must have been singing songs, and Nancy must have been ϕ too.
b. Fred must have been singing songs, and Nancy must have ϕ ϕ too.
c. Fred must have been singing songs, and Nancy must ϕ ϕ ϕ too.
(McCawley 1998^2: 217)

Taking these observations into consideration, I submit the following assumption, following and modifying Kono (2002):

(67) VP-deletion after any modal is basically possible *in syntax* be it a root modal or an epistemic modals. In the same way, VP-deletion after the infinitival marker *to* is basically possible *in syntax* be it the Control *to* or the Raising *to*.

For some people (67) is a necessary and sufficient condition (especially see (56a-c), (57a, b), (63b), (64b), (65c), and (66c)). For other people (67) is a necessary condition, thus the following condition can be seen to be sufficient (especially see (54a, b), (59a, b), (60c), (61c), and (62b)):

(68) The functions of VP-deletion are (i) omitting redundancy and (ii) showing that the remnant auxiliary is the focus. (cf. Amanuma (1988: 76))

Here let us consider semantic structure of a sentence. It is generally assumed that the sentence structure consists of at least two parts, as shown in (69) (see Kajita (1968), Nakau (1994), Sawada (1993, 1995), and Nakano (1994)):

(69) [Modality [Proposition]][24]

Moreover, it is known that the Modality part cannot normally be a focus. The cleft-sentence test shows this, as shown in (70a, b):

(70) a. *It is *certainly* that John loves Mary.
 b. *It is *probably* that she is happy. (Kono 2002: 283)

Here, turning to infinitives and modals, we can presume that epistemic modals and Raising infinitivals belong to the Modality part while root modals and Control infinitivals are included in the Proposition part in semantic structure, as shown in (71):[25]

(71) Epistemic Modals and Raising Infinitivals
 a. John must be tall.
  =MUST [John is tall]
 b. John seems to be happy.

=SEEM TO [John is happy]

(72) Root Modals and the Control Infinitivals
    a. John must be polite to his parents.
       =[John MUST be polite to his parents]
    b. John tried to win.
       =[John TRIED TO win]

That is to say, since MUST in (71a) and SEEM TO in (71b) constitute the Modality part, they cannot be the focus of the sentence just as in (70a, b), thus ungrammaticality results in (15b), (54a, b), (59a, b), (60c), (61c), and (62b). On the other hand, since MUST in (72a) and TRIED TO in (72b) constitute part of the Proposition, they can be the focus of the sentence, thus the grammaticality results in (14), (55a, b), and (58a, b). Note here that *have* and *be* (see (60a, b), (61a, b), (62a), (63a), (64a), (65a, b), and (66a, b)) or *not* (see (57a, b)) can be the focus and thus grammaticality results even in the cases of epistemic modals or Raising infinitivals.

Note interestingly that Akmajian and Wasow (1975), who judge sentences ungrammatical in the cases where two out of three auxiliary verbs are deleted (see (60c), (61c), and (62b)), still note that the following example is grammatical:

(73) Sam could have been using drugs, but could Bill (have) (been)?
                                                                      (Akmajian and Wasow 1975: 237)

Moreover, similar cases are also seen in tag questions or the answers to the questions:

(74) a. John could be sleeping, couldn't he?
    b. John could be sleeping, couldn't he be?   (Ibid.: 224-225)
(75) a. "You wouldn't have enjoyed the film." "Yes, I would."
    b. "Could you have been dreaming?" "I suppose I could/COULD have/ COULD have been."   (Swan 1995^2: 178)
(76) A: Could Tom have been at the scene of the murder?
    B: Yes, he could (have (been)).   (Kono 2002: 282)

As for this problem, Amanuma (1989) and Kono (2002) argue that the main function of questions is asking *truth-value* and the first auxiliary plays the role of that function. Namely, even if the first auxiliary is an epistemic modal, it can be the focus whether it is *true* or *false*, and thus the modal can remain alone after VP-deletion. These facts will also be evidence for our assumption.

Needless to say, the discussion above is not a comprehensive theory about VP-deletion (cf. Sag (1980), Lobeck (1995), and Imanishi and Asano (1990)), but at least I have shown that VP-deletion can basically apply *in syntax* under the same conditions whether epistemic modals or root modals, or the Raising *to* or the Control *to* are involved. This conclusion will support our assumption in (1c), i.e. that there is only one type of infinitival marker *to*.[26]

3.5 Concluding Remarks

In this chapter I claimed that the infinitival clause is a type of ModalP in syntactic structure. I proposed that unlike the generalized assumptions the infinitival marker *to* itself does not have features but the [Nonfinite T] and [Unspecified Person] features are in I^0, and thus *to* does not raise at all because it does not check any Tense or Person features. Furthermore, I assumed only one type of *to* and one type of [Nonfinite T], unlike Chomsky and Lasnik (1993), Stowell (1982), Bošković (1995), and Martin (1992, 2001). In Section 3.2 I reviewed various pieces of evidence for this claim. In section 3.3 I proposed the framework of Case checking in infinitival clauses, then discussed especially the Case checking system of *try*-type infinitivals and *want*-type infinitivals, pointing out problems with Bošković's (1995) analyses. In Section 3.4, though Martin (2001) assumes two types of the infinitival marker *to* based on the differences in deletability of VP after *to*, I showed that VP-deletion can basically apply to both the Control type infinitivals and the Raising type infinitivals *in syntax*. Moreover, I claimed that VP-deletion applying to Control type infinitivals and Raising type infinitivals is subject to the same functional condition applying to epistemic modals and root modals.

Notes to Chapter 3

1. The discussion of this chapter is partly based on Nomura (2000d).

2. Though, even in Modern English, we can find dialects where modals co-occur, especially the Southern Dialects:

   (i) a. I *might could* have gone if the weather had been better.
       b. We *might should* go check our trot lines now.
                (Dialect of the North District of Arkansas, quoted from Newmeyer (1969))

   As for many similar examples in the history of English, see Denison (2000).

3. In principle *to* cannot move *downwardly*. However, Pollock (1989), Nakajima (1989), and Hasegawa (2003) assume the downward movement of *to*, though the frameworks assumed are each different. We shall discuss this problem again in Chapter 4.

4. Judging from the facts in (7a, b) and (11a, b), we may say that the infinitival *to* is more like the modal *should* than other modals. (The similarity between *to* and *should* has been mentioned also by Chomsky in the 1970's, Radford (1997), Martin (2001), etc.)

   In this connection, I would like to consider the finiteness of *should*: as for *finiteness*, I claim that the modal *should* seems to be *less tensed* than other modals. Consider the following examples violating the *wh*-island constraint:

   (i) a. ?Which books did he want to know where *to* put?
       b. *Which books did he want to know where Mary [*Past*] put?
                                                                    (cf. Hasegawa (2001: 136))

   Hasegawa argues that the ungrammaticality in (ib) is crucially concerned with the violation of the *Tensed-S Condition* (TSC) as well as the *wh*-island constraint. (Note that his system predicts that DC (=*Degree of Complexity*) 2 is ungrammatical.) But Tonoike (2001) gives the following example, which is more acceptable than (ib), where the complement *wh*-clause is tensed:

   (ii) Which books did he want to know where he *should* put?   (Tonoike 2001: 3)

Considering (ia, b) and (ii), Tonoike indicates that the ungrammaticality (ib) is concerned with *presumed finiteness*.

However, if TSC is one of the appropriate principles in linguistic theory as Hasegawa (2003) argues (see the appendix to Chapter 9), we can conclude that the modal *should* is less tensed than the other modals in finite sentences, i.e., is similar to the infinitival marker *to* in terms of a lack of finite tense.

5. Incidentally, in this section I have explained the VP-deletion phenomena by using the notion of *self-controllable* assumed by Shumaker and Kuno (1980), but I shall try to provide other explanations in Section 3.4.

6. As for the concept of *prepositional* complementizer, see Jespersen (1924), Jackendoff (1973, 1977), Bresnan (1979), Emonds (1976, 1985), McCawley (1998^2), H. Hasegawa (1998), and K. Hasegawa (2003).

7. For the critique of the Null Case analysis of PRO (e.g. Stowell (1982), Bošković (1996), Martin (2001)), see Watanabe (1996), Hasegawa (2003), Nakamura (2003), etc.

8. Especially, the *ECM* (=Exceptional Case Marking) construction (i.e. the Raising-to-Object construction) is literally *exceptional*. As is well known, note that it is not observed in other European languages like French, Italian, or German.

9. In the cases of *arbitrary* PRO as in (ib), I will assume *generic* person, number, and gender features.

   (i) a. To see is to believe.
       b. PRO To see is PRO to believe.

10. Note that we should consider whether each verb selects object or not is an *idiosyncratic property*. That is, *try* does not take Indirect Object as its complement, as shown in (i):

    (i) a. *John tried Mary to solve the problem.
        b. John tried [$_{DP}$ Mary$_i$][$_{CP}$ φ [$_{IP}$ PRO$_i$ to solve the problem]].

    As for this problem, see also Chiba (1984a).

11. I will also assume following Hasegawa (2003) that *with* in the following examples in (i)

and (ii) is a type of prepositional complementizer as well as *for*:

(i) *With* the bus drivers on strike, we'll have to ride our bicycles.　　(McCawley 1983)
(ii) a. *With* people walking all directions, she couldn't cross the intersection.
　　b. *With* his lips tightly closed, he kept silent.
　　c. *With* his mouth wide open, he lay on the couch.　　(Tonoike 1989b: 115-116)

For this construction, note here that PRO cannot appear either just as in (24b):

(iii) a. **With* PRO coming home early, he went for a walk.
　　b. **With* PRO exhausted, he went to bed early.
　　c. **With* PRO reluctant to go home, he went to a movie.　　(Ibid.: 116)

These are also explained straightforwardly by (16a, b): the covert complementizer ϕ can check only PRO, not lexical NPs, while the overt complementizer *with* can check lexical NPs, not PRO.

In this connection, *without* can be a prepositional complementizer judging from (iva-c), but in the *without* construction PRO can occur, as shown in (va, b). Note, however, that in this case the complement is not IP (i.e. participle construction) but DP (i.e. gerund) judging from the contrast between (vc) and (vd):

(iv) a. *Without* her parents around all the time, she couldn't do anything.
　　b. *Without* his friend helping him, the student couldn't have finished his homework.
　　c. *Without* my dog happy to see me, coming home would be miserable.
　　　　　　　　　　　　　　　　　　　　　　　　　　　　(Ibid.: 115-116)
(v) a.　She never goes out *without* PRO eating breakfast.
　　b.　He went to school *without* PRO eating breakfast.
　　c.　*Without* his noticing, she slipped out of the room.
　　d.　**Without* him noticing, she slipped out of the room.

Incidentally, Tonoike (1989b) assumes that both *with* and *without* are P selecting IPs based on the *PRO Theorem* which was assumed in GB Theory. For the problems as to what the syntactic categories of various subordinate conjunctions are in English, see Dubinsky and Williams (1995), Haumann (1997), etc.

12. Here I am assuming that Accusative Case is always assigned *under a Spec-Head relation*, including the ECM construction, following Bowers (1993) and Tonoike (1993). But

note in particular that I assume that Accusative Case is assigned by V, not by *v*, unlike the standard assumption. Take an example (ia). The *v*P structure of (ia) can be shown in (ib) under the standard assumption:

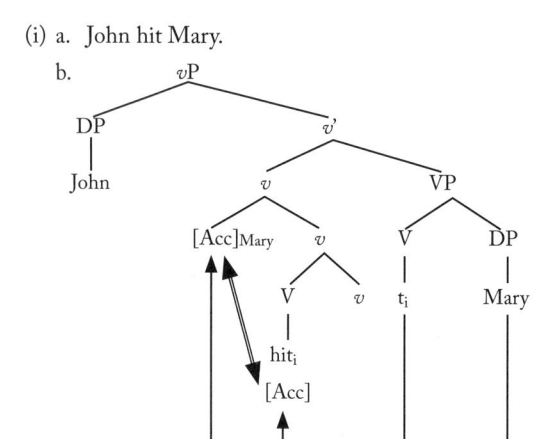

(i) a. John hit Mary.

b. [tree diagram: *v*P with DP "John" and *v*' branching into *v* and VP; *v* contains [Acc]Mary and *v* with V "hit$_i$" [Acc]; VP contains V t$_i$ and DP "Mary"]

Then, the *v*P structure of (iia) can be shown in (iib) under our assumption. (Adjunct *yesterday* is added to (ia) for the discussion.)

(ii) a. John hit Mary yesterday.

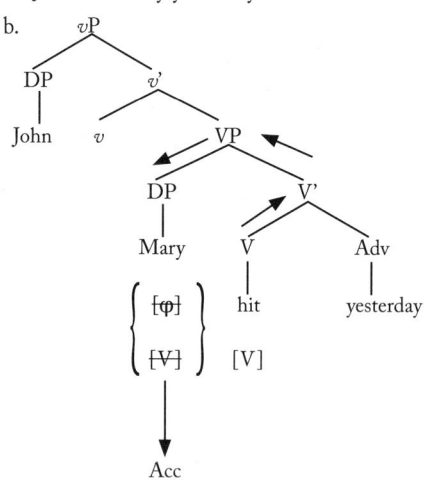

b. [tree diagram: *v*P with DP "John" and *v*'; *v*' branches into *v* and VP; VP branches into DP "Mary" and V'; V' branches into V "hit" [V] and Adv "yesterday"; Mary has {[φ], [V]} → Acc]

If we assumed (ib), however, we would have the following problems: first, features movement should be abolished as much as possible. I am not assuming feature movements either in this book. As for studies along this line, see Kayne (1998), though his discussion itself is empirically problematic, and Tonoike (2003).

Second, even if we did not assume the checking system by using feature movement in (ib), familiar complex problems will be raised: *equidistance*, *tucking-in* (causing violation of *extension condition*), *crossover* of the movements of subject and object, etc. On the other hand, assuming (iib), feature movements need not be assumed and thus *only* overt movement is assumed. Then, none of the complex problems mentioned above will be raised at all under our hypothesis. Note that there is no possibility that subject and object are crossed anywhere in the derivation.

Third, we can assume that subject and object are both merged at the Spec position uniformly. Thus we can conclude that our Accusative Case checking system in (iib) is much more appropriate than the standard assumption (ib).

Before closing this note, I should mention the following: what about the simple case (ia) where there is no adjunct before merging *hit* and *Mary* at the first stage. In this case as well, I will make the same assumption. Consider the following structure:

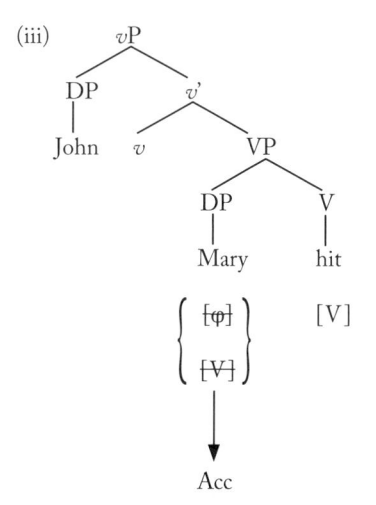

(iii)
```
            vP
           /  \
         DP    v'
         |    /  \
        John v    VP
                 /  \
               DP    V
               |     |
              Mary  hit
              { [φ] }   [V]
              { [V] }
                 |
                 ▼
                Acc
```

That is, though this is *practically* Case checking under the *Sister relation* assumed traditionally, *Mary* should be considered *Spec by definition* and thus this simple case is also compatible with our framework.

Incidentally, Chomsky has sometimes implied that adjuncts exist in *another dimension*. In reality, I will take this assumption in this book, so Accusative Case checking would be *always* shown in (iii) even in the cases including adjuncts like (iia).

13. As for *successive cyclic* NP-Movement, the subject DP moves to every I to specify the [Unspecified Person] feature, and at Spec in the highest IP it can get Nominative Case:

    (i) a. John appears to be likely to win.
    b. [IP [Pres] [VP appear [IP { [Nonfinite T] / [Person] } [ModalP to [VP be likely

    [IP { [Nonfinite T] / [Person] } [ModalP to [VP John win]]]]]]]]
    [φ]

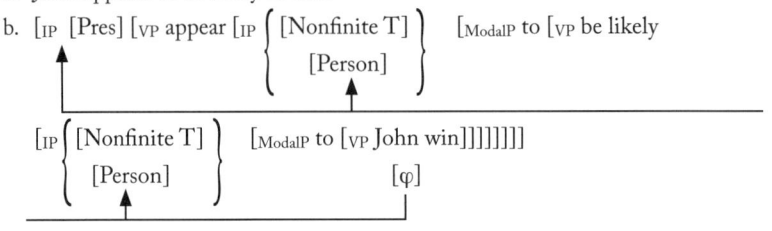

14. Chomsky's (1986) notion of *S'-deletion* is also a stipulation.

15. Incidentally, as for a more detailed classification from other viewpoints and a good review of the complement structures of infinitival clauses, see Matsuyama (2001).

16. In the cases of *manner-of-speaking* verbs as well, the complementizer *that* cannot be deleted, as shown in (i):

    (i) a. John whispered *(that) Mary stole a diamond.
    b. You grumbled *(that) John hit Susan.
    c. Mary complained *(that) the room was too hot.

    Stowell argues that *that*-clauses of manner-of-speaking verbs are syntactic *adjuncts*, not *arguments* selected by the verbs. But it would not be impossible to apply his explanation to the cases of *subjunctive verbs*.

17. We shall discuss this problem in detail again in the next section 3.3.3 and the appendix to Chapter 6.

18. Note interestingly that object clauses cannot be the topics of the cleft sentences:

    (i) *It is *that the world is round* that I believe.

However, we should assume that *syntax* allows this operation, judging from the fact that (41a) is grammatical. I will leave this problem open in this book.

19. As for the concepts of *nouniness* or *squish*, see Ross (1972, 1973) and Akimoto (1986).

20. Compared with the [want NP to VP] clause (e.g. *want, wish, would like, hate,* etc.), the complementizer *for* cannot be deleted in the [hope NP to VP] clause (e.g. *hope, long, yearn, arrange, care, wait,* etc.) (See (18a)):

(i) I hope *(for) Mary to solve this problem. (cf. (44a))

I will claim that the difference in grammaticality between (44a) and (i) should be explained by the following *lexical redundancy rules*, as shown in (ii) and (iii):

(ii) $\begin{cases} \text{[V for DP]} \\ \text{[V for DP to VP]} \end{cases} \rightarrow$ *(for)

(iii) $\begin{cases} \text{[V DP]} \\ \text{[V for DP to VP]} \end{cases} \rightarrow$ *for* is phonetically deleted in surface structure

As illustrations of (ii) and (iii), consider the following examples:

(iv) a. We do *hope/long* *(for) world peace.
　　b. I *hope/long* *(for) Mary to solve this problem.
(v) a. I *want/like* this watch.
　　b. I *want/would like* (for) Mary to solve this problem.

We might say that the complementizer *for* in (ivb) is *more prepositional* than the one in (vb) or that in this case another PP headed by the preposition P exits over CP and two *for*s are incorporated into one (cf. Bresnan (1979) and Hasegawa (1998)), but I will leave this problem open.

21. Martin (2001) mentioned an *LI* reviewer's comment in the note:

(i) One *LI* reviewer claims not to get a contrast between VP-ellipsis in raising infinitivals and VP-ellipsis in control infinitivals, finding to be acceptable. Although there does appear to be some variability among speakers of English, the majority of people I have consulted report judgments along the lines of those in the text. Most others at least find a significant contrast between raising and control in the predicted direction. I have so far encountered only two English speakers who find little or no contrast (including the reviewer cited above). (Martin 2001: 154, fn. 30)

Our discussion will agree with the reviewer and the one other English speaker.

22. Lasnik (1999: Chapter 2) has the same judgments as Martin's about VP-deletion after the Control and ECM *verbs*:

(i) a. John tried to be courageous, and Mary tries to also.
  b. I want John to be courageous, and I want Mary to also.
(ii) a. ?*I believe John to be courageous, and I believe Mary to also.
  b. ?*John is believed to be courageous, and Mary is believed to also.

(Lasnik 1999: 66)

But he argues that raising *adjectives* do not conform this pattern:

(iii) a. ? John is likely to be courageous, and Mary is *likely* to also.
  b. ? John said that he was *likely* to solve this problem, and he is *likely* to. (Ibid.)

I believe that (iiia, b) also support my hypothesis, but Lasnik claims that differences in grammaticality between (iia, b) and (iiia, b) would be basis for Lasnik and Saito's (1992) claim that Raising adjectives have *alternative Control structures* (see also Martin (2001: Section 6)).

23. Note in particular that judgments are different between Akmajian and Wasow (1975) and Akmajian, Steel, and Wasow (1979).

24. Strictly speaking, they assume at least *three layers*. (See also Cinque's (1999) assumed structure, introduced in Chapter 2):

(i) a. Incidentally, he had fortunately escaped from the death camp.
  b. [$_{S1}$ [$_{SAdv}$ incidentally] [$_{S2}$ [$_{SAdv}$ fortunately] [$_{S3}$ Tense [Tns [Past][Perfect]] [$_{S4}$ he escape from the death camp]]]] (Kajita 1968)

(ii) [$_{Meaning\ of\ Sentence2}$ [$_{Discourse\text{-}Modality}$ [$_{Meaning\ of\ Sentence1}$ [$_{Sentence\text{-}Modality}$ [$_{Poposition4}$ [$_{Polarity}$ [$_{Proposition3}$ [$_{Tense}$ [$_{Proposition2}$ [$_{Aspect}$ [$_{Proposition1}$ [$_{Predicate}$ [$_{Argument\ (n\ \geq\ 1)}$]]]]]]]]]]]]]

(Nakau 1994)

(iii) a. Probably they will be eating dinner by now, won't they?
  b. [Fα=Performative won't they? [Fβ=Attitudinal probably, will, I guess [P=Proposition they are eating dinner by now]]] (Sawada 1993, 1995)
(iv) a. You must be very careful. (Epistemic)
  b. [IP(=illocutionary point) I SAY to you [PA(=propositional attitude) I BELIEVE [TM(=truth modality) necessarily TRUE [p(=proposition) you Tns be very careful]]]] (Nakano 1994)

25. Many generative semantics linguists in the 1970's (especially see the studies introduced in note 27 in Chapter 1) assume the structures similar to (71a, b) and (72a, b) as the *syntactic* structures of modals. As an illustration of this, see the following:

(i) a. John must know the answer. (Epistemic)
  b.

```
                        S₁
                       /  \
                    NP₁    VP₁
                     |      |
                    S₂      V
                   /  \
                 NP₂   VP₂
                  |     |
                 S₃     V
                /  \
              NP₃   VP₃
               |     |
              S₄     V
             /  \
           NP   VP₄
            |   /  \
            N  V   NP
            |  |    |
                    N
            |  |    |    |     |
          John know answer PRES must PRES
```

(Imai 1975: 90)

(ii) a. John may pick the flowers.
b.

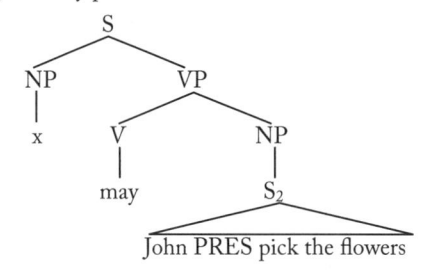

```
         S
        / \
      NP   VP
      |   /  \
      x  V   NP
         |   |
        may  S₂
             |
       John PRES pick the flowers
```

(Ibid.: 259)

We may say that these structures are, in a sense, accurate as *semantic* structures.

26. Martin also argues that the contrast of *VP-preposing* in Control infinitivals and Raising infinitivals can be evidence for his claim, as is shown in (i):

(i) a. [vp Fix the car], John tried PRO to [vp e].
b. *[vp Know the answer], I believe Bill to [vp e].

However, we can probably provide the same account in our discussion so far for the grammaticality in (ia) and (ib), judging from the following examples of VP-preposing in root modals and epistemic modals:

(ii) a. John said that he doesn't want to solve the problem, but [solve the problem] he *must* ϕ. (root use)
b. *They say John doesn't know French at all, but to my knowledge, [know French very well] he *must* ϕ. (epistemic use)

Thus, the remaining strong evidence for Stowell's (1982) and Martin's (1992, 2001) discussion is the *temporal semantics* of Control complements vs. that of Raising complements. I will leave this problem for future study, but I suspect that such temporal semantics can be reinterpreted without assuming two types of tense (or *to*) under other tense interpretation theories (see Reichenbach (1947), McCawley (1971), Comrie (1985), Enç (1987), Hornstein (1990), Declerck (1991b), Mihara (1992), and Wada (2001)). I also suspect that the temporal semantics of Control complements vs. that of Raising complements come from the *presence of the complementizer*, which connects the tense relations between the matrix clause and the complement clause.

Chapter 4

On the Position of *Not* in Infinitival Clauses[1]

4.1 Introduction

In this chapter I discuss the position of the negative *not* in infinitival clauses. As I discussed in Section 3.2.2, *not* is placed *before* the infinitival marker *to*, as shown in (1) to (3), which we considered to be evidence for the present proposal.

(1) a. Be careful *not to* catch a cold. (=(8) in Chapter 3)
   b. *Be careful *to not* catch a cold.
(2) Try *not to* be late. (NOT USUALLY ~~Try to not be late.~~)
   (Swan 1995[2]: 276)
(3) It [i.e. the group '*to*+infinitive'] cannot be split up by the negative particle *not*:
   e.g. The wisest policy would be *not to* do anything at all. (*to not* do)
   (Declerck 1991a: 467)

We can say that this rule generally applies to standard English. However, we can find the *marginal* word order <to not V> in some constructions or dialectal variations, as shown in (4) and (5):

(4) a. John wants *to not* go.
   b. Peter expects his friends *to not* object to his proposals. (Pollock 1989: 375)
(5) a. We will send enough troops *to not* let Macedonia shut down its borders.
   b. You have to learn *to not* let it start.   (Fitzmaurice 2000: 171)

What should we do with these word ordering relations between *to* and *not*? There are two possibilities: one possibility is that the word order is derived from the other. The other possibility is that both word orders are the independent constructions. Pollock (1989) and Hasegawa (2003) take the former position, as shown in (6) and (7):

(6) a. John wants *to not* go.
   b. John wants *not to* go.
   c. John wants to not ___ go. (Pollock's (1989) analysis)

(7) a. *Not to* have played football for many years is a disadvantage in a major game.
   b. *To not* have played football for many years is a disadvantage in a major game.
   c. ___ not to have played football for many years is a disadvantage in a major game. (Hasegawa's (2003) analysis)

In this chapter, however, I will argue that the latter possibility is more appropriate.

4.2 Pollock's (1989) Analysis

The main points of Pollock's (1989) analysis of infinitival clauses are shown in (8a-c):

(8) a. *To* is base-generated in INFL.
   b. *To* can be moved by Affix Movement (Chomsky's (1981) *Rule R*) and this adjoins it to VP at S-structure, where this Affix Movement is optional since *to* is not a bound morpheme.
   c. *Not* (i.e. Neg^0) does not block this lowering rule.

As an illustration of this, consider the derivation of (6a, b), as shown in (10):

(9) a. John wants *to not* go. (=(6a))
   b. John wants *not to* go. (=(6b))

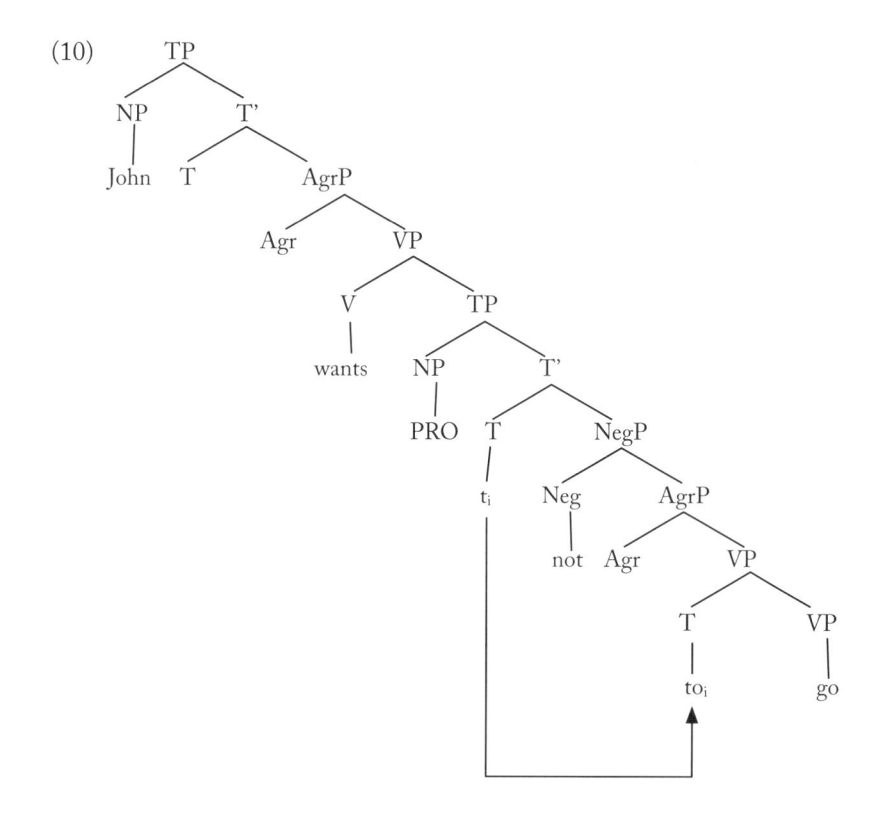

(10)
```
              TP
            /    \
          NP      T'
          |      /  \
         John   T   AgrP
                    /  \
                  Agr   VP
                       /  \
                      V    TP
                      |   /  \
                   wants NP   T'
                         |   /  \
                        PRO T   NegP
                            |   /  \
                            tᵢ Neg  AgrP
                                |   /  \
                               not Agr  VP
                                       /  \
                                      T    VP
                                      |    |
                                     toᵢ   go
```

Here, when the rule in (8b) does not apply in the underlying structure, the *marginal* word order in (9a) is derived. On the other hand, when the rule in (8b) applies in the underlying structure, the *standard* word order in (9b) is derived.

However, there are not a few problems with Pollock's analysis: first, conceptually speaking, the operation Affix Hopping (see Chapter 1) should be applied only to *affixes* (i.e. bound morphemes), not *words* (i.e. free morphemes). Second, (8c) is a stipulation and we should consider the possibility that this *not* could prevent this movement due to a violation of Travis's (1984) *Head Movement Constraint* (HMC), though Pollock assumes several *technical devices* to circumvent this from happening. Third, a serious problem is that *downward movements* such as (8b) normally cannot be permitted in any theories of generative grammar.[2] Fourth, his theory cannot properly explain the following examples of *pro-infinitives* (Jespersen (1909-1949: Part V)), pointed out by Sawada (1995) and Matsubara (1997a). Consider the following examples:

(11) a. She opened the door, though I told her not to ϕ.
   b. John must take advantage of that offer. It would be foolish not to ϕ.
(Sawada 1995: 124-125)

Since the word order in (11a, b) is <not to V>, (8b) should have been applied and thus the infinitival marker *to* should be in VP-Spec. But this result wrongly predicts that *to* itself is deleted by VP-deletion, as shown in (12a, b), following ungrammatical (13a, b):[3]

(12) a. I told her [TP PRO [T t_i][NegP not [VP to_i open the door]]]
                                                    ϕ
   b. It would be foolish
       [TP PRO [T t_i][NegP not [VP to_i take advantage of that offer]]]
                                                    ϕ

(13) a. *She opened the door, though I told her not ϕ.
   b. *John must take advantage of that offer. It would be foolish not ϕ.

As I discussed in Chapter 1, Chomsky (1995: Chapter 4) and his subsequent work has eliminated AgrP or AGRsP and AGRoP for *conceptual* and *theory internal* reasons, but the discussion above forces us to conclude that Pollock's assumption that *to* downwardly moves to VP-Spec cannot hold *empirically* either. [4), 5), 6)]

4.3 Hasegawa's (2003) Analysis

Let us begin by considering Hasegawa's analysis of the following examples:

(14) a. *To not have* played football for many years is a disadvantage in a major game. (=(7b))
   b. *To have not* played football for many years is a disadvantage in a major game. (Hasegawa 2003: 67)

Hasegawa also criticizes Pollock's *Spilt*-I *Hypothesis* itself and does not assume AgrP used in Pollock (1989) nor AGRsP and AGRoP used in Chomsky (1995:

Chapters 2-3). In Pollock's analysis (14b) should be derived from (14a), as shown in (15):

(15) To ___ not have played ... → To have not ___ played   (Ibid.)

However, Hasegawa claims that (14a) is *sentential negation* but that (14b) is *verb phrase negation* and thus the two should be distinguished (cf. Iatridou (1990)). Indeed, I agree with his claim that the two are not identical constructions, but the problem is, I claim, that Hasegawa regards not only the following (16) but also (14a) above as *sentential negation* sentences:

(16) *Not to have* played football for many years is a disadvantage in a major game.   (Ibid.)[7]

Namely, Hasegawa assumes that (14a) is derived from (16) and thus both sentences are sentential negations. Here let us review how he accounts for the derivation of (14a) from (16). First, he assumes the following Phrase Structure Rules:

(17) a. S' → (C) S
 b. S → (AdvP) S (AdvP)
 c. S → NP VP
 d. VP → (AdvP) VP (AdvP)
 e. VP → Aux V'
 f. V' → (AdvP) V' (AdvP)
 g. V' → V $\left\{ \begin{array}{l} \text{Pred} \\ \text{(NP) (PP) } \left(\left\{ \begin{array}{l} \text{S'} \\ \text{PP} \end{array} \right\} \right) \end{array} \right\}$
 h. ... (omitted)
 o. Aux → Aux_1 (Aux_2)
 p. Aux_1 → $\left\{ \begin{array}{l} \text{Tns (M)} \\ \text{to} \end{array} \right\}$
 q. Aux_2 → (have En) (be ing)   (Ibid.: 49-50)

Roughly speaking, his S', S, VP, Aux (especially Aux₁), and V' each correspond to CP, IP, I', I and ModalP, and VP respectively in this book. Based on these PS-Rules, the structure of (16) will be something like the one in (18):[8), 9)]

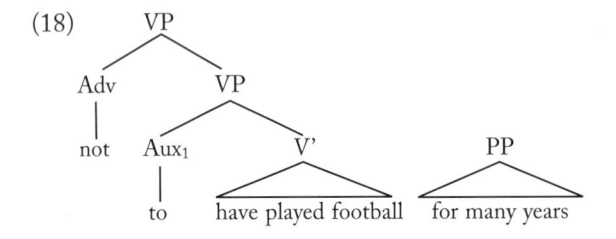

(18)
```
           VP
          /  \
        Adv   VP
         |   /  \
        not Aux₁  V'       PP
             |   / \      / \
             to have played football  for many years
```

Then, he assumes a late rule, as shown in (19), following Baker (1989, 1991):

(19) a. ┌──► [vp Adv Aux₁ X] → Aux₁ [vp Adv __ X] (Optional)
        └──────────────┘

   Condition: Aux₁ has no stress.

   b. John [vp probably will help us]. → John wĭll [vp probably help us].
      (˘ means no stress)

   c. Rule Ordering: *Not* attraction(=(ii) in note 31) →V'-deletion→Affix Hopping/*do*-support→Stress Assigning→(19a)[10)]

(Ibid.: 65)

Interestingly, he mentions that, although the rule in (19a) is similar to *not* attraction, (19a) is rather different from *not* attraction since it applies later than *not* attraction and is subject to a phonological condition as well.

That is, when (19a) applies to (18), (14a) is derived, as shown in (20):[11)]

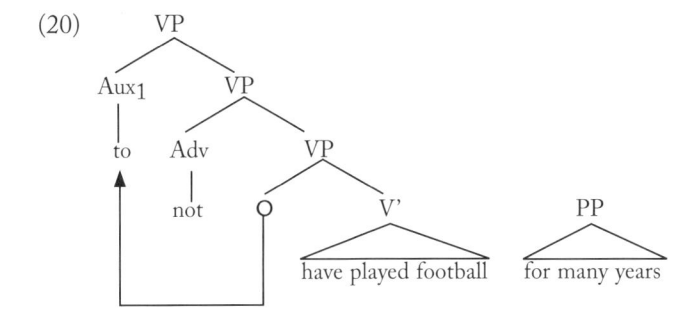

(20)
```
              VP
            /    \
         Aux₁    VP
          |     /  \
          to  Adv   VP
               |   /  \
              not  ∅   V'         PP
                      / \        /  \
              have played football  for many years
```

Hasegawa's explanation above is coherent under his framework, but I would like to point out two problems: first, though his framework can indeed generate the marginal word order <to not V>, at the same time, it wrongly predicts that the <to not V> word order like in (1b), (2), and (3), which are ungrammatical sentences in standard English, is grammatical:

(21) a. *Be careful *to not* catch a cold. (=(1b))
  b. *Try *to not* be late. (=(2))
  c. *The wisest policy would be *to not* do anything at all. (=(3))

Note here that (19a) can apply *freely* so long as the phonological condition in (19a) is met.

Second, his system cannot explain the ungrammaticality of (22b) either:

(22) a. Carol told Dan to leave, but Jim told him *not to* ___.
  b. *Carol told Dan to leave, but Jim told him *to not* ___.   (Ernst 1992: 128)

As the rule ordering in (19c) shows, the rule in (19a) applies *later than V'-deletion*. Thus, Hasegawa's framework should predict that (22b) can be derived from (22a) with no problems and be grammatical, contrary to the fact. This discussion forces us to conclude that Hasegawa's explanation about the <to not V> word order is also insufficient.

4.4 An Alternative Analysis

Now we are in the position to provide an alternative analysis, but the alternative is not new at all, but rather it is a traditional position, as shown in (24a,b):

(23) a. *Not to have* played football for many years is a disadvantage in a major game. (=(16))
    b. *To not have* played football for many years is a disadvantage in a major game. (=(14a))
    c. *To have not* played football for many years is a disadvantage in a major game. (=(14b))

(24) a. *Not* in (23a) is sentential negation *not*, which is in Spec-NegP, i.e., this *not* negates the whole infinitival clause.
    b. *Not* in (23b) is a verb phrase negation *not*, which is adjoined to PerfP (=a type of VP), i.e., this *not* negates only PerfP.[12]
    c. *Not* in (24b) is main verb phrase negation *not*, which is adjoined to VP, i.e., this *not* negates only VP.

The structures of the infinitival clauses in (23a-c) are each shown in (25a-c) respectively.[13] Note that I will omit the *v*P node below in this chapter because we need not express it in particular for the discussion, and will ignore the *for* phrase just as in (18) and (20) but this problem will be discussed later.

(25) a.
```
         CP
        /  \
       C    IP
           /  \
          DP   I'
          |   / \
         PRO I   NegP
            [Nonfinite T] / \
                        Adv  Neg'
                        |   /  \
                       not Neg  ModalP
                           |   /   \
                          NE  Modal  PerfP
                              |     /  \
                              to  Perf  VP
                                  |    /\
                               have-en play football
```

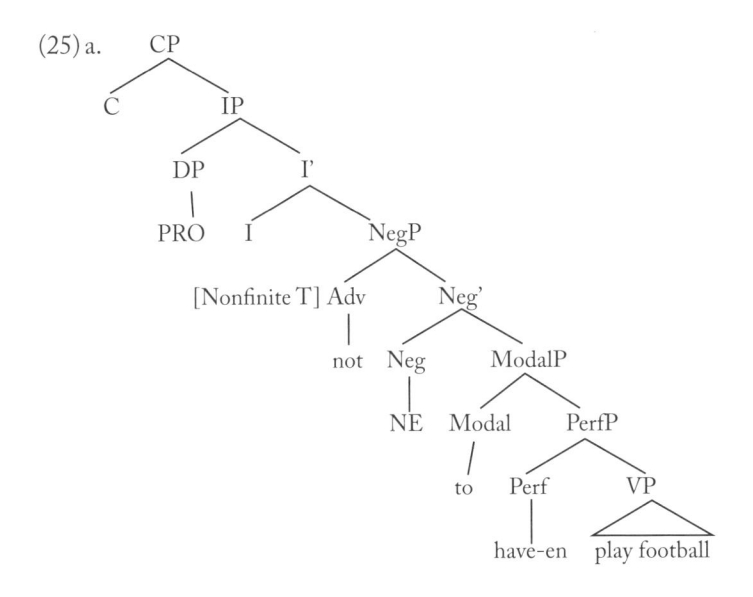

b.
```
         CP
        /  \
       C    IP
           /  \
          DP   I'
          |   / \
         PRO I   ModalP
            [Nonfinite T] / \
                       Modal  PerfP(=VP)
                       |     /   \
                       to   Adv   PerfP
                            |    /  \
                           not  Perf  VP
                                |    /\
                             have-en play football
```

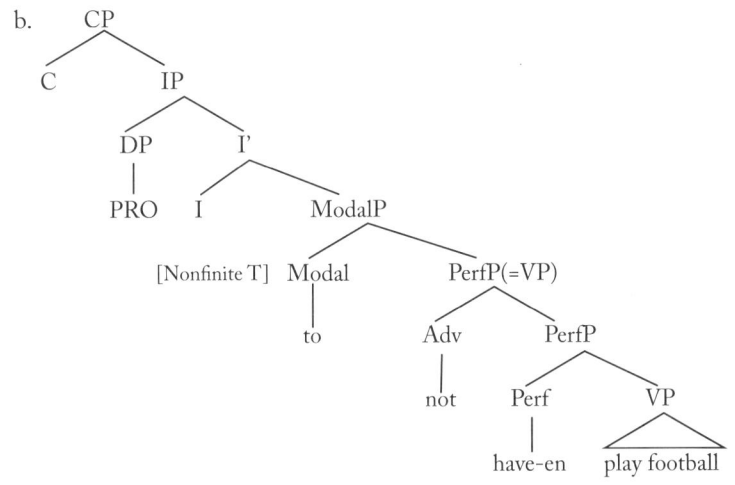

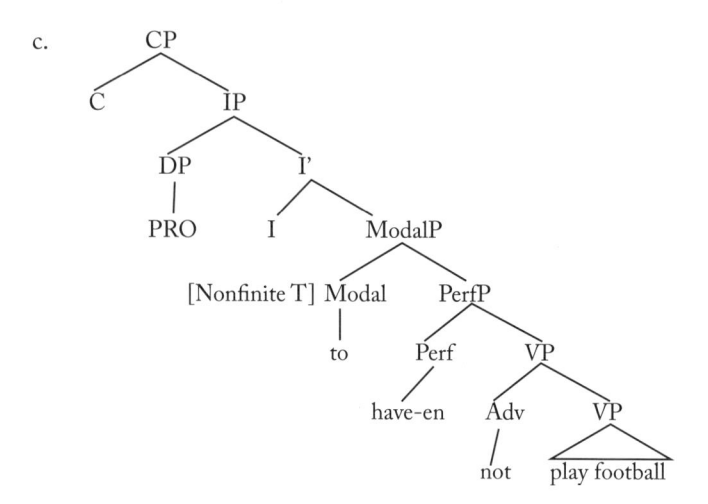

c.
```
              CP
             /  \
            C    IP
                /  \
              DP    I'
              |    /  \
             PRO  I    ModalP
                       /    \
           [Nonfinite T] Modal  PerfP
                        |      /    \
                        to   Perf    VP
                            /       /  \
                        have-en   Adv   VP
                                   |   /  \
                                  not play football
```

Last, I should mention the *scope relations* in (23a-c). In fact, since Hasegawa (2003) adopts a rather traditional version of generative theory (see Nomura (2000c, 2005b)), he can possibly make a similar assumption to mine as well, but he does not do so; the reason is, I suppose, that (23a, b) have two interpretations while (23c) has only one interpretation, as shown in (26):

(26) a. { To not / Not to } have played football for many years is a disadvantage in a major game.
Ambiguous: (i) If you have played football for not so many years, it is a disadvantage in a major game. (For example, only two years have passed since you stared playing football.: not (many)) (ii) If you have stopped playing football many years ago, it is a disadvantage in a major game. (For example, fifteen years have passed since you stopped playing football.: many (not))

b. To have not played football for many years is a disadvantage in a major game.
Not ambiguous: only (ii) in (26a)

(Hasegawa 2003: 67, translations are mine)

How should we deal with these differences in semantic interpretation under our framework? I propose the following assumption, as shown in (27), instead of using the recent general assumption of *LF Quantifier Raising* in line with May (1985) or Aoun and Li (1993).

(27) The adverbial phrase for many years can adjoin to both IP and VP.[14]

Given (27), consider each case in (23a-c):

(28) *Not to have* played football for many years is a disadvantage in a major game. (=(23a))
   a. the case where the *for* phrase adjoins to IP→MANY>NOT

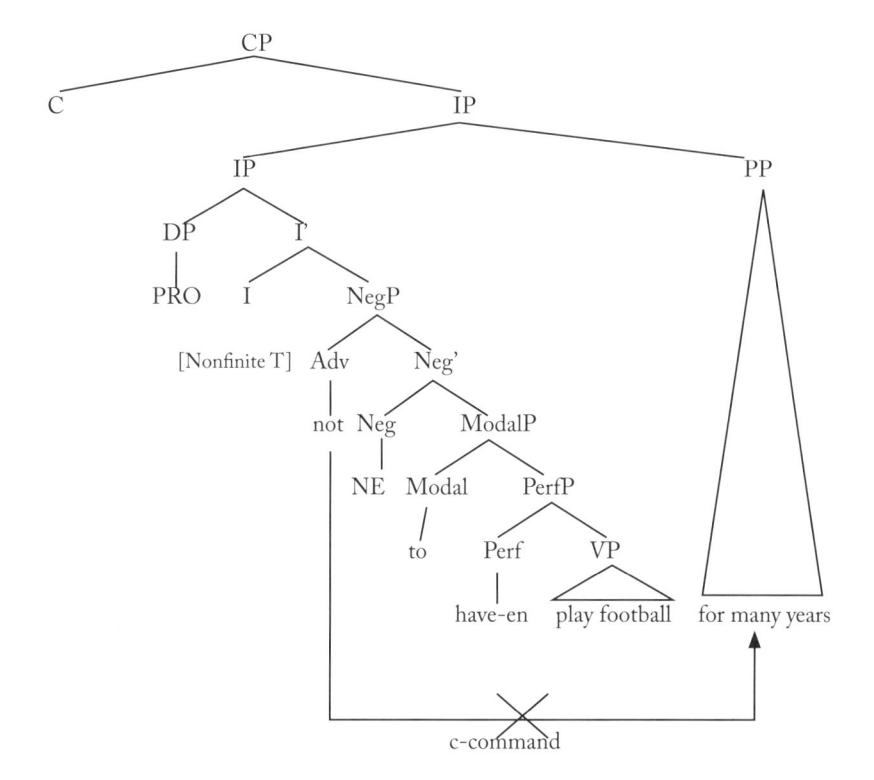

```
                        CP
                   /         \
                  C           IP
                         /          \
                        IP            PP
                      /    \           |
                    DP      I'         △
                    |      /  \
                   PRO    I    NegP
                              /      \
                    [Nonfinite T]  Adv    Neg'
                                   |    /     \
                                  not  Neg    ModalP
                                       |     /      \
                                       NE  Modal    PerfP
                                           |       /    \
                                           to    Perf    VP
                                                  |     /\
                                               have-en play football   for many years
                                                          ↑
                                                    ╳
                                                c-command
```

b. the case where the *for* phrase adjoins to VP→NOT > MANY

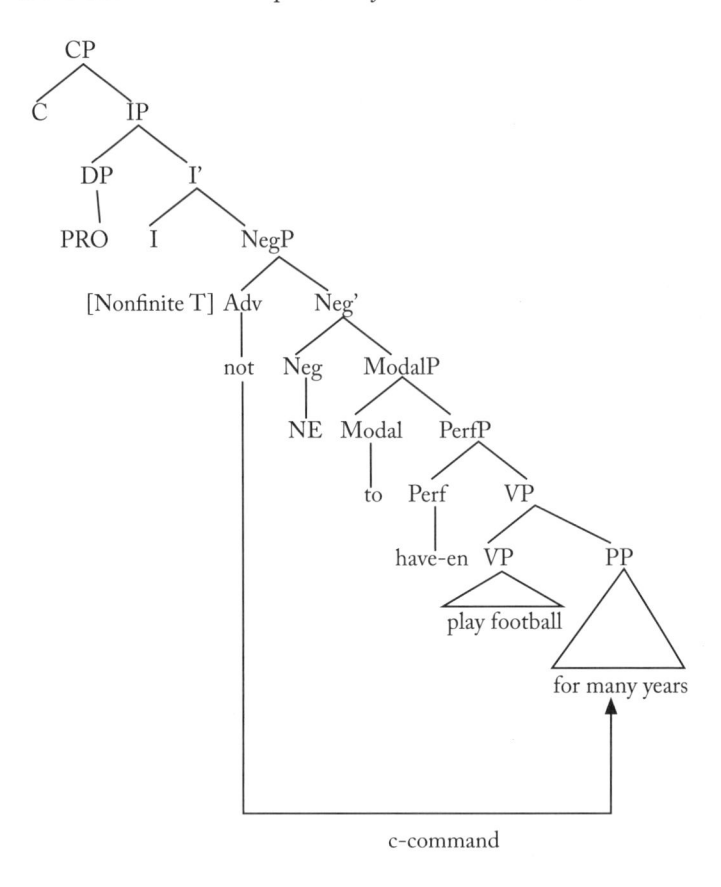

[Tree diagram:
CP
├── C
└── IP
    ├── DP
    │   └── PRO
    └── I'
        ├── I
        │   └── [Nonfinite T]
        └── NegP
            ├── Adv
            │   └── not
            └── Neg'
                ├── Neg
                │   └── NE
                └── ModalP
                    ├── Modal
                    │   └── to
                    └── PerfP
                        ├── Perf
                        │   └── have-en
                        └── VP
                            ├── VP
                            │   └── play football
                            └── PP
                                └── for many years

c-command (arrow from *not* to *for many years*)]

(29) *To not have* played football for many years is a disadvantage in a major game. (=(23b))

Chapter 4   On the Position of *Not* in Infinitival Clauses   109

a. the case where the *for* phrase adjoins to IP→MANY > NOT

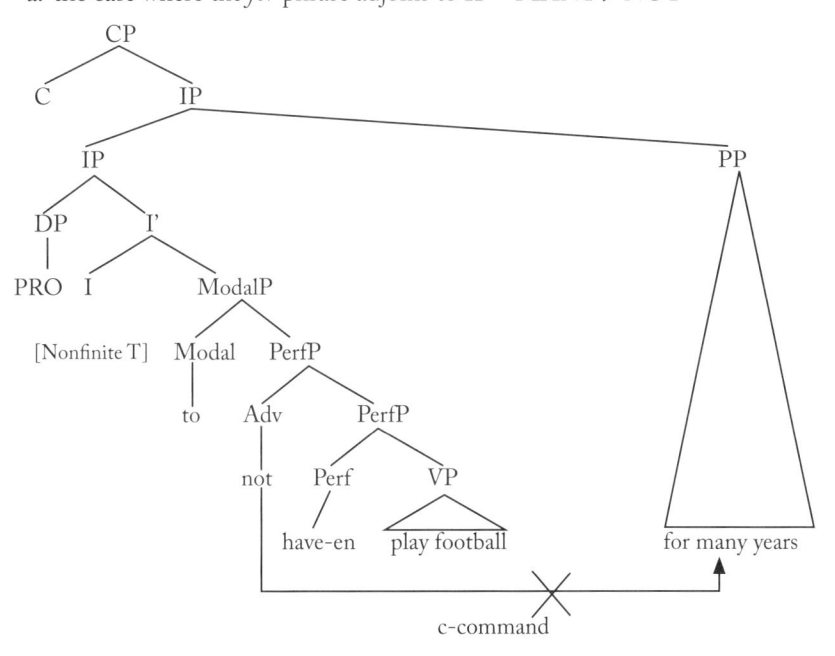

b. the case where the *for* phrase adjoins to VP→NOT > MANY

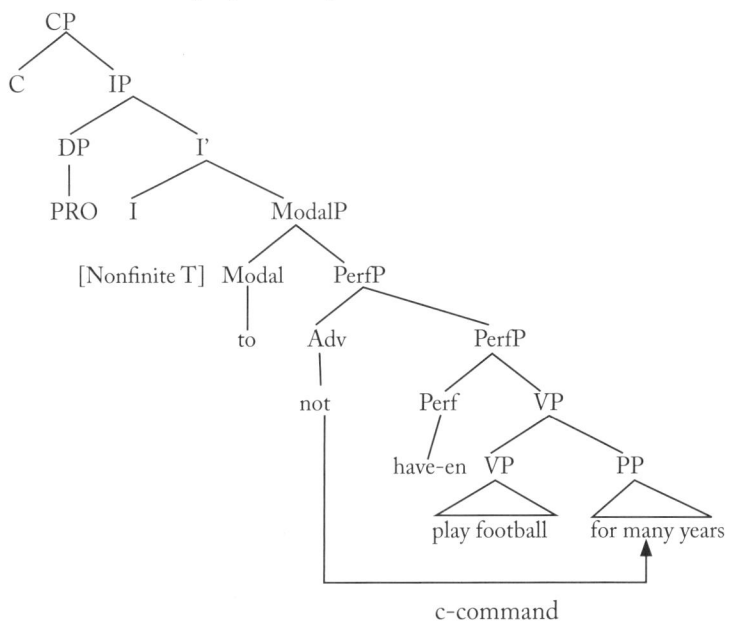

(30) *To have not* played football for many years is a disadvantage in a major game. (=(23c))
   a. the case where the *for* phrase adjoins to IP→MANY>NOT

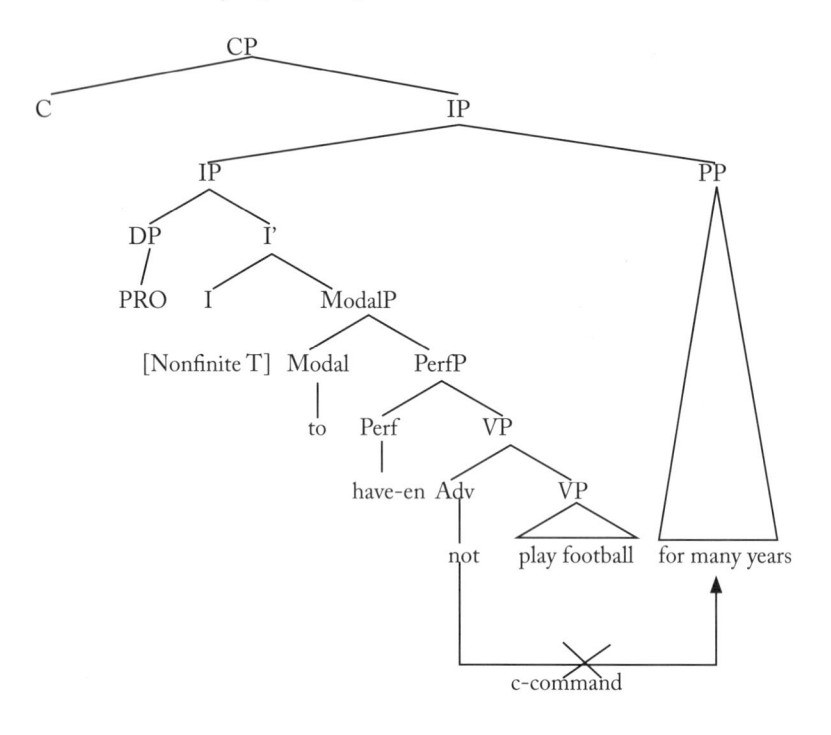

b. the case where the *for* phrase adjoins to VP→MANY＞NOT

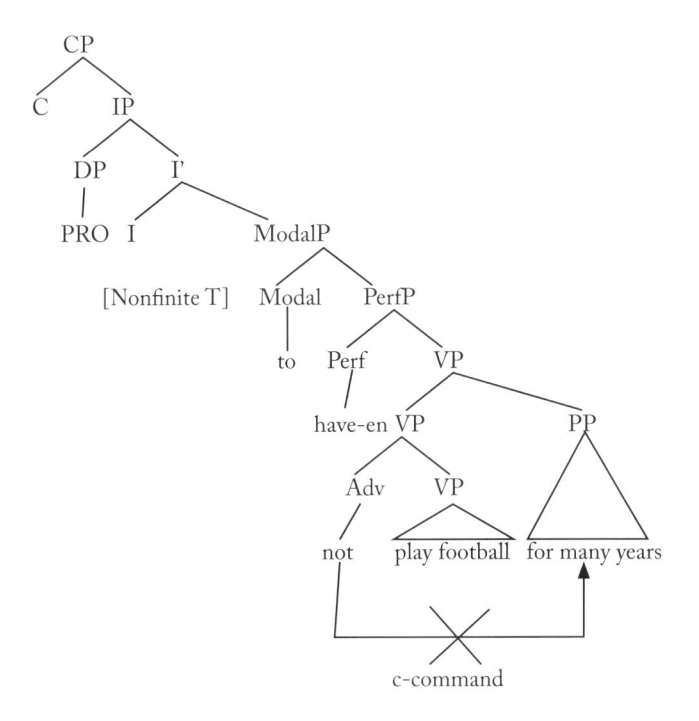

```
                    CP
                   /  \
                  C    IP
                      /  \
                    DP    I'
                    |    /  \
                   PRO  I    ModalP
                        |    /    \
                 [Nonfinite T] Modal  PerfP
                              |     /    \
                              to  Perf    VP
                                   |     /  \
                               have-en  VP   PP
                                       /  \   △
                                      Adv  VP
                                      |
                                     not  play football  for many years
```

c-command

Here I will show the summary below:

(31)   IP-Adjunct   VP-Adjunct
    a. Not to have…=Sentential Negation →MANY＞NOT   NOT＞MANY
    b. To not have…=VP Negation   →MANY＞NOT   NOT＞MANY
    c. To have not…=VP Negation   →MANY＞NOT   MANY＞NOT

In conclusion, given that the adverbial phrase *for many years* can be both IP-adjunct and VP-adjunct, our alternative analysis can properly account for the differences in scope interpretations in (23a-c).[15]

4.5 Concluding Remarks

In this chapter I discussed the position of *not* in infinitival clauses. Pollock (1989) assumes that the standard <not to V> order is derived from the marginal

<to not V> order and conversely Hasegawa (2003) assumes that the <to not V> word order is derived from the <not to V> order, but I showed that both analyses are empirically problematic. In conclusion I claimed that the two word orders are *not identical constructions* and thus the <not to V> order alone is *the negation of the whole infinitival clause* and the <to not V> word order is *verb phrase negation*. Furthermore, assuming that the adverbial phrase *for many years* can be both IP-adjunct and VP-adjunct, our framework can properly account for the differences in scope interpretations that Hasegawa (2003) observes.[16]

Notes to Chapter 4

1. The discussion in this section is mainly based on Nomura (2001a)

2. In GB Theory this was assumed to be a violation of *ECP*, as shown in (i), which causes *strong deviance* (see Chomsky (1986), Rizzi (1990), and Lasnik and Saito (1992)):

   (i) Empty Category Principle
      a. A nonpronominal empty category must be properly governed.
      b. α properly governs β iff α θ-governs or antecedent-governs β.

      (Chomsky 1986: 17)

   However, as I discussed in Section 3.3.2, now that government is abolished entirely in the Minimalist Program, ECP itself cannot exist. But no *downward movements* are allowed in principle all the same in the Minimalist Program, because sentence building (i.e. Merge and Move) is implemented in a *bottom-up* way.

   Incidentally, *downward movements* are ruled out by *antecedent government*. As for the *that*-trace effect, on the other hand, which was also assumed to be the violation of ECP, Hasegawa (1993-1994) and Pesetsky and Torrego (2000) attempt to give other explanations without assuming ECP, though their directions are rather different.

3. However, Shigeo Tonoike (personal communication, 2005) suggested that in (13a, b) VP-deletion cannot apply because the identity condition on VP-deletion does not apply in this case.

4. Additionally, Sawada (1995) and Matsubara (1997a) argue that Pollock's analysis of the infinitival clauses itself is wrong, on the basis of the fact that he fails to explain not only the violation of ECP and VP-deletion in the <not to VP> construction discussed here but also other types of VP-deletion and the positions of adverbs in *split infinitives*.

5. Nakajima (1989) supplies almost the same explanation as Pollock's about the <to not V> word order under the standard IP structure in GB Theory, though he does not assume AgrP. Consider the following examples in (ia, b) and their underlying structure (ii):

(i) a. I warned Bill [not to eat fish]. (Nakajima 1989: 37)
   b. %I warned Bill [to not eat fish] (cf. (ibid.: 38))

(ii) 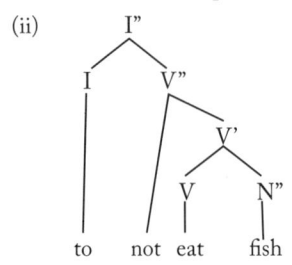
```
        I"
       /  \
      I    V"
      |    |
      |    V'
      |   /  \
      |  V    N"
      |  |    |
      to not eat fish
```
(Ibid.)

He also assumes that (ii) is the underlying structure and that *to* moves to the *left-edge of V'* by Affix Hopping, as shown in (iii), resulting in the standard word order (ia).

(iii) [I' ..t.. [V" not [V' to eat fish]]]   (Ibid.: 39)

This explanation will also cause the same problems as we discussed concerning Pollock's analysis in this section, though I suspect that Nakajima does not assume this structure and derivation any more.

6. It does not seem that even our framework can explain the following examples in French:

(i) a. *Pierre ne   pas   mange.
       Peter   NE   not   eats
    b. Pierre ne   mange pas.
       Peter   NE   eats   not   (Pollock 1989: 393)
(ii) a. Ne   pas   manger...
        NE   not   to eat
     b. *Ne   manger pas...
        NE   to eat not   (Ibid.: 394)

The examples show that in French the word order is <ne + V + pas> in finite sentences, while it is <ne + pas + V> in infinitival clauses. The structures in (i) and (ii) will be shown each in (iii) and (iv) in our framework:

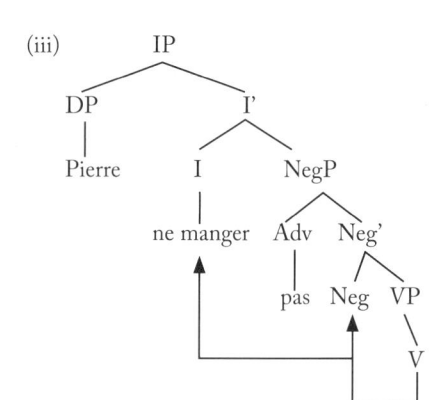

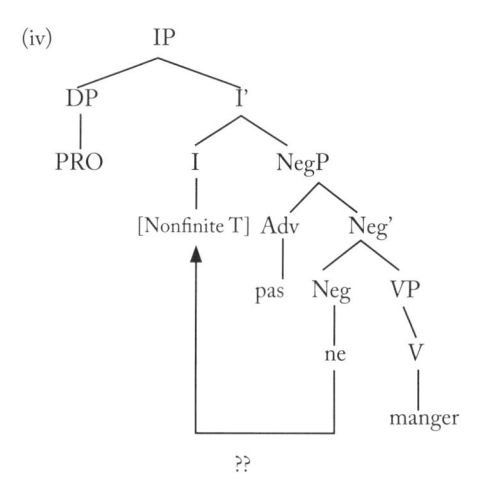

(iii) IP
      ╱ ╲
     DP   I'
     │   ╱ ╲
   Pierre I NegP
          │ ╱ ╲
     ne manger Adv Neg'
               │ ╱ ╲
              pas Neg VP
                      ╲
                       V

(iv) IP
      ╱ ╲
     DP   I'
     │   ╱ ╲
    PRO I NegP
         │ ╱ ╲
   [Nonfinite T] Adv Neg'
                 │ ╱ ╲
                pas Neg VP
                     │ ╲
                     ne V
                         │
                       manger
         ??

Note that Hasegawa (2003) also notices the problems as to the positions of adverbs in infinitival clauses in French, such as shown in (v), and proposes the following rule in (vi) instead of assuming Agr:

(v) ⎧ Souvent mal faire ⎫ ses devoirs, c'est stupide.
    ⎨ Faire souvent mal ⎬
    ⎩ Souvent faire mal ⎭
    'To frequently do one's homework badly is stupid.' (Hasegawa 2003: 215)

(vi) Adjoin V to the left of VP optionally in the structure of [_VP Adv V …].
                                                          (Ibid.: 217, fn. 1)

I will leave this problem for future study.

7. Note that Iatridou discusses (14b) and (16) but does not deal with (14a) in her discussion.

8. Here I am ignoring the *for* phrase (=*for many years*) for the purpose of simple notations. Needless to say, for Hasegawa's explanation, the position of the *for* phrase is crucial: he assumes that since the *for* phrase and *not* are both VP-adverbs, either can freely merge beforehand.

9. Note that he assumes that *not* is not the head of NegP but is one of the VP-adverbs:

(i) a. X Adv=Adverbial elements adjoined to X

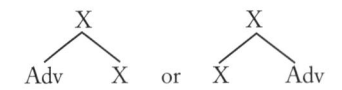

```
     X              X
    / \            / \
  Adv  X    or    X  Adv
```

b. S Adv=perhaps, probably, frankly, obviously, strangely, naturally, ...
c. VP Adv=just, never, rarely, hardly, often, always, ever; not

(Hasegawa 2003: 57)

But he claims that *not* is a VP-adverb but has *special properties*, as shown in (iia, b):

(ii) *Not*-Placement [Attraction] Rule

a. Adjoin [+Finite] Aux₁ to the left of VP beginning with *not*:

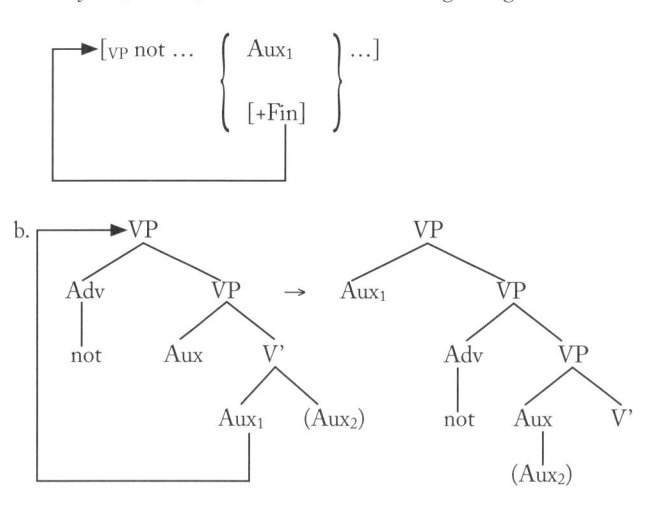

[VP not ... { Aux₁ / [+Fin] } ...]

b.

```
        VP                              VP
       /  \                            /  \
     Adv   VP         →            Aux₁    VP
      |   /  \                            /  \
     not Aux  V'                        Adv   VP
            /  \                         |   /  \
          Aux₁ (Aux₂)                   not Aux  V'
                                             |
                                           (Aux₂)
```

(see (ibid.: 59, 43))

Given this assumption, though *often* and *not* are both VP-adverbs, Affix Hopping applies in (iiia) and thus derives (iva), while *not* Attraction applies in (iiib) and thus derives (ivb):

(iii) a. John often [Pres go to New York]

b. John not [Pres go to New York]

(iv) a. John often [__ go+Pres to New York]
    b. John Pres not [__ go to New York]

Consequently, *go*+Pres in (iva) becomes *goes* in (va), while *do*-support (see Hasegawa (2003: 39)) applies to the stranded Tense in (ivb) and thus gives (vb):

(v) a. John often *goes* to New York.
   b. John *does* not go to New York.

10. I will leave it open whether the rule in (19a) is really needed in linguistic theory or English Grammar. But it is true that it has a rather wide descriptive coverage, judging

from the fact that it can explain all the following contrasts in grammaticality:

(i) a. He always has been very kind to me.
   b. He hǎs always been very kind to me.
   c. He always hǎs been very kind to me. /
      He never hǎs been very polite.
   d. *He hǎs always been very kind to me. /
      *He hǎs never been very polite.
   e. He always hás. / He never will.
   f. *He hás always. / *He will never.
   g. He hásn't. / He wón't.

   (˜means the contrastive stress; ´ means the primary stress.)
   (Hasegawa 2003: 66)

11. Note that the *not* attraction rule does not apply in (18) since Aux₁ (=the infinitival marker *to*) is not [+Finite] in this case.

12. In other words, I am assuming that *not* in (23b) is the same type of adverb appearing in *split infinitivals*, as shown in (ia-e):

(i) a. It is necessary to *clearly* understand Chomsky's theory.
   b. It will be found possible to *properly* describe why dinosaurs died out.
   c. You expect me to *never* remember my past.
   d. She wished to *thoroughly* enjoy her dinner.
   e. He proposes to *further* characterize his nation. (Matsubara 1997a: 51)

Incidentally, normative grammar says that we should not use split infinitives, but Fitzmaurice (2000) reported that the uses of this split word order <to not V> in negative infinitival clauses have been increasing in number. Interestingly, according to her, not a few educated people use this word order as well:

(i) a. Some departments *seem to not* be very interested in developing a writing intensive course.
      (male university professor of Linguistics I, department meeting, Jan. 13, 1999)
   b. It's only superficial *to not* have objectives as outcomes for this [writing] course if we're focusing on the process [of writing]
      (female university professor of Sociology, Jan. 7, 1999)

c. The students *hope to not* get calls at that office.
(male university professor of Linguistics II, Jan. 14, 1999)
d. It forces them *to not* run large classes and let them do journals instead.
(male university professor of Linguistics I, Jan. 14, 1999)

(Fitzmaurice 2000: 179-180)

13. Technically speaking, I am assuming that adjuncts exist *in another dimension* in this book (see note 12 in Chapter 3), as Chomsky sometimes suggests, so adjuncts cannot prevent Affix Hopping from applying to V, as shown in (iia), unlike *Specifier* elements in (ia):

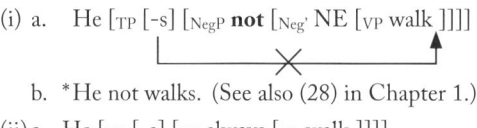

(i) a. He [$_{TP}$ [-s] [$_{NegP}$ **not** [$_{Neg'}$ NE [$_{VP}$ walk]]]]
 b. *He not walks. (See also (28) in Chapter 1.)
(ii) a. He [$_{TP}$ [-s] [$_{VP}$ always [$_{VP}$ walk]]]]
 b. He always walks.

Thus, since *not* in (25c) is not a *Specifier* but an *Adjunct*, this *not* does not prevent the perfect affix *–en* from attaching to *play* by Affix Hopping.

14. Hasegawa formalizes this fact by the following lexical redundancy rule (see also note 8 and (i) in note 9):

(i) S Adv → VP Adv (not vice versa)
(ii) a. *Probably*, John will wash the dishes.
 b. John *probably* will wash the dishes.
 c. John will *probably* wash the dishes. (Hasegawa 2003: 58)

15. Before closing this section, I will briefly mention Shigeo Tonoike's question (personal communication, 2005) as to *why IP and VP and not other constituents* apply in my assumption (27).
 In this connection I also wondered if *not* could be merged at a point before the phrase *for many years* is merged in the derivation of (30b). If possible, (30) would be ambiguous as are (28) and (29). In fact, as I have discussed in this chapter, (30) is commonly considered to be unambiguous, i.e., to have only the (iib) reading:

(i) To have *not* played football for *many* years is a disadvantage in a major game. (=(30))

(ii) a. If you have played football for not so many years, it is a disadvantage in a major game. (For example, only two years have passed since you stared playing football.: not (many))

  b. If you have stopped playing football many years ago, it is a disadvantage in a major game. (For example, fifteen years have passed since you stopped playing football.: many (not))

On the contrary, however, according to D. L. Smith (personal communication, 2005), the following sentences have only the (iia) reading:

(iii) a. To have not played football *very many years* is a disadvantage *in the major leagues*.
  b. To have not played football *many years* is a disadvantage *in the major leagues*.

Taking the readings of (i) and (iiia, b) into consideration, we should consider (i) to be ambiguous syntactically. Moreover, I suspect that native speakers' intuitions are somewhat bothered by an aversion to using *many* in that *much* and *many* go better with negatives in current usage, as shown in (iv):

(iv) a. I *don't* have *much* money.
  a'. ??I *have* much money. (=I have a lot of money.)
  b. I *don't* have *many* friends.
  b. ?? I have *many* friends. (=I have lots of friends.)

Especially with the preposition *for*, the negative context seems better:

(v) a. I have *not* played *for many years*.
  a'. ?? I have played *for many years*. (=I have played many years./I have played for years.)

Note here that when we use *for a whole season* instead of *many* to avoid this problem, the sentence will be ambiguous, as shown in (vi):

(vi) To have *not* played football *for a whole season* is a disadvantage in the major leagues.

(D. L. Smith (personal communication, 2005))

In sum, we may say that (i) (=(30)) is, in fact, ambiguous, and it follows that we can eliminate the stipulation (27) (=The adverbial phrase *for many years* can adjoin to both *IP* and *VP*), though I will leave details relating to this problem for future study.

16. For the grammatical and semantic conditions on the <to not do> word orders in infinitival clauses, see Nomura and Smith (2006).

Chapter 5

Ought to and *Be to*[1]

5.1 Introduction

I discussed the syntactic status of the infinitival marker *to* in detail in Chapter 3. In fact, in the history of generative grammar, *to* was often considered to be an AUX element in the 1970's or an I(NFL) or T element in the 1980's. As is well known, the INFL(ection) system was proposed instead of AUX in Chomsky (1981):

(1)…, an element (call it "INFL," suggesting "inflection") indicating in particular whether the clause is finite or infinitival. Suppressing the distinction between indicative and subjunctive, we will say that INFL has the values [Tense], where [+Tense] stands for finite and [-Tense] for infinitival.

(Chomsky 1981: 18-19)

Since then (i.e. since the 1980's), it seems to me that *to* is tacitly considered to be base-generated in I (or T) in much of the literature.[2] But this assumption raises a serious problem (other than the one concerning the position of *not*): the problem with *ought to* and *be to*, pointed out by Sawada (1985, 1995) and Ando (1996, 2003). Consider the following examples:

(2) a. You *ought to* go.
b. John *is to* come back to Japan on September 1st.

We must regard *ought* in (2a) and *be* in (2b) as modals for various reasons, as we shall discuss below. But then, the problem arises that the present proposal would predict that the infinitival marker *to* and *ought* or *be* in (18a, b) cannot co-occur by the general principle, as shown in (3):

(3) Modals do not co-occur. (See (31g) in Chapter 1.)

In this chapter I will attempt to solve this problem.

5.2 Improper Analyses

To begin with, let us consider three seemingly obvious solutions that we can easily dispense with. One is to assume that both *ought* or *be* and *to* are base-generated under Modal^0:

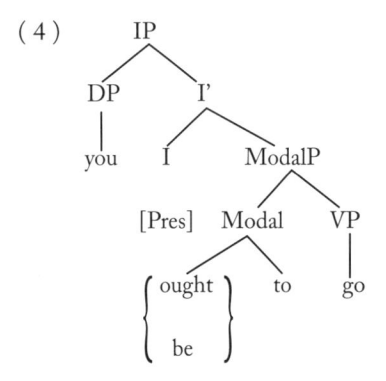

(4)
```
        IP
       /  \
      DP   I'
      |   /  \
     you I   ModalP
        [Pres] /   \
            Modal  VP
            /  \    |
         {ought} to go
         { be  }
```

However, there are many problems with this analysis: first, conceptually speaking, this structure will raise the problem of *double heads*.[3], [4] Second, this assumption will wrongly generate ungrammatical negative and interrogative sentences, as illustrated in (5b), (6b), (7b), and (8b):

(5) a. You *ought not to* go.
    b. *You *ought to not* go.   (Swan 1995^2: 398)
    c. *You [I [Modal ought to]] not go.
(6) a. John *is not to* come back to Japan on September 1st.
    b. *John *is to not* come back to Japan on September 1st.
    c. *John [I [Modal is to]] not come back to Japan on September 1st.
(7) a. *Ought we to* go now?
    b. **Ought to we* go now?

c. *[c [I [Modal ought to]]] we go now?
(8) a. *Is John to* come back to Japan on September 1st?
   b. **Is to John* come back to Japan on September 1st?
   c. *[c [I [Modal is to]]] John come back to Japan on September 1st?

Third, given this assumption, no elements should not intervene between *ought* or *be* and *to*, but it is not the fact:

(9) a. We ought *always* to carry some spare money.   (Sawada 1995: 130)
   b. You ought *always* to carry some spare money.   (Swan 1995^2: 398)
   c. I felt nervous because I was *soon* to leave home for the fist time. (Ibid.: 90)

Fourth, this assumption should also predict that the *to*-infinitival is *not a constituent*, but this is not the case either:

(10) Right Node Raising
   a. Mondale ought—but Regan ought not—[to go to Beirut in June].
       (Sawada 1995: 134)
   b. Mondale is—but Regan is not—[to go to Beirut in June].   (Ibid.)
(11) Deletion of *to*-infinitival
   a. Kim ought [to leave] and Sandy ought [φ], also.
       (Gazdar *et al.* 1982: 606)
   b. We ought [to wake Helen], oughtn't we [φ]? (NOT ... oughtn't we to)
       (Swan 1995^2: 398)
   c. We ought [to go] and so *ought* you [φ]. (*and *ought* you *to*)
       (Declerck 1991a: 379)
   d. Kim is [to leave] and Sandy is [φ], also.   (Gazdar *et al.* 1982: 602)
   e. Bill is to leave at once, and Alice is (to) also.   (McCawley 1998^2: 252)
(12) Conjoined Structures of *to*-infinitivals
   a. Kim is [to go to Rome on Tuesday] and [to fly to Istanbul on Friday].
       (Ibid.)
   b. Societies require centers of independent thought and criticism if they are [to progress] or [even to survive].   (Sawada 1995: 135)

In sum, we can conclude that the assumption that *ought* or *be* and *to* are both base-generated in Modal^0 is clearly implausible.

The second solution is to assume that *ought to* and *be to* are not modals at all but *main verbs* such as *want to*, *try to*, etc. However, this hypothesis is clearly wrong as well, as Coates (1983) and Sawada (1995) observe. Here let us apply Coates's (1983: 4) *Seven Formal Characteristics of Modals* (see (31) in Chapter 1) to *ought to* and *be to*:

(13) *ought to*
    (i) Takes Negation directly
        a. We *oughtn't* to help him. (McCawley 1998[2]: 252)
        b. He *oughtn't* to leave tomorrow. (Sawada 1995: 130)
    (ii) Takes inversion without DO (*can I?*, *must I?*)
        a. *Ought we* to help him?
        b.* *Do we ought* to help him? (Ibid.)
    (iii) 'Code'[5]
        a. Kim ought [to leave] and Sandy ought [ϕ], also. (=(11a))
        b. We ought [to wake Helen], oughtn't we [ϕ]? (=(11b))
        c. We ought [to go] and so *ought* you [ϕ]. (=(11c))
    (iv) Emphasis
        a. We OUGHT to help him.
        b.*We DO ought to help him. (McCawley 1998[2]: 252)
    (v) No *-s* form for third person singular
        *John *oughts* to go now.
    (vi) No non-finite forms
        *He regrets *oughting to* leave tomorrow. (Sawada 1995: 130)
    (vii) No co-occurrence
        *I want very much for you *to ought* to leave tomorrow. (Ibid.)

In sum, *ought to* meets *all* the seven characteristics of modals and thus exactly like a modal, except in selecting *to*-infinitives rather than root infinitives. Then, how about *be to*?

(14) *be to*
   (i) Takes Negation directly
       He *isn't* to leave tomorrow.   (Sawada 1995: 130)
   (ii) Takes inversion without DO (*can I?*, *must I?*)
       a. *Is he* to leave tomorrow?
       b. **Do he be* to help him?
   (iii) 'Code'
       a. Kim is [to leave] and Sandy is [φ], also. (=(11d))
       b. Bill is to leave at once, and Alice is (to) also. (=(11e))
   (iv) Emphasis
       Bill IS to leave at once.
   (v) (*Be to* has a form for third person singular.)
       a. *John *be to* leave at once.
       b. John *is to* leave at once.
   (vi) No non-finite forms
       *He regrets *being to* leave tomorrow.   (Sawada 1995: 130)
   (vii) No co-occurrence
       *I want very much for you *to be to* leave tomorrow.   (Ibid.)

Be to meets as many as six characteristics, just as the periphrastic *do* does (see (32) in Chapter 1). This then leads us to conclude that *be to* is also a type of modal.[6] In conclusion, the hypothesis that *ought to* and *be to* are not modals but main verbs lacks support as well.

The third solution might be to assume that *ought* or *be* selects IPs:

(15) [IP You [ModalP ought [IP to leave now]]].

But there are two serious problems with this proposal: first, modals can never select an IP:

(15) a. *You can [IP to go home].
     b. *You may [IP you will go home].

Second, the structures of (15) force us to assume that there are no main verbs in the matrix clauses, as Sawada (1995) and Ando (2003) point out. To quote Ando:

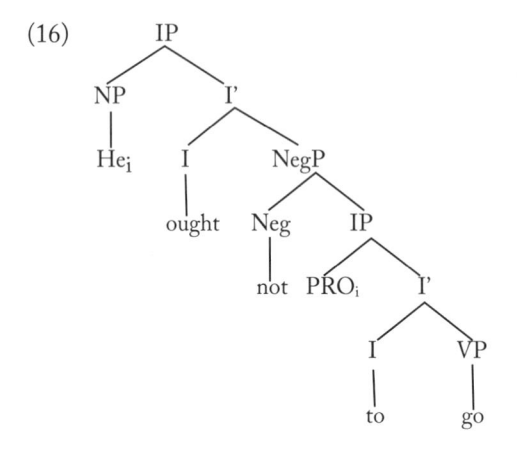

(16)
```
              IP
           /      \
         NP        I'
         |       /    \
        He_i   I       NegP
               |      /    \
             ought  Neg     IP
                    |      /  \
                   not  PRO_i  I'
                              /  \
                             I    VP
                             |    |
                             to   go
```

Indeed, this structure might generate the right surface structure, but it is fundamentally wrong in that there is no VP in the main clause.

(Ando 2003: 633, translations are mine)

In sum, none of the three tentative analyses discussed above are appropriate.

5.3 Previous Analyses

Next, here let us consider Sawada's (1985, 1995) and Ando's (1996, 2003) analyses, where they point problems with *ought to* and *be to* in detail.

5.3.1 Sawada's (1985, 1995) Analysis

Sawada's (1985, 1995) works are important studies where he attempts to treat infinitival clauses and the Aux system uniformly based on GB Theory. He assumes the following phrase structure:

(17) S → NP (INFL) (not) $\left\{ \begin{array}{c} \text{VP} \\ \text{VP'} \end{array} \right\}$

(Sawada 1995: 136)

Given this form, the structure of (18a) can be shown in (18b):

(18) a. Regan ought to go to Beirut.
   b.

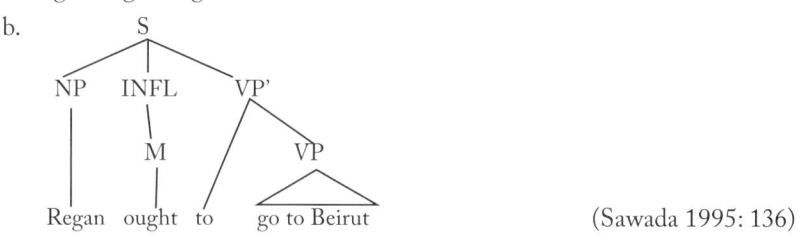

```
              S
       ┌──────┼──────┐
      NP    INFL    VP'
       │     │     ╱  ╲
       │     M        VP
       │     │         △
      Regan ought to  go to Beirut
```
(Sawada 1995: 136)

Note here that INFL selects not CP but VP'.[7] Thus, the VP' analysis presupposes the following rule:

(19) INFL is subcategorized for VP or VP'. (Ibid.: 137)

Sawada claims that this rule can explain the occurrences of both VP and VP' in *pseudo-cleft sentences* and the two forms of *need*, as shown in (20):

(20) a. All I did was [VP give her a little push].
   b. All I did was [VP' to give her a little push].
   c. What a fire-door does is [VP delay the spread of a fire].
   d. What a fire-door does is [VP' to delay the spread of a fire].
   e. Need I [VP come early this morning]? (Modal)
   f. Do I need [VP' to come early this morning]? (Verb)   (Ibid.: 137-138)

However, there are some important problems with this analysis: first, the phrase structure rule in (17) cannot rule out the following ungrammatical sentences:

(21) a. *You *cannot to* go to the party.
   b. *John *must to* go at once.

Second, if Sawada assumed only one type of syntactic category VP' (=InfP) as a subcategory of infinitival clauses, as compared to the generally assumed classification of CP (=Control) and IP (=Raising),[8] the following examples in

(23a, b) should be all grammatical just as the example one in (22), but this is not the case at all:

(22) What John tried was [$_{VP'}$ to win].
(23) a. *What John seems is [$_{VP'}$ to be happy].
   b. *What you ought is [$_{VP'}$ to go at once].

As discussed above, we cannot but conclude that Sawada's analysis is insufficient.

5.3.2 Ando's (1996) Analysis

Ando (1996) assumes that the infinitival marker *to* is base-generated in VP-Spec. Given this assumption, the structure of (24a) will be as shown in (24b):

(24) a. I consider John to be honest.
   b.

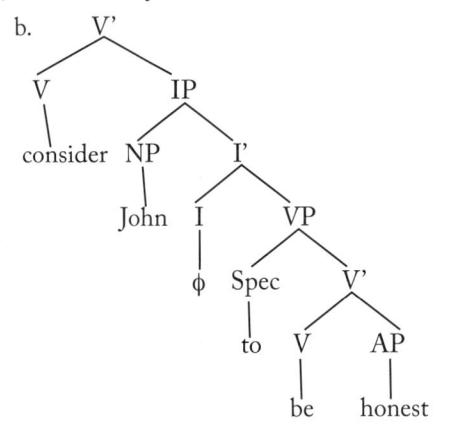

```
            V'
           /  \
          V    IP
          |   /  \
      consider NP  I'
              |   / \
            John  I   VP
                  |  / \
                  φ Spec V'
                     |  / \
                     to V   AP
                        |   |
                        be honest
```
                                                    (Ando 1996: 160)

He then claims that this assumption follows from the following three facts: first, as for the complements of *perception verbs* or *causative verbs*, *to* appears *optionally* in older English, but *to* appears *obligatorily* in Preset-Day English:

(25) a. Or didst thou see my friend *to* take his death. (Marlowe, *Edward II* 1401)
   b. When shall you see a Iew commit the like? (Id., *Iew of Malta* 1707)

(26) a. While hunger make you eate. (Id., 1 *Tamburlaine* 1695)
   b. Whose lookes make this inferior world *to* quake, (Id., 2 *Tamburlaine* 2708)
   (All quoted from Ando (1996: 160))

Second, as for the *passives* of perception verbs or causative verbs, *to* appears *obligatorily* in Preset-Day English:

(27) a. He was seen *to* come.
   b. He was made *to* come.
   c. He was heard *to* come.   (Ando 1996: 161)

Third, *to* appears optionally in the following constructions:

(28) a. I helped him (to) find his things.
   b. I helped (to) do his homework.
   c. Go (to) see him.   (Ibid.)

Note here that Ando's crucial supposition is that the Specifier is an *optional* node (see Ando (1996: 161)). But some problems can be raised with his analysis: first, his assumption can successfully account for (25a, b), (26a, b), and (28a-c) due to the optionality of the Spec *to*, but conversely his system will not rule out the following ungrammatical sentences, just as is the case in Sawada (1985, 1995):

(28) a. *You cannot [vp *to* go to the party]. (=(21a))
   b. *John must [vp *to* go at once]. (=(21b))
(29) a. *They saw him [vp *to* come]. (cf. (27a))
   b. *They made him [vp *to* come]. (cf. (27b))
   c. *They heard him [vp *to* come]. (cf. (27c))

Second, in connection with the first problem, we should recall that the bare infinitive complements and the *to*-infinitive complements after perception verbs or causative verbs are different constructions at least in Present-Day English, as is pointed out by Declerck (1982), Felser (1998), and Matsuyama (2001). For example, the active perception verbs cannot select perfect aspect as a complement, but the passive voice can do so, as stated below:

(30) a. *We saw the library *have burned down*.
   b. The library was seen to *have burned down*. (Matsuyama 2001: 123)

However, this would not be problematic if we assumed that (30b) is derived from the following grammatical clause in (31), rather than ungrammatical clause in (30a):

(31) We saw the library *to* have burned down. (Ibid.)

These facts force us to conclude that Ando's (1996) analysis is not on the right track.

5.3.3 Ando's (2003) Analysis

Actually, Ando's (2003) analysis is conceptually similar to the proposal to be submitted in the next section based on Nomura (2000d). Consider his assumed structure in (32):

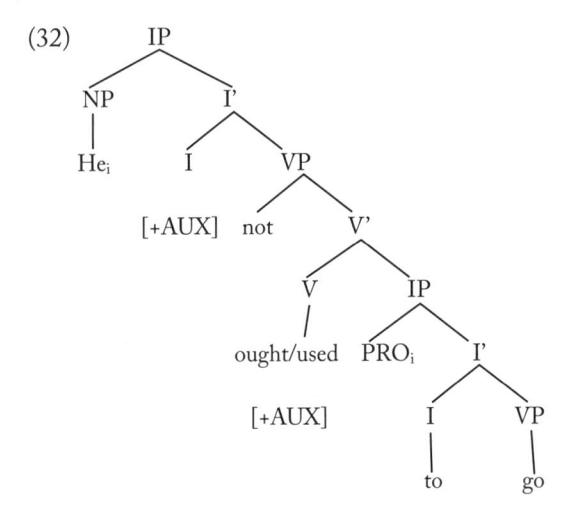

(32)
```
            IP
           /  \
         NP    I'
         |    /  \
         He_i I    VP
            [+AUX] / \
                 not  V'
                     / \
                    V   IP
                    |  /  \
              ought/used PRO_i  I'
                    [+AUX]    /  \
                             I    VP
                             |    |
                             to   go
```

Ando crucially assumes that this structure is the same as the control structure of the *try*-type verbs, but that *ought* and *used* exceptionally have the [+AUX] feature unlike main verbs, with the result that *ought* and *used* must raise to I⁰ to check off the [+AUX] feature in I⁰.

However, I would like to point out two problems with his analysis: first, if this structure represented a control structure, the complement structure should be not an IP but a CP, as I discussed in detail in Section 3.3.2. Even if it were a CP, however, his system could not account for the following contrast all the same that we discussed in section 5.3.1:

(33) a. What John tried was [CP PRO to win]. (=(22))
　　b. *What you ought is [CP PRO to go at once]. (=(23))[9]

Additionally, this CP analysis would contradict the general assumption that modals can never select CPs (cf. (15)):[10]

(34) a. *You ought [CP for John to leave at once].
　　b. *You can [CP that you will go home].

Second, as a more serious problem, the subjects of *to*-infinitivals cannot be PRO, since the expletive *there* can appear as the subject (of the matrix clause):

(35) a. *There* ought to be some nonsmoking seats here.
　　b. *There* ought to be traffic lights at this crossroads.

Note here that the expletive *there* cannot be the controller of PRO:

(36) a. *There_i tried [PRO_i to be many flowers in the garden].
　　b. *There_i decided [PRO_i to be solutions to this problem].

Consequently, our discussion conclusively shows that a *to*-infinitival clause after *ought* cannot be CPs, nor can PRO appear as the subject.[11), 12)]

5.4 An Alternative Analysis

Keeping the problems with previous studies in mind, I will offer an alternative analysis in this section.

5.4.1 *Ought to*

I propose the following hypothesis about the behavior of *ought to*:

(37) There are three types of *ought*:
   (i) a fully modal *ought*, which is generated in the head of ModalP just the same as other ordinary modals (e.g. *can*, *may*, *must*, etc.)
   (ii) an intermediate modal *ought to*, which is base-generated in the head of a main VP but will raise to Modal^0 in order to get an uninterpretable Tense feature and be pronounced as a full form in PF, and further to I^0 to check off that uninterpretable Tense feature
   (iii) a main verb *ought to*, which is generated in the head of a main VP and has the control structure just as the same as the *try*-type control verbs (e.g. *try*, *intend*, *decide*, etc.)

First, let us consider the case of (37i). We can consider that the following examples, especially *non-assertive* ones, correspond to this case:

(38) Maybe he *oughtn't* go into the street like that. (Arthur Miller, *Chinese Encounters*, p. 139)   (Quoted from Asakawa and Kamata (1986: 103))
(39) *Ought you* smoke so much?   (Leech and Svartvik 1994[2]: 210)
(40) Elicitation tests on young people have shown that, for both AmE and BrE, in nonassertive contexts the *to*-less *ought* construction is widely acceptable, and for some speakers even preferable to the construction with *to* in nonassertive contexts; eg:
   They *ought not* (*to*) do that sort of thing.
   Ought we (*to*) have done it?
   Oughtn't we (*to*) send for the police?[13]

(Quirk *et al*. 1985: 139-140, fn. (a))

In this case the underlying structure of (41a) will be as shown in (41b):

(41) a. You oughtn't go.
b.

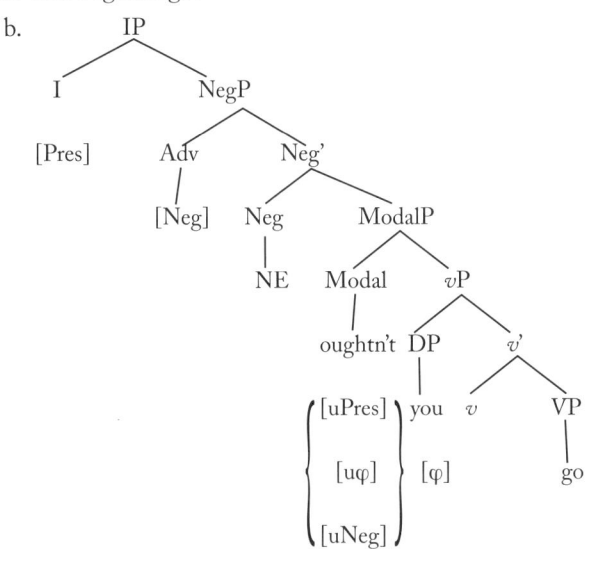

```
                    IP
                   /  \
                  I    NegP
                /     /    \
            [Pres]  Adv    Neg'
                    |     /    \
                  [Neg]  Neg   ModalP
                         |    /      \
                         NE  Modal    vP
                             |       /  \
                          oughtn't  DP   v'
                                    |   / \
                                [uPres] v  VP
                                 you       |
                                [uφ] [φ]  go
                                [uNeg]
```

Second, let us consider the case of (37ii). We can consider that the following examples correspond to this case, which are the uses most familiar to us:

(42) a. You ought to go. (=(2a))
 b. You ought not to go. (=(5a))
 c. Ought we to go now? (=(7a))

As an illustration of this, let us consider the derivation of the simple example in (42a): its underlying structure will be something like the one shown in (43):

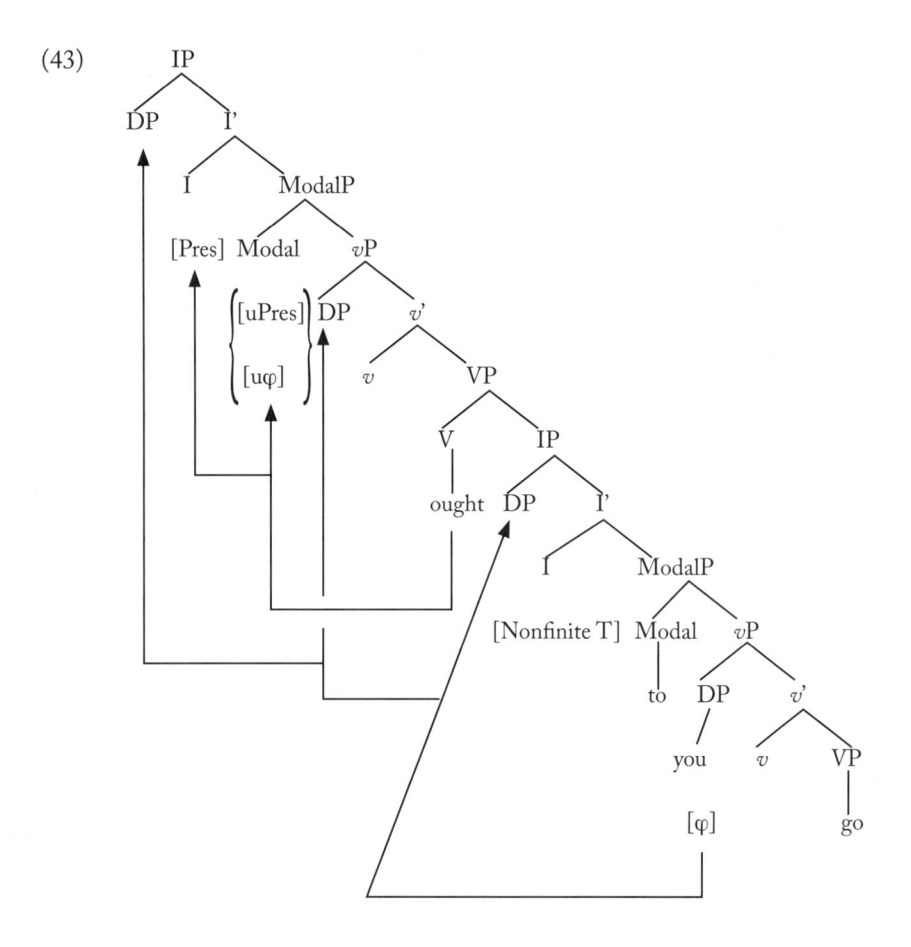

(43) [Syntactic tree diagram showing IP structure with DP and I', where I contains [Pres] Modal, ModalP dominates vP with [uPres] and [uφ] feature bundles on DP, V "ought" selecting IP complement with [Nonfinite T] Modal "to", DP "you" with [φ], and VP "go". Arrows indicate movement.]

Here the crucial assumptions are the following two points:

(44) a. *Ought* is the *bare* form and is base-generated in the head of the *main VP*, selecting a *raising* infinitival as a complement.
  b. Only the features (i.e. [uPres] and [uφ]) are merged in Modal^0 exceptionally. Since these are only feature bundles and thus not concrete lexical items constituting a modal, they lack the feature [Root] needed for affixation.

Given (44b), the *bare form* of *ought* is selected by Modal^0, but is not assigned [Root] by the feature bundles of the modal, thus cannot be pronounced in this position.

Consequently, *ought* raises to Modal to get [uPres] and [uφ] for the purpose of pronouncing it as a full form in PF (see (23) in Chapter 1). Then, *ought* must further raise to I to check off the [uPres] and [uφ]. As for the subject, *you* raises to IP-Spec in the matrix clause in successive cycles.

Needless to say, this behavior of *ought* is *exceptional*, but we must *stipulate* it somewhere in the particular grammar of English. I suspect that this exceptional behavior comes from the following two causes:

(45) a. *Ought* has not fully developed as compared to other ordinary modals.
  b. After the time *to*-infinitives and root-infinitives were in competition (cf. Ando's (1996) examples as in (25) and (26)), the *to*-infinitive has accidentally remained as a complement in the case of *ought* in the history of English.

As for (45a), let us quote Ando (2003):

(46) Though the grammaticalization of *can, may, shall, will*, etc. to modals began about 800 in the OE period, it was not until the ME period that the grammaticalization of *ought* and *used* began; according to *OED*, the first example of *ought* and *used* appeared as late as c1175 and 1303.
(Ando 2003: 633, fn. 3, translations are mine)

As for (45b), we can find many examples like the following, where root-infinitives were used rather than *to*-infinitives:

(47) a. nothynge that *ought* of reason be rekened (=reckoned) for the cause (1533 More, *Apologye*)
  b. I *ought* craue pardon (1590-6 Spenser, *Faerie Queene*, 1. 12. 18)
  c. You *ought* not walke (1599 Shakespeare, *Julius Caesar*, I. i. 3)
  d. all men *ought*, as well as most men do, obey him (1661 Cowley, *Cromwell*, 366)   (All quoted from H. Ono and Ito (1993: 105-106))

We will not discuss this problem any further in this book, but as for the historical development of *ought*, see especially S. Ono (1969, 1989).

Turning to the main discussion, let us consider the third case of (37iii). We can observe that the following *dialectal* or *non-standard* examples that correspond to this case:[14]

(48) a. % He didn't ought to leave.
    b. % Did he ought to leave.   (Asakawa and Kamata 1986: 102)

(49) The form *didn't ought to* is occasionally used, but is generally considered to be nonstandard.   (Declerck 1991a: 378)

(50) Treating *ought* as a main verb with DO-support, which is usually described as a dialectal usage, proved to be the least popular alternative in a test with BrE teenage informants:

    They *didn't ought to* do that sort of thing.

    Did we *ought to* have done it?

However, the existence of this construction, even if it is not part of Standard English, is an indicator of the marginal status of *ought to* which, like the other marginal modals, shows some tendency to pattern as a main verb.

    (Quirk *et al.* 1985: 140)

(51) "You *didn't ought to* have brought a woman like that into my house" (1947 Maugham, *The Kite*, 19)   (Quoted from Ono and Ito (1993: 106))

In this case the structure of (52a) is shown in (52b), which is the same structure as that of *try*-type control infinitivals:

(52) a. You didn't ought to leave.

b.

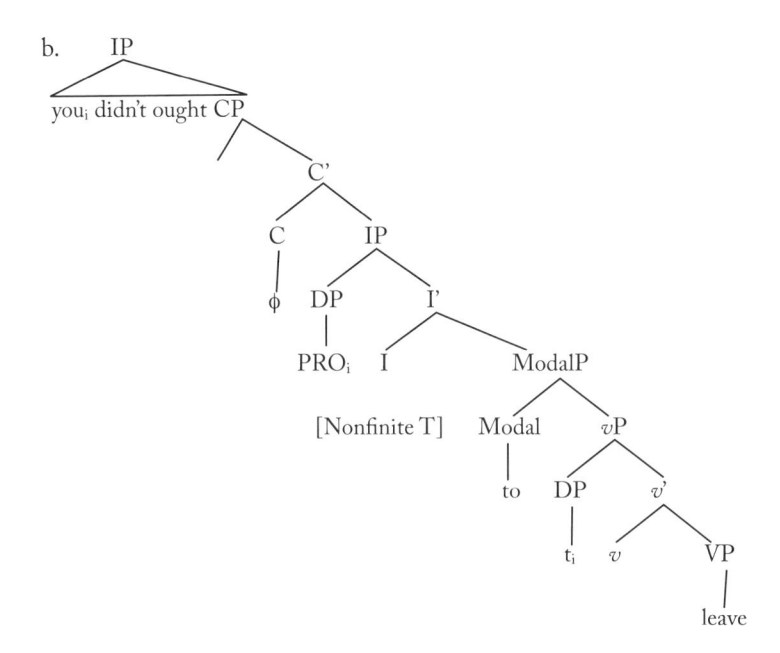

```
         IP
        / \
you_i didn't ought  CP
                   / \
                  C'
                 / \
                C   IP
                |  / \
                φ DP  I'
                   |  / \
                 PRO_i I    ModalP
                       |    / \
                 [Nonfinite T] Modal  vP
                               |     / \
                               to   DP  v'
                                    |  / \
                                    t_i v  VP
                                           |
                                         leave
```

In this section I have shown that we can naturally provide an account for the exceptional behavior of *ought* (*to*) assuming three types of *ought* in a non *ad hoc* fashion.

5.4.2 *Be to*

As for *be to*, we can assume the following two types corresponding to (37ii, iii) in the case of *ought to*, as shown in (53):[15), 16)]

(53) There are two kinds of *be to*:
 (i) an intermediate modal *be to*, which is base-generated in the head of a main VP and is pronounced as a full form in PF, but raises to Modal⁰ in order to get an uninterpretable Tense feature, and further to I⁰ to check off that uninterpretable Tense feature
 (ii) main verb *be to*, which is generated in the head of main VP and has the PrP[17)] as its complement

Needless to say, all the examples of *be to* are classified into (53i), and thus there will be no problems raised. Consider the following examples again.

(54) a. John *is to* come back to Japan on September 1ˢᵗ. (=(2b))
 b. He *isn't to* leave tomorrow. (=(14i))

The question is whether examples of (53ii) really exist or not. As for this problem, Yagi (1996: Chapter 3) interestingly argues that the following examples are, in fact, not what we call *modal* 'be' but should be regarded as *main verb* like in (53ii):

(55) a. He *is to* blame. (Passive)
 b. The porter *was* nowhere *to* be found. (Possibility)
 c. This letter *is to* tell you that... (Purpose) (Yagi 1996: 244)

The reason why he claims this is that these uses of *be to* have nonfinite forms or can co-occur with modals. Consider the following examples:

(56) a. My father mightn't *have been to* blame.
 b. The lawyer must *have been* nowhere *to* be found.
 c. As far as I can tell, this letter *must be to* inform me that he was going to kill himself. (Ibid.)

Taking this fact into consideration, the structure of (55c) will be shown as in (57) where the main verb *be* heads the main VP:

(57) [IP [Pres] [VP is [PrP this letter [Pr' e [ModalP to tell you that ...]]]]][18)

Last, I would like to mention the meanings of *be to*. As is well known, *be to* is said to have various kinds of meanings. To quote Swan (1995²):

(58) Plans and Arrangements
 a. The President *is to* visit Nigeria next month.
 b. We *are to* get a 10 per cent wage rise next month.

(59) 'Fate'
   I thought we were saying goodbye for ever. But we *were to* meet again, many years later, under very strange circumstances.
(60) Pre-conditions
   a. If we *are to* get there by lunchtime we had better hurry.
   b. He knew he would have to work hard if he *was to* pass his exam.
(61) Orders
   a. You *are to* do your homework before you watch TV.
   b. She can go to the party, but she's not *to* be back late.

   (All quoted from Swan (1995[2]: 87))

It would be very strange if we assumed that the single lexical item *be to* has all these meanings in the Lexicon; here I will propose that these meanings, including both cases of modal *be* and main verb *be to*, are caused not by the meaning *be to* itself but by pragmatic inference. Consider the following model:

(62) You *are to* do your homework before you watch TV.
(63) Operation in Syntax
   __ are [you to do your homework before you watch TV].
(64) Pragmatic Inference after LF Representation
   a. [A certain event] *always* exists.
   b. [The event] is [for you to do your homework before you watch TV].
   c. Therefore, you *must* always do your homework before you watch TV.

This model will also strengthen our assumption that in underlying structure some lexical items having concrete meanings does not originate in the head of ModalP and thus, for example, *be* raises to Modal^0, where it acquires no lexical meanings but only the modal properties.

5.5 Concluding Remarks

In this chapter I discussed *ought to* and *be to*. Indeed, as Sawada (1985, 1995) and Ando (1996, 2003) claim, the assumption that the infinitival marker *to* is a type of modal raises a serious problem; the infinitival marker *to* and *ought* or *be* should not co-occur by a general principle that modals do not co-occur. However, I showed that we can explain the exceptional behavior of *ought to* and *be to* by assuming two or three types of *ought* or *be* in a non *ad hoc* fashion.[19]

Notes to Chapter 5

1. This chapter is mainly based on Nomura (2000d).

2. Though, note that, as I mentioned in note 9 in Chapter 2, Chomsky himself has never mentioned the base-generated position of the infinitival marker *to* since then, as far as I know.

3. Note that we may say that one of the motivations of Pollock's (1989) Split-I Hypothesis is to avoid *double (or triple) heads*. Consider the following examples:

    (i) a. John could swim very fast (when he was young).

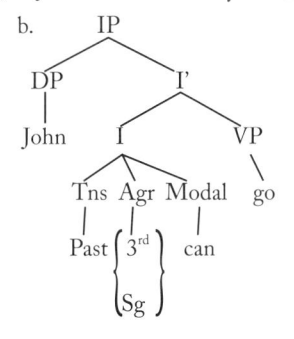

    b.
```
           IP
          /  \
        DP    I'
        |    /  \
      John  I    VP
           /|\    \
        Tns Agr Modal go
         |   |    |
        Past {3rd} can
             {Sg}
```

    (ii) a. Thou shalt not kill. (Early Modern English)
    b. Du sollst nicht töten. (German)
       you shall not kill
       'You must not kill.'

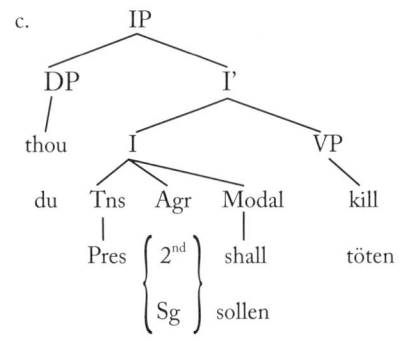

    c.
```
              IP
             /  \
           DP    I'
           |    /  \
          thou  I    VP
               /|\    \
           du Tns Agr Modal kill
               |   |    |
              Pres {2nd} shall töten
                   {Sg}  sollen
```

4. As Ando (2003) points out, assuming that *not* is also generated in I^0, the structure will further be a triple head:

   (i) a. We ought not to help him.

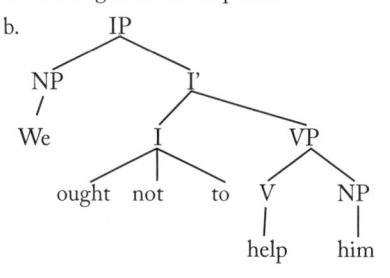

   b.
```
              IP
           /      \
         NP        I'
         |       /    \
         We     I      VP
              /|\     /  \
         ought not to V   NP
                      |   |
                     help him
```
   (Ando 2003: 633)

5. Interestingly, McCawley (1998²) does not accept *to*-deletion (cf. (11e)); he claims that *to* must be stranded:

   (i) You ought to help us, and your brother $\left\{\begin{array}{l}{}^*\text{ought}\\ \text{ought to}\\ {}^*\text{does}\end{array}\right\}$ also.

   (McCawley 1998²: 252)

   I suspect that this 'Code' usage is a British one. (Note that Michael Swan, Renaat Declerck, and Gerald Gazdar are all British and James D. McCawley is a Scottish American.)

6. Emonds (1976) calls this use of *be* in *be to* infinitives Modal '*be*'.

7. Sawada assumes that VP' is semantically parallel to CP, as shown in (i):

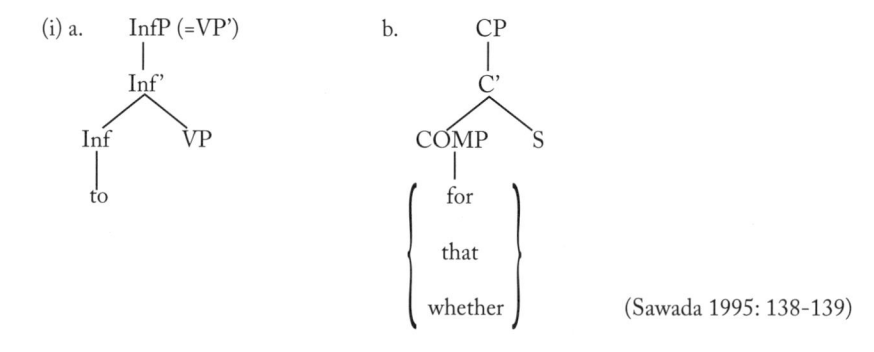

   (i) a. InfP (=VP')
           |
           Inf'
          /   \
        Inf   VP
         |
         to

   b. CP
       |
       C'
      /   \
    COMP   S
     |
   $\left\{\begin{array}{l}\text{for}\\ \text{that}\\ \text{whether}\end{array}\right\}$

   (Sawada 1995: 138-139)

This idea is originally based on Bresnan (1979) and Sawada assumes that *to* functions as a *verb-phrasal complementizer*, and thus further assumes that complementizers can be divided into two types, i.e. *clausal* and *phrasal*:

(ii) complementizers ⟨ Clausal (=COMP)
　　　　　　　　　　　　 Phrasal (=Inf) 　　　　　　　　　　　　(Ibid.: 139)

In this sense Sawada's analysis is similar to Bošković's (1996) analysis in that the *try*-type infinitivals are not CPs but IPs, which I criticized in Section 3.3.2.

8. Note that he does not assume PRO and thus assumes that the *try*-type predicates directly select *to*, as shown in (ia), just as *wonder* selects *whether*, as shown in (ib):

(i) a. John tried [InfP [Inf to] [VP win the race]].

　　b. Mary wondered [CP [COMP whether] [S he was coming]].
　　　　　　　　　　　　　　　　　　　　　　　　　　(Sawada 1995: 142)

9. Though, as for (33b), it might be ruled out due to the fact that *ought* does not have an independent transitive verb use (unlike *try*), as shown in (i):

(i) a.　I like to try *different kinds of food*.
　　b.　*I ought *money* for your service.

10. Sawada (1993) clearly denies this possibility as well:

(i) We have much difficulty trying to show this *to*-infinitive [i.e. *to* appearing in *ought to* construction] to be an infinitival *clause* by hypothesizing PRO, as shown in (81):
(81) We ought [S PRO to start before it rains].
The reason why we cannot assume this structure is that modals cannot possibly select *clauses*.　　　　　　　　　　(Sawada 1993: 116, translations are mine)

11. Incidentally, in the 1970's some generative semantics linguists (see note 27 in Chapter 1) assumed that *root modals* have a *control* structure while *epistemic modals* have *raising* structure (see note 23 in Chapter 3), but it is now assumed that root and epistemic modals *both* have *raising* structures, judging from various facts including the occurrence of the expletive *there* discussed here. As for the study and a good review of this

problem, see Kaneko (1999).

12. Incidentally, Ishihara (1998) discusses the occurrences of root infinitives in English based on *Optimality Theory*. She mentions *ought to* and *have to* in notes such as the following:

> (i) We can observe cases where auxiliaries such as *has to* or *ought to* obligatorily select *to*, but it can be assumed that these auxiliaries select control complements CP, and thus these cases are not violations of NRFC [i.e. No Redundant Functional Categories].
>
> (Ishihara 1998: 70, fn. 6, translations are mine)

However, as we discussed extensively in this section, her analysis of *ought to* will face the same problems as Ando's (2003) does. (Note that in the case of *have to* her analysis is possible, because *have to* is syntactically a *main verb*, not a modal at all; none of Coates's (1983) Seven Formal Characteristics of Modals apply to *have to*.)

13. Note that after noting the examples in (40) Quirk *et al.* also state the following:

(i) In assertive contexts, however, the *to*-less form is unacceptable:
We $\begin{Bmatrix} ought\ to \\ {}^*ought \end{Bmatrix}$ give him another chance.

(Quirk *et al.* 1985: 139-140, fn. (a))

Judging from this, we should note that the environment where fully modal *ought* is used is the same as the one where the periphrastic *do* is used. (See also note 25 in Chapter 1.)

14. We should pay attention to the fact that all the examples in (48) to (51) are *past* forms of *ought*. Probably this has something to do with the fact *ought* does not have a past form *morphologically*. Note that, historically speaking, *ought* is an example of a *preterite-present verb*, and originally comes from the *past* form of *āgan* in Old English.

15. In the cases of *used (to)* as well, we could assume two classifications. Consider the following examples:

(i) intermediate modal *used to*
  a. Used you to play football at this school? (Swan 1995[2]: 577)

b. Used you to play crickets at school? (Sawada 1995: 130)
   c. I used not to like opera, but now I do. (Swan 1995²: 577)
(ii) main verb *use(d) to*
   a. Did you use to play football at this school? (Swan 1995²: 577)
   b. I didn't use to like opera, but now I do. (Ibid.)
   c. *Did* you *use to* see her in town? (Malamud 1979, *Dubin's Lives*, p. 334)
   d. She's a lot more serious about herself in a way she *didn't used to* be. (Ibid., p.274)
   e. *Didn't* we *used to* have fun?
   f. I *did used to* think about doing just that. (e, f; Jespersen 1914-49: IV, 1.9(3))
   (c-f; quoted from Asakawa and Kamata (1986: 102))

16. Note that fully modal *be*, which is generated in the head of ModalP, is not allowed:

(i) *You *are leave* at once.

17. Here I will assume *PrP* (=Predication Phrase) following Bowers (1993), though in this case it would be almost the same if we assumed *Sc* (=Small Clause).

18. Here I am not assuming *v*P in structures where PrPs occur, following Shigeo Tonoike's (personal communication, 2002) suggestions.

19. As for the discussion in this chapter, Shigeo Tonoike (personal communication, 2005) suggested the following alternative idea:

(i) a. Main verbs *ought* and *be* occur, both of which are Raising verbs selecting *to*-infinitives (=ModalP) as complements.
   b. *Be* is the same as normal *be*-verbs, and always raises to I^0.
   c. *Ought* can exceptionally raise to I^0 or select *do*-support (just as the use of *have* in British English), though it has the single morphological form *ought*, i.e., does not have a 3rd person singular form such as **oughts*.
   d. For the problem as to whether to select *to* or not, there are two types of *to*, i.e. overt *to* and covert *to*, following Radford's (1997) approach.

Chapter 6

The General Properties of the Subjunctive Present

6.1 Introduction

Before discussing the subjunctive present in detail in the next chapters, I will, in this chapter, review (i) the terminology of *mood*, *modal*, and *modality*, (ii) the status of subjunctive mood in Present-Day English, and (iii) the general properties of the subjunctive present.

6.2 Mood, Modal, and Modality

In this book I will define *mood* as follows:

(1) Mood
  the inflectional forms of verbs or their system for expressing modality

Here we find the term *modality* in (1). *Modality* is, needless to say, the adjectival form of *modal* morphologically, but I will define *modal* as follows in parallel to (1):

(2) Modal (noun)
  the auxiliary verbs expressing modality

Note in particular that I am not assuming the following:

(3) Modality is expressed in the meanings of modals (or moods).

This is because *modality* is expressed not *only by modals* (or *only by mood*) but by of other means as well, as shown in (4):

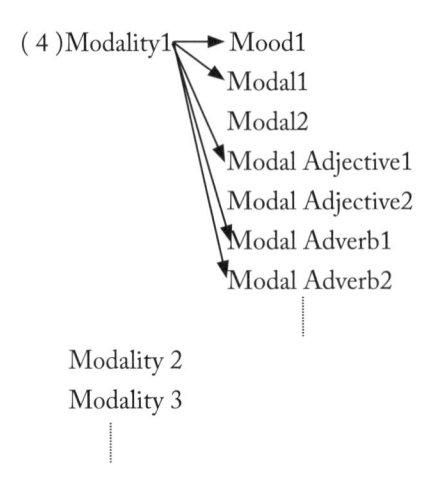

(4) Modality1 ⟷ Mood1
    ↖ Modal1
     Modal2
     Modal Adjective1
     Modal Adjective2
     Modal Adverb1
     Modal Adverb2

Modality 2
Modality 3

As an illustration of this phenomenon, consider the following examples:

(5) Possibility
 a. John *may* be a teacher. (Modal)
 b. It is *possible* that John is a teacher. (Modal adjective)
 c. *Possibly* John is a teacher. (Modal Adverb)

Taking this into consideration, I will define *modality* as follows:

(6) Modality
 the expression of the speaker's belief, opinion, or attitude towards his or her utterance

Based on (6), we should replace (3) with (7):

(7) Modality is expressed by mood, modals, modal adjectives, modal adverbs, or other linguistic forms.

In sum, it is true that *mood*, *modal*, and *modality* are related to one another in many respects, but at the same time they should be carefully distinguished.[1] I will leave details relating to the exact formalization of mood and modality for future study, and will go on to our discussion below using the definitions in this section.

As for the general discussion of *mood* and *modality*, see especially Jespersen (1924), Sawada (1993), and Palmer (1990^2, 2001^2).

6.3 Types of Mood

As is well known, there are said to have been *four moods* in the Proto-Indo-European language: *Indicative*, *Subjunctive* (or *Conjunctive*), *Optative*, and *Imperative* (see, e.g., Kozu (1954)). Optative merged into subjunctive as early as in Latin.

Note here that the meanings of *modals*, *modal adjectives*, or *modal adverbs* are comparatively easy to define (e.g. possibility, ability, permission, obligation, etc.), but the meanings of *moods* are vague and rather difficult to define. As for this problem, it would be useful to consider the terms for *moods* used by Sweet (1898):

(8) a. Indicative Mood —Fact-Mood
    b. Imperative Mood —Will-Mood
    c. Subjunctive Mood —Thought-Mood

The *core* albeit *vague* meanings of the three moods are well expressed by the terms of *fact*, *will*, and *thought*. We can further say that indicative is *objective* while imperative and subjunctive are *subjective*. For this problem, see further Jespersen (1924), Hosoe (1933), and Ando (1999, 2004).

Now, in Old English we can clearly recognize the above three moods, i.e. indicative, imperative, and subjunctive, *morphologically*. Consider the following conjugation table of the weak verb *fremman* '*do*' in Old English:

(9)   Present Indicative
     Sg. 1 fremme
          2 fremest
          3 fremeþ
     Pl.   fremmaþ

             Imperative
     Sg.   freme

Pl.   fremmaþ

        Present Subjunctive
Sg.   fremme
Pl.   fremmen

        Preterite Indicative
Sg. 1   fremede
    2   fremedest
    3   fremede
Pl.   fremedon

        Preterite Subjunctive
Sg.   fremede
Pl.   fremeden

Inf.   fremman
Infl. Inf.   tō fremmenne
Pres. Ptc.   fremmende
Past Ptc.   (ġe-)fremed   (Mitchell 1965: 43-44)

But English has lost its inflections through its history. The three periods of the history of English are often characterized from the viewpoint of inflection as follows:

(10) a. Old English   —the period of full inflection
     b. Middle English   —the period of leveled inflection
     c. Modern English   —the period of lost inflection
                                            (Baugh and Cable 1993[4]: 50)

Here the problem is whether the three moods really exist in Present-Day English. Keeping this problem in mind, we shall discuss the status of subjunctive mood in Present-Day English in the next section.

6.4 The Presence of Subjunctive Mood in Present-Day English

It is widely accepted that three moods exist in Present-Day English; indicative, imperative, and subjunctive. Consider the following examples:

(11) a. Indicative
   I *studied* mathematics very hard in my school days.
   b. Imperative
   Study math every day.
   c. Subjunctive
   If I *studied* mathematical linguistics, I could understand the model of Chomsky's (1957) *Syntactic Structures* much better.

But note here that the *original* inflected forms of each mood no longer exist in (11a-c) unlike in the cases of Old English in (9). Namely, we could possibly regard the imperative form *study* as a *root* or *infinitival* form, and the subjunctive form *studied* as a (indicative) *past* form.

In fact, this problem was much discussed among traditional grammarians. Roughly speaking, we could classify the grammarians into the following two groups:

(12) a. those who accept subjunctives based on *meaning*, including periphrastic uses—Curme (1931), Sonnenschein (1916, 1927), Onions (1932[6]), Poutsma (1904-29), etc.
   b. those who accept only a few uses of subjunctives based on *form*—Jespersen (1924, 1933), Kruisinga (1932[6]), Scheurweghs (1959), Sweet (1892-98), etc.

As for the examples of (12a), to quote Curme, Poutsma, and Sonnenschein:

(13) a. Mood is a grammatical form denoting the style or manner of predication.
   (Curme 1931: 393)
   b. As the simple subjunctive forms in the course of a long phonetic development lost their distinctive endings, modal auxiliaries were

pressed into service to express the same ideas. In large measure they are subjunctive forms, although not recognizable by distinctive endings. In fact, however, whether indicative or subjunctive in form, they perform the function of the older simple subjunctive and are here treated as our modern subjunctive forms. (Ibid.: 393)

(14) ... expressing the speaker's mental attitude regarding the fulfillment of the predication. The forms which correspond to this attitude are called moods.
(Poutsma 1904-29, 2-2: 9)

(15) It is impossible to frame a definition of such terms on the basis of distinction in *form*. They are essentially terms of syntax; that is to say, they denote categories of *meaning*, not categories of *form*. And this is just as true of Latin grammar as it is of English grammar.... And from this point of view the supposed inapplicability of such terms to languages which have lost many of their old inflexions disappears. (Sonnenschein 1916: 3f)

Sonnenschein (1927) further argues that *context, word order, phrasing*, and *intonation* as well as *form* function to distinguish moods.

On the other hand, grammarians in (12b) claim that mood should be defined on the basis of *form*, not *meaning*. To quote Jespersen:

(16) A mood, in accordance with PhilGr ([i.e. Jespersen (1924)]) 313, may be defined as a grammatical form, or the function of such a form, which expresses a certain attitude of the mind of the speaker or the writer towards the contents of the sentence, though in some cases the choice of the mood is determined not by the attitude of the actual speaker, but by the clause itself and its relation to the main nexus on which it is dependent.
(Jespersen 1909-49, Part VII: 623)[2]

(17) Further it is very important to remember that we speak of "mood" only if this attitude of mind is shown in the form of the verb: mood thus is a syntactic, not a notional category. (Jespersen 1924: 313)

It is well known that Jespersen and Sonnenschein had a heated discussion about the definition of *mood* and *case*. To quote Jespersen's criticism:

(18) If we pass on to the Indicative and the Subjunctive, the first remark that obtrudes itself is that the treatment of this subject has been needlessly complicated by those writers who speak of combinations with auxiliary verbs, e.g. *may he come/he may come/if he should come/he would come*, as if they were subjunctives of the verb *come*, or subjunctive equivalents. Scholars would hardly have used these expressions if they had had only the English language to deal with, for it is merely the fact that such combinations in some cases serve to translate simple subjunctives in German or Latin that suggests the use of such terms, exactly as people will call *to the boy* a dative case.
(Ibid: 315)

As a result, he claims that <modal + verb> dose not represent the mood of the verb, and that what is called subjunctive past should be regarded as one of the uses of tense; he calls it *imaginative tense* in Jespersen (1909-49, Part IV) or *imaginative use of tense* in Jespersen (1933).

Here let us sum up the terms of each traditional grammarian including the ones discussed so far:

(19) those who accept subjunctives based on *meaning*, including periphrastic uses
   a. Curme (1931)—optative subjunctive, potential subjunctive
   b. Onions (1932[6])—subjunctive equivalent (e.g. *shall/should, may/might*)
   c. Poutsma (1904-29)—conditional mood
(20) those who accept only few uses of subjunctives based on form
   a. Jespersen (1909-49, 1924, 1933)—imaginative tense, imaginative use of tense
   b. Kruisinga (1932[6]), Zandvoort (1966[4]), Scheurweghs (1959), etc.—modal preterite, modal preterite perfect
   c. Sweet (1892-98)—tense mood[3)]

But note that even Jespersen accepts the subjunctive past form *were* and subjunctive present as uses of subjunctive mood, because they have different forms from indicatives. Moreover, Quirk *et al.* (1985) in Present-Day English grammar studies accept three uses of subjunctive mood as follows:

(21) a. mandative subjunctive
   b. formulaic subjunctive
   c. *were*-subjunctive   (Quirk *et al.* 1985: 155)

We can roughly say that (21a, b) represent subjunctive present and (21c) subjunctive past. In conclusion *at least* the *were*-subjunctive and the *subjunctive present* should be recognized as subjunctive *mood* even in Present-Day English.

As for the general discussion of subjunctive mood in English, see Jespersen (1909-49, Part V, 1924), Hosoe (1933), Harsh (1968), Quirk *et al.* (1985), James (1986), Declerck (1991a), and Chiba (2000).

6.5 The Uses of the Subjunctive Present

Next, let us review the uses of the *subjunctive present* in Present-Day English. Following Nomura (2004a), I assume four subcategories of the subjunctive present. First, the subjunctive present is used in clauses of *condition*, *concession*, and *negative purpose*, though it is restricted to very formal usage:

(22) Condition
   a. If any person *be* found guilty, he shall have the right of appeal.
   b. (Even) if that *be* the official view, it cannot be accepted.
(23) Concession
   a. Though that *be* true, you must not give up your plan.
   b. Though he *be* the President himself, he shall hear us.
   c. Whatever *be* the reasons for their action, we cannot tolerate such disloyalty.
   d. Whether she *be* right or wrong, she will have my unswerving support.
(24) Negative Purpose
   a. The President must reject this proposal, lest it *cause* strife and violence.
   b. They removed the prisoner in order that he not *disturb* the proceedings any further.
               (All quoted from Quirk *et al.* (1985: 158, 1012))

Second, the subjunctive present is used in *optative* sentences.[4]

(25) a. God *be* praised!
   b. Lord *have* mercy upon us! (Leech 1987²: 113)
(26) a. God *save* the Queen.
   b. Heaven *preserve* us from that!
   c. Long *live* the king!
   d. (God) *bless* you!
   e. The devil *take* that man.
   f. God *help* you. (Declerck 1991a: 353)

However, we should also consider that these expressions are used only in fixed expressions in Present-Day English. To quote Imai *et al.* (1995):

(27) However, this usage of the subjunctive only occurs in "fossilized" expressions: when you, for instance, want very much for John to come, you don't say, "*John come!" but "I do hope John will come" etc. (Imai *et al.* 1995: 21)

Third, the subjunctive present survives in some *stereotype expressions*:[5]

(28) a. *Come* what may, we will go ahead with our plan.
   b. *Suffice* it to say that you win.
   c. Heaven *forbid* that I should let my own parents suffer.
   d. *Be* it noted that this offer was made in good faith.
   e. *Be* that as it may, we have nothing to lose.
      (Quirk *et al.* 1985: 157-158)

Fourth, the most important uses of the subjunctive present are what is called *mandative subjunctive*, which is *the only productive use* remaining in Present-Day English, as compared to the three uses above.[6] Consider the following examples:

(29) a. The council has decided [decreed, insisted] that a special committee *be* set up to investigate the matter.
   b. I suggest that you *say* nothing to her about it.[7]
   c. It is essential that there *be* no shortage of food.
   b. They are anxious that this infamous letter *remain* unpublished.

(Declerck 1991a: 353-354)
(30) a. The committee {proposes / proposed} (that) Mr Day *be* elected.
   b. I demand(ed) that the committee *reconsider* its decision.
   c. His sole requirement is/was that the system *work*.

(Quirk *et al.* 1985: 158)
(31) a. John demands that Susan *leave* immediately.
   b. President Carter is very eager that the talks among these world leaders *be* held.
   c. That she not *know* this before tomorrow is crucial.
   d. I have no quarrel with this conclusion that particles *be* assigned to the category Preposition. (Chiba 1987: 1)

To borrow a statement from Quirk *et al.* (1985), we can define the mandative subjunctive as follows:

(32) a. Terms for the two categories of the present subjunctive are the MANDATIVE and the FORMULAIC subjunctive. These are realized, like the imperative, by the base form of the verb. (Quirk *et al.* 1985: 155)
   b. The present subjunctive is also used in *that*-clauses (esp AmE) after verbs, adjectives, or nouns that express a necessity, plan, or intention for the future: …. (Ibid.: 1012)
   c. The following are among those expressions which commonly introduce a *that*-clause containing the mandative subjunctive:

   VERBS: *decide, insist, move, order, prefer, request*
   ADJECTIVE: *advisable, desirable, fitting, imperative*
   NOUNS: *decision, decree, order, requirement, resolution*

(Ibid.: 157)
   d. They *recommended*
      It is *appropriate*   } that this tax *be* abolished.
      We were faced with the *demand*

(Ibid.: 156)

Here I will show the fuller lists of the subjunctive-taking verbs, nouns, and adjectives (cf. (32c)) that Chiba (1987) compiled (see also Quirk *et al.* (1985: 1182, 1224)):[8]

(33) Subjunctive-Taking Verbs
accept, adjure, advise, advocate, agree, allow, approve, argue, arrange, ascertain, ask, authorize, beg, beseech, bid, care, cause, caution, challenge, choose, claim, command, concede, consent, consider, contract, contrive, counsel, crave, cry out, decide, declare, decree, deduce, demand, desire, destine, determine, dictate, direct, disapprove, emphasize, enact, encourage, enjoin, ensure, entail, enter, entreat, envisage, exhort, expect, favor, fix, forbid, gesture, grant, guarantee, had better, had rather, hint, hope, implore, indicate, insist, instruct, insure, intend, intimate, involve, lay down, look to it, maintain, manage, mandate, matter, motion, move, necessitate, need, occasion, offer, opine, opt, ordain, order, permit, petition, plan, plead, pledge, postulate, pray, preclude, predestine, prefer, premise, prescribe, presuppose, pronounce, propose, provide, recommend, request, require, resolve, rule, sanction, say, scheme, second, see (to it), see fit, settle, specify, state, stipulate, submit, suffer, suffice, suggest, support, take care, understand, urge, vote, want, warn, warrant, will, wish, would rather, write   (Chiba 1987: 3)

(34) Subjunctive-Taking Adjectives
fitting, fortunate, good, ideal, impatient, imperative, impolite, important, impossible, inadvisable, inappropriate, inconvenient, inevitable, insistent, interested, logical, mandatory, necessary, needful, normal, obligatory, opportune, optimal, politic, preferable, proper, relevant, right, satisfactory, sufficient, unnatural, unnecessary, urgent, usual, vital, willing, wise

(Ibid.: 3-4)

(35) Subjunctive-Taking Nouns
advantage, advice, alternative, appeal, arrangement, assumption, call, challenge, check, claim, command, concern, conclusion, condition, constraint, contention, control, convention, criterion, decision, demand, desideratum, desire, determination, dictum, edict, expectation, hope, hypothesis, idea, (of) importance, innovation, insistence, instruction, intention, (in) interest, (in) nature, necessity, objective, order, plea, point, possibility, prayer, preference,

prerequisite, principle, property, proposal, recommendation, regulation, (of) relevance, request, requirement, restriction, rule, ruling, sacrilege, solution, specification, suggestion, (high) time, tenet, understanding, view, wish

(Ibid.: 4)

In the next chapters we shall especially focus on the mandative subjunctive.

Here let us review the general characteristics of the *mandative subjunctive*, ignoring the formal ones which we shall discuss in the next section. First, the uses of the subjunctive present are generally *non-productive set-phrases*. Even if this is argued not to be the case, such expressions give us the impression of being *formal*, *literal*, or *archaic* in style. Second, note that *indicative mood* or *modals* are often used as *alternatives* to the mandative subjunctive in Present-Day English. Consider the following examples:

(36) a. The employees have demanded that the manager
   { *resign*   <esp AmE>
     should resign   <esp BrE>
     resigns. }
  b. { Our decision is that the school *remain* closed. [subjunctive]
       Our decision is that the school *remains* closed. [indicative]
  c. { They insisted that we *not* eat meat. [subjunctive]
       They insisted that we *do not* eat meat. [indicative] }[9]

(Quirk *et al.* 1985: 157)

Third, in connection with the second point, it is generally assumed in traditional grammar that the mandative subjunctive is used mainly in American English, while the quasi-subjunctive *should* is used in British English. But in reality, we should note that the uses of the mandative subjunctive have been increasing in number recently (see Övergaard (1995), Asahara (1994, 1995, 1999), and Nomura (1999)). Fourth, only the uses of the mandative subjunctive are clearly productive today.

As for other general properties of the subjunctive present, see especially Chiba (1987, 2001).

6.6 Three Formal Characteristics of the Subjunctive Present

In this section I discuss three formal characteristics of the subjunctive present (see also Chiba (1987: Chapters 2-3) and Hasegawa (2003: 48)). Several interesting formal characteristics are seen in subjunctive clauses, but the following three are especially important: first, subjunctive verbs always take the root forms regardless of Tense, Person, and Number. Consider the following examples:

(37) a. John demands that <u>Susan</u> *leave* immediately.   (Chiba 1987: 1)
  b. I demand<u>ed</u> that the committee *reconsider* its decision.
                                         (Quirk *et al.* 1985: 156)

(37a) shows that there is the lack of concord between the subject of the 3rd person singular and the subjunctive verb. (37b) shows that though the matrix clause is past tensed, there is no backshifting of tense.

Second, *do*-support does not apply and modals cannot occur in subjunctive clauses either, except the quasi-subjunctive modals *should* (or *shall*). To quote Culicover (1971), which, to my knowledge, is the first systematic study on the subjunctive present in the framework of generative grammar:

(38) a. I demand that you {*will be/*are/*might be/be} here.
  b. I demanded that you {*would be/*are/*were/*might be/*will be/be} here.
                                         (Culicover 1971: 38)
(39) a. I {*order/believe} that you {don't/do not} take much of an interest in this place.
  b. I order that you (*do) take some pains to keep this place clean.   (Ibid.: 40)
(40) *It is imperative that you {*will/can/must/would/could/might*} leave on time.
                                         (Ibid.: 42)[10]

Third, the word order of negation in subjunctive clauses is <not + V>, and not <V + not> in standard English, including the cases of *have* and *be*.[11] Moreover, *do*-support is not used either in forming negative sentences. Consider the following examples:

(41) His father insisted that John {*not smoke/*smoke not/*do not smoke*} at home.
(42) It is essential that this mission *not fail*. (Quirk *et al*. 1985: 156)
(43) We considered it desirable that he *not leave* school before finishing his exams.
(Swan 1995²: 541)
(44) a. He demands that the organisation *not dictate* thought.
 b. *He demands that the organisation *dictate not* thought. (James 1986: 124)
(45) a. I demand that you *not be* such a fool.
 b. *I demand that you *be not* such a fool. (Culicover 1971: 41)
(46) a. I suggest that you *not be* over-confident.
 b. *I suggest that you *don't be* over-confident. (Tonoike 1989c: 127)
(47) a. He suggested that he *not have* finished the work before 10 o'clock.
 b. *He suggested that he *have not* finished the work before 10 o'clock.
(Beukema and Coopmans 1989: 429)

These three characteristics seem to be *quite peculiar* compared to *indicative finite sentences*, but giving adequate accounts for them is one of the main aims of this book, which will be discussed in detail in the next chapters.

6.7 Concluding Remarks

In this chapter I defined the three terms, *mood*, *modal*, and *modality*, which are similar to each other but should be distinguished. Then I discussed the problem as to whether subjunctive mood still exists or not in Present-Day English, reviewing the argumentations among traditional grammarians. Last, before discussing the syntactic structures of the subjunctive present in the next chapters, I reviewed the uses and the general properties of the subjunctive present, and discussed the three important formal characteristics seen in subjunctive present clauses.

Notes to Chapter 6

1. As for the problem with this terminology, see also Onoe (2001), where he discusses the terms of *mood*, *modal*, and *modality* in Japanese Linguistics, compared with the uses in English (Linguistics).

2. I think that the following part of Jespersen's view on mood in (16) is of great importance:

    (i) … though <u>in some cases the choice of the mood is determined</u> not by the attitude of the actual speaker, but <u>by the clause itself and its relation to the main nexus on which it is dependent</u>. (Underlines are mine)

    For example, indeed, the choice of subjunctive or indicative in (iia, b) is determined by the speaker's belief or attitude toward the proposition, and thus we can express this as (iii):

    (ii) a. If John *is* honest, I will employ him.
    　 b. If John *were* honest, I would employ him.
    (iii) Meaning (or Modality) determines Mood.

    However, when the speaker has heard Mary say, "I am sick," he must use the indicative mood irrespective of his belief or attitude to the proposition, as shown in (iva). Even if he doubted that she was actually sick, he could not use subjunctive mood *at least* in Present-Day English such as in (ivb).

    (iv) a. Mary said that she *was* sick.
    　 b. *Mary said that she *be* sick.

    This means that in the complement *that*-clause of *say* the indicative forms *must* be used regardless of the speaker's belief or attitude toward the proposition, and thus we can express this as (v):

    (v) Meaning (Modality) does not necessarily determine Mood. (i.e. (iii) is not always true.)

Needless to say, the reverse is true, because moods necessarily express some subjective or objective meanings or other:

(vi) Mood determines Meaning (Modality).

From this viewpoint as well, we should conclude that Jespersen's claim that mood is basically a *grammatical* notion is more appropriate.

Additionally, based on Jespersen's view in (i), which means (v) and (vi), we should crucially modify the definition of mood in (1) as follows:

(vii) Mood is the verbal inflectional forms or their system for expressing modality, but the choice of mood is determined by modality or *by the clause itself and its relation to the matrix clause.*

3. Since the inflection of *subjunctive past* is very weak, the interpretation needs *pragmatic support*. As for this problem, see Nomura (2000e). For example, the following (i) has two interpretations, but we cannot distinguish them by the inflections alone:

(i) If it *rained*, the match would be cancelled.   (Palmer 1974: 144)
   a. present counterfactual condition (=subjunctive past)
   b. past open condition (=indicative past, i.e., "Whenever it rained in those days, the match would be cancelled.")

4. Incidentally, the term *subjunctive mood* originates from the Latin word *modus subjunctivus* (=mood to be subjoined), which implies that subjunctive is the mood used in *subordinate clauses*. However, it is clear that subjunctive is also used in *root clauses* judging from the uses of optative sentences. Onions (1932[6]) also argues that this term is misleading in two respects; one is that indicative rather than subjunctive is used in subordinate clause, and the other is that subjunctive is needed in many root clauses and many matrix clauses as well. As for the problem of the terminology of subjunctive, see further Hosoe (1933) and Ando (1999).

5. Quirk *at al.* (1985) consider two uses in our classification, i.e. *optative sentences* and some *stereotype expressions*, to be *formulaic subjunctive*.

6. Incidentally, it is well known that Bradley (1904) predicted the future of English subjunctive just a century ago, as shown in (i):

(i) The only feature in the simplification of English accidence that remains to be mentioned is the disappearance of the subjunctive mood. In Old English the subjunctive played as important a part as in modern German, and was used in much the same way. Its inflexion differed in several respects from that of the indicative. The only formal trace of the old subjunctive still remaining, except the use of *be* and *were*, is the omission of the final *s* in the third person singular of verbs. And even this [i.e. the only formal trace of the Old subjunctive still remaining] is rapidly dropping out of use, its only remaining function being to emphasize the uncertainty of a supposition. <u>Perhaps in another generation the subjunctive forms will have ceased to exist except in the single instance of *were*</u>, which serves a useful function, although we manage to dispense with a corresponding form in other verbs.

(Bradley 1904: 52-53, underlines are mine)

However, it is very interesting that the mandative subjunctive survives in Present-Day English contrary to his prediction.

7. Hiroki Tsuchiya asked me whether we could regard *say* in (29b) as a use of *indicative mood* at the presentation of Nomura (2003b). As for this question, we can answer that it should be regarded as a subjunctive use, because if this were an indicative use, *will say* rather than *say* should be used so long as it has a non-habitual interpretation.

This problem is complex, however, as we discussed in Section 6.4. Assuming the standpoint based on *strict morphological form* like Jespersen, *say* in (29b) would be regarded as indicative mood. As for this problem, note that Visser (1966) calls uses like *say* in (29b) *modally zero forms* or *modally non-marked forms*, and thus distinguishes clear subjunctive uses by calling them *modally marked forms*, as shown in (i):

(i) I suggest<u>ed</u> that you *say* nothing to her about it.

8. Note, however, that the problem as to what lexical items require a subjunctive clause is in fact very complex (see Chiba (1991)). We shall discuss this problem later in Chapter 10.

9. Yuzaburo Murata asked me what we should think of *do* in (36c) at the presentation of Nomura (2003b). In fact, this is not so easy a question to answer; note that not *did* but *do* is used in (36c). One answer is assuming that, though *do* is an indicative use, not *did* but *do* is used because this sentence has a *habitual* interpretation. Another answer is

assuming that *do* is one type of subjunctive alternative use of auxiliary as well as *should* (only when we can consider that this sentence does not have a habitual interpretation). As supporting evidence, notice that *do* was used as an alternative use of subjunctive present in older English. Consider Chiba's (1987: 177, fn. 1) examples:

(i) a. ... a public *admonition* to Michael Parrot, that he *do* not presume any more to mention a certain worm .... And oh! let me watch myself, that my prosperous state do not make me forget to look up, with due thankfulness to Providence.
(Charleston 1941: 139-140)
b. I am now going down to Garden City and New York till the President send for me; or, *if* he *do* not send for me, I'm going to his house and sit on his front steps till he come out! (Curme 1931: 407)
c. I *move* that the House *do* now adjourn. (Visser 1966: 836)

Furthermore, even in Present-Day English, these uses of *do* are sometimes seen. Consider the following examples:

(ii) a. I *insist* that he DO not take the medicine.
b. I *insist* that he DO take the medicine.
c. I *suggest* that you DO try to be more helpful. (Bolinger 1977: 189-195)
(iii) I believe your chances of getting a grant are better than a full fellowship as there is no fixed age limit on grants, so I *suggest* you DO apply for a Fellowship grant.
(Chiba 1987: 177, fn. 1)
(iv) Anderson goes on to call for a radical reformation of ..., *requiring* that analysts *do* not seek to .... (Lightfoot (1979), *Principle of Diachronic Syntax*, 148-149)
(v) a. John was able to play first violin, so I'm requesting that you *do*, too.
b. Just as it's *important* that Harry *see* this film, so it's *necessary* that everyone else *do*, too.
c. I *order* that everyone *get* out of the pool, and I *demand* that you *do*, too, Bobby Poobah. (Culicover 1971: 130, fn.12)

Note that all these examples are *clearly in subjunctive environments* (cf. Visser's (1966) *modally marked forms* in note 7) except for (iic), (iii), and (iv).

Incidentally, Kyoko Asahara (personal communication, 2003) pointed out that in the cases where the main clause is past tensed like in (36c) <should + root form> rather than <not + subjunctive present> or <do not + root form> is mainly a use in the attested examples in British English. I am grateful to her for pointing out this fact. As for this problem, see further Asahara (1999, 2000, 2001).

10. However, as we discussed in Section 6.5, indicative, *do*-support, and modals can *all* appear in subjunctive present clauses. As for this problem, Chiba (1987: Chapters 2-3) reports many attested examples where indicative, *do*-support, or modals appear in subjunctive present clauses. Needless to say, we should consider such examples as *indicative* uses, but the problem is not so easy. As an illustration of this, consider the case of *insist*:

(i) a. insist1: to assert or maintain firmly
    b. insist2: to demand or persist in demanding (cf. Chiba (1987: 11))

(ii) insist ─┬─ indicative use (insist1) ─── indicative form
             └─ subjunctive use (insist2) ─┬─ subjunctive form
                                            └─ indicative form (cf. (ibid.: 14))

What is complex is that subjunctive use (insist2) in (ii) takes not only subjunctive forms but also indicative forms. As for this point, consider the attested examples in Chiba:

(iii) a. It is surely premature to *insist* that the basis of linguistic theory *be* extended to include obscure and intuition-bound concepts, on the grounds that .... (Culicover *et al.* (1977), *Formal Syntax*, p.5)
      b. One can thus firmly *insist* (by using MUST) that he *says* what he wants for a present, or that he *pays* a visit .... (Palmer (1979), *Modality and the English Modals*, p.62) (Quoted from Chiba (1987: 7))

Namely, even in complement *that*-clauses selected by predicates like those in (33-35) we might not find clear differences in grammaticality like in Culicover's judgments so easily in attested examples. As for this problem, Chiba shows lexical items selecting subjunctive clauses obligatorily for many speakers:

(iv) Lexical Items Which Obligatorily Take Subjunctive Clauses
    Verbs: *demand, desire, request*
    Adjectives: *anxious, imperative, mandatory*
    Nouns: *desire, intention, wish* (Chiba 1987: 6)

However, as Chiba himself shows, indicative, *do*-support, and modals can appear even in complement *that*-clauses selected by the typical predicates in (iv). Consider the following examples of *demand* where modals appear:

(v) a. I demand that John *must* help me. (Aijmer 1972: 74)
 b. We demand that this burden *must* be removed. (Curme 1931: 401-402)
 c. Therefore we must now ascertain whether these as yet unanalyzed items and constructions are consistent with our general hypothesis or if they *demand* that some modification of our hypothesis, or perhaps even a quite different hypothesis, *must* be adopted. (Hogg (1977), *English Quantifier Systems*, p.141)
 d. This in turn *demands* that the writer *can* see his performance as the reader will see it. (Lester (1970), *Readings in Applied Transformational Grammar*, p.208)

(All quoted from Chiba (1987: 70, 73))

We should take all these facts into consideration in constructing the syntax of subjunctive present.

11. However, the cases of *have* and *be* are in fact very complex. We shall discuss this problem in detail later in Chapter 12.

Appendix to Chapter 6

On Phonetic *That*-Deletion in Mandative Subjunctive Clauses

In this book I am assuming two types of *that*; the indicative *that* and the subjunctive *that*. To support this I pointed out the fact that the subjunctive *that* is normally not deleted in Nomura (2000b). However, as I mentioned in note 28 in Nomura (2000b), we can still find cases where *that* is deleted even in mandative subjunctive present clauses. Since then, I have found many other examples where the subjunctive *that* is missing.

Thus I will modify my assumption on *that*-deletion in mandative subjunctive clauses and propose the following:

(1) The conditions on *that*-deletion in mandative subjunctive clauses are the same as in indicative *that*-clauses.

I will continue assuming two types of *that*; the indicative *that* and the subjunctive that. Note incidentally that our standpoint is different from Ando's (2004) conclusion that two types of *that* do not exist in English, though he also points out that the assumption that the subjunctive *that* cannot be deleted is empirically wrong.

Appendix 6.1 Studies Assuming That the Subjunctive *That* Cannot Be Deleted

So far many linguists have assumed that the subjunctive *that* cannot be deleted. As an illustration of this, I quote Chomsky and Lasnik (1977):

(2) … and in subjunctive clauses, deletion of *that* is not permitted.
(Chomsky and Lasnik 1977: 485-486)

Taking this into consideration, observe the following examples:

(3) a. I ask that John be allowed to come.
 b. *I ask John be allowed to come.   (Rosenbaum 1967: 92, fn. 3)
(4) She demands *(that) he think of a clever sentence.   (Wilkins 1977: 123)
(5) a. *I ask (order) you be taken away.
 b. *I ask (order) the offenders be taken away.

c. *I ask all of them be there.
d. *I order they be there.
e. *I urge (beg) you (urge the offenders) be taken away.
f. *I urge (beg) they reconsider.
g. *I adjure (implore) you take heed.
h. *I wish the report be turned in. (Bolinger 1972: 48-49)

(6) John
a) *asked
b) *ordered
c) *dictated
d) (*)advised
e) (*)requested
f) (*)required
g) insisted
h) demanded
Tom leave immediately.

(Chiba 1987: 151)

(7) a. The committee may insist [that he resign].
b. *The committee may insist [he resign]. (Radford 1988: 308)
(8) *I suggested to John α he should leave early. (Nakajima 1996: 154)
(9) a. I demand *(that) he see the president now.
b. I think (that) he works in a hospital. (Haegeman and Guéron 1999: 107)
(10) a. I request *(that) John be given the leave to go.
b. The Selection Committee may insist *(that) he resign by the end of September.

(Hiroe 1999: 57)

(11) a. I recommended {that / ?φ} he take the medicine.
b. It is necessary {that / ?*φ} he take the medicine.
c. I asked {that / *φ} he take the medicine.

(Murakami 2000: 85)

The above data appears to support the hypothesis that the subjunctive *that* cannot be deleted but there are many exceptions that I will discuss below.

Appendix 6.2 Examples Where the Subjunctive *That* Is Deleted

Despite the examples in the previous section, we can also find many examples, including many *attested examples*, where the subjunctive *that* is deleted. Consider the following examples:

(12) a. they demanded he get the R. works going
  b. the doctor insisted he remain in bed
  c. he had insisted the vile stuff be served
  d. he proposed they try fishing
  e. I propose a temporary chairman be named
  f. I rather a man be anything than a woman be mean
  g. I'd rather you wait
  h. T. suggested it be provided with lightning rods
  i. he suggested I draft a scheme
  j. I suggested we fly to S.
  k. I wasn't suggesting you not do it
  l. he suggested he wait a year
  m. (they) urged W. Combe at the College not enclose (Kirchner 1970-72: §105.1$_3$)

(13) a. I ask they all be there. (cf. (5a-c))
  b. ?I ask they reconsider. (cf. (5a-c))
  c. I order they be taken away. (cf. (5d))
  d. ?I urge (beg) they be taken away. (cf. (5e,f))
  f. ??I urge (beg) they reconsider. (cf. (5e,f))
  g. I adjure (implore) you be cautious. (cf. (5g))
  h. ?I prefer you leave now.
  i. ?I prefer the children leave now.
  j. I prefer they leave now.
  k. ?I wish he be taken there. (cf. (5h))
  l. ?I wish they be shown the way. (cf. (5h))
  m. I want only that you be happy. (cf. (5i))   (Bolinger 1972: 48-49)

(14) I insist (that) Bob be fired.   (Postal 1974: 87, fn. 6)

(15) Mary demands (that) Fred leave immediately.   (Culicover and Wexler 1977: 52)

(16) John, who it's essential [she talk to t]   (Chomsky (1981: 246), Kayne (1980))

(17) a. who is it essential [John see t]
  b. who is essential [t see John]   (Ibid.: 247)

(18) The committee { proposes / proposed } (that) Mr Day be elected.   (Quirk *et al.* 1985: 156)

(19) a. Who did John { insist / demand } Tom kill t?

    b. John $\left\{\begin{array}{l}\text{insisted}\\ \text{demanded}\end{array}\right\}$ Tom leave immediately.

    c. Who did John $\left\{\begin{array}{l}\text{insist}\\ \text{demand}\end{array}\right\}$ t leave immediately?

                                                                        (Chiba 1987: 151)

(20) These analyses demand φ these higher predicates be transparent to deep structure constraints, assuming such constrains exist. (Newmeyer (1975), English Aspectual Verbs, p.33)   (Quoted from Chiba (1995:25))

(21)a. ?The King decreed the rebels be drawn and quartered.

    b. ?I requested John help me.   (McCawley 1998[2]: 149)

These examples show that even in subjunctive clauses the complementizer *that* can be deleted *syntactically*. As for this point, we should note McCawley's (1998[2]) comment after pointing out that (21a, b) and (22b-d) are not so bad as (22a), where *that* is deleted in the sentential *that*-clause:

(22)a. That/*φ Perot will be elected is unlikely.

    b. It is unlikely that/(?)φ Perot will be elected.

    c. John said sarcastically that/?φ he was glad he had such good friends.

    d. Frank assured us yesterday that/?φ the trouble was over.   (Ibid.)

(23) Omission of the *that* is generally possible when the *that*-clause immediately follows a verb or adjective of which it is the object. Its omission from a non-extraposed subject complement is highly deviant, and its omission from a subjunctive *that*-clause or from a *that*-clause that is separated from the verb or adjective by intervening material is mildly odd.   (Ibid.: 148)

All these data appear to be direct counter examples to the hypothesis that the subjunctive *that* cannot be deleted that was claimed by, e.g., Chomsky and Lasnik (1977), Haegeman and Guéron (1999), Hiroe (1999), Murakami (2000), and Nomura (2000b). Incidentally, as for the claim that *that*-less clauses are not CPs but IPs (see Doherty (1997)), complement clauses should be basically CPs from the viewpoint of the uniformity of syntactic structures, and moreover we need to examine whether the claim is empirically appropriate (see also Section 3.3.2).

Appendix 6.3 The Phonetically Deleted Complementizer *That*

Based on the empirical data in the previous section, I tentatively make the following assumption (see also Section 3.3.3):

(24) The complementizer *that* can be *phonetically* deleted in surface structure, whether it is the indicative *that* or the subjunctive *that*.

I will further assume two functional conditions on *that*-deletion: (i) the *Parsing Condition* and (ii) the *Semantically Transparent Condition*. As for (ii), I am grateful to Ken-ichi Takami (personal communication, 1999) for pointing out this possibility (cf. Kuno and Takami's (1993: 44) *Constraint on Extraction from Embedded Clause*).

The *Parsing Condition* means that acceptability is degraded by the potential of *ambiguity in parsing*, which can explain not only the indicative cases in (24a-c) but also the subjunctive cases (25a, b):

(25) a. *φ Perot will be elected is unlikely. (=(21a))
 b. *I believe very strongly φ Mary will solve this problem. (=(52c) in Chapter 3)
 c. *John expressed the feeling φ the meeting should not be held.
  (Chomsky 1986b: 36)
(26) a. *I asked you be there.
 b. I demanded you be there. (Bolinger 1972: 24)

Bolinger argues that (26a) is unacceptable due to the potential ambiguity with the possible construction in (27a) while (26b) is acceptable due to the impossibility of (27b):

(27) a. I asked you *to* be there.
 b. *I demanded you *to* be there.

Next, the *Semantically Transparent Condition* means that *that*-deletion is allowable when the main clause is *semantically transparent*, i.e. *that* cannot be deleted when it is selected by the verb having *semantically more important information* than the rest of the sentence. As is well known, *that* cannot be deleted after *non-bridge verbs*, as shown in (28):

(28) a. John whispered *(that) Mary stole a diamond.
 b. You grumbled *(that) John hit Susan.
 c. Mary complained *(that) the room was too hot.

Here we can consider the subjunctive cases in (2-11) to be parallel to the cases of non-bridge verbs in (28a-c), because the subjunctive verbs are considered to have rather important information (e.g. *insist*=demand (sth) *forcefully, not accepting a refusal*). Moreover, since *semantically more important information* is a relative concept in a sense, the actions of *insist, demand, propose, suggest*, etc. are not necessarily semantically more important for those who do not consider or feel those actions important. We could consider that such assumptions allow *that*-deletion even in mandative subjunctive clauses. Note that the verbs seen in (1-10) are *typical* subjunctive verbs.

Incidentally, in this connection, Kinsuke Hasegawa (TEC lecture in 1999) pointed out that *wh*-extraction is possible even in *that*-clauses selected by non-bridge verbs for those who *always* complain, grumble, murmur, etc. in their daily life. Considering this to be parallel to *that*-deletion as well, we can naturally consider that the frequency of the uses of the subjunctive present is not so high as with indicative sentences, judging from the fact the mandative subjunctive is a *formal* or *literary* expression in Present-Day English. Consequently, the subjunctive *that* is *normally* resistant to deletion. As supporting evidence for this, we can easily find examples in the Early Modern English period where the subjunctive *that* is deleted; Murakami (2000) reported many examples of such types as the following:

(29) a. … she sayd therto agayne φ ye be not wyse therin.
 b. … if I finde φ you bee not intangled to any other, ….
 c. Then said they to him, φ We be not borne of fornication, wee haue one father, euen God.
 d. But the men that went vpp with him, sayde: φ We be not able to goo vpp agenst the people, ….
 e. But the men that went vp with him, said, φ Wee be not able to goe vp against people, ….
 f. I hope, φ it be not so
 g. Pray heauen φ it be not full of knight againe.
 h. If you bite one another, take heed φ you be not deuoured one of another ….
 i. … take heede φ you bee not deuoured one of another, ….
 j. … but I dred φ it be not
 k. … for I understand φ +tay be not wardes ….
 l. … we wold φ she be not wronged in hir right:
 m. Sir, as me thinks, φ your rowls thear be not kept as they ought to be;
 n. God grant φ it be not a prognostication of some great storme to this noble kingdome.
 o. I think φ ther be not the lyke places agayn for England to be founde.

p. I praye God ϕ this opportunytye be not lost, ….
q. I wisch ϕ his wife be not a widowe againe.
r. … therefore me thinks still it weare well ϕ we be not all togeither swallowed up in the contemplation of ….
s. I beseech ϕ you be not discouraged in proceeding to ….

(Murakami 2000: 91-92)

Since subjunctive verbs were used much more frequently in this period, we can consider that people in those days could delete the subjunctive *that* rather easily, though Murakami arrives at a different conclusion based on the data above.

Needless to say, since we can explore various other approaches to this problem, it will be best to leave this question open for future study. As for other possibilities of explaining *that*-deletion, see Bolinger (1972), Erteschick (1973), Stowell (1981), Pesetsky (1995), Chiba (1995), Nakajima (1996), and Doherty (1997).

Last, incidentally, Ando (2004) also submits the following example of subjunctive *past*, where *that* is missing, as another counterexample against the assumption that the subjunctive *that* cannot be deleted, as shown in (30):

(30) I wish ϕ I were taller. (Ando 2004: 31)

Indeed, contrary to subjunctive *present*, *that* is *normally* deleted in the subjunctive *past that*-clause selected by *wish*. But, as for this problem, Minoji Akimoto (personal communication, 2003) pointed out the possibility that the complementizer *that* has come to be deleted in Present-Day English as a marker where *wish* complement clauses has become the construction expressing *nonfactual events* resulting from *grammaticalization*. Though we need further investigation, I agree with him at present, since *wish* also selected a subjunctive *present* clause expressing *open condition* with the *overt* complementizer *that* in earlier English. Consider the following example:

(31) I wish *that* this matter *be* disposed of with as little scandal as may be. (Arthur Conan Doyle, 19th Century)

Appendix 6.4 The Null Complementizer vs. the Phonetically Deleted Complementizer

Before closing this appendix, we should point out the difference between the complementizer *that* which is phonetically deleted in surface structure and the null complementizer ϕ. Note that we took the same standpoint in the discussion as to infinitival clauses in Section 3.3.3, as shown in (32):

(32) a. I want [CP ϕ for Mary to solve this problem].
(phonetically deleted *that* in the surface structure)
b. John tried [CP ϕ PRO to solve this problem].
(the null prepositional complementizer base-generated in the underlying structure)

Just as in the case of infinitival clauses, I also assume that a null complementizer is base-generated in the underlying structure in the following examples:

(33) a. ϕ God *be* praised!
b. ϕ Lord *have* mercy upon us! (=(25a, b) in Chapter 6)

We can assume that *archaic uses* of present subjunctive verbs having [uSubj] raise to C to check off the [uSubj] feature, in the following types of examples:

(34) a. *Come* what may, we will go ahead with our plan.
b. *Suffice* it to say that you win.
c. *Be* it noted that this offer was made in good faith.
d. *Be* that as it may, we have nothing to lose.

Note here that with these verbs raising to C cannot occur in mandative subjunctive clauses, as shown in (35b):

(35) a. The committee demanded [that John should resign].
b. *The committee demanded [should$_i$ John t$_i$ resign].

(Nomura 2000b: 57)

This is because the complementizer *that* does exist though it is phonetically deleted unlike the null prepositional complementizer ϕ in (34a-d). That is to say, (35b) is *practically* ruled out by what is called the *Doubly-filled COMP Filter*, as shown in (36):

(36) *I demand [CP [C should$_i$ that] John t$_i$ resign].

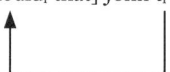

Appendix 6.5 Concluding Remarks

In this appendix I modified my assumption on *that*-deletion in mandative subjunctive clauses proposed in Nomura (2000b). Though many linguists have assumed that the subjunctive *that* cannot be deleted, I have shown that the assumption is empirically wrong by submitting many examples where the subjunctive *that* is deleted. Then I proposed that the complementizer *that* can be *phonetically* deleted in surface structure whether it is the indicative *that* or the subjunctive *that*, though *that*-deletion is subject to two functional conditions on *that*-deletion: (i) the Parsing Condition and (ii) the Semantically Transparent Condition. Last, just as in the cases of infinitival clauses, I assumed two types of complementizers in subjunctive present clauses as well: (i) phonetically deleted *that* in surface structure and (ii) the null complementizer φ, base-generated in the underlying structure.

Chapter 7

The Structure of Subjunctive Present Clauses[1]

7.1 Introduction

In this chapter I discuss the syntactic structure of subjunctive present clauses, especially mandative subjunctive clauses. The purpose of this chapter is to explain the three formal characteristics discussed in Chapter 6, which seem to be quite peculiar compared to those of indicative finite sentences, and to account for various phenomena in subjunctive present clauses. After presenting my proposal in the next section, I will examine in detail various characteristics of subjunctive present clauses and show that the present proposal is appropriate.

7.2 Proposals

First of all, I propose the following points about the syntactic structure of the subjunctive present clauses based on the ModalP Hypothesis that I proposed and discussed in Chapter 2:

(1) In subjunctive present clauses the covert modal M_ϕ has the [uSubj(unctive)] and [uPres] features which move to I^0, thus the verb itself does not move in Present-Day English. This means that the category of the subjunctive present is *modal*, though this modal is *covert* (i.e. phonetically empty) unlike ordinary modals (e.g. *may*, *can*, *must*, etc.).
(2) Subjunctive present clauses have, in fact, *present tense* (the [uPres] feature) even in Present-Day English.
(3) The subjunctive covert modal M_ϕ raises to I to check off [uSubj] and [uPres] as *the last resort*.[2]

On these assumptions, the underlying structure of the simple sentence illustrating the mandative subjunctive (4) is as shown in (5):

(4) I insisted [CP that he not go there].

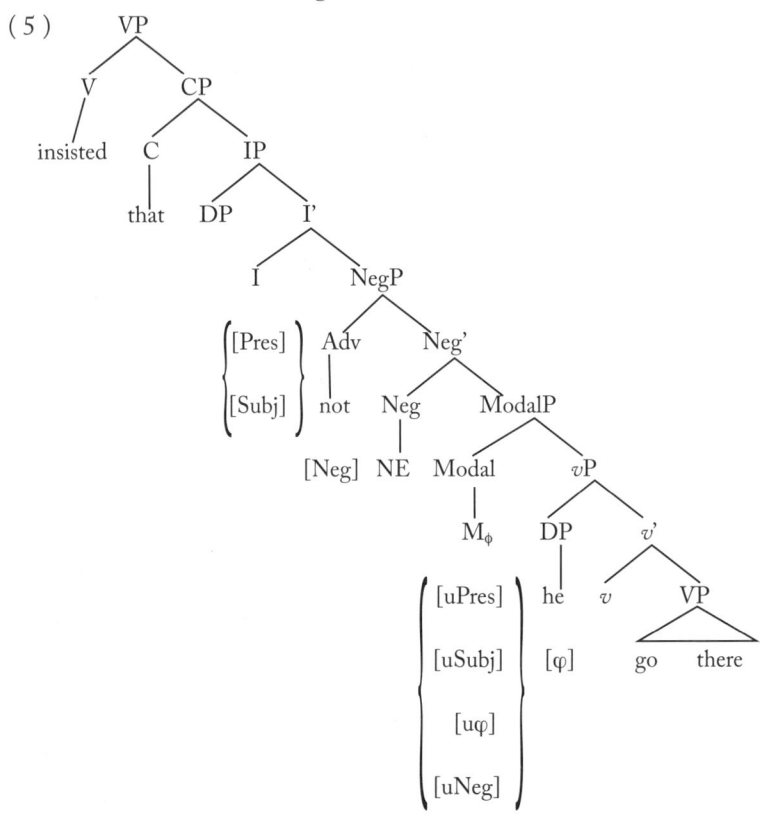

(5)

```
         VP
        /  \
       V    CP
    insisted / \
            C   IP
            |  / \
          that DP  I'
                  / \
                 I   NegP
          {[Pres]} / \
          {[Subj]} Adv  Neg'
                   |   / \
                  not Neg  ModalP
                       |   / \
                    [Neg] NE Modal  vP
                              |    / \
                              Mφ  DP  v'
                           {[uPres]} he  / \
                           {[uSubj]} [φ] v  VP
                           {[uφ]}          /\
                           {[uNeg]}       go there
```

Let us consider the derivation of (5). First, *he* raises to IP-Spec to get a Case and become a full form (see (16a) in Chapter 1). Second, [Pres] and [Subj] in I are copied to I', IP, the raised DP (=*he*), and [φ] in *he* is copied to IP, I', and I due to Feature Dribbling (see (17) in Chapter 1).[3] This is shown in (6) below:

(6)

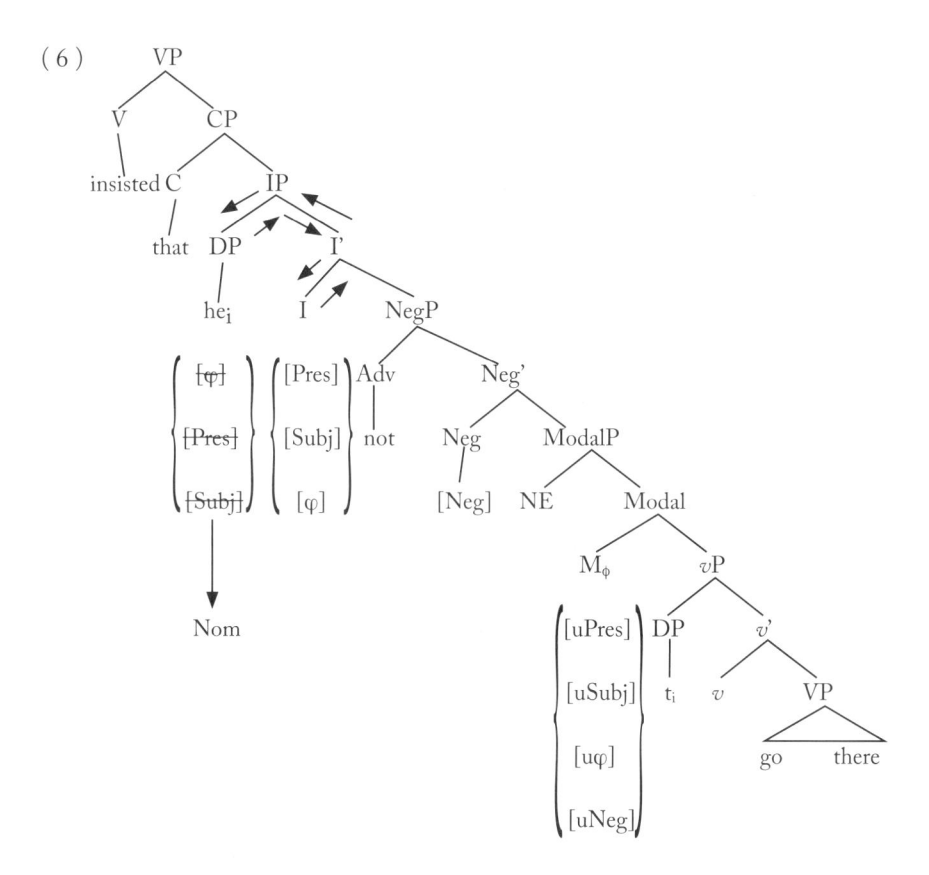

[tree diagram showing:
VP → V (insisted), CP
CP → C (that), IP
IP → DP (he_i), I'
I' → I, NegP
I features: {[φ], [Pres], [Subj]} and {[Pres], [Subj], [φ]}
Adv: not
NegP → Adv, Neg'
Neg' → Neg, ModalP
Neg: [Neg], NE
ModalP → Modal
Modal → M_φ, vP
M_φ: {[uPres], [uSubj], [uφ], [uNeg]}
vP → DP (t_i), v'
v' → v, VP
VP → go there
Arrow from I features to "Nom"]

Here I will modify the assumption about Nominative Case assigning in (16bii) as follows:

(7) Nominative Case Assignment (Revised)
Nominative Case is a reflex of [φ] and the finite I feature complex (i.e. [Tense] and [Mood]).

Given this, Nominative can be assigned in the following cases:

(8) a. [φ]+[Ind(icative)]+[Pres]
    b. [φ]+[Ind(icative)]+[Past]
    c. [φ]+[Subj(unctive)]+[Pres]

d. [φ]+[Subj(unctive)]+[Past]
e. [φ]+[Imp(erative)]+[Pres]⁴⁾

Thus, it follows from (8c) that *he* is assigned Nominative Case as a reflex of [φ]+[Subj]+[Pres], with the result that these features are all deleted.

Let us turn to the main discussion: third, the subjunctive covert modal M_ϕ raises to Neg to check off [uNeg], and further raises to I to check off the uninterpretable features [uPres], [uSubj], and [uφ] as a last resort.

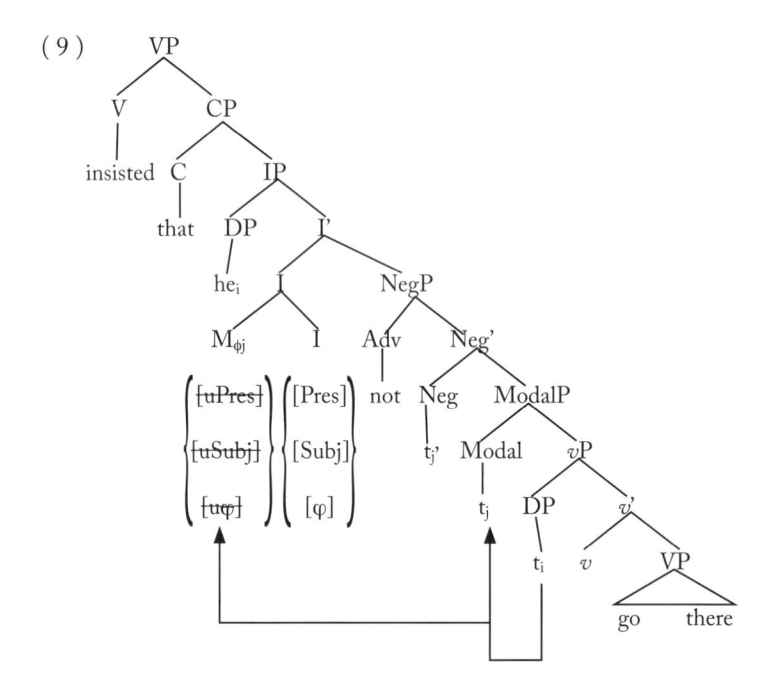

(9)

[Tree diagram: VP dominating V "insisted" and CP; CP dominating C "that" and IP; IP dominating DP "he_i" and I'; DP containing M_{φj} with features [uPres], [uSubj], [uφ] (all struck through); I' dominating I with features [Pres], [Subj], [φ] and NegP; NegP dominating Adv "not" and Neg'; Neg' dominating Neg "t_j'" and ModalP; ModalP dominating Modal "t_j" and vP; vP dominating DP "t_i" and v'; v' dominating v and VP "go there"]

Here note that, as I assumed in Chapter 1, [Pres], [Subj], and [φ] are all interpretable for I. Additionally, these features are also copied to IP due to Feature Dribbling, which is compatible with the selection by C, having the same features:

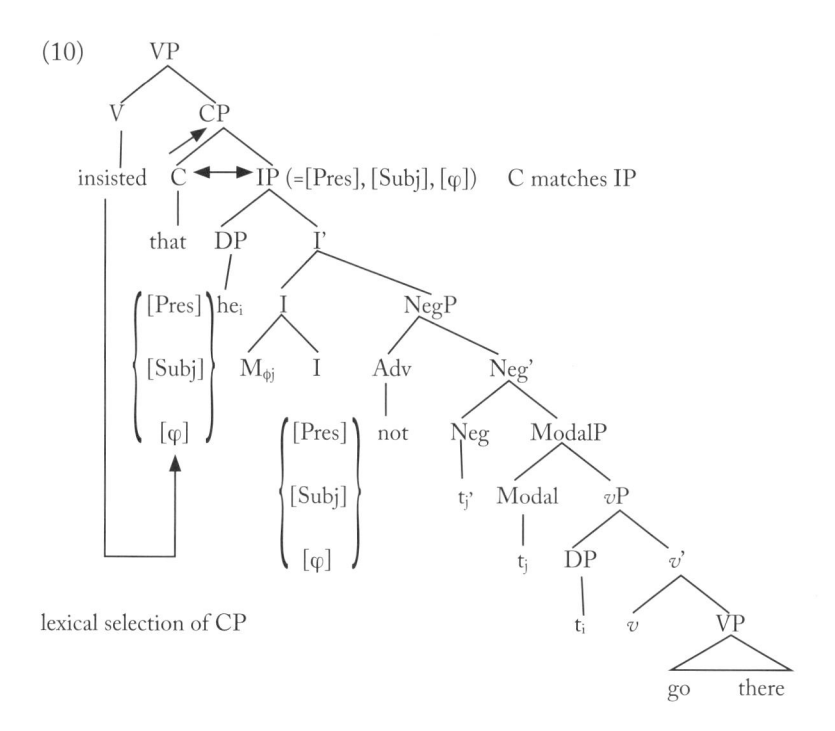

(10) [tree diagram]

VP
├── V: insisted
└── CP
    ├── C: that
    └── IP (=[Pres], [Subj], [φ])   C matches IP
        ├── DP: he_i {[Pres], [Subj], [φ]}
        └── I'
            ├── I
            │   ├── M_φj
            │   └── I
            └── NegP
                ├── Adv: not {[Pres], [Subj], [φ]}
                └── Neg'
                    ├── Neg: t_j'
                    └── ModalP
                        ├── Modal
                        └── vP
                            ├── DP: t_i
                            └── v'
                                ├── v
                                └── VP: go there

lexical selection of CP

Last, CP having the [Pres], [Subj], and [φ] features is merged to the main verb *insisted*, which can lexically select such a CP, and thus the derivation converges. Note that since the indicative *that* mismatches IP having [Subj] due to Feature Dribbling, the derivation will crash. Consider the following example:

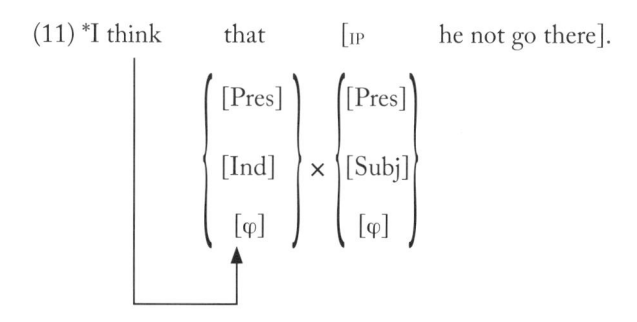

(11) *I think that [_IP he not go there].

{[Pres], [Ind], [φ]} × {[Pres], [Subj], [φ]}

Additionally, note that the relation between the matrix subjunctive verb and the *that*-clause having [Subj] is not checked but *lexically selected*. That is to say, the [Pres], [Subj], and [φ] features in the *that*-clause are *not erased by feature checking*. This assumption is supported by the presence of non lexically selected complementizers having [Subj], as illustrated in (12). As for other examples than *if*, consider the examples, as shown in (13):[5)]

(12) a. *If* any person *be* found guilty, he shall have the right of appeal. (=(22a) in Chapter 6)
    b. [CP   If   [IP   any person be found guilty], he shall....

$$\begin{Bmatrix}[\text{Pres}]\\ [\text{Subj}]\\ [\varphi]\end{Bmatrix} \quad \begin{Bmatrix}[\text{Pres}]\\ [\text{Subj}]\\ [\varphi]\end{Bmatrix}$$

(13) a. *Though* that *be* true, you must not give up your plan. (=(23a) in Chapter 6)
    b. *Whether* she *be* right or wrong, she will have my unswerving support. (=(23d) in Chapter 6)

Moreover, in the cases of *optative sentences*, we should consider that the *zero complementizer* C_ϕ is present in root sentences:

(14) [CP C_ϕ [IP   God save the queen]].

$$\begin{Bmatrix}[\text{Pres}]\\ [\text{Subj}]\\ [\varphi]\end{Bmatrix} \quad \begin{Bmatrix}[\text{Pres}]\\ [\text{Subj}]\\ [\varphi]\end{Bmatrix}$$

In the next sections I will examine the adequacy of the above hypothesis by reviewing various aspects in the subjunctive clauses.

7.3 Tense and Three Formal Characteristics of Subjunctive Clauses

To all appearances, the three formal characteristics seen in subjunctive clauses given in Chapter 6 might be taken as evidence that subjunctive clauses have *no tense*. Let us examine them once again:

(15) a. The forms of subjunctive verbs are always the *root forms* irrespective of Tense and Agr.
  b. There is no *do*-support. Note that the auxiliary *do* has been thought of as a *tense-bearer* to support a stranded Tns in traditional transformational grammar.
  c. In negative subjunctive clauses the word order is <not + have/be>, and not <have/be + not>.

However, assuming the proposals presented in the previous section, we can explain all three of the peculiar characteristics of subjunctive present clauses as follows:

(16) a. Supposing that the subjunctive present is one type of covert modal, the following verbs must be, needless to say, the root forms.
  b. Supposing that the auxiliary *do* is also a type of modal as we discussed in Chapter 1, it will follow that *do* does not appear in subjunctive clauses, since modals (i.e. the covert subjunctive modal M_ϕ and the auxiliary *do* in this case) do not co-occur (see (31g) in Chapter 1).
  c. Since the verb itself does not move, it follows that *not* and V remain in situ, so the word order is always <not + V> in all the cases including those with *be* and *have*.

The explanations in (16a-c) are entirely consistent, but as for (16b, c) we shall further discuss this topic again and reformulate them in Section 8.3 and Chapter 12.

7.4 On the Non-cooccurrence of Modals

Interestingly, as we mentioned, modals do not appear in mandative subjunctive clauses,[6] except for the quasi-subjunctive *should*.[7] Observe the examples in Section 6.3 again and the following additional ones:

(17) a. *I demand that you {*will be/might*} be here.
　　b. *I demanded that you {*would be/might be/will be*} here.
(Culicover 1971: 38)
(18) *It is imperative that you {*will/can/must/would/could/might*} leave on time.
(Ibid.: 42)
(19) a. He says that John *must* read that book.
　　b. He demands that John (**must*) read that book.　　(Emonds 1976: 197)
(20) *His mother urged that John *ought to* wear a raincoat.　　(Weeda 1981: 405)
(21) a. *I require that {John / each student} {*will / would / might*} {leave. / fill out forms.}
　　b. *The requirement that John {*will / would / might*} leave is obvious.
　　c. *It is necessary that John {*will / would / might*} leave.
(Safir 1982: 454-455)
(22) a. *He demanded that the successful candidate *can* speak German.
　　b. *The police require that the spectators *must* stand behind the barricade.
(Potsdam 1997: 535)

We can naturally explain this important characteristic as well by assuming a covert subjunctive modal M_ϕ: it will follow that ordinary modals do not appear in subjunctive clauses due to the general principle of non-cooccurrence of modals.

7.5 The Position of Adverbs

Chiba (1984b, 1987: Chapter 3) first observes in detail that in mandative subjunctive clauses the position of adverbs, which he calls *preverbs*, is different from that in indicative finite sentences. Consider the following examples:

(23) Although there is independent motivation for NP subcategorization for these cases, it is not really necessary that there {a)*be always / b) always be} independent evidence.

(24) John disregarded her requirement that he {a)*have really / b) really have} completed the job by 10:00 today.

(25) I demand that the students {a) *have always / b) always have} finished their assignments when they come to the class.

(26) Such a formation would not require that there {a) *be actually / b) actually be} a prepositional phrase in the verb phrase underlying the passive.

(27) Vennemann's model cannot account for cases such as these, since it requires that the adpausal form {a) *be always / b) always be} the underlying form.

(28) It is not necessary that there {a) *be actually / b) actually be} objects in the world for a nominal concept to identify.

(29) John required that they {a) *be actually / b) actually be} accepted.

(30) I demand that filthy hippies {a)*be always / b) always be} shot.

(All quoted from Chiba (1987: 85))

Radford (1988) and Potsdam (1997, 1998) observe a similar phenomenon, as illustrated below:

(31) a. I insist that he *definitely have* finished by tomorrow.
　　 b. *I insist that he *have definitely* finished by tomorrow. (Radford 1988: 457)

(32) a. *It is recommended that you *be normally* approved by the committee first.
　　 (Cf. Participants *are normally* approved by the committee first.)

b. *It is crucial that we *be absolutely* paying attention to his every word.
(Cf. We *were absolutely* paying attention to his every word.)
c. ?It is mandatory that everybody *have certainly* read at least the introduction.
(Cf. Everybody *had certainly* read at least the introduction.)

(Potsdam 1997: 537)

These ungrammatical word orders (i.e. <V + Adv>) would be fully grammatical if these sentences were indicative finite clauses. It follows from the assumption that the moved elements are members of the covert subjunctive modal M_ϕ alone, and that the verb itself remains in situ. Assuming that the verb does not move, the word order naturally should be the same as in the underlying structure (i.e. <Adv + V>).

7.6 Negative Inversion

The following example illustrates what is generally called *Negative Inversion* (NI) in generative syntax:

(33) With no job is he happy.

NI is a kind of *Topicalization*, but characteristically *obligatory Subject-Aux Inversion* is seen with Negative Preposing. As is well known, Topicalization, including NI, also occurs in subordinate clauses. Observe the following examples:

(34) a. I think that *to Lee*, Robin gave a book. (Culicover 1991: 5)
b. I said that *under no circumstances* should he be arrested. (Rizzi 1990: 117)

The sentence structure of (34b) is analyzed as follows:

(35) I said [$_{CP}$ that [$_{TopP}$ under no circumstances$_j$ [$_{Top'}$ should$_i$ [$_{IP}$ he [$_{I'}$ t$_i$ [$_{ModalP}$ t$_i$

[$_{vP}$ be arrested t$_j$]]]]]]].

That is, the negative element *under no circumstances* moves to TopP-Spec and the modal *should* moves to the head of TopP.[8]

However, interestingly, NI does not appear in mandative subjunctive clauses:

(36) a. *It is required that *with no job* be he happy. (Steele *et al.* 1981: 193)
　　b. *I demand that *under no circumstances* be he arrested. (Rizzi 1990: 117)

Note also interestingly that the following sentences are grammatical, where Subject-Aux Inversion *does not apply* despite the presence of the negative preposing:

(37) a. It is required that with no better job *he be* happy.[9]
　　b. I demand that under no circumstances *he be* arrested.[10]

This shows convincingly that the verb cannot raise to I (and thus Top) in Present-Day English, which is compatible with the present proposal that the covert subjunctive modal M_ϕ moves alone and the verb itself remains in place.

7.7 Phonological Support

Observe the following examples of *contraction* in indicative finite sentences:

(38) a. *They have* completed the job.
　　b. *They've* completed the job.

Interestingly, such contraction is not allowed in subjunctive present clauses:

(38) a. She insists that {*they've / they have} completed the job by 10:00 today.[11]
　　b. I demand that {*they've / they have} removed their shoes before entering.
　　c. We request that {*you've / you have} departed by no later than Wednesday. (Selkirk 1980: 104-105)
(39) We request that {a) you have / b) *you've} left/gone by no later than Wednesday. (Chiba 1987: 59)

(40) a. I demand that *he have* a second chance.
   b. *I demand that *he've* a second chance. (Radford 1988: 458)
(41) a. The major ordered that *he have* completed the operation by midnight.
   b. *The major ordered that *he've* completed the operation by midnight.
(Radford 1997: 160-161)

Based on our framework, in all the ungrammatical sentences above, what exists in the head of IP is not the aspectual verb *have* but the covert subjunctive modal M_ϕ; in any case *have* is blocked from cliticizing onto the subject by the presence of the features which intervene between *they/you/he* and *have*. It can be observed that these examples reflect the same phenomenon seen in *wanna*-contractions:[12]

(53) a. Who₍ᵢ₎ do you want t₍ᵢ₎ to meet Bill?
   b. *Who do you *wanna* meet Bill?

Additionally, the following example also shows that the main verbs in subjunctive clauses are not finite but root forms:

(54) a. The director requires that all the actors *want to* give their most.
   b. *The director requires that all the actors *wanna* give their most.
(Brame 1981: 286, fn. 13)

The reason for this is that this kind of contraction applies between *finite* verbs and certain other elements, as illustrated in (55):

(55) a. To *have not* been on time was a spy.
   b. *To *haven't* been on time was a spy.
(56) a. He may *have not* been listening.
   b. *He may *haven't* been listening. (Fiengo 1980: 73)

The cases discussed in this section show that the present proposal is reasonable from the phonological viewpoint as well.

7.8 VP-Deletion

In subjunctive present clauses VP-deletion with *do*-support does not apply:

(57) a. *John was unable to play first violin, so I'm requesting that Harry *do*.
 b. *Just as it's important that Harry see this film, so it's necessary that Bill *do*, too.
 c. *I prefer that you leave now and that Bill *do* tomorrow.
  (Culicover 1971: 130, fn. 11)

These examples are also the basis for the present proposal; they are all ruled out by the general principle of the non-cooccurrence of modals, just as in the cases in Sections 7.4 and 7.5.[13)]

Incidentally, VP-deletion is possible if any *non-modal* Aux element (i.e. *be* and *have*) or the negative *not* remains, as illustrated below:

(58) a. I demand that you be taking Kippy for a walk and that Susan *be* ϕ, too.
  (Weeda 1981: 408)
 b. I demanded that you have removed your shoes before entering and that Mary *have* ϕ, too. (Asakawa and Kamata 1986: 73)
(59) a. A: Should we wake Dad?
   B: No! It's absolutely imperative that you *not* ϕ.
 b. Kim needs to be there but it is better that the other organizers *not* ϕ.
 c. Ted hoped to vacation in Liberia but his agent recommended that he *not* ϕ.
  (Potsdam 1997: 538)

As for this problem, we shall discuss it in detail later in Chapter 11.

7.9 Concluding Remarks

In this chapter I argued that the subjunctive present in Present-Day English is a type of covert modal, and that movement in subjunctive present clauses is the movement of the covert modal and thus the main verb itself remains in situ. Moreover, I showed that under the present proposal, we can naturally account for various characteristics of subjunctive present clauses, i.e. tense and three formal characteristics of subjunctive clauses, the non-cooccurrence of modals, the position of adverbs, Negative Inversion, contraction phenomena, and the impossibility of VP-deletion with *do*-support.[14]

Notes to Chapter 7

1. This chapter is mainly based on Nomura (2000b, 2004b), but I will modify some important points here.

    Nomura (2000b) is a revised version of a paper presented at the TACL meeting held at the University of Tokyo on October 9th, 1999. I have benefited from discussion with the participants, among whom were Heizo Nakajima and Ken-ichi Takami. I am also deeply indebted to Ken-ichi Takami, Shigeo Tonoike, and Kinsuke Hasegawa for their insightful and helpful comments on earlier versions of Nomura (2000b).

    Nomura (2004b) is a revised version of Nomura (2003b), a paper presented at Symposium, "Kateehoo o Megutte [Problems in the Subjunctive Mood]", 11th General Meeting of the Society of English Grammar and Usage, held at Kansai Gaidai University on October 25th, 2003. I have benefited from discussion with the other three panelists, Harumi Sawada, Sadao Ando, and Masayuki Higuchi, and the participants, among whom were Minoji Akimoto, Kyoko Asahara, Kenji Kashino, Yuzaburo Murata, Hiroki Tsuchiya, and Shiro Wada.

2. Note that Ando (1996, 2004) and Matsubara (1997a, b) conclude that I contains [+Tense], [+Agr], and [+Mood] as a feature complex:

    (i) IP

    Spec I'

    I VP

    $\begin{bmatrix} +\text{Tense} \\ +\text{Agreement} \\ +\text{Mood} \end{bmatrix}$

    (Matsubara 1997a: 71)

3. As for the idea that the [Subj] feature is percolated, see also Haegeman and Guéron (1999: 108).

4. As for the subjects of imperatives, see the appendix to this chapter below.

5. As for *that*-clauses as well, we can find archaic uses of *that* not selected by any elements.

(i) a. O *that* a rescue party might come soon!

b. *That* he should go back on me at the critical moment!

In other languages we can find many examples like this. As an illustration of this, consider the following example of *que* (=that) in French:

(ii) *Qu*'il reussisse!
    that he succeed
    'May he succeed!'

Moreover, Akira Watanabe (TEC lecture in 1999) pointed out similar phenomena with the Japanese complementizer *koto*, as illustrated in (iii):

(iii) Hayaku shigoto-o sumasu *koto*!
    at once work Acc finish that
    'Finish your work at once!'

6. However, as we discussed in note 9 in Chapter 6, modals in fact appear in subjunctive clauses, but I regard these examples as *indicative* cases, which I will put aside here, just as in the case of *do* in (36c) in chapter 6. As for this problem and many attested examples, see especially Chiba (1987: Section 2.4).

7. As for the quasi-subjunctive *should* (or *shall*), we shall discuss it in detail in Chapter 8.

8. The structure of Topicalization has been discussed in many studies (e.g. Culicover (1991)), but in this paper I assume TopP following Nakajima (1996).

9. D. L. Smith (personal communication, 2000) pointed out the following:

(i) "It is required that *with no job* he be happy" is a bit hard to take semantically. Better would be "It is required that with no *better* job he be happy," i.e., "he should accept things as they are".

10. However, naturally, Negative Inversion is possible if the quasi-subjunctive modal *should* exists in mandative subjunctive clauses:

(i) I demand that under no circumstances *should he* be arrested.

11. Note that even if the same word sequence is seen in *that*-complement clause selected by *insist*, the contraction can apply in the case of *indicative* clauses, as illustrated in (ia):

(i) a. She insists that $\left\{ \begin{array}{l} \textit{they've} \\ \textit{they have} \end{array} \right\}$ completed the job.
  b. I know that *they've* already left.
  c. We realize that *you've* been here before. (Selkirk 1980: 104-105)

12. Though, note that since *trace* has been abolished in Chomsky (2000, 2001a, b), it remains unknown whether explanations like those in (53) so far discussed should be reformulated in the present Minimalist framework. However, the evidence discussed here will not be lost.

13. Incidentally, Culicover (1971) notes that VP-deletion with *do*-support is sometimes seen, though not accepted by all speakers. Consider the following examples:

(i) a. John was able to play first violin, so I'm requesting that you *do*, too.
  b. Just as it's important that Harry see this film, so it's necessary that everyone else *do*, too.
  c. I order that everyone get out of the pool, and I demand that you *do*, too, Bobby Poobah. (Culicover 1971: 130, fn.12)

Since these examples would be far less acceptable if the subject were not *you*, he mentions that sentences semantically similar to imperative sentences using *do*-support might render these sentences acceptable.

14. Though the direction of studies in the treatment of periphrastic *do* and modals and VP-deletion in subjunctive present clauses is appropriate, I will change the assumptions of quasi-subjunctive modals, ordinary modals, and periphrastic *do* in a more appropriate way in the next chapter; see Section 8.3.

Appendix to Chapter 7

The Subjects of Imperative Sentences

In finite sentences in Present-Day English *root forms* are used not only in *subjunctive present clauses* but also in *imperative sentences*. Many linguists have been studying imperatives since the beginning of generative grammar, but we may say that a decisive conclusion has not been found because the exact formalization of imperatives is very difficult. As for the most cited studies of imperatives, see Lees (1964), Katz and Postal (1964), Hasegawa (1965), Culicover (1971, 1976), Ukaji (1978), Bolinger (1977), Imai and Nakajima (1978), Sawada (1983), Davies (1986), Tonoike (1989c), Pollock (1989), Zhang (1990), Arimoto (1994), Potsdam (1998), and Rupp (2003).

Indeed, the exact formalization of imperatives will not be discussed in this book, either, but if I were to consider some possibilities coherently, we could assume that the covert modal M_ϕ has the feature [uImp] just as in the cases of the subjunctive present. This means that imperative verbs are, in fact, not *finite forms* but *root forms* including the cases of *have* and *be*, and we have good reason to assume this. Consider the following examples.

(1) a. *Be not foolish.
 b. *Have not finished the homework before I come back.
(2) a. Never be there at five. (Lees 1964: 34)
 b.??Be never there at five. (Arimoto 1994: 264)
(3) a. Leave. I don't want to.
   cf. Mary left. I don't want to.
 b. Be quiet. I don't want to.
   cf. *Mary is quiet. I don't want to. (Lasnik 1999: 114)

Additionally, assuming the covert modal M_ϕ in imperative sentences, it naturally follows that there are no imperative sentences employing modals in English:

(4) a. *Must study hard.
 b. *Can swim very fast.

Imperative issues are very complex (including *do* and *don't* imperatives, inversion seen in imperatives, etc.), so I will leave them for future study, but here we need to mention the subjects of imperative sentences in the connection with note 4 in this chapter.

Based on (8e) in Chapter 7, I will assume that the covert imperative modal M_ϕ also has [uPres] just as ordinary modals or subjunctive covert modals. Note that, semantically speaking, imperatives cannot have [Past] tense. As an illustration of the assignment of Nominative Case in imperatives, consider the following examples:

(5) a. *Somebody* help me.
 b. *Somebody* please catch me.
 c. *Men* over 50 please stand up.
 d. *Those* applying for the job stand in this line. (Tonoike 1989c: 126)

It is certain that these NPs are *subjects* not *vocatives* judging from the following tests:

(6) Intonation
 a. Everybody ↘ behave yourselves. (Fall)
 b. Everybody, ↘↗ behave yourselves. (Fall-Rise)
(7) Co-occurrence of *you*
 You, you stand in the corner.
(8) Reflexive Pronoun
 a. Everybody behave yourselves/*themselves*.
 b. Everybody, behave yourselves/*themselves.

Furthermore, I will assume that [φ=2ndPerson, Sg or Pl Person]+[Imp(erative)]+[Pres] is realized as *pro* (as well as *you*) in the cases of unmarked imperative sentences. As for the possibility of the occurrence of *pro* in imperatives, see Tonoike (1989c).

(9) pro Stand up!

Incidentally, Radford (1997) argues for the possibility that the imperative subject remains in *v*P in Belfast English based on the data in Henry (1995). Consider the following examples in Belfast English:

(10) Unaccusative
 a. Go you to school!
 b. Run youse to the telephone!
 c. Walk you into the garden! (Radford 1997: 396)
(11) Unergative

    a. You read that book!   a'. *Read you that book!
    b. You protest!   b'. *Protest you!   (Radford 1997: 398)

If we assumed that imperative subjects also remain vP and thus do not raise to IP-Spec, we might assume that they are assigned some *default Case*, not *Nominative Case*. However, assuming (8e) in this chapter, we should think that the imperative subjects do not remain in vP-Spec but raise to IP-Spec, because they are assigned Nominative Case, not a default Case judging from the following examples:

(12) a. You stand by the door and *she/*her* watch the window!
     b. *He/*Him* who carries the machine gun step away from the car. (Rupp 2003: 25)

Though, it seems that the test of reflexive pronouns like in (8) implies both possibilities: overt subjects raise to IP-Spec, or *pro* exists in IP-Spec rather than any overt subject:

(13) a. [$_{IP}$ Everybody$_i$ behave [$_{vP}$ t$_i$ *themselves$_i$*]].
     b. [$_{IP}$ pro$_i$ [$_{vP}$ Everybody behave *yourselves$_i$*]].

So far I have shown some possibilities that have promise, but I will leave details relating to these problems for future study.

Chapter 8

On the Modal *Should* in Mandative Subjunctive Clauses[1]

8.1 Introduction

As is often said, the modal *should* appears in mandative subjunctive clauses especially in British English. Consider the following examples and statements:

(1) The employees have demanded
that the manager { resign (esp AmE) / *should* resign (esp BrE) / resigns } (Quirk *et al*. 1985: 157)

(2) It's a good thing that he *should* recognise his faults.
It's a good thing that he recognise his faults. (rare, archaic)
(Leech 1987[2]: 114)

(3) In formal British English, *should* can be used in *that*-clauses after adjectives and nouns expressing the importance of an action (e.g. *important, necessary, vital, essential, eager, anxious, concerned, wish*).
  It's important that she *should* talk to me when she gets here.
  Is it necessary that my uncle *should* be informed?
  I'm anxious that nobody *should* be hurt.
  It is his wish that the money *should* be given to charity.
This also happens after verbs expressing similar ideas, especially in sentences about the past.
  He insisted that the contrast *should* be read aloud.
  I recommended that she *should* reduce her expenditure.
(Swan 1995[2]: 518)

In this chapter I discuss various topics relating to quasi-subjunctive modals appearing in subjunctive present clauses.[2]

8.2 The Obligation Meaning of *Should* in Mandative Subjunctive Clauses

To begin with, let us consider the following question in (4), which is a delicate problem for many non-native speakers:

(4) Does the auxiliary *should* appearing in mandative subjunctive clauses have the *obligation* meaning?

To put it differently, which is appropriate as the Japanese translation of (5), (6a) or (6b)?

(5) His boss suggested that he *should* change his plan.
(6) a. Jooshi-wa kare-ni keekaku-o henkoosuru-koto-o teeanshi-ta.
       boss-Top him-Dat plan-Acc change-Comp-Acc suggest-Past
       'His boss suggested that he change his plan.'
   b. Jooshi-wa kare-ni keekaku-o henkoosu-bekida-to teeanshi-ta.
       boss-Top him-Dat plan-Acc change-should-Comp suggest-Past
       'His boss suggested that he ought to change his plan.'

The answer is that there is likely to be no implication of obligation when we consider that *suggest* selects mandative subjunctive clauses. Thus, the Japanese translation should be not (6b) but (6a).[3] To quote Leech (1987[2]) and Coates (1983):

(7) Where SHOULD functions as a pure quasi-subjunctive, it is semantically empty. (Coates 1983: 68)
(8) As one would expect from the above discussion, *that*-clauses with the Subjunctive may be converted into *that*-clauses with *should* without any change of meaning: *The Law-Lords have decided/decreed/insisted/voted that the existing law (should) be maintained.* In this sense, the *should* + Infinitive construction might be called, historically speaking, a 'subjunctive substitute'.
(Leech 1987[2]: 115, fn. c)

However, what is complex in this matter is that in the sentence (5) itself *should* might, nevertheless, carry the meaning of obligation when it is considered that *suggest* selects indicative clauses, as illustrated in the Japanese translation in (9):

(9) Jooshi-wa   kare-ni   keekaku-o   henkoosu-bekida-to   shisashi-ta.
    boss-Top   him-Dat   plan-Acc   change-should-Comp   imply-Past
    'His boss implied that he should change his plan.'

Our discussion above is also supported by Leech (1987²) and Coates (1983). Note that they argue that even native speakers sometimes have difficulty in deciding between (6a) and (7) in interpretation. To quote them again:

(10) 'Putative' *should* has to be carefully distinguished from *should*='ought to'; and yet in many instances it is difficult to tell from context which meaning is meant to apply. Does one interpret *They agree that the rules should be changed* as 'They agree that the rules should be changed' or 'They agree that the rules be changed'? In practice, there is little difference between these interpretations.   (Leech 1987²: 116, fn. d)

(11) Where SHOULD functions as a pure quasi-subjunctive, it is semantically empty. But in many contexts, where the preceding adjective or verb is not incompatible with the sense of weak obligation expressed by Root SHOULD, we have merger. That is, it is not clear which of the two uses the speaker/writer intended, as both are possible. However, comprehension is not affected since the two meanings are not mutually exclusive.

(83) *It is /… / essential that on this point the churches should learn from each other* (Lanc 2)
   (= 'it is essential that they learn …' (quasi-subjunctive)
   = 'they ought to learn' (Root))

(84) *I sug/gèsted# that ə that /they should#. put ((a))round /each 'carriage do̊or#əm-a /piece of beáding#* (S.1.9.23)
   (= 'I suggested that they put …' (quasi-subjunctive)
   = 'you ought to put a piece of beading around each door' (Root))
   Adjectives like *essential* and verbs such as *suggest* do not preclude Root meaning and therefore in such contexts the two meanings

co-exist. (Coates 1983: 68-69)

Moreover, such ambiguity is not necessarily seen in mandative subjunctive clauses. That is, such ambiguity is seen only when the words having the lexical property compatible with the obligation inference take *that*-clauses. Coates lists such predicates; she assigns * to them in the following list:

(12) *Adjectives etc. Preceding That-clauses with Quasi-subjunctive SHOULD in Samples*

Adjectives	Verbs	Nouns
appropriate	agree	basis
better	ask(2)	condition
distasteful	decide(3)	danger
*essential	*suggest	determination
expedient	think	idea
*fitting		notion
funny		*suggestion
*important		wish
ironical		
inevitable		
keen		
legitimate		
natural(2)		
*necessary(2)		
*right		
sad		
shameful		
understandable		
undesirable		

(Ibid.: 69)

As discussed above, we can conclude that the quasi-subjunctive *should* is semantically empty and thus does not imply obligation. In *that*-clauses selected by some predicates we can interpret the sense of obligation meaning in *should*, but we should regard such a use of *should* as an indicative use.[4]

8.3 The Syntactic Status of the Quasi-Subjunctive Modals

Taking the discussion above into consideration, I make the following assumption about the quasi-subjunctive modals including *should*:

(13) Only *should* (or *shall*) and *may* (or *might*) in subjunctive present clauses have the [uSubj] feature among overt modals. (Other overt modals can have only the [uInd] feature.)

Here I will submit further statement and examples in this use other than (1-3):

(14) In very formal (especially official and legalistic) texts *shall* is often used instead of *should*:
e.g. The council hasn't decided yet which firm *shall* build the bridge.
 The committee have agreed that the agenda *shall* be changed.
 I demand that the existing rules *shall* be observed.
This use of *shall* is only possible if the head clause is not one of the past tenses. (Declerck 1991a: 420)

(15) a. We hired a guide lest we *should*/(*might*) get lost in the jumble of alleys.
 b. Mr Rushdie decided to go into hiding lest he *should* be killed by a Muslim.
 c. He always bolts the door so that nobody *shall* enter. (archaic)
(Ibid.: 442)[5]

(16) EXCLAMATORY WISH (very rare)[6]
May he never set foot in this house again!
May God grant you happiness! (Leech 1987^2: 76)

Technically speaking, we could assume that these modals have the [uInd] feature just as ordinary modals, as was suggested by Shigeo Tonoike (personal communication, 1997) and Madoka Murakami (personal communication, 2002).

In that sense it would only be a *notational problem* as to which feature to assume, [uSubj] or [uInd]. However, in this book I am assuming that these modals alone can have the [uSubj] feature in that (i) they are formally inserted as *place-holder* modals and that (ii) they are *semantically empty*. In this connection, Watanabe (1993b) mentions the possibility that the periphrastic *do* is not a mere tense-bearer as assumed traditionally but a *substitute modal for the indicative mood*. Following him, I will assume the following auxiliaries to be *substitute modals for mood* in Present-Day English:

(17) a. [uInd, uTense, uφ] → do, does, did
　　b. [uImp, uPres, uφ] → do
　　c. [uSubj, uTense, uφ] → should (shall), may (might)

Assuming this, I should change the approach to explanation in Chapter 7, namely that periphrastic *do* does not appear ((16b) in Section 7.3), nor do ordinary modals (other than quasi-subjunctive modals) occur (Section 7.4), nor can VP-deletion with *do*-support apply (Section 7.8), and there are no imperative sentences employing modals in English (Appendix 7.1). I explained them all by using the following general principle:

(18) Modals do not co-occur. (See (31g) in Chapter 1.)

Instead, the phenomena discussed in Chapter 7 should be explained by the following properties in the lexicon in English:[7]

(19) a. *Do* having [uSubj] does not exist in the lexicon.
　　b. Modals having [uImp] do not exist in the lexicon.
　　c. Modals having [uSubj] do not exist in the lexicon except for the subjunctive substitute modals *should* (or *shall*) and *may* (or *might*)

Considering the whole system of mood in English, the explanations based on this revised assumption will be preferable and more appropriate, and thus the assumptions in (17) and (19) should be included in the conclusions reached in this book.[8]

8.4 Dialectal Variations

It is generally assumed that subjunctive present forms (i.e. root forms) are used in American English while the quasi-subjunctive *should* is used in British English. However, the facts are not so simple; first, both constructions are differently used according to *style* in American and British English. Moreover, the *feelings* towards the two constructions are also different in American and British English. Consider the following statements:

(20) <u>In Great Britain this use of the present subjunctive is considered "pedantic"</u>. Englishmen prefer to use the auxiliary *should*, as *I suggested he should take it with him*. In the United States the simple subjunctive is the form used most often in natural speech. <u>The construction with *should* appears, too, but is felt to be "bookish" or "British"</u>.
(Evans and Evans 1957: 484, underlines are mine)

(21) In general, the present subjunctive occurs more frequently in AmE than in BrE; <u>in BrE it occurs chiefly in formal style</u>.
(Quirk *et al.* 1985: 1013, underlines are mine)

(22) In (very) formal English (i.e. BrE), the present subjunctive can be used instead of *should*. (Declerck 1991a: 421, fn. 1)

Considering (20-22), we can sum up in the following way:

(23)

	American English	British English
the subjunctive forms	normal use	(very) formal style pedantic
quasi-subjunctive *should*	bookish "British"	normal use

Furthermore, many linguists point out that recently the uses of the present subjunctive forms have been increasing *even in British English* resulting from the influence of American English, as stated below:

(24) a. The mandative subjunctive is more characteristic of AmE than of BrE, where it is formal and rather legalistic in style. There are indications, however, that it is reestablishing itself in BrE, probably as a result of AmE influence. (Quirk *et al*. 1985: 157, underlines are mine)

b. The use of the present subjunctive seems to be increasing in BrE in *that*-clauses. There is a greater use of the subjunctive than the indicative if the agentive (perhaps implied) in *that*-clauses is shown to be willing to perform the action. Contrast:

The committee was impressed by the candidate, but recommended that she *reapply* when she had been awarded her PhD.

He was very *reluctant* to leave, but I recommended that he *went*.

But in both instances the usual form for BrE is the *should*-construction, here *should go*. (Ibid.: 1013, fn. [a], underlines are mine)

(25) Fowler (1965) states that this use [i.e. the subjunctive present forms] has appeared in newspapers, and Foster (1968: 212) points out that the younger generation novelists have come to like this usage.

(Wakatabe 1985: 133, translations are mine)

As for the *statistical study* of this problem, see especially Övergaard (1995), Haegeman (1986), and Asahara (1994, 1995, 1999, 2000, 2001). Övergaard (1995) discusses the mandative subjunctive constructions in American and British English in the 20th century (i.e. the 1900's, the 1920's, the 1940's, the 1960's, and 1990's) in detail. He reports that the uses of the subjunctive present forms have remarkably increased both in American English and in British English. Haegeman (1986) discusses the examples appearing in Survey of English Usage Corpus in Contemporary British English. Asahara (1994) discusses the frequency changes of the mandative subjunctive forms over the past three centuries. According to her, in American English modals were frequently used in the 18th and 19th centuries, but the uses of the present subjunctive forms increased gradually until at last in the 20th century the uses of the present subjunctive forms have become much greater than the modal uses. In British English modals were dominantly used and the uses of the present subjunctive forms were very rare in the 18th and 19th centuries, but the uses of the present subjunctive forms have been increasing gradually from the 20th century on.

In conclusion, though both the subjunctive present forms and the quasi-subjunctive *should* are used both in American English and in British English, the *style* and the *feelings* towards the two constructions are different in the two varieties. Despite this fact, we should notice the recent tendency where the uses of the subjunctive present forms have been increasing both in American English and in British English.

8.5 Quasi-Subjunctive *Should* and Emotional *Should*

First, consider the following examples:

(26) a. I'm surprised that your wife *should object*.
 b. I'm surprised that your wife *objects*. (Leech 1987[2]: 115)

Jespersen (1909-49: Part VII) calls the use of *should* as in (26a) 'emotional' *should*, Aijmer (1972) calls it 'emotive' *should*, Palmer (1987[2]) calls it 'evaluative' *should*, and Sawada (1998) uses the term SHOULD (=Emotion). Here I will use the term 'emotional' *should* following Jespersen.

Now Quirk *at al.* (1985), Leech (1987[2]), or Hosoe (1933) regard both the quasi-subjunctive *should* and emotional *should* as the same use; Quirk *et al.* and Leech call them 'putative' *should*, and Hosoe calls them 'disguised' subjunctive, but are the two types of *should* really identical? In this section I make the following assumption:

(27) The quasi-subjunctive *should* has the feature [uSubj] and is semantically empty, while emotional *should* has the feature [uInd] and expresses a somewhat vague emotional meaning.

First, emotional *should* cannot have the [uSubj] feature, because the subjunctive present forms cannot occur in *that*-clauses where emotional *should* occurs. Consider the following statements and examples:

(28) In this use [i.e. the use of emotional *should*], *should* cannot be replaced by the subjunctive.
   e.g. I was anxious that he should be well cared for. (*that he be ...)
   (Declerck 1991a: 422, fn. 2)
(29) Note, however, that the *should* construction is usable in many *that*-clauses where the Subjunctive is impossible: *It is interesting that the play should be a huge success.* The Subjunctive appears to be restricted to *that*-clauses expressing some element of wish or intention. (Leech 1987[2]: 115, fn. c)
(30) Sentences like these can also be constructed without *should*. <u>Subjunctives cannot be used.</u>
   It's astonishing that she *says/said* that sort of thing to you.
   (BUT NOT It's astonishing that she say ...)
   I was shocked that she *didn't* invite Phyllis.
   (Swan 1995[2]: 519, underlines are mine)

Second, as we discussed in Section 8.2, the mandative subjunctive construction and the quasi-subjunctive *should* construction are identical in meaning; both auxiliaries are *semantically empty*. However, emotional *should* has some kind of *emotional meaning* that the corresponding *indicative* sentences do not have. For example, Leech (1987[2]) argues that in (26a) it is the 'very idea of it' that surprises the speaker while in (26b) the speaker is surprised by the objection itself, which he takes to be a known 'fact'. Similar discussions are seen in Leech and Svartvik's (1994[2]: 114) or Declerck's (1991a: 422) distinction between *theoretic* and *putative*.[9]

Third, emotional *should* can express *past event* by selecting perfect infinitives as well as simple infinitives, but the subjunctive *should* cannot. Consider the following examples:

(31) a. I was surprised that he *should feel* lonely when he was in California.
   b. I was surprised that he *should have felt* lonely when he was in California.
   (Quirk *et al.* 1985: 1015)
(32) *He demanded that I *should have gone* there.[10]

In sum, we can conclude that the quasi-subjunctive *should* and emotional *should* are not identical in many respects.

8.6 *Should*-Deletion

Many linguists have considered the possibility that the subjunctive present is derived by *should*-deletion, as is noted in Chiba (1987: 68) quoted in (33):

(33) Note incidentally that based on a linguistic fact such as the one shown in (60) above, Kiparsky and Kiparsky (1970, p.171) proposed that "a future *should* is optionally deleted by a late rule, leaving a bare infinitive." For similar ideas of *should*-deletion in traditional grammar, see Visser (1966, pp.788-89; p.844) and Traugott (1972, p.180). (Chiba 1987: 68)

In this section, however, I point out that this proposal is rather problematic.[11] First of all, supposing that such a proposal as in (32) is correct, we should be able to make the assumption such as in (34):[12]

(34) Tense+*should* deletes freely in subjunctive present clauses. (Non-obligatory Transformation)[13]

(35) a. I command [that you Tns+should go there]. (D-structure)
　　b. I command [that you　　φ　　go there]. (S-structure 1)
　　c. I command [that you should　　go there]. (S-structure 2)

The crucial point is that *freely* in (34) implies that the presences of *should* does not change the grammaticality and the meaning of subjunctive sentences. However, there are many counter-examples; first, when the modal *should* appears in the following subjunctive present sentences, i.e. (36a) and (37a), the meaning of the resulting sentence (36b) is different from that of (36a), and the resulting sentence (37b) is totally ungrammatical:

(36) a.　God bless you!
　　　b. ??God *should* bless you! (not the same meaning)
(37) a.　Be it noted that this offer was made in good faith.
　　　b. *Should it be noted that this offer was made in good faith.

Next, as we discussed in Section 8.3, the modals used as an alternative to the subjunctive present are not only *should*; *shall*, *may*, and *might* are also used. In these cases we cannot possibly assume that *should* exists in the underlying structure. Observe the examples in (14-16) again:

(38) a. The council hasn't decided yet which firm *shall* build the bridge.
   b. The committee have agreed that the agenda *shall* be changed.
   c. I demand that the existing rules *shall* be observed.
(39) a. We hired a guide lest we *should*/(*might*) get lost in the jumble of alleys.
   b. Mr Rushdie decided to go into hiding lest he *should* be killed by a Muslim.
   c. He always bolts the door so that nobody *shall* enter. (archaic)
(40) a. *May* he never set foot in this house again!
   b. *May* God grant you happiness!

If we dared to assume a deletion rule, we should assume not only *should*-deletion but also *shall*-deletion, *may*-deletion, and *might*-deletion.

Third, historically speaking, the mandative subjunctive construction was not derived by the *should*-construction; the subjunctive present form already existed in the Old English period.[14] As an illustration of this, I quote examples of the mandative subjunctive in the Early Modern English period:

(41) a. I charge thee That thou *attend* me: (Shakespeare, *Tempest*, I. ii. 452-3)
   b. But I have prayed for thee, that thy faith *faile* not.
                                    (Authorized Version, Luke xxii. 32.)

Fourth, contrary to the second point, mandative subjunctive clauses with *should* are sometimes ungrammatical or less acceptable especially in American English. As for this problem, see especially Hojo (1971), Matsui (1981), and Chiba (1987: Section 4-4). Consider the following excerpts:

(42) For most speakers of American English, *should* in the embedded sentences after such verbs as *demand, order, recommend* is obligatorily deleted.
   (44a) *I demand that you *should* do the dishes.

(44b) I demand that you do the dishes.

(Hojo 1971: 103-104)

(43) a. I prefer that I not be asked to do the work.
  b. ?*I prefer that I *should* not be asked to do the work.
  c. I asked that Mary come here at once.
  d. ?*I asked that Mary *should* come here at once.
  e. Mary obeyed the command that she come here.
  f. ?*Mary obeyed the command that she *should* come here.
  g. It is crucial that the war between Iran and Iraq be settled.
  h. ?*It is crucial that the war between Iran and Iraq *should* be settled.

(Matsui 1981: 46-47)

(44) However, the reverse seems to be true with verbs such as *ask*, *order*, *request*, and *require*. That is, the sentence in (103), in which *should* appears, are unacceptable or less acceptable than those with the present subjunctive, for many of the nine American and Canadian informants who I consulted:

(103) *John { a) asked / b) ordered / c) requested / d) required } that Tom *should* leave immediately.

(Chiba 1987: 146)

Here I will quote an interesting result of informant checks that the Obunsha Dictionary Editorial Office Editors (1999) asked:

(45) QUESTION: Do you ever say or write, "I asked that she (should) go at once." to mean, "I asked her to go at once."? Yes/No
  a. American/Ed. D, M. A./40/NY
    No. [I would use the subjunctive with the verb *suggest*; e.g. "I suggested she go."]
  b. American/M. A./40/NW
    Yes. [But because the former is wordy, I would use the latter.]
  c. American/M. A., J. D./50/NY
    Yes [But without "should"]
  d. American/B. A./20/Ohio
    Yes [But without "should"]

e. American/B. A./20/NY
[But prescriptively incorrect]
f. American/Ph. D./UCLA
[Only as formal usage, probably written only. Without 'should.']
g. American/B. A./20/Hawaii
Yes [But not often]
h. British/M. A./60/London
No [Personally, I don't use this expression, but I don't find it offensive.]
i. British/B. A, M. A/40/ London
No [Never]
j. British/ Ph. D/40/London
Yes [I would probably write it rather than say it.]
k. British/B. A./20/North Eng.
Yes [Although I have read it more often than said or written it. I'd imagine that you'd find this sort of sentence in the works of Jane Austin, where...]
l. Canadian/B. A./Ottawa
No [But that's just me. I've read many times and it sounds fine.]
m. Australian/Tourism/20/Canberra
No

What is very interesting is that most of the Americans answered *No*, and that even the Americans who answered *Yes* said that *should* is unnecessary.

As discussed above, we can conclude that the subjunctive present constructions clearly cannot be derived by *should*-deletion. Even if we confined the proposal relating to the derivation of the mandative subjunctive constructions, they cannot be derived by *should*-deletion, *at least in American English*.[15]

8.7 Concluding Remarks

In this chapter I discussed the quasi-subjunctive *should* and related topics. After pointing out that the quasi-subjunctive *should* is semantically empty, I proposed that only the quasi-subjunctive modals *should*, *shall*, *may*, and *might* have the [uSubj] feature as placeholder auxiliaries. On the other hand, I assumed that emotional *should* is a modal having [uInd]. Moreover, I claimed that emotional *should* has some emotional meaning and thus the quasi-subjunctive *should* and emotional *should* are not identical. Last, though many linguists assume *should*-deletion in the derivation of subjunctive present clauses, I concluded from various facts that the subjunctive present cannot be derived by *should*-deletion, at least in American English.

Notes to Chapter 8

1. This chapter is partly based on Nomura (1999a)

2. Though Quirk *et al.* (1985) and Leech (1987[2]) use the *putative* (*should*), and Hosoe (1933) uses *Disguised Subjunctive*, I will use the term the *quasi-subjunctive* following Coates (1987) here. The reason will be discussed in Section 8.5.

3. In my feeling, the Japanese translation in (3a) itself is unacceptable, since *teeansuru* (=suggest) and *beki(da)* (=should) are not compatible:

    (i) ??Jooshi-wa   kare-ni   keekaku-o   henkoosu-bekida-to   teeanshi-ta.
        boss-Top   him-Dat   plan-Acc   change-should-Comp   suggest-Past
        'His boss suggested that he ought to change his plan.'

    Incidentally, Akira Watanabe (1999 in TEC lecture) showed the following classification:

    (ii) -yooni vs. -koto
        a. -yooni/*-koto
            iu (=say)
            simukeru (=induce, force, tempt)
            settokusuru (=persuade)
            unagasu (=urge, prompt)
        b. -yooni/-koto
            meejiru (=order)
            susumeru (=advice, recommend)
        c. *-yooni/-koto
            sentential subject
            e.g. Mainichi   tabako-o   suu-koto-wa   karada-ni warui.
                                        *suu-yooni-wa
                every day   cigarette-Acc   smoking-Comp-Top   body-for bad
                'It is bad for the health to smoke every day.'
            { teeansuru (=suggest, propose)
              booshisuru (=prevent)   } with lexical subjects
              kitaisuru (=expect) }

For subject and object control in Japanese, see further Watanabe (1996b).

4. Hiroki Tsuchiya (see also Tsuchiya (2003: Chapter 15)) asked me the following question at the presentation of Nomura (2003b):

   (i) I wonder if the root form (i.e. the subjunctive present form) and *should* are different in meaning. I think that the root form is a *distant* expression while *should* shows *empathy*. What do you think of this problem?

   The discussion in this section will be my answer.
   However, we should also note that when more than one form or expression can have one meaning (i.e. the same meaning intellectually), differentiation in meaning often occurs. As for this problem, see Bolinger (1977) and Tsuchiya (2003).

5. Also pay attention to Declerck's note:

   (i) The conjunction *lest* (which is very formal and has a negative meaning ('so that not', 'for fear that')) is usually followed by *should*, occasionally by *might*, <u>never by another auxiliary</u>.   (Declerck 1991a: 442, fn. 1, underlines are mine)

6. *May* is not used in mandative subjunctive clauses at least in Present-Day English, but in Pre-Modern English *may* was also used in mandative subjunctive clauses (see Nomura (2001b)):

   (ii) a. Here, father, take the shadow of this tree
           For your good host; pray that the right *may* thrive.
           (Shakespeare, *King Lear*, V. ii. 2)
       b. And, sir, to-night
           I do entreat that we *may* sup together.   (Shakespeare, *Othello*, IV. i. 262)

7. Interestingly, we can see placeholder auxiliaries in Old Japanese. As I noted in Tadao Nomura (2002c: 98, fn. 8)), Takashi Nomura (1995) argues that we cannot but regard the *mu*-type auxiliaries in "----*ka* ----*mu*" constructions in the *Man-yooshu* (the Nara Period) as the ones agreeing with *ka* in *Kakarimusubi* constructions. It is often said that the *mu*-type auxiliaries basically express *possibility* or *volition*, but he argues that the *mu*-type auxiliaries in "----*ka*----*mu*" constructions in the *Man-yooshuu*

are semantically empty. (Note in particular that English *should* normally expresses possibility or volitional obligation.)

Furthermore, Onoe (2001) claims that *mu* in <mizenkee (imperfective form) + *mu*> in Old Japanese is not an *auxiliary* having particular lexical meanings but a verbal *affix* of *mood* expressing irrealis or non-factive situations.

8. Though, considering note 9 in Chapter 6 carefully, we may assume that *do* has the [uSubj] feature for some speakers. Then we should modify (16) as follows:

   (i) a. [uInd, uTense, uφ] → do, does, did
   b. [uImp, uPres, uφ] → do
   c. [uSubj, uTense, uφ] → should (shall), may (might), *do (for some speakers)*

9. Note that Sawada (1998) argues that the distinction of *idea* vs. *fact* or *theoretic* and *putative* is insufficient and submits the following hypothesis:

   (i) Principle of Psychological Conflict
   SHOULD (=Emotion) expresses the psychological conflict between the propositional content presented as a topic and the assumption that the speaker holds. (Sawada 1998: 166-167, translations are mine)

10. A possible interpretation of (32) is that of the *back-shifted future perfect*, as stated below:

    (i) His demand was PAST [that I WILL HAVE GONE there (by a certain past time)].

11. As for other critiques of *should*-deletion in the present subjunctive clauses, see Hasegawa (1963, 2003), Araki *et al.* (1977: Section 5.1), and Chiba (1987: Section 4.4).

    Hasegawa (1963), whom I believed was the first to discuss the mandative subjunctive under the framework of transformational generative grammar, offers the following view:

    (i) First of all, I would like to mention the idea that this construction [i.e. not + subjunctive] is derived by *should*-deletion. We cannot find any syntactic supports that this construction is derived by the deletion of *should* or other modals from the diachronic viewpoint, and as we would have to restrict this syntactic analysis to American English (and we should do so because we can regard this construction as an "American usage"). Though we might find more or less evidence that *should* is deleted if this construction is compared to "British English" as a *different dialect*, it goes without saying that we could not account for the overall system of the language (or the dialect) if we dealt with different dialects together.

(Hasegawa 1963: 609, translations are mine)

12. In the following discussion in this section, we use the framework of the pre-Minimalist Model for the purpose of discussion only.

13. Even if we admit a transformational rule of deletion, the rule for deleting a specific lexical item *should* is very dubious in itself.

14. Incidentally, it is often said that modal auxiliaries developed as substitutes for the subjunctive mood in the history of English, but Ogawa (1989) discusses Old English modal verbs in detail and concludes that the facts are not so simple and thus the *substitution theory* is dubious.

15. Minoji Akimoto (personal communication, 1997) and Kazuo Nakazawa (personal communication, 1997) pointed out the possibility of *should*-deletion. We could assume *should*-deletion only in *mandative* subjunctive clauses in *British* English. Consider the following examples:

(i) a. I *asked* that I (*should*) be allowed to see her.
 b. I *demand* that John (*should*) go there at once!
 c. The officer *ordered* {that the men (*should*) fire the guns/that the guns (*should*) be fired}.
 d. I *recommend* that everyone (*should*) buy this dictionary.
 e. I *request* that he (*should*) leave.
 f. He *requires* that they (*should*) work all night.
 (From *Longman Dictionary of Contemporary English*,
 all quoted from Chiba (1987: 148))

Note that in *British* English *should* can occur in *that*-clauses even after *ask*, *demand*, *recommend*, *request*, or *require*.

Chapter 9

Tense in Subjunctive Present Clauses[1]

9.1 Introduction

One of the biggest issues about subjunctive present is whether subjunctive present clauses are tensed or not. As is well known, it is widely accepted in traditional grammar and many previous studies that subjunctive present clauses have no tense in Present-Day English. However, as I discussed in Chapter 7, I am assuming in this book that subjunctive present clauses, in fact, have *present tense*. In this chapter, after reviewing previous studies and pointing out their problems, I show that the present proposal is more appropriate from various viewpoints.

9.2 Previous Studies and Issues Raised (I)

9.2.1 Studies Where Aux (=Tns (Mod)) is Deleted or Lacking

Hasegawa (1963), who was the first, to my knowledge, to focus on the subjunctive present in the framework of transformational grammar, argues that Tns is deleted in subjunctive present clauses by a transformational rule. Consider his assumed transformational rule in (1) and the example in (2):

(1) $\left. \begin{array}{l} H + NP + Y \\ Nom\ (Pred)\ Tns + MV \end{array} \right\} \rightarrow H + that + Nom\ (Pred)\ MV + Y$

where NP = T + Nf = the + reason, etc.; H = Nom + Aux $\left(\begin{array}{l} V_{tac'} + P; \\ V_{tah} \end{array} \right)$

$V_{tac'}$ + P = insist on, etc.; V_{tah} = ask, command, demand, move, request, require, suggest, urge, etc. (Hasegawa 1963: 609)

(2) $\left. \begin{array}{l} \text{I insist on it} \\ \text{He not Pres smoke at home} \end{array} \right\} \rightarrow$ I insist on that he not smoke at home.

(Ibid.)

(According to Hasegawa, P(reposition) is deleted afterwards by a late obligatory transformation.)

Hasegawa (2003: 47-48) also concludes that Aux₁ (see (17) in chapter 4) is deleted in subjunctive clauses, as shown in (3):

(3) Aux₁ will be deleted where
$$\begin{pmatrix} X^0 \\ +\text{Subjunctive} \end{pmatrix} \text{ that NP (not) } [_{\text{Aux1}} \triangle] \, X$$
(X^0 = V, A, N. [+Subjunctive])   (Hasegawa 2003: 48)

As for a similar idea, Asakawa and Kamata (1986: 71) mention that the subjunctive lacks Aux (=Tense and Modal).

9.2.2 Studies Where INFL Is Lacking

Zanuttini (1991) argues that subjunctive present clauses lack an I projection and Sawada (1993, 1995) argues that subjunctive present clauses (as well as the infinitival clauses and participle constructions) lack INFL in IP, both of which are kind of notational variants shown in the previous section in Principles and Parameters Theory, since I(NFL) is generally assumed to contain both Tense and Modal.

9.2.3 Studies Where Subjunctive Is Assumed as a Disjunctive Category with Aux (=Tense and Modal)

A relatively large number of studies assume the syntactic category *Subj* or *SUBJ* is assumed as a disjunctive category with Tense and Modal. Note that these studies also assume that present subjunctive clauses have no tense.

Culicover (1971, 1976), who studied the subjunctive present extensively in the framework of generative grammar (cf. Hasegawa (1963)), assumes a category SUBJ which is *disjunctive* with Tense (Modal), as shown in (4a-c):

(4) a. one indicator of the subjunctive is the lack of tense and modal.
(Culicover 1976: 151)

b. To summarize, we can achieve considerable generalization in the grammar if we derive both the imperative and the subjunctive from an Aux-less structure. (Ibid.: 152)

c. $\text{Aux} \rightarrow \left\{ \begin{array}{l} \text{TENSE (M)} \\ \text{for-to} \\ \text{poss-ing} \\ \text{SUBJ} \end{array} \right\}$ (have+en) (be+ing)

(Culicover 1971: 34)

Ukaji (1978), who did an extensive study on imperative sentences in Early Modern English, assumes almost the same phrase structure as Culicover's, as shown in (5):

(5) a. Subj is assumed to be disjunctive with Tense M, not just with Tense alone, ... (Ukaji 1978: 38)
b. ..., we assume that the base component of the grammar of early Modern English had the phrase structure rules 2.11, ...
(2.11) 1) S → (Neg) (Emph) NP Aux VP (Place) (Time)
2) $\text{Aux} \rightarrow \left\{ \begin{array}{l} \text{Tense (M)} \\ \text{Subj} \end{array} \right\} \left(\left\{ \begin{array}{l} \text{have} \\ \text{be} \end{array} \right\} \text{-en} \right) (\text{be-ing})$
3) .... (Ibid.: 12)
c. The AUX of an imperative is analyzed as containing Subj(unctive) which is disjunctive with Tense M. (Ibid.)

As for other studies holding similar assumptions, see Araki *et al.* (1977: Section 5.1), Imai and Nakajima (1978: 421), Hayashi (1988: 200), Tonoike (1989c: 127), Arimura (1993: 80, fn. 15), etc. As an illustration, to quote Tonoike:

(6) I → $\begin{Bmatrix} \text{Present (Mod)} \\ \text{Past (Mod)} \\ \text{IMP} \\ \text{to} \\ \text{ing} \\ \text{SUBJ} \end{Bmatrix}$

(Tonoike 1989c: 127)

9.2.4 Problems with the Studies in Sections 9.2.1-9.2.3

As observed in the various studies in the previous subsections, we may say that the *intuitions* that some Aux elements are lacking in subjunctive present clauses are basically right, but I would like to point out some problems mainly from the present point of view: first, in the light of the *uniformity* of syntactic structures, we should assume the basic uniform syntactic structures as much as possible. Under the hypotheses described above, we could not but assume different structures for each sentence type, i.e. indicative, imperative, subjunctive, infinitives, etc.

Second, as Kuwabara (2001) argues, if the I-projection were lacking in subjunctive present clauses, sentential adverbs could not appear there since they appear within the I-projection, but in fact sentential adverbs can appear in subjunctive present clauses (see Chiba (1987) and Potsdam (1997, 1998)), as shown in (7):

(7) a. The guide urges that one *certainly* go to the local museum.
  b. The doctor proposed that the patient *probably* be examined a second time.
  c. My teacher insists that I *normally* work on my homework before bedtime.
(Potsdam 1998: 140)

Note here that sentential adverbs (e.g. *certainly*, *entirely*) cannot appear within VP unlike VP adverbs. Consider the following examples:

(8) Sentential Adverbs
  a. *George has been {certainly/probably} ruined by the tornado.
  b. *George is being {certainly/probably} trailed by the FBI.
(9) VP Adverbs

a. George has been {completely/entirely} ruined by the tornado.
b. George could have been {safely/effortlessly} rescued.

(Kuwabara 2001: 176)

Consequently, we can say that (7a, b) clearly show that an I-projection exists in subjunctive present clauses as well.

Third, a serious problem is raised with Case checking with the above assumptions. Observe the following example:

(10) I insisted that *he* leave at once.

This example clearly shows that the subject NP takes *Nominative* Case in subjunctive present clauses, but none of the studies mentioned above can explain this fact: under the general assumption in P & P Theory, Nominative Case could not be assigned or checked without a Tns or INFL element in subjunctive clauses.[2), 3)]

Fourth, considering the fact that quasi-subjunctive modals *should* (and *shall*) (see Chapter 8) or even ordinary modals can, in fact, appear in subjunctive present clauses (see note 9 in Chapter 6), there should be an allowance for a position for modals in these clauses. Furthermore, as we shall discuss in detail in Chapter 12, *have-be* raising applies in subjunctive present clauses; this fact will force us to allow for an INFL position as well.

9.3 Previous Studies and Issues Raised (II)
9.3.1 Studies Assuming Empty or Null Modal

Contrary to the studies discussed above, several linguists have assumed an *empty* or *null modal* in subjunctive present clauses, which standpoint is similar to the proposal in this book.

As I mentioned in note 3 in Chapter 1, Chomsky has hardly discussed subjunctives in English up to now, but he may be the first person to mention the possibility that the subjunctive present has tense. Consider the following comments:

(11) To purse the matter further, let us assume following in essentials, Bresnan (1970), that there is a universal element COMP and that the base system of English includes the rules in (16):

(16) a. S → COMP NP $\begin{Bmatrix} \text{T (M)} \\ \text{(for) -to} \\ \text{'s -ing} \end{Bmatrix}$ VP

b. .....

(Chomsky 1973=1977: 87)

(12) We may assume that <u>one realization of M is the element subjunctive</u> discussed in Culicover (1971) in his analysis of imperatives and related structures (and thus <u>subjunctives are assumed here to be tensed</u>).

(Ibid.=Chomsky (1977: 87, fn. 13), underlines are mine)

(13) For example, I have said nothing about <u>subjunctives</u>, a somewhat marginal construction in English that <u>behaves in the manner of tensed clauses with regard to binding, though there is no overt AGR element</u>.

(Chomsky (1981: 230, fn. 73), underlines are mine)

As for other studies assuming a null or empty modal in the subjunctive present, see Roberts (1985), Rizzi (1990), Haegeman (1986), Chiba (1987), Potsdam (1997, 1998), and Nomura (1999b, 2000b, 2004b). Though, note in particular that these studies, unlike mine, do not assume ModalP.

9.3.2 Studies Assuming Generalized IP Structures

As I discussed in detail in Chapter 1, we may say that Chomsky (1995, 2000, 2001a, b) assumes almost the same structure for IP as Chomsky's (1986) IP, since he has abolished the syntactic node Agr. In connection with the subjunctive present, as for studies assuming the normal IP structure, see Murakami (1995a, b, 1998, 2000, 2002), Chiba (1994), Ando (1996, 2003, 2004), Matsubara (1997a, b), etc. As an illustration of this, observe Matsubara's phrase structure again, mentioned in note 2 in Chapter 7:

(14)   IP
      / \
   Spec   I'
         / \
        I   VP

$\begin{bmatrix} +\text{Tense} \\ +\text{Agreement} \\ +\text{Mood} \end{bmatrix}$

(Matsubara 1997a: 71)

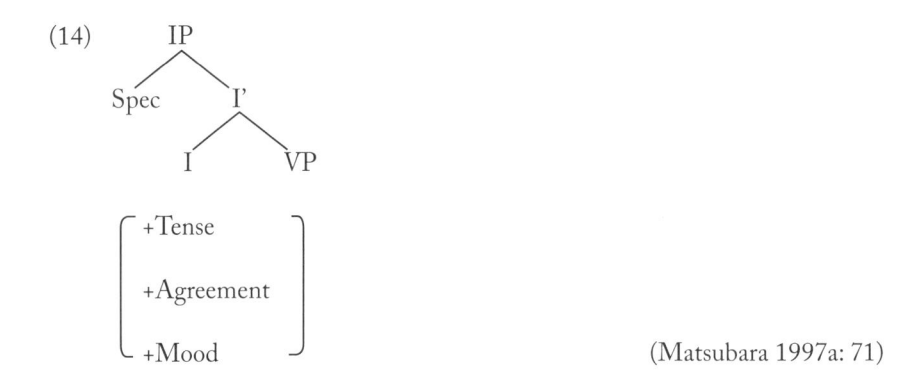

9.3.3 Problems with the Studies in Sections 9.3.1-9.3.2

The studies reviewed in Sections 9.3.1-9.3.2 make assumptions similar to our framework in a sense. However, since they do not assume anything like the ModalP Hypothesis proposed in this book, they do not provide adequate accounts for many syntactic phenomena discussed in the previous chapters; the problems with Modal Negation and Propositional Negation (Chapter 2), the position of *not* in infinitival clauses (Chapters 3-4), *ought to* and *be to* (Chapter 5), etc. Judging from these phenomena, we can conclude that AgrP, which is problematic both conceptually and empirically, should not be assumed in linguistic theory, but ModalP should be assumed as empirically required at least in Present-Day English.

9.4 Syntactic Supports for the Assertion That Subjunctive Clauses Have Tense

Taking the reviews in the previous sections into consideration, we will present syntactic support for the assertion that subjunctive present clauses in fact have tense. First of all, we should mention the three formal characteristics seen in subjunctive present clauses discussed in Chapters 6-7. To all appearances, these three formal characteristics might be taken as evidence that subjunctive present clauses have no tense; (i) The forms of the subjunctive verbs are always the root forms irrespective of matrix tense or the 3rd person singular present subject, (ii) there is no *do*-support, which has been thought of as a tense-bearer to support a stranded Tns in traditional transformational grammar, and (iii) in negative sentences of subjunctive present clauses the word order is <not + have/be>, and not <have/be + not>. However, as we discussed in Sections 7.3 and 8.3 (revised assumption), we can explain all three of the peculiar characteristics in mandative subjunctive clauses as shown in (15):

(15) a. Supposing that the mandative subjunctive is one type of covert modal, the form of the following verbs must, needless to say, be the root forms.
    b. Since the auxiliary *do* having the [uSubj] feature does not exist in the lexicon considering the whole system of mood and modals in English, *do* cannot appear in subjunctive present clauses. (In Present-Day English only *should* (*shall*) and *may* (*might*) exist as quasi-subjunctive modals in the lexicon.)
    c. Since the verb itself does not move, it follows that *not* and V remain in situ, so the word order will always be <not + V> in all the cases including with *be* and *have*.

Next, consider additional syntactic support for the assertion that subjunctive clauses have Tense. First, from the UG point of view, it is reasonable to assume that the subjunctive present has tense, because in the cases of French, German, Italian, Spanish, Rumanian, etc., and historically speaking Old English as well, the subjunctive has, without doubt, distant present tense forms. Observe the following examples from Old English:

(16) a. Ic *gebæd*   for þe þæt ðin geleafa ne *geteorige*
       I prayed (past) for you that your faith not fail (subj. pres)
       'I have prayed for you that your faith may not fail.'
                   (Luke 22, 32. (in *The Gospel according to Saint Luke.*))
    b. Ure hælend *lyfde*   þæt mann his life *gebeorge*
       Our saviour permitted (past) that man his life preserve (subj. pres)
       'Our Saviour permitted that a man should preserve his life.'
                   (*Ælfric's Lives of Saints* 138, 332) (Quoted from Visser (1966: 845))

Ando (2004) also claims that subjunctive present clauses are finite based on the cross linguistic facts. As an illustration, he submits the following examples from Spanish, as shown in (17a, b). (Note that *SB* means the *space builder* assumed in the Mental Space Theory (cf. Fauconnier (1997: 39).)

(17) a. *Exijo* que Juan   *parta* para Hawaii manana.
     [SB]   [SUBJ 3 Sing Pres]
     'I-demand that Juan leave for Hawaii tomorrow.'
   b. Exigi que Juan   *partiese* para Hawaii el dia siguiente.
     [SB]   [SUBJ 3 Sing Past]
     'I-demanded that Juan leave for Hawaii the following day.'
                                                       (Ando 2004: 31)

Indeed, these examples might not be direct evidence for the usage in Present-Day English, but they can be strong supporting evidence.

Second, subjunctive clauses can be considered to be tensed from the viewpoint of *Binding Theory*, as I quoted from Chomsky (1981) under (13) in this chapter. I will repeat this comment again as (18):

(18) … subjunctives, a somewhat marginal construction in English that behaves in the manner of tensed clauses with regard to binding, though there is no overt AGR element.   (Chomsky 1981: 230)

Considering this, observe the following examples:

(19) John_i demanded that Bill like himself*_i/j_.
(20) a. *I suggested that myself be invited.
    b. *They demanded that each other be released.
       (cf. They each demanded that the other be released.)
    c. He_i demanded that he_i be given the money.   (Haegeman 1986: 72)
(21) An American couple, both alcoholics, decided to split up, and
     { a) each of them insisted that the other } take responsibility
     { b) *they insisted that each other   }
     for their 14-year-old daughter.   (Chiba 1987: 79)

Third, as we have seen in (10), only Nominative Case appears in subjunctive present clauses (and tensed indicative sentences), not Genitive or Accusative Case:

(22) a. I demand [that *they/*them/*their* leave for Hawaii tomorrow].[4]
 b. I know [that *they/*them/*their* leave for Hawaii tomorrow].

(Radford 1988: 292)

This fact shows that subjunctive present clauses are tensed since Nominative Case is assigned in the IP-Spec position, that is, [+Nom] is licensed only if the sentence has tense, as we discussed in the previous chapters.

Fourth, in contrast to Nominative Case, PRO does not appear in subjunctive present clauses (and tensed indicative sentences):[5]

(23) a. *I knew [that PRO leaves for Hawaii tomorrow].
 b. *I demand [that PRO leave for Hawaii tomorrow].
 c. I intend [PRO to leave for Hawaii tomorrow].
 d. I intend [PRO leaving for Hawaii tomorrow].　　(Ibid.: 291)

Fifth, Chomsky (1973) claims that subjunctives also satisfy the *Tensed-S Condition* (TSC), which leads us to conclude that subjunctive present clauses have tense. The TSC is defined in Chomsky (1973) as follows:[6]

(24) No rule can involve X, Y in the structure
　　…X…[α…Y…]…, where α is a tensed sentence.　(Chomsky 1973=1977: 74)

For example, this condition explains the contrast between grammatical and ungrammatical sentences in (25):

(25) a. I believe the dog to be hungry.
 b. I believe (that) the dog is hungry.
 c. The dog$_i$ is believed [t$_i$ to be hungry].
 d. *The dog$_i$ is believed [t$_i$　is hungry].　　　(Ibid.: 88)

Additionally, Chomsky (1973) notes that the subjunctive present is also subject to the TSC, as shown in (26):

(26) For English, tensed sentences and subjunctive fall under α [i.e. α is the definition of the TSC in (24)].   (Chomsky (1973=1977: 176, fn. 22))

Considering this, observe the following examples:[7]

(27) a. Mary demands (that) Fred leave immediately.
    b. *Fred$_i$ is demanded (that) t$_i$ leave immediately (by Mary).
                                         (Culicover and Wexler 1977: 52)
(28) *John is demanded (that) leave immediately.   (Chiba 1994: 327)

In sum, there are many linguistic facts that lead us to conclude that subjunctive clauses are in fact tensed.

9.5 Tense or Agr?

Before giving our conclusion, here we should examine the possibility that subjunctive present clauses have *Agr* rather than *Tense*. As for this perdpectve, see Murakami (1995a, b, 1998, 2000, 2002) and Chiba (1994).[8] As an illustration of this, let us review Murakami's system. She submits the following table of the change of the verbal features (i.e. Tense, Agr, and Mood) in the history of English, where Agr is identified by the presence of morphological markers and Tense is identified by the presence of *do*-support:

(29) Feature Reinterpretation in English History
    Indicative: [+Tense, +Agr, +Mood] →[+Tense, +Agr, -Mood]
    Subjunctive: [+Tense, +Agr, +Mood] →[-Tense, +Agr, -Mood]
    Imperative: [+Tense, +Agr, +Mood] → [+Tense, -Agr, -Mood]
                                                (Murakami 2002: 167)

Then, following Raposo's (1987) Nominative Case checking system for Portuguese inflected infinitives, she assumes a Nominative Case checking system in subjunctive present clauses, where Agr is a dependent Case checker which *must be activated* by another head *under head-to-head adjacency*, as shown in (30):

(30) I asked [CP [C that] [IP he [I +Agr] take the medicine]].   Case checking
head-to-head activation (Ibid.)

She further assumes that if the complementizer *that* is missing as in (31) ungrammaticality results because the empty C breaks the chain of Agr activation upon head adjacency:

(31) I asked [C that/*ϕ] he take the medicine. (Ibid.)

Since the difference between our framework and hers comes from which Nominative Case checking we should take, we might say that her system is a notational variant in a sense, but here I would like to point out empirical problems with her Nominative Case checking system. First, as we discussed in the appendix to Chapter 6, we can easily find many examples where *that* is missing even in subjunctive present clauses, as shown in (32):

(32) a. Mary demands (that) Fred leave immediately. (=(27a))
 b. These analyses demand ϕ these higher predicates be transparent to deep structure constraints, assuming such constrains exist. (Newmeyer (1975), *English Aspectual Verbs*, p.33)   (Quoted from Chiba (1995: 25))

This means that the subject can be assigned Nominative Case even if the overt complementizer *that* does not exist in subjunctive present clauses.

Second, in connection with the first point, her system should not be able to check Nominative Case in optative sentences, as shown in (33):

(33) a. *God* Save the Queen!
 b. *Heaven* forbid that I should let my own parents suffer.
(Quirk *et al.* 1985: 157)

Note that the overt complementizer itself, which she assumes can activate Agr for

Nominative Case checking, cannot exist in these examples.[9]

Third, we should assume that the following constructions have at least some Infl or Agr element:

(34) Accusative Gerund
  a. [*Him* preparing dinner seldom] is good for her health.
  b. [*Him* not preparing dinner] is good for her health.
  (Ross 1973: 163)
  c. [*Him* having to sing the song] worried John very much.
  (Tonoike 1989b: 94)
  d. [Susan/?Her/*She solving the problem] would be a stroke of luck.
  (Culicover 1997: 48)

(35) Participle Construction
  Him having left, Mary left sad. (Bouchard 1982: 450)

(36) Small Clause
  a. [Susan/?Her/*She angry] is a terrible sight.
  b. [Susan/?Her/*She in the Vatican] made history. (Culicover 1997: 48)

These examples show that Nominative Case is not necessarily assigned even if Infl or Agr are present. In other words, the presence of Agr is not a *sufficient* condition albeit a *necessary* condition for assigning Nominative Case.

In conclusion, we can assume that the *sufficient* condition for assigning Nominative Case is the presence of Tense rather than Agr.[10), 11)] As for the claims that Nominative Case checking is crucially concerned with Tense, see further Tonoike (1999), Pesetsky and Torrego (2001), and Radford (2004).[12]

9.6 Concluding Remarks

In this chapter I discussed the role of tense in subjunctive present clauses. Though it is widely accepted in traditional grammar and many previous studies that subjunctive present clauses have no tense in Present-Day English, I claim that subjunctive present clauses do, in fact, have present tense. As for the three formal characteristics of the subjunctive present, I showed that based on the proposals in Chapter 7, we can adequately explain why subjunctive present clauses behave as if they had no tense.[13] Then I showed that there are many additional linguistic facts that force us to conclude that subjunctive present clauses are tensed. Additionally I showed that the assumption that Nominative Case checking is based on the presence of Agr rather than Tense is empirically problematic, and thus I conclude that the necessary condition for assigning Nominative Case is the presence of Tense.

Notes to Chapter 9

1. This chapter is partly based on Nomura (1999b, 2000b, 2004b).

2. Hasegawa (2003: 220) assumes that Nominative Case is assigned to the subject NP by its sister [+Finite] VP. Moreover, he mentions several times that Aux_1 is the marker showing that the sentence is [+Finite] (e.g. Hasegawa (2003: 44)). On the other hand, he also admits that subjunctive present clauses are [+Finite] in Hasegawa (2003: 220). However, as I pointed out in Nomura (2000c: 195), his claims are contradictory to his formalization of the present subjunctive, because Aux_1 should be deleted in subjunctive present clauses.

3. Though, note that Sawada (1995) (and Matsubara (1997a, b) and Ando (1996)) claims that Case checking is based not on *syntax* but reflects the speaker's *epistemological* attitude toward the world.

4. In this connection, we could consider this to be evidence that *that* appears as a complementizer, since *that* can select only tensed clauses:

    (i) a. I think that he is honest.
        b. *I think that him to be honest.
        c. *I think for him is honest.
    (ii) a. I demand that he be honest.
        b. *I demand that him to be honest.
        c. *I demand for him be honest.

    Though, we might give another account for these examples based on our framework discussed in the previous chapters.

5. Considering these facts, the subjunctive present in Present-Day English is considered to be an intermediate element between tensed clauses and infinitival clauses. As additional evidence for this from language variation, note that Terzi (1997) and Watanabe (1993a, b) mention that the PRO subject is allowed in subjunctive clauses in the Balkan languages. Note also that infinitival clauses in Portuguese take inflections (i.e. Agr) and Nominative subjects, as is discussed in Chomsky (1981). We can summarize the varieties found approximately as follows:

(i) "More" Tensed

↑ <finite-S>	...Nom	inflected	tensed
<*were* (past)-subjunctive>	...Nom	inflected	tensed
<the subjunctive present>	...Nom	no inflection	tensed
<Balkan subjunctive>	...PRO	inflected	no tensed
<infinitive in Portuguese>	...Nom	inflected	no tensed
↓ <infinitive>	...PRO, Acc.	no inflection	no tensed

"Less" Tensed

This is an interesting problem, but I will leave details relating to this problem for future study.

6. As for the status of the TSC, we shall discuss it again in the appendix to this chapter.

7. It can be assumed that (27b) and (28) are ungrammatical mainly because of the TSC, but other factors may also account for the ungrammaticality. Note that the acceptability in (27b) and (28) will be degraded regardless of the presence of *that*. First, consider the following sentence (ia) with the complementizer *that*:

(i) a. *Fred$_i$ is demanded *that* t$_i$ leave immediately (by Mary).
   b. *Who$_i$ do you think *that* t$_i$ saw John?

In this case the extraction of the embedded subject produces severe deviance, which is generally called the *that*-trace effect, though I will leave open how it can be reformalized in the Minimalist framework (see note 3 in Chapter 4).

Next, consider the example in (ii) without the complementizer *that*:

(ii) *Fred$_i$ is demanded t$_i$ leave immediately (by Mary).

In this case the sentence will be ungrammatical all the same, because the underlying structure itself is, generally speaking, unacceptable when the complementizer *that* is deleted. (As for this problem, see the appendix to Chapter 6). Consider the following example:

(iii) *Mary demands φ Fred leave immediately.

(Though, we should consider the fact that Culicover and Wilkins regard (iii) as grammatical because *that* is placed in parenthesis in (27a).)

Thus, it follows that the ungrammaticality (or unacceptability) of (27b) and (28) comes from several factors including the TSC.

Incidentally, Kinsuke Hasegawa (personal communication, 1999) also claims that the ungrammaticality of (27b) or (28) is caused by the TSC. However, his view is that subjunctive present clauses are not *tensed* but *finite* sentences (see note 2), so that the Tensed-S condition should be called the *Finite-S Condition* to include these subjunctive cases.

8. Note that Chiba (1987: 109) assumes the present subjunctive to be [+Tense, -Agr] but Chiba (1991) assumes it to be [-Tense, +Agr].

9. She could give an account for the following examples under her framework:

(i) a. *Suffice* it to say that we won.
    b. *Be* it noted that this offer was made in good faith. (Quirk *et al.* 1985: 157-158)

In these examples she might assume that the subjunctive verbs themselves move to C and thus C is activated.

However, note that in the cases of (33a, b) the subjunctive verbs do not move. See also the following ungrammatical sentences:

(ii) a. *Save God the queen! (cf. (33a))
     b. *Forbid Heaven that I should let my own parents suffer. (cf. (33b))

10. Our system should predict that the following constructions have Tense:

(i) Gerund
    He singing the song was a nuisance to his family. (cf. (31d))   (Tonoike 1989b: 94)
(ii) Absolute Nominative
    a. *He* waiting for her in the hall below, she had to find another way of leaving the hotel.
    b. *She* being the next of kin, she inherited everything. (Declerck 1991a: 462, fn. 4)

As for (i), I suspect that it is a marginal example where Nominative appears by analogy because *he* is in the *sentence initial position*. Pay attention to Culicover's judgment in

(34d). Additionally, consider the following example:

(iii) I can't imagine *he/his/him* singing the sonata.

As for (ii), I think it reasonable to assume Tense in these examples; this implies that participle constructions can have tense, judging from the fact that participle constructions are rather similar to (tensed) subordinate clauses.

Incidentally, Murakami might claim that Nominative Case is checked only by Agr in these examples, but even so, note that she could not give an adequate account for (34-36).

11. I think that Murakami's claim on V raising itself is interesting; she claims that overt V raising in European languages is crucially concerned with the morphology of mood rather than Agr.

12. Incidentally, note that Pesetsky and Torrego (2001) assume that C bears an uninterpretable T feature [uT], and that *that* is not a complementizer itself but an instance of T that has moved to C in order to delete the [uT] feature, as shown in (i):

(i) a. Mary thinks that Sue will buy the book.
    b. Mary expects (*sic*) [CP [T that]$_j$ + [C, u̶T̶][IP Sue will$_j$ buy the book]].
    (Pesetsky and Torrego 2001: 373)

Here if I were to adopt their type of approach, I would make the following assumption about the syntactic structure of mandative subjunctive clauses based on the ModalP Hypothesis (cf. Section 7.2):

(ii) C bears an uninterpretable subjunctive feature [uSubj], and *that* is not a complementizer itself but an instance of [Subj] (i.e. subjunctive mood) that has moved to C in order to delete the [uSubj] feature.

Given (ii), the underlying structure of a simple sentence of the mandative subjunctive (iii) will be as shown in (iv):

Chapter 9 Tense in Subjunctive Present Clauses 237

(iii) I insisted [$_{CP}$ that he not go there].

(iv)
```
         VP
        /  \
       V    CP
       |   /  \
   insisted C   IP
           |  /  \
      [uSubj] DP  I'
                 /  \
                I    NegP
              [Pres] / \
                    Adv  Neg'
                    |   /   \
                   not Neg   ModalP
                      [Neg] NE  /  \
                             Modal  vP
                              |    /  \
                              M_φ  DP  v'
                            [uPres] |  / \
                            [Subj]  he v   VP
                            [uφ]      [φ] / \
                            [uNeg]       go  there
```

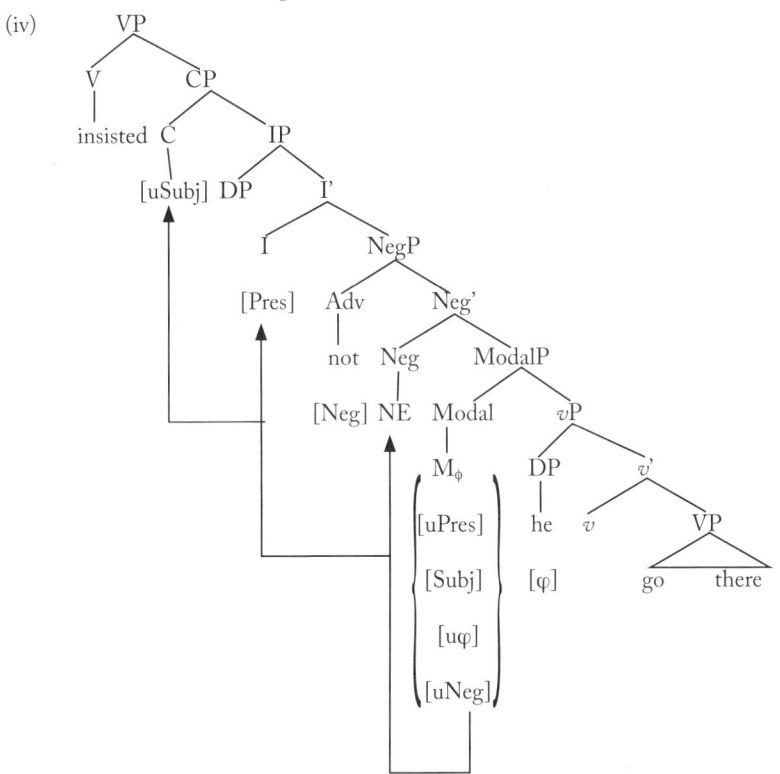

This means that the complementizer *that* introducing a subjunctive clause is a reflex of the covert modal M$_φ$ having the feature of subjunctive mood.

Furthermore, if I were to adopt Pesetsky and Torrego's type of approach about the structure of infinitival clauses as well, I would make the following similar assumption about the syntactic structure of infinitival clauses based on the ModalP Hypothesis (cf. Section 3.3):

(v) C bears an uninterpretable subjunctive feature [uIrrealis], and that *for* is not complementizer itself but an instance of [Irrealis] that has moved to C in order to delete the [uIrrealis] feature.

Given (v), the underlying structure of a simple sentence of the infinitival clause (vi) will be as shown in (vii):

(vi) John longed for Mary to come back.

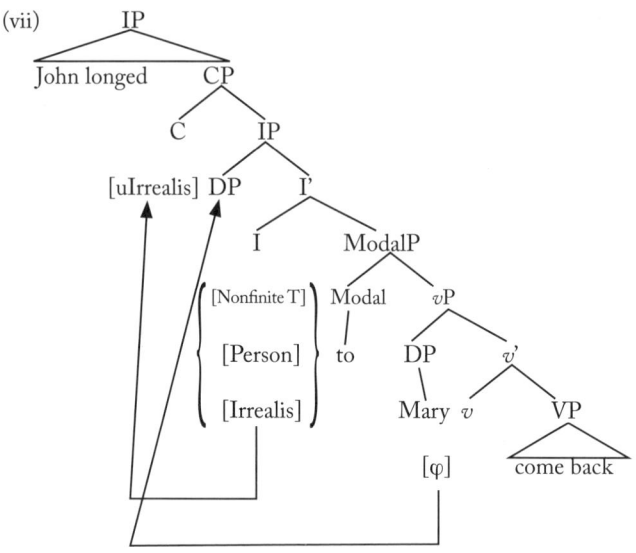

(vii) [tree diagram: IP dominating "John longed" and CP; CP dominating C [uIrrealis] and IP; IP dominating DP and I'; I' dominating I and ModalP; I containing {[Nonfinite T], [Person], [Irrealis]}; ModalP dominating Modal "to" and vP; vP dominating DP "Mary" and v'; DP with [φ]; v' dominating v and VP "come back"]

This means that the complementizer *for* introducing an infinitival clause is a reflex of the covert I having the uninterpretable feature of [uIrrealis].

It follows from the above discussion that C always indicates or is a reflex of the type of *force* or *mood*. Though the direction mentioned in this note is interesting indeed, I will leave it for future study.

13. Incidentally, for the first formal characteristic of the subjunctive present, i.e., the forms of the subjunctive verbs are always in the root forms irrespective of matrix tense or the 3rd person singular present subject, as shown in (i), I showed in this chapter that if we assume that the mandative subjunctive is one type of covert modal, the following verbs must be the root forms.

(i) a. John demands that Susan M$_\phi$ *leave* immediately.
    b. John demand<u>ed</u> that Susan M$_\phi$ *leave* immediately.

Considering the (ib) type of example, in particular, it is often claimed in school grammar and traditional grammar that there is no *sequencing of tenses* and no *backshifting of tense* in subjunctive clauses.

As for this claim, however, Shigeo Tonoike (personal communication, 2005) suggested the following:

(ii) M_ϕ in (ia) is a *present* tensed modal, and on the other hand, M_ϕ in (ib) is a *past* tensed modal. In other words, sequencing of tenses or backshifting of tense does, in fact, apply even in subjunctive clauses, just as in indicative finite clauses.

I agree with him in this respect. I am grateful to him for suggesting this idea.

Appendix to Chapter 9

A Note on Hasegawa's (2003) Tensed-S Condition

In Chapter 9 I crucially used the *Tensed-S Condition* (TSC) as support for the assertion that subjunctive present clauses have in fact Present Tense.

However, it is generally assumed that the TSC does not exist as an independent principle in the present form of generative theory; the TSC developed into the *Propositional Island Condition* or the *Nominative Island Condition* in Chomsky (1980). Furthermore, it is said that *Binding Principle (A)* includes the TSC in Binding Theory in Chomsky (1981). But, strictly speaking, the status of the TSC remains unknown in the Minimalist Program, because Chomsky implies several times after Chomsky (1995: Chapter 3) that Binding Theory is not a pure syntactic phenomena but should be treated as a substantial postcyclic interpretation rule in LF, as shown in (1):

(1) Operations lacking overt counterparts and apparently not interacting with CHL might be among the principles of interpretation of LF, hence "postcyclic," inspecting a representational level in the manner of many other systems (including binding theory, on the assumptions of MP). (Chomsky 2000: 144, fn. 44)

If this line of thought is on the right track, which I am not sure of now, then the TSC will be possibly reinterpreted as an independent syntactic condition in the Minimalist framework. In this appendix I briefly discuss the possibilities and problems with Hasegawa's (2003) TSC. This appendix is partly based on Nomura (2000c, 2005a).

Appendix 9.1 The Definitions of the TSC

As I discussed in note 10, the TSC is defined in Chomsky (1973) as follows:

(2) No rule can involve X, Y in the structure
...X...[$_\alpha$...Y...]..., where α is a tensed sentence. (Chomsky 1973=1977: 74)

As I noted above, Chomsky (1981) claimed that the TSC is not needed as an independent condition any longer because we can reduce it into *Binding Principle (A)*, but Hasegawa (2003) claims that there are some cases where we can account for ungrammaticality *only* with the TSC itself and thus the TSC should be maintained in the following form:

(3) Operations of a rule R on Y and A in:
...Y...[α...A...]...Y...
where α is the first Tensed S over A and A is not dominated by an NP in α
....DC 1 (DC = Degree of Complexity)
(Hasegawa 2003: 139, translations are his)

Appendix 9.2 Basic Supporting Data

Hasegawa submits many examples as evidence for the TSC, for which the grammaticality judgments are revealing as they can be directly explained by the TSC. Consider the following examples:

(4) *Tough*-construction
   a. It is hard [PRO to believe [that Mary loves John]].
   b. *John is hard [PRO to believe [that Mary loves _]]?
      cf. Who did Bill say it's hard to believe that Mary loves _]]? (Hasegawa 2003: 30)
(5) Reflexive Pronouns as the Subject
   a. John believes [himself to be a genius].
   b. *John believes [(that) himself is a genius].   (Ibid.: 158)
(6) Reflexive Pronouns in the Picture Nouns
   *These pictures of himself show [that Snoopy is an excellent pilot].   (Ibid.: 168)
   cf. These pictures of himself show [Snoopy to be an excellent pilot].
(7) The Complex NP Constraint Violation
   a. *Who did John deny [$_{NP}$ the rumor [$_S$ that he had dated _]]?
   b. Bush must do two things that he showed [$_{NP}$ no inclination [$_S$ PRO to do _]] during the campaign.
   c. a negotiated settlement which the opposition forces expressed [$_{NP}$ desire [$_S$ PRO to take part in _]] during the campaign.
   d. Which race did John see [$_{NP}$ a chance [$_S$ for us to win _]]?   (Ibid.: 186)

(8) Extraction from Adjunct
   a. * Who did John accept the job (so) [s that he might please _]]?
   b. * Who did he get so angry [s that he fired _]]?
   c. * Who was he so exhausted [s that he couldn't speak to _]]?
   d. What did he go all the way to Brazil [s PRO to buy _]]?
   e. a man whom Israel moved heaven and earth [s PRO to get _ out of jail]]
   f. It's the children that we are staying home [s PRO to take care of _] that are going to be tomorrow's leaders.
   g. the working-class benefits they (=socialists) fought so long [s PRO to achieve _]]

   (Ibid.: 188-189)

It can be concluded that the difference in grammaticality among these sentences depends on whether the complement sentences have tense or not. Thus Hasegawa claims that the TSC operates is in some syntactic analyses and is needed as an independent condition.

Appendix 9.3 Comparison between the TSC and the Extraction from NP

In Hasegawa's bounding theory he claims that the following type of sentences should be ruled out due to *DC* (=Degree of Complexity) 2 because of the two NPs from which something is extracted:

(9) *Who did they hear [NP some funny stories about [NP picture of _]]?   (Ibid. 192)

However, his system counts the TSC *only once* as DC no matter how many times the Tensed-S appears, as is shown by definition in (3). I think it inconsistent to differentiate the two cases in applying the TSC and the extraction from NP, but I do not know why he assumes so. As an illustration of this, consider the following example of *unbounded wh*-movement:

(10) What [s1 do you think that [s2 John believes that [s3 Tom bought ___]]]?

Needless to say, Hasegawa does not count DC 3 in (10), which should cause the full ungrammaticality in his theory. Note here that he does not assume *successive-cyclic* movement but assume that *what* moves straightforwardly to the sentential-initial position from the in-situ position (see also Hasegawa (1981, 2001, 2002, 2003)).

In this connection, Hasegawa (1981) criticizes Chomsky's (1973) definition of TSC by arguing that (c) and (d) in (11) are only *ad hoc* conditions:

(11) No rule can involve X and Y (X superior to Y) in the structure
$\ldots X \ldots [_\alpha \ldots Z \ldots -WYV \ldots] \ldots$
where (a) Z is specified subject of WVV
or (b) α is a subject phrase properly containing MMC(Y) and Y is subjacent to X
or (c) Y is in Comp and X is not in Comp
(d) Y is not in Comp and α is a Tensed S.

(Chomsky 1973=1977a: 112)

However, it appears to me that Hasegawa's (2003) TSC definition has practically the same problem he criticized Chomsky for in Hasegawa (1981).

Appendix 9.4 Extraction of *Wh*-phrase from Tensed-S vs. Non-tensed-S

As I discussed in note 4 in Chapter 3, Hasegawa's system predicts that the following (12b) is ruled out by DC 2, i.e. the TSC and the *wh*-island constraint as a subtype of GAoA (=the *Generalized A-over-A Principle*):

(12) a. ? Which books did he want to know where *to* put _ _?
b. * Which books did he want to know where Mary put _ _?

(Hasegawa 2001: 136)

However, as I noted in note 4 in chapter 3, Tonoike (2001) gives the following example (13), as more acceptable than (12b), where the complement *wh*-clause is tensed:

(13) Which books did he want to know where he should put?   (Tonoike 2001: 3)

Considering (12a, b) and (13), Tonoike indicates that the ungrammaticality of (12b) is concerned with *presumed finiteness*. If his line of thought is on the right track, we could give other accounts for the grammaticality seen in *wh*-movement.

However, as I pointed out in the note, we can explore the possibility that the modal *should* is less tensed than the other modals in finite sentences, i.e., is similar to the infinitival marker *to* in terms of a lack of finite tense. Moreover, we should reconsider whether or not Hasegawa's many examples in (7-8) can be explained in terms of the concept of presumed finiteness that Tonoike pointed out. We will leave these problems for future study.

Appendix 9.5 Reflexive Pronouns as the Subject in Tensed-S

We may say that in Binding Theory the grammaticality in (5b) has been an issue:

(14) a. John believes [himself to be a genius]. (=(5a))
　　b.*John believes [(that) himself is a genius]. (=(5b))

As I discussed in Nomura (2000c, 2005a), at present, Chomsky does not have any way to account for the ungrammaticality in (14b) in a principled way; since Chomsky (1986a) proposed the idea of *CFC* (=Complete Functional Complex), his system wrongly predicts that (14b) is grammatical because the *governing category* will be *the whole sentence* by definition, unlike the definition of the governing category in Chomsky (1981). Consequently, Chomsky (1986a) and Chomsky and Lasnik (1993) took the strategy based on the ECP, as shown in (15):

(15) *John self+I believe [$_{CP}$ [$_{IP}$ (that) t is a genius]].

Assuming the LF movement of reflexive pronouns, they claimed that (15) should be ruled out since the trace t cannot be properly governed in any way; it was assumed in GB Theory that (i) I (=Agr) in the complement clause governs the subject but cannot *properly* govern it, (ii) the complementizer *that* cannot govern the subject whether it is overt or not, and (iii) the matrix verb *believes* cannot govern t across CP and IP. However, now that *government*, *binding*, and *trace* are all eliminated in the Minimalist Program, this explanation itself cannot hold, either. In that sense I think that Hasegawa's simple explanation by the TSC is well worth reconsidering.

However, I would like to point out an even simpler possibility as follows:

(16) English reflexive pronouns do not have Nominative Case lexically.

This is supported by the fact that *each other* is not so bad as reflexive pronouns even when it occurs in the same subject position of Tensed-S. To quote Culicover (1997):

(17) In the text it was noted that the following sentences are not equivalent in acceptability.

(1) a.*John believes (that) herself is intelligent.
   b.*John and Susan believe (that) each other is intelligent.
Sentence (1b) is not as bad as (1a).
Along with these judgments we have the following, shared by many speakers.
(2) a. [John and Susan]$_i$ were wondering exactly what each other$_i$ was going to do when the balloon hit the ground.
   b. [John and Susan]$_i$ were extremely concerned about what was going to happen to each other$_i$ when the balloon hit the ground.
   c. [John and Susan]$_i$ were extremely concerned about the dangers that each other$_i$ was facing.
   d.?[John and Susan]$_i$ were amazed at what each other$_i$ was wearing to the beach.
(Culicover 1997: 86-87)

Though, I must add the following comment as well he made.

(18) Nevertheless, there are some cases that seem to be completely impossible:
   (3) a.*[John and Susan]$_i$ were wondering what you said to each other$_i$.
      b.*[John and Susan]$_i$ were extremely concerned about what you did to each other$_i$. (Ibid.: 87)

Appendix 9.6 Reflexive Pronoun Interpretations in the Picture Nouns

In Hasegawa's theory the presence of examples like (19b) is very crucial:

(19) a. * These pictures of himself show [that Snoopy is an excellent pilot].
    b. These pictures of himself show [Snoopy to be an excellent pilot].

Here I would like to add several comments about this example. I am much obliged to D. L. Smith (personal communication, 2001) for his crucial comments. First, according to him, *prove* is better than *show*. Indeed, Hasegawa (1983) submitted the following examples where *prove* is used:

(20) a. * This picture of himself *proves* [that John is a football player].
(Culicover 1976: 271)
    b. This picture of himself *proves* John to be a football player.
(Hasegawa 1983: 103)

Next, D. L. Smith judged *himself* to be better than *him*:

(21) a. *This picture of *him* proves John to be a football player.
 b. This picture of *himself* proves John to be a football player.

Third, importantly enough, he pointed out that the picture must be taken by *John* himself in order for (21b) to be acceptable. (As for related problems, see Smith (1981). See also Kuno (1987) and Kuno and Takami (1993).) If this is the case, the following (22) can be assumed to exist behind (21b):

(22) This picture of himself *that he took* proves John to be a football player.

This also implies that we can assume the presence of PRO in the front of the subject NP, as shown in (23):

(23) [PRO$_i$ This picture of *himself*] proves John$_i$ to be a football player.

If this is on the right track, it will follow that *himself* is not *directly* coindexed to *John* but PRO is coindexed to *John*. Note also that Hasegawa himself assumes PRO in gerunds, as shown in (24a,b):

(24) a. *[PRO contradicting himself] will prove [that Mr. Jones is a liar].
 b. [PRO contradicting himself] will prove Mr. Jones to be a liar.
 (Hasegawa (2003: 168), quoted from Bresnan (1982))

Of course, a more detailed formalization is needed, but I think that this direction, assuming PRO in the picture nouns, is well worth exploring.

Appendix 9.7 Language Universals

I consider that the TSC is well motivated in English, but what about other languages? In connection with the types of the subjunctive expressions discussed in this book, consider the following examples of subjunctives from other languages:

(25) Jon$_i$ segir (subj) að Maria telji (subj) að Haralldur vilji (subj) að Billi heimsæki (subj) sig$_i$.
 'John$_i$ says (subj) that Mary believes (subj) that Harold wants (subj) that Bill visits

(subj) himself$_i$.'   (Mailing 1984: 213)
(26) Toti baietii$_i$ s-au nimerit (*ca) t$_i$ sa fie bolnavi.
  'All the boys$_i$ refl-have (pl) happened (*that) t$_i$ be (subj) sick.'
  (Grous and Horvath 1984: 351)

(25) is an example from Icelandic where the *Long Distance Binding* is seen in subjunctive clauses. (26) is an example from Rumanian where NP-movement applies *across the complement Tensed-S* for Nominative Case checking. Hasegawa's TSC should predict that both (25) and (26) are grammatical, but this is not the case. If we took Hasegawa's theory literally, we should also assume the *Mood-S Condition* as well as the TSC. (As for other attempts to solve this problem, see Progovac (1993), who deals with reflexive pronouns by assuming two types of reflexive pronouns, i.e. the XP type and the X^0 type reflexive pronouns, and Watanabe (1993b), who propopses a *Layered Case Theory*.)

Appendix 9.8 Concluding Remarks

In this appendix I discussed the possibilities and problems with Hasegawa's (2003) Tensed-S Condition very briefly. We will leave it for future study whether this interesting condition is really needed as an independent condition in grammar.

Chapter 10

On Lexical Items Requiring a Subjunctive Present Clause[1]

10.1 Introduction

In this chapter I discuss the problem as to what lexical items can select a subjunctive present clause. I gave the full lists of the subjunctive-taking predicates that Chiba (1987) studied in Chapter 6. I will list them again as (1-3).

(1) Subjunctive-Taking Verbs
  accept, adjure, advise, advocate, agree, allow, approve, argue, arrange, ascertain, ask, authorize, beg, beseech, bid, care, cause, caution, challenge, choose, claim, command, concede, consent, consider, contract, contrive, counsel, crave, cry out, decide, declare, decree, deduce, demand, desire, destine, determine, dictate, direct, disapprove, emphasize, enact, encourage, enjoin, ensure, entail, enter, entreat, envisage, exhort, expect, favor, fix, forbid, gesture, grant, guarantee, had better, had rather, hint, hope, implore, indicate, insist, instruct, insure, intend, intimate, involve, lay down, look to it, maintain, manage, mandate, matter, motion, move, necessitate, need, occasion, offer, opine, opt, ordain, order, permit, petition, plan, plead, pledge, postulate, pray, preclude, predestine, prefer, premise, prescribe, presuppose, pronounce, propose, provide, recommend, request, require, resolve, rule, sanction, say, scheme, second, see (to it), see fit, settle, specify, state, stipulate, submit, suffer, suffice, suggest, support, take care, understand, urge, vote, want, warn, warrant, will, wish, would rather, write   (Chiba 1987: 3)

(2) Subjunctive-Taking Adjectives
  fitting, fortunate, good, ideal, impatient, imperative, impolite, important, impossible, inadvisable, inappropriate, inconvenient, inevitable, insistent, interested, logical, mandatory, necessary, needful, normal, obligatory, opportune, optimal, politic, preferable, proper, relevant, right, satisfactory,

sufficient, unnatural, unnecessary, urgent, usual, vital, willing, wise (Ibid.: 3-4)
(3) Subjunctive-Taking Nouns
advantage, advice, alternative, appeal, arrangement, assumption, call, challenge, check, claim, command, concern, conclusion, condition, constraint, contention, control, convention, criterion, decision, demand, desideratum, desire, determination, dictum, edict, expectation, hope, hypothesis, idea, (of) importance, innovation, insistence, instruction, intention, (in) interest, (in) nature, necessity, objective, order, plea, point, possibility, prayer, preference, prerequisite, principle, property, proposal, recommendation, regulation, (of) relevance, request, requirement, restriction, rule, ruling, sacrilege, solution, specification, suggestion, (high) time, tenet, understanding, view, wish

(Ibid.: 4)

However, as Chiba (1991) discussed in detail, the problem as to determing what lexical items require a subjunctive present clause is in fact very complex. In this chapter I will attempt to solve this problem.

10.2 Chiba (1991)

Chiba (1991) is the most important study on this question. He observes many examples of matrix verbs that are not properly c-commanded by the element requiring the [+Subj] feature semantically. For example, (4a) is normally considered ungrammatical because *write* is not a verb which requires a subjunctive clause, but even this sentence is acceptable if it is given a proper context and modifier, as shown in (4b). Note in particular that the adverbial modifier *in her will*, which makes (4b) very natural, is not a *complement* but an *adjunct*:

(4) the relevance of adverbial modifiers
    a. ?The widow *wrote* that Ball *be* given part of her property.
    b. Ball is arrested for the murder of a rich widow. The widow wrote *in her will* that Ball *be* given part of her property. (Chiba 1991: 26)[2)]

He further gives examples where not only adverbial modifiers (i.e. adjuncts) but also *subjects, modals, coalescence of two verbs, whole NPs*, etc. are relevant to the acceptability of subjunctive sentences. Consider the following examples:

(5) the relevance of subjects
   a. ?John *says* that the one who wears the ring *be* offered as a sacrifice.
   b. (The Beatles are pursued by a mysterious Eastern religious sect because of the ring Ringo Star wears.) *The law of the religion says* that the one who wears the ring *be* offered as a sacrifice. (Ibid.: 24)
(6) the relevance of modals
   a. *It *was recognized* that a number of critical meteorological parameters *be* met for an aerosol to exhibit optimum effect.
   b. In considering BW defense, it *must be recognized* that a number of critical meteorological parameters *be* met for an aerosol to exhibit optimum effect. (Ibid.: 29)
(7) coalescence of two verbs
   a. *Bill *brought it about that* Harry *go* or *be* allowed to go.
   b. *Bill will *bring it about that* Harry *go* or *be* allowed to go.
   c. I {am asking / ordered} Bill to bring it about that Harry *go* or *be* allowed to go. (Ibid.: 30)
(8) the relevance of the whole NP
   a It is [a matter of some *disappointment* to me] that still many of my own countrymen {*be/are} too shortsighted to ascribe any symbolic significance to the plight of a minority, such as artists, in any social order.
   b. It is [a matter of prime *importance*] that these elements be defined relatively to the other elements and to the interrelations among all of them. (Ibid.: 32)

After attempting to solve some cases by proposing *feature transfer*, Chiba treats and discusses these examples in detail as a problem of *non-localizable contextual features* discussed in Kajita (1976, 1977).

10.3 Konno (2002)

Konno (2002) claims that subjunctive present clauses are licensed not by *syntactic* conditions but by *semantic* and *pragmatic* conditions. As an illustration of this, he argues that (9b) can be explained by Chiba's (1991) mechanism of feature transfer in (10), but that (11a-d) cannot be explained in the same way because the licensing elements are *across* the subjunctive present clauses or outside the sentences themselves:

(9) a. *We add that the selection procedure be psychologically plausible.
   b. We add *to this requirement* that the selection procedure be psychologically plausible. (Chiba 1991: 27)

(10) We add to this requirement that the selection procedure be psychologically plausible.
 [+Subj]

(11) a. I'm *demanding* something. It's that you *be/*are* there on time.
(Jacobson 1992: 288)
   b. The entrance *condition*, which I would like to call the entrance "burden," imposed by the university consists of two requirements. One is that every candidate turn in three papers by the end of January. The other is that the three papers *be* concerned with syntax, semantics and phonology, respectively.
   c. We established *requirements* for the Ph.D. candidacy. Afterwards, we added that candidacy *be* limited to those students who have completed papers in all three of the main areas — syntax, semantics and phonology.
   d. A: What's written in Mr. Arai's *will*?
      B: That his wife *be* given all of his property. (Konno 2002: 43)

Konno then proposes the following semantic and pragmatic condition:

(12) *Uttaekake no Jooken* (=The Condition of an (Underlying) Appeal)
    Present subjunctives in Present-Day English must contain an underlying *appeal* of some sort. (Konno 2002: 44, translations are mine)

He explains that the most important point is "demanding that some event will be realized" in licensing the subjunctive present and thus uses the term appeal to express the point. Additionally, he argues that this *Condition of an Underlying Appeal* can explain not only the non-localizable examples above but also the *optative sentences* and what he calls *if you be constructions*, as shown in (13) and (14):

(13) a. God save the Queen.
  b. God bless America.
  c. God damn you.
  d. "God rot you to hell," said Finn and vomited. (Ibid.: 46)
(14) a. If you be nice, I'll give you a big kiss.
  b. If you be a good girl, I'll give you a piece of candy.
  c. If you never be naughty again, I won't tell your father that you broke the vase. (Ibid.)

He concludes that his *semantic* or *pragmatic condition* is more comprehensive than *syntactic explanations*.

10.4 Problems with Konno (2002)

Despite the discussion in the previous section, I claim that Konno's (2002) explanation is insufficient. First of all, as both Madoka Murakami and I pointed out at his presentation, the following examples in (15) are not concerned with his Condition of an Underlying Appeal at all. We should notice that *complementizers* license subjunctive present clauses in these examples:

(15) a. *If* any person be found guilty, he shall have the right of appeal.
    (Quirk *et al.* 1985: 1112)
  b. The President must reject this proposal, *lest* it cause strife and violence.
    (Ibid.: 158) (Quoted from Konno (2002: 47))

Though, Konno claims that these examples are *literary* expressions and do not reflect the semantic features of the subjunctive present in Present-Day English and thus should be excluded from his explanations. He claims, as supporting evidence, that the following examples are inappropriate in *colloquial* speech in Present-Day English:

(17) a. #If it *rain* tomorrow, I won't go to school.
   b. #Taro will not go on if his effort not *be* rewarded.   (Konno 2002: 46)
(18) #Take an umbrella with you, lest it *rain*.   (Ibid.: 47)

However, this argument is also flawed; we can easily find many *attested examples* where subjunctive present forms are allowed in Present-Day English. Observe Chiba's (1987) examples:

(19) a. But *if* that *be* the case, then how could these highly abstract principles possibly be learned inductively? (Newmeyer (1980), *Linguistic Theory in America*, p. 42)
   b. But all of the assumptions (3)-(5) are moot (to say the least), and *if* any one of them *be* not accepted, C's argument for the necessary correctness of (1) falls through. (*Lingua* 50 (1980), p. 126)
   c. If the air flow is of sufficient magnitude, voicing will set in, *provided* only that the vocal cords not *be* held as widely apart as they are in breathing or in whispering. (Chomsky and Halle (1968), *The Sound Pattern of English*, pp. 326-27)
   d. Moreover, *even if* it *be* granted that the indexing of question words is necessary, there is not a priori reason to accord OP segmental states. (*Foundations of Linguistics* 11 (1974), p. 6)
   e. No -*ly* adverbials *whether* they *be* analyzed as manner, frequency, or some other kind (e. g. *cleverly*, occasional intervals) are permitted. (Jacobs and Rosenbaum (1970), *Readings in English Transformational Grammar*, p 90)
   f. Notice, also that the rules must be realized in some form *in order that* the game *be* playable. (Searle (1969), *Speech Acts*, p. 39)
   g. [P]risoners are afraid to report assaults, *lest* they *be* singled out as snitches. (*Time*, June 8, 1981, p. 17)

(All quoted from Chiba (1987: 45))

Moreover, if we assumed that *literary* expressions do not reflect the semantic features in Present-Day English, then *no* uses of the subjunctive present should reflect the semantic features of today's English since all uses of the subjunctive present are *more or less literary*. Rather, what Konno should account for is why his examples in (17a, b) and (18) are *not ungrammatical* even if they are *not acceptable* in colloquial style as compared to a *fully ungrammatical* example as in (20):

(20) **Since* no one *agree* to my proposal, I will give it up.　　(Araki *et al*. 1977: 448)

Next, his condition should predict that *all* optative sentences that contain an appeal are gramatical, but this is not the fact at least in Present-Day English, as shown in (21):

(21) a. *John *come*!　　　　　　　　　　　　　　　　　　(Imai *et al*. 1995: 21)
　　b. *She *study* very hard!
　　c. *He *pass* the entrance examination to the university!

Third, note that *think* and *believe* cannot possibly select a subjunctive present clause however much we change or modify the sentence or the context. For example, even if we attempt to modify Konno's examples in (22) in some way to make them more acceptable, they are still not improved in any way, as shown in (23):

(22) a. *The pope *believed* that God *save* the cruel world.
　　b. *I *think* that Taro *be* angry (*sic*) [about] what you said.　　(Konno 2002: 42)
(23) a. *The pope *hoped* for world peace. He *believed from the bottom of his heart* that God *save* the cruel world.
　　b. *If Taro is angry about what you said, then I will be not reprimanded by him. I *want* this to be the case, and I *think* that Taro *be* angry about what you said.

This suggests that *think* or *believe* cannot select a subjunctive clause *syntactically* irrespective of the sentence meanings.

As discussed above, we can conclude that Konno's semantic and pragmatic condition is insufficient for accounting for all the cases of the subjunctive present. Rather, judging from the examples above, we should consider that what his semantic condition covers is *only* mandative subjunctive cases.[3)]

10.5 An Alternative Account

Then, what should we do with this complex problem? I assume that both *syntactic* conditions and a *semantic* condition are necessary. Namely, we should crucially consider that *after* the syntactic conditions apply, semantic conditions must apply as well.

10.5.1 Syntactic Condition

As for the syntactic conditions, I make the following assumption:

(24) Subjunctive complementizers must or can select subjunctive present clauses.

Here I will assume that the subjunctive complementizers consist of the following:

(25) a. the *optative* null complementizer ϕ
 b. the complementizers expressing *condition, concession*, and *purpose*
    e.g. *if, though, whether, wh-ever, so that, for fear, lest,* etc.
 c. the mandative subjunctive complementizer
    i.e. *that*, the phonetically deleted *that*

Based on this classification, we can define (24) more accurately as follows:

(26) a. The optative null complementizer ϕ *must* select a subjunctive present clause.[4)]
 b. The complementizers expressing *condition, concession*, and *purpose can* select a subjunctive present clause.
 c. The mandative subjunctive complementizer *must* or *can* select a subjunctive present clause.[5)]

Incidentally, as for older forms of English, we could assume that "the subjunctive complementizers *must* select a subjunctive present clause", but as the indicative forms developed, this constraint has changed into the present form in (26a-c).

Needless to say, *can* in (26b, c) implies the following assumption in (27), as is shown by (28) and (29):

(27) The complementizers that *can* select a subjunctive present clause can select an indicative clause at the same time as a *default* in Present-Day English.

Observe the following examples:

(28) a. If it *rains* tomorrow, the picnic will be put off.
 b. Though John *is* young, he is rather conservative.
 c. He has been studying hard so that he *can* get into the university of his choice next year.

(29) a. One can thus firmly *insist* (by using MUST) that he *says* what he *wants* for a present, or that he *pays* a visit. (Palmer (1979), *Modality and the English Modals*, p. 62)
 b. In fact, it has been *proposed* that there *is* a universal condition blocking such rules. (Chomsky (1972), *Studies in Semantics in Generative Grammar*, p. 184)

(Quoted from Chiba (1987: 7))

10.5.2 Semantic Condition

Next, let us consider the semantic conditions. First, I make the following assumptions:

(30) a. Since the optative null complementizer ɸ in (26a) and the complementizers expressing *condition*, *concession*, and *purpose* in (26b) contain the clear lexical subjunctive meanings in the lexicon, they can select a subjunctive present clause *without any semantic support*.
 b. Since the mandative subjunctive complementizer *that* is *semantically empty*, though it has the subjunctive feature syntactically, constructions containing *that* must be semantically supported to allow a subjunctive clause.

Here I propose the following semantic condition:

(31) When the subjunctive *that* is introduced, the sentence must express an *unspecified desirable future event* by way of linguistic elements or contextual meanings.

As for the semantic condition in (31), we can say that similar ideas to mine have been proposed in the past including Konno's condition of underlying appeal in (12); Onions's (1932[6]) *Will*, Hosoe's (1933) *Thought*, Lyons's (1977) *Non-Factivity*, Hooper's (1975) *Assertiveness*, Pesetsky's (1982) or Givón's (1994) *Irrealis Event*, James's (1986) *Blueprint*, etc.[6),7)] However, I claim that the important thing is that the semantic condition in (31) or others are a *necessary and sufficient condition* for the case of (30b) but not so for (30a) (see (15a, b) and (19a-g)).[8] As for this problem, we should review Chomsky's (1975) comments on Jespersen's view of subjunctives, as shown in (32a, b):

(32) a. Similarly many languages have a subjunctive mood, but "it would be perfectly impossible to give definition ... as would at the same time cover its employment in all the languages mentioned."

(Chomsky 1975=1977: 27-28) [Quoted part is from Jespersen.]

b. Jespersen also holds that it is "impossible to give such a definition of the subjunctive in any of these languages as would assist us in deciding where to use it and where to use the indicative." I do not understand exactly what he means by this, or why he holds this view. The arguments he gives do not relate to it, so far as I can see. His discussion of the subjunctive and its expression seems to presuppose that there is a general notion of "subjunctive" relating to "the world of ideas," and if a grammar tells us how this notion is expressed in some language, then it would seem that we do have a "definition" that "would assist us in deciding where to use it."

(Chomsky 1975=1977: 28, fn. 5)

In my understanding, if we apply our present analysis, Jespersen would claim that the *semantic* condition in (31) does not specify *all* the environments where the subjunctive is used, while Chomsky would claim *syntax* can specify the *potential* subjunctive complementizers as seen in (25). That is, we should consider that both Jespersen and Chomsky are right though each observes language phenomena from different point of views.

10.5.3 Potential Subjunctive-Taking Verbs

If the direction discussed so far is on the right track, then what is most important is the problem as to what lexical items can select (mandative) subjunctive clauses. As for this, I make the following assumption:

(33) a. Deontic verbs can potentially select subjunctive present clauses.
　　b. Epistemic verbs cannot select subjunctive present clauses.

What I mean by *deontic* and *epistemic* verbs is shown as listed below:[9]

(34) Deontic Verbs
　　a. Verbs of WILL
　　　advise, arrange, ask, challenge, command, compel, decide, determine, encourage, force, insist, intend, move, order, persuade, propose, recommend, request, suggest, tell, urge, etc.
　　b. Verbs of WANTING
　　　beg, beseech, care, desire, hope, like, love, prefer, pray, want, wish, etc.
(35) Epistemic Verbs
　　assume, believe, consider, expect, feel, know, prove, show, suppose, think, understand, etc.

Needless to say, what category is realized as a complement clause selected by these verbs is different from word to word. As Chiba (1984a, 1987: Chapter 4) and Yagi (1996) discuss in detail, this is also a complex problem. Consider the following examples:

(36) a. John $\left\{\begin{array}{l}\text{decreed} \\ \text{*ordered} \\ \text{demanded}\end{array}\right\}$ that Bill leave.

b. John $\left\{\begin{array}{l}\text{*decreed} \\ \text{*ordered} \\ \text{demanded}\end{array}\right\}$ of Bill that he leave.

c. John $\left\{\begin{array}{l}\text{*decreed} \\ \text{ordered} \\ \text{*demanded}\end{array}\right\}$ Bill to leave.

d. John $\left\{\begin{array}{l}\text{*decreed} \\ \text{*ordered} \\ \text{demanded}\end{array}\right\}$ PRO to leave.

(Chiba 1987: 114)

It is true that the exact formalization of this problem itself is important, but at the same time we should consider the possibility that the absence of certain linguistic forms is an *accidental gap* concerning various *historical*, *semantic*, or *phonological* conditions.[10)] In other words, we should consider that all the deontic verbs can *potentially* select a subjunctive present clause.

As an illustration of this, let us consider the case of *want*. As is often claimed, *want* normally cannot select a subjunctive present complement but only an infinitival clause. Consider the following examples:

(37) *I want that you be happy. (Bolinger 1972: 49)
(38) I want you to do it. (*I want that you should do it.)   (Declerck 1991a: 421)
(39) Do you want me to make you some coffee?
     (NOT ~~Do you want that I make you some coffee?~~)   (Swan 1995[2]: 584)

Bolinger argues that the only exceptions are the cases of (i) *that*-clauses with the adverbs *only*, *merely*, *solely*, and *just* etc., and (ii) quasi-cleft sentences (because we can interpret *all I want* to be *I want only*), as shown below:

(40) a. I want *only* that you be happy.
     b. *All I want* is that you be happy.   (Bolinger 1972: 49)

However, Chiba (1991) observes additional examples other than the types (i) and (ii) that Bolinger points out, as shown in (41):

(41) a. John wants *very much* that the fighting stop.
   b. I *never* wanted *it* that they be treated like that.
   c. John wants *it of Bill* that he clean the house.   (Chiba 1991: 42, fn. 22)

Furthermore, Yagi (2002) argues that we can find many *attested examples* where even *very much* or the complementizer *that* is missing. Consider his examples:

(42) a. ... ; they decided that; 'God *wanted* that they *should* be French'; and French they became. [BNC]
   b. You *want* she *should* trip over and break her neck? [BNC]
   c. ..., and he told her, 'Please don't ever run away from me. I *want* we *should* always talk. ....' [BoE (COBUILDdirect) ukbooks]
   d. You *want* we *should* go bankrupt. [*OED2*, s.v. SHOULD (1960)]
   e. They *want* they *should* take you away. [*OED2*, s.v. SHOULD (1978)]
   f. KNIGHT: When my time on Earth is gone and my activities here are past, I *want* they *bury* me upside down and my critics can kiss my ass. [LKL 2001]   (All quoted from Yagi (2002: 45))

From the uses of *want*, we can conclude that *all* deontic verbs can *potentially* select a subjunctive present clause.

On the other hand, as we discussed in (22a, b) and (23a, b), we should consider that epistemic verbs in (35) cannot select a subjunctive present clause *syntactically*. Here note interestingly that the epistemic verbs in (35) are also the verbs that trigger the *Raising-to-Object*. From this fact, we can assume the following correlations, as shown in (43-45) (see also note 5 in Chapter 9):

(43) a. Deontic Verbs — *can* assign Null Case — *can* select a subjunctive present clause
       (=Control Infinitivals)
   b. Epistemic Verbs — *cannot* assign any Case — *cannot* select a subjunctive present clause
       (=Raising Infinitivals)

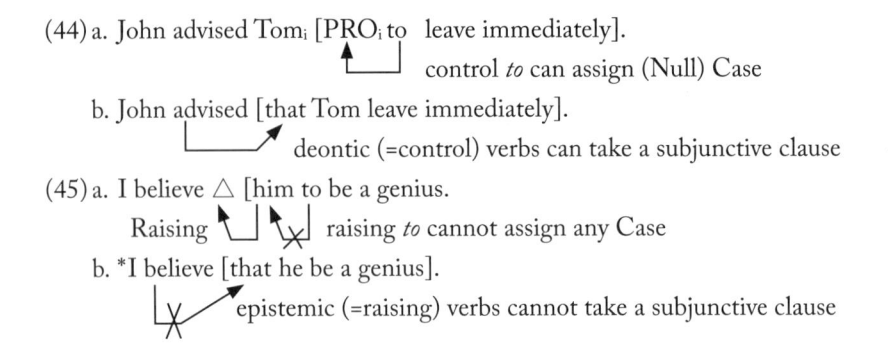

(44) a. John advised Tom_i [PRO_i to leave immediately].
      control *to* can assign (Null) Case
   b. John advised [that Tom leave immediately].
      deontic (=control) verbs can take a subjunctive clause

(45) a. I believe △ [him to be a genius.
      Raising   raising *to* cannot assign any Case
   b. *I believe [that he be a genius].
      epistemic (=raising) verbs cannot take a subjunctive clause

Additionally, as we discussed in Chapter 3, since ECM (=Raising) predicates are literally *exceptional*, other verbs *automatically* belong to Control predicates. Applying this specification to *that*-clauses, the verbs selecting a *that*-clause other than epistemic verbs should all belong to the class of deontic verbs, which implies that they can potentially select subjunctive present clauses as well. However, in this case they must be *semantically* supported to be acceptable (see (30b)). Consequently, (46a) will be unacceptable while (46b) will be acceptable.

(46) a. ?The widow *wrote* that Ball *be* given part of her property. (=(4a))
   b. Ball was arrested for the murder of a rich widow. The widow *wrote in her will* that Ball *be* given part of her property. (=(i) in note 1)

10.6 Concluding Remarks

In this chapter I discussed the rather complex question as to what lexical items can select a subjunctive present clause. After reviewing Chiba (1991) and Konno (2001), I argued that Konno's Condition of an Underlying Appeal is insufficient. Instead, I proposed that both syntactic conditions and semantic conditions are needed; assuming three types of subjunctive complementizers, (i) the optative null complementizer φ and the complementizers expressing condition, concession, and purpose, can select a subjunctive present clause without any semantic support, while (ii) the use of mandative subjunctive complementizer *that*, which is semantically empty, must be semantically supported as well. As for the semantic condition, I assumed that when the subjunctive *that* is introduced, the sentence must express an *unspecified desirable future event* by linguistic elements or contextual meaning. Last, concerning the important problem as to what lexical items can select subjunctive present clauses, I proposed that deontic verbs can *potentially* select subjunctive present clauses but epistemic verbs cannot select subjunctive present clauses *syntactically*.

Notes to Chapter 10

1. This chapter is mainly based on Nomura (2005b). I am grateful to two anonymous reviewers of *Eego Gohoo Bunpoo Kenkyuu* [Studies in English Grammar and Usage] for their helpful comments on an earlier version of this paper, but time limitation forced me to restrict myself to only partial revision.

2. According to D. L. Smith (personal communication, 2000), in order to make the whole (4b) more acceptable, the past form *was* should be used instead of the present form *is*, as shown in (i):

    (i) Ball *was* arrested for the murder of a rich widow. The widow wrote in her will that Ball be given part of her property.

3. Though, I think it important to note that Konno (2002) points out that examples like in (11a-d) are acceptable.

4. However, as I showed in (21a-c), optative sentences are, in fact, not productive in Present-Day English. It follows that we might consider that the optative null complementizer ϕ is already *fossilized* today. Note here that Konno (2002) claims that optative sentences as subjunctive uses are productive, but I claim that it is not optative (=subjunctive) verb uses themselves (see (21a-c)) but some fixed constructions that are productive, as shown in (i):

    (i) a. God bless [ ]!
        b. [ ] be hanged!

    In other words, since various words can be filled into the bracket part (e.g. *the Queen, the King, America, money, grammar*, etc.), optative sentences themselves may appear to be productive, but only in this limited way.

5. The cases of *must* in (26c) are the examples listed in (i):

    (i) Lexical Items Which Obligatorily Take Subjunctive Clauses
        Verbs: *demand, desire, request*
        Adjectives: *anxious, imperative, mandatory*

Nouns: *desire, intention, wish* (Chiba 1987: 6)

However, even these lexical items can take *indicative clauses*, as I noted in note 10 in Chapter 6. That is to say, in Present-Day English we may as well make the same assumption on the mandative subjunctive complementizer *that* as (26b), as shown in (ii):

(ii) The mandative subjunctive complementizer *can* select a subjunctive present clause.

6. Note also that Kajita (1968) claims that mandative subjunctive clauses have *future* tense in deep structure, as shown in (i):

(i) In this study, however, the position is taken that the embedded sentences of this type [i.e. mandative subjunctive clauses] have Tense, in particular, Future, in the deep structure. (Kajita 1968: 51)

7. An anonymous reviewer raises a question whether the *unspecified desirable future event* in (31) is almost synonymous with the term *mandative*. Indeed, this is true in certain respects and I will not claim at all that the concept of an unspecified desirable future event is a new concept, as is also shown by other studies so far including Konno's. The important thing is, however, that this semantic condition must apply after the syntactic conditions apply, as I stated above in this section. But I will leave the exact formalization of the unspecified desirable future event for future study.

8. An anonymous reviewer suggests that a part of my semantic condition should be a pragmatic one, if we can consider Konno's condition in a different way. As for this problem, I consider that the *semantic* condition that I use covers both *semantic* cases (in a narrower sense) and *pragmatic* ones.

9. I think that the classifications of (34b) (=Verbs of WANTING) and (35) (=Epistemic Verbs) each correspond to what Postal (1974) calls *W-verbs* and *B-verbs*.

10. As an example of a *historical* coincidence, consider the following examples:

(i) a. John *ordered that* the children *be* not noisy when he gets home from work.
(Nomura 2004: 51) (cf. (36a))
b. He *demanded* the traitor *to* give up his lovely prize. (1795, *OED*) (cf. (36c))

These examples also force us to conclude that *decreed/force/demand* can *all* potentially take a subjunctive clause, a control infinitival, and PRO.

Note also that Ogawa (1988) points out the possibility that the ungrammaticality in (i) is related to the fact *demand*, *dictate*, and *insist* cannot take a *human* NP solely as an object, as is shown in (ii), unlike *command, order, request, require, ask, beg, urge,* and *advise*:

(i) *They {demanded, dictated, insisted} the man to leave.
(ii) *They {demanded, dictated, insisted} the man. (Ogawa 1988: 149)
 cf. He demanded *an apology/a reform*.

Chapter 11

NegP and VP-Deletion in Subjunctive Present Clauses

11.1 Introduction

In this chapter I discuss the problem of the presence of NegP and the controversial problem as to which position *not* occupies, the Spec position or the Head position. Then, in connection with this problem, I discuss the licensing condition on VP-deletion in subjunctive present clauses: Potsdam (1997, 1998) claims that *only* the negative *not* licenses VP-deletion in subjunctive present clauses and therefore concludes that *not* is the Head of NegP. However, I argue that not only the negative *not* but also other elements can license VP-deletion in subjunctive present clauses. Moreover, I claim that the licensing condition on VP-deletion in subjunctive present clauses is the same as that in indicative sentences, and consequently conclude that the VP-deletion phenomenon in subjunctive present clauses cannot be taken as decisive evidence for the claim that *not* is the Head of NegP.

11.2 The Presence of NegP

Since Pollock (1989) proposed the Split-I Hypothesis, many linguists have assumed that the negative *not* constitutes its own projection NegP; Pollock (1989), Laka (1990), Rizzi (1990), Ouhalla (1990), Iatridou (1990), Belletti (1990), Zanuttini (1991), Roberts (1992), Haegeman (1995), Chomsky (1995: Chapters 2-4), Potsdam (1997, 1998), etc. Judging from the fact *not* is very different from other adverbs as well as from the syntactic phenomena of negation in other European languages, it seems rather reasonable to me to assume NegP, and in this book I follow this assumption as well.

On the other hand, there are not a few linguists that do not assume NegP in English; Baker (1991), Ernst (1992), Murakami (1995a, b, 1998, 2000, 2002),

Sawada (1993, 1995), Ando (1996, 2003, 2004), Matsubara (1997a, b), Hasegawa (2003), etc. Especially, Murakami, Sawada, and Matsubara assume similar standard IP structures where *not* is adjoined to I, following Radford (1988).[1] As an illustration of their assumed structures, consider the structure in (1b) assumed by Murakami (1995a):

(1) a. John does not smoke.
b.

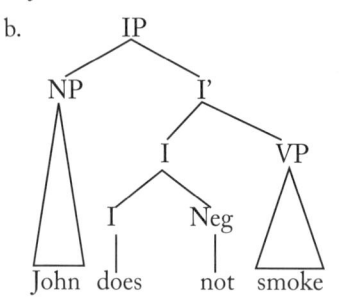

```
              IP
             /  \
           NP    I'
           /\   /  \
              I      VP
             / \      \
            I   Neg    \
            |    |      \
          John does   not smoke
```
                                                              (Murakami 1995a: 103)

However, I would like to point out the following problems with their assumed structure: first, as I mentioned above, for many other European languages, we have good reason to assume NegP. If this line of thought is on the right track, in the light of *the uniformity of syntactic structures* or the *null hypothesis*, we can and should assume NegP in English as well, though we cannot but assume one other functional category in the process. Second, their IP analyses cannot provide an adequate account for why *not* can be adjoined to I but other adverbs cannot. Even if we assume that other adverbs can be adjoined to I, we cannot explain why *not* alone triggers *do*-support, as shown in (2a, b):

(2) a. John does *not* smoke.
　　b. *John does *never* smoke.

Third, as we discussed in Chapter 2, their IP analysis cannot generate Propositional Negation, just as Chomsky's (1995, 2000, 2001a, b) phrase structure cannot. Observe the following example:

(3) You must [not go]. (MUST＞NOT)

Under the IP analysis *must* always must be c-commanded by *not*. In order to generate the interpretation of Propositional Negation, we should at least assume a structure where modals *asymmetrically* c-command *not*.

As discussed above, we can clearly conclude that NegP should be assumed in English, although Matsubara (1997a, b) offers further arguments that NegP cannot be assumed judging from two standard tests for phrasal constituency. In the next section I will examine his discussion.

11.3 Matsubara (1997a, b)

Matsubara (1997a, b) uses two standard tests for phrasal constituency, i.e. *Fronting* and *Deletion*, which were introduced by Radford (1988: 90), in order to decide whether NegP has phrasal constituency or not. Consider his examples:

(4) a. John did [$_{NegP}$ not go to Kyoto].
    b. John did [$_{NegP}$ not kiss Mary softly].
    c. John did [$_{NegP}$ not eat an apple for breakfast].
    d. John will [$_{NegP}$ not kill Bill in the car].
    e. John will [$_{NegP}$ not write a letter to his father].
    f. John should [$_{NegP}$ not show these pictures to Mary].
                                                                (Matsubara 1997a: 65)

(5) NegP Fronting
    a. *[$_{NegP}$ Not go to Kyoto]$_i$ John did t$_i$.
    b. *[$_{NegP}$ Not kiss Mary softly]$_i$ John did t$_i$.
    c. *[$_{NegP}$ Not eat an apple for breakfast]$_i$ John did t$_i$.
    d. *[$_{NegP}$ Not kill Bill in the car]$_i$ John will t$_i$.
    e. *[$_{NegP}$ Not write a letter to his father]$_i$ John will t$_i$.
    f. *[$_{NegP}$ Not show these pictures to Mary]$_i$ John will t$_i$.   (Ibid.)

(6) NegP Deletion
    a. A: Will the President of the United States [$_{NegP}$ not talk about racial discrimination]?
       B: *No, he will ϕ. (ϕ= not talk about racial discrimination)
    b. A: He can [$_{NegP}$ not swim 60 yards].

B: *I can ɸ, either. (ɸ= not swim 60 yards)

c. *John does [NegP not want to leave], and Bill does ɸ, either. (ɸ= not want to leave) (Ibid.: 66)

To all appearances, his discussion is appropriate, but the following basic premise is needed to prove that his discussion is right:

(7) If a given sequence of words constitutes a phrasal constituent (=XP), then it can always be fronted or deleted whatever category it may be.

But this premise is clearly wrong empirically. To illustrate this, consider the following examples:

(8) IP Deletion
   a. *I don't know if [IP John will come], and Bill also wonders if ɸ. (ɸ= John will come)
   b. *I think that [IP John will come], and Bill also thinks that ɸ. (ɸ= John will come) (Tonoike 1989d: 228)
   c. A: Did John leave London?
      B: I wonder if [IP he did].
      B': *I wonder if ɸ. (ɸ=*he did*, or *he left London*)
(9) IP Fronting
   a. I think that [IP John left London].
   b. *[IP John left London]$_i$ I think that t$_i$.

Matsubara uses IP throughout his thesis, but if he assumed the premise in (7), then he would have to conclude that IP does not have phrasal constituency as well.[2]

From these examples we can draw the following inference:

(10) If a given sequence of words can be fronted or deleted, then it is a phrasal constituent (=XP), but *the converse is not always true*.
(11) Deletion or Fronting is a necessary and sufficient condition for testing constituency concerning lexical categories (e.g. VP, DP, AP, PP), but not so

concerning functional categories (e.g. IP, CP, NegP).[3]

As discussed above, we cannot but conclude that Matsubara's argument is faulty after all.[4], [5]

11.4 *Not* as a Spec or *Not* as a Head?

Another controversial problem is the position of *not* in NegP: which position does *not* occupy, the Spec or the Head? As for a good review of this problem, see Murakami (1995a) and Mori (1995a, b). First, as for the studies assuming *not* as the Head of NegP, the following linguists explore the following posibilities in (12) through (17) (the single-bar level projection is omitted following Murakami (1995a)):

(12) Pollock (1989)

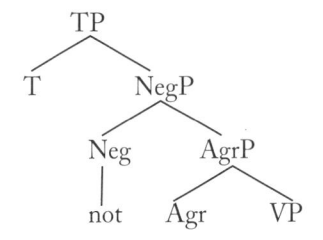

```
        TP
       /  \
      T    NegP
           /  \
         Neg   AgrP
          |    /  \
         not  Agr  VP
```

(13) Ouhalla (1990)

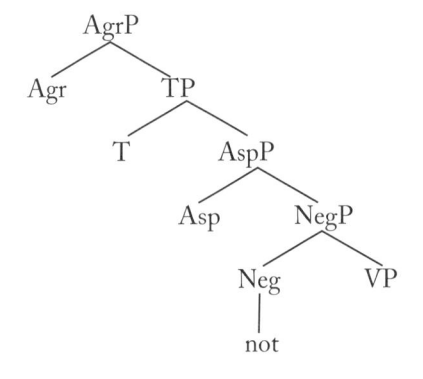

```
         AgrP
        /    \
      Agr     TP
             /  \
            T    AspP
                /    \
              Asp    NegP
                     /   \
                   Neg    VP
                    |
                   not
```

(14) Iatridou (1990)

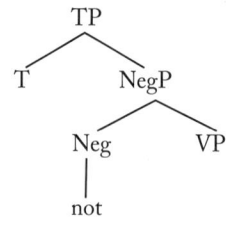

```
        TP
       /  \
      T    NegP
           /  \
         Neg   VP
          |
         not
```

(15) Zanuttini (1991)

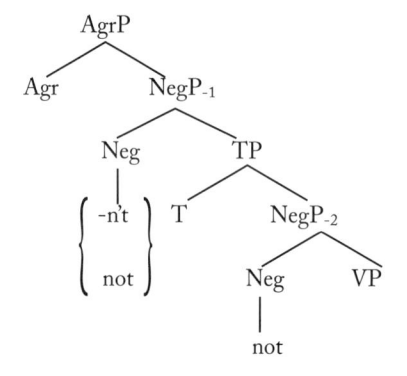

```
         AgrP
        /    \
      Agr    NegP₋₁
             /    \
           Neg     TP
            |     /  \
         ⎧-n't⎫  T   NegP₋₂
         ⎨    ⎬       /   \
         ⎩ not⎭     Neg    VP
                     |
                    not
```

(16) Laka (1990)

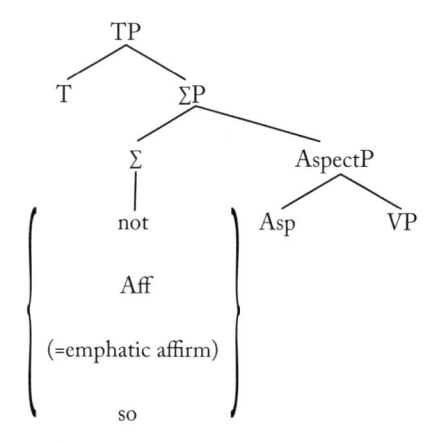

```
            TP
           /  \
          T    ΣP
              /  \
             Σ    AspectP
             |    /    \
  ⎧  not  ⎫  Asp     VP
  ⎪        ⎪
  ⎪  Aff   ⎪
  ⎨(=emphatic affirm)⎬
  ⎪        ⎪
  ⎩   so   ⎭
```

(17) Chomsky (1995: Chapters 2-3)

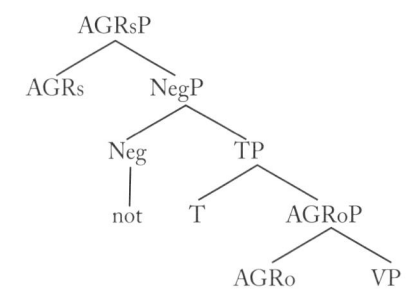

```
            AGRsP
           /    \
        AGRs    NegP
               /    \
             Neg     TP
              |     /  \
            not   T    AGRoP
                       /    \
                    AGRo    VP
```

Next, on the other hand, the following linguists explore the possibility of assuming *not* as the Spec of NegP as illustrated in (18) through (20):

(18) Rizzi (1990)

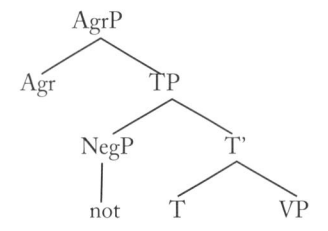

```
            AgrP
           /    \
         Agr    TP
               /  \
            NegP   T'
              |   /  \
            not  T    VP
```

(19) Belletti (1990)

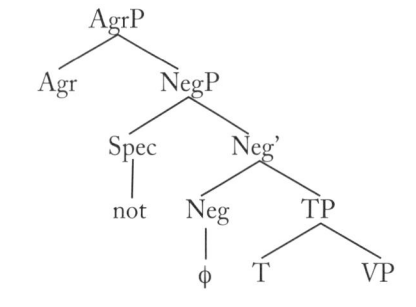

```
            AgrP
           /    \
         Agr    NegP
               /    \
             Spec    Neg'
              |     /    \
            not   Neg    TP
                   |    /  \
                   φ   T    VP
```

(20) Roberts (1992)

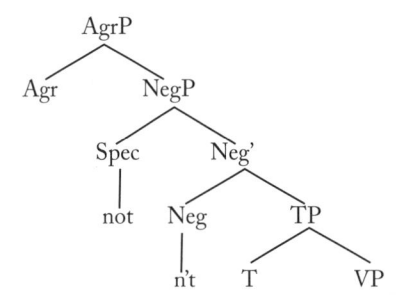

```
        AgrP
       /    \
     Agr    NegP
           /    \
         Spec    Neg'
          |     /    \
         not  Neg     TP
               |     /  \
              n't   T    VP
```

Third, as for studies assuming that *not* is a certain kind of modifier, which belong to neither group shown above, see Radford (1988), Baker (1991), Ernst (1992), Murakami (1995a, 1998, 2003), Sawada (1993, 1995), Ando (1996, 2003, 2004), Matsubara (1997a, b), and Hasegawa (2003). Here, since we already mentioned most of these studies in Sections 11.2-11.3, I will show only Baker's assumed structure, which is different from the one assumed by Radford, Murakami, Sawada, and Matsubara in that *not* is not assumed to be adjoined to I, as stated Section 11.2:

(21) Baker (1991)

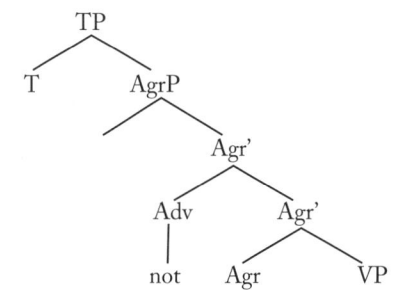

```
      TP
     /  \
    T    AgrP
          \
           Agr'
          /    \
        Adv    Agr'
         |    /    \
        not  Agr    VP
```

Now, which possibility should we adopt? Needless to say, we will not assume the third possibility, where NegP itself is not posited, for the reasons discussed in the previous sections. Then, the crucial issue is the *Head Movement Constraint* (HMC) proposed by Travis (1984). The HMC was defined in Chomsky (1986b) as follows:

(22) Movement of a zero-level category β is restricted to the position of a head α that governs the maximal projection γ of β, where α θ-governs or L-marks γ if α ≠ C. (Chomsky 1986b: 71)

However, now that government is eliminated in the present framework, we may safely say that the following definition will suffice for the purpose of discussion:

(23) Head movement cannot pass over the closest c-commanding head.[6)]
(cf. Chomsky (1995: 49))

Here let us take a simple example, as shown in (24):

(24) John is not happy.

If we assumed the first possibility, this sentence should wrongly be ruled out by the HMC, since the head *is* must pass over the closest c-commanding head *not*, as shown in (25):

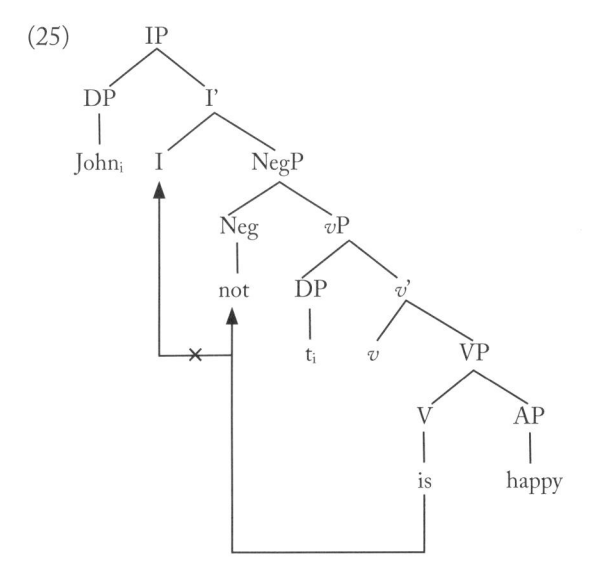

(25)

```
          IP
         /  \
       DP    I'
       |    /  \
     Johnᵢ  I   NegP
              /   \
            Neg    vP
             |    /  \
            not  DP   v'
                 |   / \
                 tᵢ  v  VP
                       / \
                      V   AP
                      |   |
                      is  happy
```

As for this problem, the studies illustrated in (12-17), taking the first possibility, assume complex but *ad hoc* solutions. We can then consider that the best way to solve this problem is to take the second possibility assuming *not* as the Spec of NegP, where the HMC is not relevant.[7] As I have discussed throughout this book, I am assuming the following structure for NegP, as shown in (26a, b):[8]

(26) a.

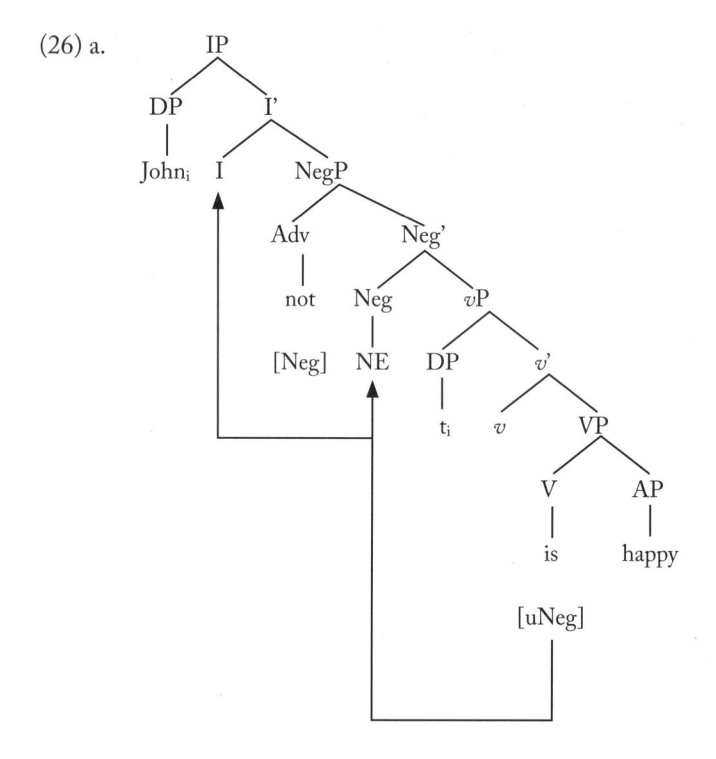

```
            IP
           /  \
         DP    I'
         |    /  \
       John_i I   NegP
              ↑  /    \
              | Adv    Neg'
              | |     /    \
              | not  Neg    vP
              |      |     /  \
              |    [Neg] NE DP   v'
              |         ↑  |    / \
              |         |  t_i v   VP
              |         |        /  \
              |         |       V    AP
              |         |       |    |
              |         |       is  happy
              |         |
              |         [uNeg]
```

b.

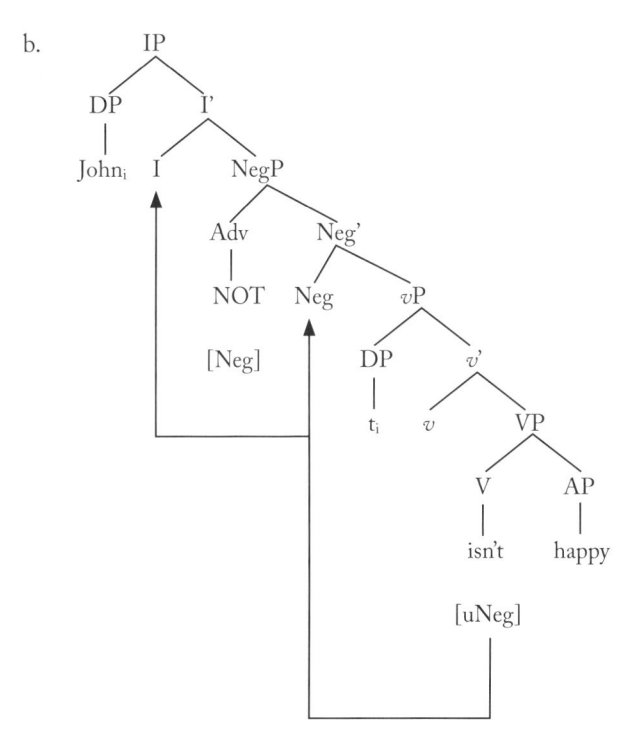

```
           IP
          /  \
        DP    I'
        |    /  \
      Johnᵢ I   NegP
              /    \
            Adv    Neg'
             |    /    \
            NOT  Neg    vP
                [Neg]  /  \
                     DP    v'
                     |    / \
                     tᵢ  v   VP
                            /  \
                           V    AP
                           |    |
                         isn't happy
                         [uNeg]
```

As supporting evidence for assuming the covert negative element NE, we can submit the negative structure <ne + V + pas> in French and <ne +V + noht> in earlier stages of English. Consider the following examples and their corresponding structures:

(27) a. Jean *n'*aime   *pas*   Marie.   (French)
     Jean NE loves   not   Marie
     'Jean doesn't love Marie.'
  b. [ɪᴘ Jean I [NegP pas [Neg' ne   [vP aime Marie]]]]
                           [Neg]   [uNeg]

(28) a. thou *ne*   knowest *nat* what is the   eende of thynges? (Middle English)
       thou NE   know   not   what is the   end   of things
       'you don't know what the end of the things is?'
       (Chaucer, *Boece* I, pr6, 48-49,
                    quoted from Nakao and Koma eds. (1990: 160))

b. [ᵢₚ thou I [NegP nat [Neg' ne [vP knowest ...]]]]
         [Neg]   [uNeg]

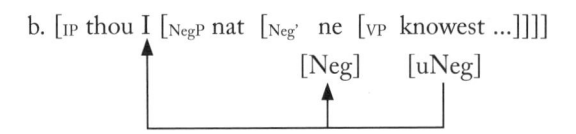

Note that English *not* was not a purely negative element but an *emphatic word* whose function is almost the same as *at all* like in *I don't like him at all*, and that French *pas* is not the main negative element either but originates from *passum* (=a step).⁹⁾,¹⁰⁾

Moreover, as Pollock (1989) points out, *ne* is often dropped in colloquial Modern French, as shown in (29):

(29) Jean (*n'*)aime par Marie.
    Jean (ne) loves not Marie
    'Jean does not love Marie.'   (Pollock 1989: 393)

As for an interesting aside, Jespersen (1924) and Pollock (1989) argue that the historical development in negative structures in French is similar to that in English, as shown in (30) (see also Mori (1995a, b)):

(30) a. Ic ne sege   > I ne sye not   > I say not
        I ne say   I ne say not   I say not
        OE   EME   the 14th century English
     b. Jeo ne di   > Je ne dis pas   > Je dis pas
        I ne say   I ne say not   I say not
        Old French   Standard French   Colloquial Modern French

(cf. Pollock 1989: 367, Jespersen 1924: 335-336)

From this fact as well, we have good reason to take the second possibility assuming *not* as the Spec of NegP.

Before closing this section, I would like to mention Madoka Murakami's question at the presentation of Nomura (2002b). She asked me why *not* does not block the movement of the subject to IP-Spec if I assume that *not* exists in the Spec of NegP (see (26a)). For her question, we can propose two answers: the first possibility is to assume that since the movement of the subject to IP-Spec is

A-movement while the Spec of NegP is an *A'-position*, *not* should not block this movement. The other possibility is to assume that since the movement of the subject to IP-Spec is *XP-movement* while *not* can be assumed to be an X^0 *category*, both are relativized and thus *not* should not block this movement. The following fact shows that *not* is not an XP category but an X^0 category:[11), 12)]

(31) *John is *very not* happy.

I believe that either possibility will answer her question, but in my opinion we should adopt the second possibility. This is because I consider that the crucial distinction is not A vs. A' but XP vs. X^0; if the distinction between A and A' were crucial, *not* would block *wh*-movement. To all appearances, this would be appropriate considering the phenomena of *Negative Islands* (see Ross (1984) and Rizzi (1990)), as shown in (32a, b):

(32) a. *[How much money]$_i$ *didn't* he earn t$_i$?
    b. *[How much]$_i$ *didn't* you pay t$_i$ for the new car?
                                                     (Kuno and Takami 1997: 558)

However, as Kuno and Takami (1997) discuss in detail, we should recognize that NegP or *not* does not necessarily block *wh*-movement, as is shown in (33a, b):

(33) a. [How much money]$_i$ *wasn't* he willing to contribute t$_i$? (cf. (32a))
    b. [How much money]$_i$ *shouldn't* I pay t$_i$ for the new car? (cf. (32b))   (Ibid.)

In conclusion, we can best assume that since the movement of the subject to IP-Spec is *XP-movement* and *not* is an X^0 *category*, *not* will not block this movement.

11.5 VP-Deletion in Subjunctive Present Clauses[13)]

As for the problem as to whether *not* is the Head of NegP or not, Potsdam (1997, 1998) provides an interesting discussion.[14)] Potsdam's (1997, 1998: Chapter 2) proposal is roughly as follows:

(34) a. The only element which can license an elided VP in subjunctive clauses is the sentential negative element *not*.
  b. Consequently, Potsdam concludes that sentential *not* is the head of NegP.

In this section, however, I discuss licensing conditions on VP-deletion in subjunctive present clauses, raising a partial objection to Potsdam (1997, 1998).

11.5.1 Potsdam (1997, 1998)

First of all, as I discussed in Section 9.3.1, Potsdam assumes the structure of subjunctive present clauses is as follows:

(35) Subjunctive present clauses have an IP whose head is a morphologically independent zero modal. (cf. Potsdam (1997: 535))

Next, many linguists have discussed the licensing conditions on VP-deletion since the 1970's, but have not reached a conclusion. However, following Bresnan (1976), Gazdar *et al.* (1982), and Lobeck (1995), Potsdam submits the following generally assumed licensing condition on VP-deletion:

(36) VP-Ellipsis Licensing Condition
  An elided VP must be the complement of a morphologically realized head.
  (Potsdam 1997: 534)

This condition can naturally give an account for the following contrasts in grammaticality:

(37) a. I'll try the guacamole ice cream if I *must* ϕ.
  b. Boxer auditioned for the choir and his roommate *did* ϕ.
  c. A baby llama will go anywhere its mother *has* ϕ.
  d. No one else will support the candidate despite the fact that the mayor *is* ϕ.
  e. *John didn't leave but Mary ϕ.   (Potsdam 1997: 534)

Moreover, Potsdam argues that *not* also seems to license an ellipsis cite, as shown in (38):

(38) a. Mary wants to go to the fashion show but her husband might *not* ϕ.
b. Some of the guests tried the appetizers but most did *not* ϕ.   (Ibid.)

Here he wants to conclude that *not* is the Head of NegP since the elided VP in (38a, b) seems to be licensed by *not*, but it is not straightforward to deduce from these examples that the element responsible for licensing the elided VP is *not*, since a modal, auxiliary, or supporting *do* are also obligatorily present in negated finite clauses. However, Potsdam claims that VP-deletion in subjunctive present clauses provides crucial evidence for assuming that *not* alone can license the elided VP; first, he shows that under the condition in (36) the following examples of subjunctive present clauses in (39) are all ungrammatical unlike the indicative sentences in (38a, b):

(39) a. John would prefer that Fred leave, and Bill would prefer that he *(leave).
                                                    (Lobeck (1995: 188, fn. 7))
b. *Kim needn't be there but it is imperative that the other organizers ϕ.
c. *We think that Mary should present her case to the committee and we ask that Bill ϕ, too.   (Potsdam 1997: 538)

Furthermore, he claims that even when auxiliaries are stranded the examples are ungrammatical. Consider Potsdam's (1997) examples:

(40) a. *We can't count on Josh to be waiting for us at the airport so we request that you *be* ϕ instead.
b. *The bridges were repaired before the engineers could even insist that the supporting structure *be* ϕ first.
c. *When the laborers have reached a decision, it is important that the leader *have* ϕ as well.   (Ibid.: 537, fn. 5)

Potsdam (1998) gives many examples other than (40a-c) as follows:

(41) PROGRESSIVE BE
    a. *I don't know if Mary is taking care of the plants while we're gone so I would ask that you *be* ϕ.
    b. *My running partner is training for the marathon and it's imperative that I *be* ϕ too.   (Potsdam 1998: 153)

(42) PASSIVE BE
    a. *The doctor didn't think that Jesse needed to be examined by a specialist but he's going to suggest that Joan *be* ϕ.
    b. *Bill was interviewed before he quit and I want to insist that you *be* ϕ too.
    c. *Jack's room was given a thorough cleaning and I suggest that yours *be* ϕ too.
    d. *The clients were told everything I suggested that they *be* ϕ.   (Ibid.)

(43) COPULA BE
    a. *You should be happy with the results even though I can't insist that you *be* ϕ.
    b. *If the whole system is to be on time, it is necessary that the connecting flights *be* ϕ as well.   (Ibid.: 154)

(44) PERFECTIVE HAVE
    a. ?By the time Wanda finishes, it is necessary that Bob *have* ϕ too.
    b. ?Jim memorized the piece and I suggest that, by next lesson, you *have* ϕ too.   (Ibid.)

On the other hand, when sentential *not* is present, ellipsis *is* grammatical as shown in (45); he says this phenomenon is very surprising:

(45) a. A: Should we wale Dad?
      B: No! It's absolutely imperative that you *not* ϕ.
    b. Kim needs to be there but it is better that the other organizers *not* ϕ.
    c. Ted hoped to vacation in Liberia but his agent recommended that he *not* ϕ.
    d. We think that Mary should present her case but we will ask that Bill *not* ϕ.
    e. A: Should I attend the meeting?
      B: I suggest that you *not* ϕ.   (Potsdam 1997: 539)
    f. John would prefer that Fred leave, and Bill would prefer that he not [e].

(Lobeck 1995: 188, fn. 7)

Consequently, Potsdam (1997, 1998) arrives at the conclusion (34a, b).

11.5.2 Problems with Potsdam (1997, 1998) and an Alternative Analysis

Despite the discussion by Potsdam (1997, 1998) reviewed in the previous section, I claim the following (46) in this section:

(46) a. The licensing conditions on VP-deletion in subjunctive present clauses are basically the same as those in indicative sentences.
b. In particular, (34a) is empirically wrong.

Here I propose the following licensing conditions on deletion (47) unlike Potsdam's (36):

(47) The Licensing Conditions on Deletion[15]
Deletion must be licensed by a morphologically identifiable head.

What I mean by *morphologically identifiable* is the following:

(48) (i) *A morphologically realized Head* must be left before a deleted XP. Or (ii) if the Head is not realized morphologically, *a morphologically realized Spec* must be left before the deleted XP so that the presence of the covert Head can be recognized.

Now let us examine Potsdam's data again under these assumptions. First, as for the cases where only the subjunctive *covert* M_ϕ is left, my informants also judge (39a, b) ungrammatical as does Potsdam:

(49) a. *Kim needn't be there but it is imperative that the other organizers ϕ. (=(39a))
b. *We think that Mary should present her case to the committee and we ask that Bill ϕ, too. (=(39b))

Under our framework (see Chapter 7) the structure of (49b) will be shown in (50):

(50) *We think that Mary should present her case to the committee and we ask [$_{CP}$ that [$_{IP}$ Bill [$_{I'}$ I [$_{ModalP}$ M$_\phi$ [$_{VP}$ ϕ too]]]]].

In this case what is left before deleted VP ϕ is the covert M$_\phi$ solely, so neither a morphologically realized Head nor a morphologically realized Spec exists, consequently ungrammaticality results.

Next, we should consider VP-deletion with *do*-support, though Potsdam does not discuss this (see also Section 7.8). Generally speaking, in subjunctive present clauses VP-deletion with *do*-support does not apply. Consider the following examples:

(51) a. *John was unable to play first violin, so I'm requesting that Harry *do*.
 b. *Just as it's important that Harry see this film, so it's necessary that Bill *do*, too.
 c. *I prefer that you leave now and that Bill *do* tomorrow.
(Culicover 1971: 130, fn.11)

These examples are ruled out by the assumption that *do* having [uSubj] does not exist in the lexicon in Present-Day English, as we discussed in Section 8.3, irrespective of VP-deletion.

Additionally, as I mentioned in note 8 in Chapter 6, we can assume that *do* having [uSubj] is assumed for some speakers. For them the following type of VP-deletion with *do* is allowed:

(52) a. John was able to play first violin, so I'm requesting that you *do*, too.
 b. Just as it's important that Harry see this film, so it's necessary that everyone else *do*, too.
 c. I order that everyone get out of the pool, and I demand that you *do*, too, Bobby Poobah.
(Culicover 1971: 130, fn.12)

Third, let us consider the cases where non-modal auxiliaries, i.e. *have* and *be*, are left. My opinion is that Potsdam gives *pragmatically unacceptable* examples or his judgment is *inaccurate*. To begin with, consider Potsdam's (1998) examples under (40a-c), which will be repeated as (53a-c) here:

(53) a. *We can't count on Josh to be waiting for us at the airport so we request that you *be* ɸ instead.
  b. *The bridges were repaired before the engineers could even insist that the supporting structure *be* ɸ first.
  c. *When the laborers have reached a decision, it is important that the leader *have* ɸ as well.   (Potsdam 1997: 537, fn. 5)

My informant checks show that these sentences are unacceptable not because VP-deletion cannot apply to them, but because of other factors: in (53a) *to be* and *that* are not parallel, in (52b) it is hard to interpret what *first* would precede, and (53c) is rather good or almost acceptable. Consequently, (53a) and (53b) can be improved if they are changed as follows:

(54) a. We can't count on Josh *to be* waiting for us at the airport so we request you *to be* ɸ instead. (cf. (53a))[16]
  b. The bridges were *completely* repaired before the engineers could even *recommend* that the supporting structure be ɸ *first*. (cf. (53b))
  c. OK/? When the laborers have reached a decision, it is important that the leader have ɸ as well. (=(53c))[17]

Next, let us consider Potsdam's (1998) examples under (41-44). Here I will submit Potsdam's original examples as the *a*-examples and my slightly modified examples as the *b*-examples below. As for the judgments for each *b*-example, the first judgment is by Donald L. Smith, and the second judgment is by Loretta Church.

(55) PROGRESSIVE BE
  a. *I don't know if Mary is taking care of the plants while we're gone so I would ask that you be ɸ. (=(41a))

    b. OK/* I don't know if Mary is taking care of the plants while we're gone so I would *like to* ask that you be ϕ *instead*.

(56) PROGRESSIVE BE

    a. *My running partner is training for the marathon and it's imperative that I be ϕ too. (=(41b))

    b. (D. L. Smith mentioned that (41b) itself is OK, but L. Church said no.)

(57) PASSIVE BE

    a. *The doctor *didn't think* that Jesse *needed* to be examined by a specialist but he's going to suggest that Joan be ϕ. (=(42a))

    b. OK/OK The doctor didn't *suggest/say* that Jesse *needs* to be examined by a specialist but he's going to suggest that Joan be ϕ.

(58) PASSIVE BE

    a. *Bill was *interviewed* before he quit and I want to insist that you be ϕ too. (=(42b))

    b. OK/OK Bill was *debriefed* before he quit and I insist that you be ϕ too.

(59) PASSIVE BE

    a. *Jack's room was given a thorough cleaning and I suggest that yours be ϕ too. (=(42c))

    b. OK/OK Jack's room was given a thorough cleaning *after the (dust) storm* and I suggest that yours be ϕ too.

(60) PASSIVE BE

    a. *The clients were told everything I suggested *that* they be ϕ. (=(42d))

    b. OK/OK The clients were told everything I suggested they be ϕ.

(61) COPULA BE

    a. *You *should* be happy with the results even though I can't insist that you be ϕ. (=(43a))

    b. OK/OK You *will probably* be happy with the results even though I can't insist that you be ϕ.

(62) COPULA BE

    a. *If *the whole system* is to be on time, it is necessary that the connecting flights be ϕ as well. (=(43b))

    b. OK/OK If *your arrival* is to be on time, it is necessary that the connecting flights be ϕ as well.

(63) PERFECTIVE HAVE

a. ?*By the time Wanda finishes*, it is necessary that Bob have ϕ too.(=(44a))

b. ?/* *For Wanda to have finished*, it is necessary that Bob have ϕ *first*.

(64) PERFECTIVE HAVE

  a. ?Jim memorized the piece and I suggest that, by next lesson, you have ϕ too. (=(44b))

  b. OK/OK Jim memorized the piece and I suggest that, by *the* next lesson, you have ϕ too.

The examples above clearly show that VP-deletion can apply syntactically when *be* or *have* remain. Though some examples are unacceptable for L. Church, the following more simple examples that I made (except for (67b) quoted from Okuno (1999)) are all acceptable for her (and D. L. Smith as well):

(65) PROGRESSIVE BE

  OK/OK I demand that you *be waiting* upstairs when I get home and that Susan *be* ϕ, as well.

(66) PASSIVE BE

  OK/OK I ordered that John *be demoted* and that Susan *be* ϕ, too.

(67) COPULA BE

  a. OK/OK I insist that you *be captain*, but I don't insist that John *be* ϕ, too. (Complement = DP)

  b. OK/OK I demand that you *be honest* and that Mary *be* ϕ, as well. (Complement = AP) (Okuno 1999: 178)

  c. OK/OK I insist that John *be in the room*, but I don't insist that you *be* ϕ. (Complement = PP)

(68) PROGRESSIVE BE

  OK/OK I demand that you *be waiting* upstairs when I get home and that Susan *be* ϕ, as well.

(69) PERFECTIVE HAVE

  OK/OK I demand that by the time I come home you *have completed* your homework and that Mary *have* ϕ, too.

My opinion is also supported by the following examples seen in the literature:

(70) a. I demand that you *be taking* Kippy for a walk and that Susan *be* ϕ, too.
(Weeda 1981: 408)
b. I demanded that you *have removed* your shoes before entering and that Mary *have* ϕ, too. (Asakawa and Kamata 1986: 73)

Our framework will naturally predict all the examples above are grammatical since the morphologically realized Heads *have* or *be* are left (see (48i)).

Incidentally, I am assuming that in the cases of auxiliaries *have* and *be*, VP-deletion can apply, but that in the cases of copula *be* (e.g. (67a-c)), *PrP* (=Predication Phrase)-*deletion* can apply,[18] but not DP-deletion, AP-deletion, or PP deletion.[19], [20] As an illustration of this, consider the following structure:

(71) I demand [CP that [IP you_i I[ModalP M_ϕ [VP be [PrP t_i [Pr' e [AP honest]]]]]]]
(=(67b))

Lastly, let us turn to the main discussion and consider VP-deletion using *not*. It is descriptively correct to say that VP-deletion using *not* is possible in subjunctive present clauses. Under our framework we can confirm that *ModalP-deletion* applies in these examples. As an illustration of this, consider the structure of (45e) as (72):

(72) A: Should I attend the meeting?
B: I suggest [CP that [IP you [I' I [NegP *not* [Neg' NE [ModalP M_ϕ [VP ϕ]]]]]]].

In this case, though a morphologically realized *Head* is not left in NegP (i.e. NE is covert), the morphologically realized *Spec*, i.e. *not*, is left and thus NE is identifiable. Consequently, the deleted ModalP is licensed by a morphologically *identifiable* head NE (see (48ii)).[21], [22]

Before closing this section we should mention the following examples:

(73) a. *Kim needn't be there but it is imperative that the other organizers
$$\begin{Bmatrix} \phi. \\ \text{certainly } \phi. \end{Bmatrix}$$

b. *Ted didn't want to vacation in Hawaii but his agent suggested that he
$\left\{\begin{array}{l}\phi. \\ \text{definitely } \phi.\end{array}\right\}$

b. *We think that Mary should present her case to the committee and we ask that Bill $\left\{\begin{array}{l}\phi, \\ \text{absolutely } \phi,\end{array}\right\}$ too.   (Murakami 1998: 42-43)

(74) a. Kim needs to be there but it is better that the other organizers
$\left\{\begin{array}{l}\text{not } \phi. \\ \text{*never } \phi.\end{array}\right\}$

b. Ted hoped to vacation in Liberia but his agent recommended that he
$\left\{\begin{array}{l}\text{not } \phi. \\ \text{*never } \phi.\end{array}\right\}$

c. We think that Mary should present her case but we will ask that Bill
$\left\{\begin{array}{l}\text{not } \phi. \\ \text{*never } \phi.\end{array}\right\}$

d. A: Should I attend the meeting?
B: I suggest that you $\left\{\begin{array}{l}\text{not } \phi. \\ \text{*never } \phi.\end{array}\right\}$ (Ibid.: 43)

These examples are interesting in that they show that since *adverbs* are not *Spec* but *Adjunct* they cannot license any deletion by definition in (47) and (48).

Considering all the discussion in this section, I submit the following conclusion: (i) not only the sentential negative *not* but also auxiliary *have* and *be* and the copula *be* allow VP-deletion in subjunctive present clauses (i.e., Potsdam's (34a) is empirically wrong). (ii) The licensing conditions on VP-deletion in subjunctive present clauses are basically the same as those in indicative sentences. The differences between indicatives and subjunctives come from the presence of the covert subjunctive modal M_ϕ in subjunctive present clauses. (iii) VP-deletion using sentential *not* is not decisive evidence for Potsdam's conclusion that *not* is the head of NegP under (34b). As for the conclusion in (iii), note that I show many pieces of evidence that support the assumption that *not* occupies the Spec of NegP as I put forth in the previous sections.

11.6 Concluding Remarks

In this chapter I claimed that we have good reason to assume NegP and furthermore that *not* is in the Spec of NegP, not in the Head of NegP. Then, in connection with this problem, I discussed the licensing condition on VP-deletion in subjunctive present clauses. Though Potsdam (1997, 1998) claims that negative *not* alone licenses VP-deletion in subjunctive present clauses and therefore concludes that *not* is the Head of NegP, I showed that not only the negative *not* but also other elements can license deletion (i.e. VP-deletion, PrP-deletion, and ModalP-deletion) in subjunctive present clauses. After showing that the licensing condition on VP-deletion in subjunctive present clauses is the same as in indicative sentences, I concluded that the VP-deletion phenomena in subjunctive present clauses do not constitute decisive evidence for the claim that *not* is the Head of NegP.

Notes to Chapter 11

1. As for Hasegawa's (2003) treatment of *not*, see Section 4.3. As for Ando's (1996, 2003) treatment of *not*, as we observed in Sections 5.3.2-5.3.3, he assumed that the sentential negative *not* is generated in VP-Spec. Note also that Ando (2003) assumes that *not* as in (ia) is *constituent negation*, unlike our assumption in Chapters 3-4, and further assumes that this type of *not* is adjoined to I', as shown in (ib):

(i) a. John wants [not to go].
    b.
```
            IP
           /  \
          NP   I'
          |   /  \
        John_i I  VP
               /  \
              V    IP
              |   /  \
           wants PRO_i I'
                     /  \
                   not   I'
                        /  \
                       I    VP
                       |
                       to   go
```
                                                            (Ando 2003: 634)

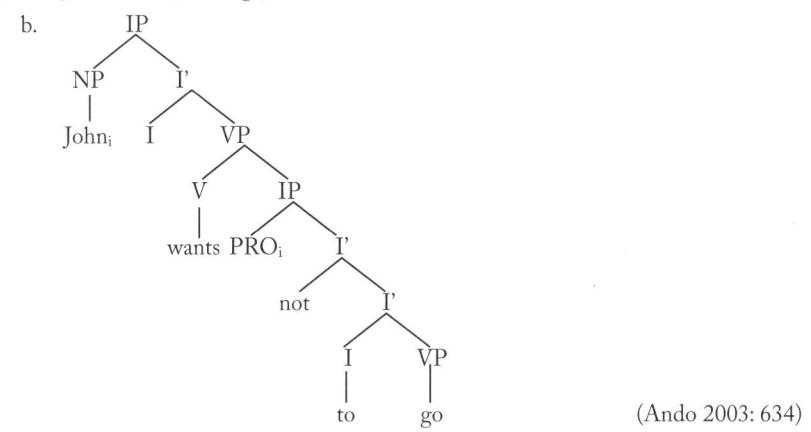

2. Hasegawa (2003) does not assume NegP either. However, he is consistent in a sense in that he does not assume IP and CP either, based on the Distribution or Replacement test. Consider the following examples:

(i) a. I think that { [_α John will come].
                     *[_α will], *[_α can]. }   (Hasegawa 2003: 205)
       → α(=S) is not the projection of Infl or Aux (=IP).
    b. I think { [_β that John will come].
                 *[_β that], *[_β ϕ]. }   (Ibid.)
       → β(=S') is not the projection of C (=CP).

Thus he concludes that S and S' are not *endocentric* constructions (=the projection of any word) but *exocentric* constructions (cf. Bloomfield (1933)).

3. As for a similar proposal as (11), see also Radford's (2004) *Functional Head Constraint*, as shown in (i):

   (i) Functional Head Constraint/FHC
   The complement of a certain type of functional head F (e.g. a determiner or complementiser) cannot be moved on its own (without also moving F)
   (Radford 2004: 89)

4. Needless to say, we could give other syntactic accounts for the ungrammaticality of NegP-Deletion or Fronting under our framework. As for NegP-Deletion e.g., since the [uNeg] feature that modals have cannot be checked off by the deleted *not* having [Neg], ungrammaticality results, as shown in (i):

   (i) A: Will the President of the United States [$_{NegP}$ not talk about racial discrimination]?
   B: *No, he will   φ= [NegP   not   NE talk about racial discrimination]
              [uNeg]   [Neg]

5. As is shown by the fact that I am not assuming AgrP in this book, I agree with his claim that assuming AgrP is empirically wrong (see note 3 in Chapter 2). However, NegP is rather different from AgrP in that the former has much to do with semantic interpretations but the latter does not have anything to do with semantic interpretations.

6. If we modified (23), we could make a more generalized assumption as follows:

   (i) Moved elements cannot pass over the closest *possible* c-commanding landing cite.

   This *intuition* has been one of the most important principles in the history of generative grammar, though the formalization has changed many times; i.e. Chomsky's (1964) *A-over-A Principle* (named by Ross (1967=1986)), Chomsky's (1973) *Superiority Condition*, Hasegawa's (1974, 1983, 2003) *Generalized A-over-A Principle* (GAoA), Bresnan's (1976) *Relativized A over A Principle*, Travis's (1984) *Head Movement Constraint* (HMC), Rizzi's (1990) *Relativized Minimality*, Chomsky's (1995) *Minimal Link Condition* (MLC), and Chomsky's (2000, 2001a, b) *Defective Intervention Constraint* (DIC).

7. Murakami (1995a, 2003) claims that the following example shows that *not* is an Infl modifier:

(i) [Could not]ᵢ the President tᵢ ratify the treaty?   (Murakami 1995a: 104)

However, as she herself comments, this is (undoubtedly) *rare*, and we therefore should consider this type of sentence to be ungrammatical at least in Present-Day English. Consider the following examples:

(i) a. **Can not* he drive?
   b. **Is not* Mary a student?
   c. **Has not* the rain stopped?   (Celce-Murcia and Larsen-Freeman 1983: 111)
(ii) a. **Do not* you like dogs?
   b. **Does not* anyone live here?
   c. **Have not* you finished?   (Davies 1986: 113)

If we assumed that this type of sentence is acceptable, we should consider *not* as in (i) to be practically the same as the affix *n't* in (iii), since no elements can intervene between the modal and *not* in this case, as is shown in (iv):

(iii) *Couldn't* the President ratify the treaty?   (Murakami 1995a: 104)
(iv) **Could possibly not* the President ratify the treaty?

8. Here we should note Lasnik's (1995=1999: Chapter 5) comment on this matter, as shown in (i):

(i) The first possibility, along the lines of Roberts (1993 [1992]; 1994), is that Neg and V are heads of different sorts (A' vs. A) and that relativized Minimality is even more relativized than in the original proposal of Rizzi (1990). If a head only blocks movement of a head of the same type, Neg would then not block movement of V. The second possibility is that Neg is *not* a head, but a modifier.
(Lasnik 1995=2000: 108)

We will not consider Lasnik's implied first *ad hoc* proposal that Neg and V are heads of different sorts. As for his second implied proposal that Neg is not a *head* but a *modifier*, we may say that Radford (1988), Baker (1991), Ernst (1992), Murakami (1995a, 1998, 2003), Sawada (1993, 1995), Ando (1996, 2003, 2004), Matsubara (1997a, b),

Hasegawa (2003), etc. take this possibility seriously. On the other hand, Rizzi (1990), Belletti (1990), Roberts (1992), and I do not consider this possibility a serious problem since Spec positions can be considered to have the nature of *modifier* rather than *head*.

9. As for the development of the negative structure in the history of English, see, e.g., Ishikawa (1995).

10. Murakami (2003) assumes the negative structure in older English to be the following:

(i)

```
         I'
        / \
       I   VP
      / \   \
     I  Neg  V
         |   |
       na/not ne+V
```

(Murakami 2003: 4)

However, at the presentation of Murakami (2003) Masachiyo Amano pointed out that two lexical items cannot be merged under the V^0 node. On this point I agree with Amano.

11. Here I am assuming a similar notion of Spec assumed in early X-bar theory (cf. Chomsky (1970), Jackendoff (1977), and Emonds (1985)). Consider the following examples:

(i) NP-Spec

```
              N"
             /  \
           Det   N'
            |     \
    {some/this/a/the/---}  N
                            \
                           book
```

(ii) AP-Spec

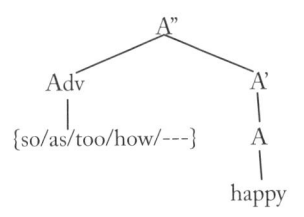

```
         A"
        /  \
      Adv   A'
       |    |
{so/as/too/how/---}  A
                     |
                   happy
```

(iii) PP-Spec

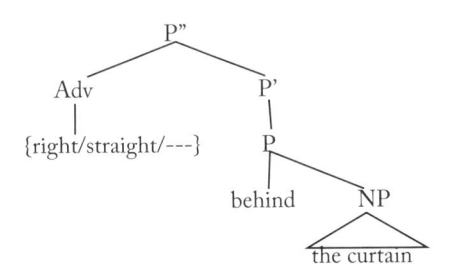

```
          P"
         /  \
       Adv   P'
        |    |
{right/straight/---}  P
                     / \
                 behind  NP
                         |
                    the curtain
```

(iv) VP-Spec

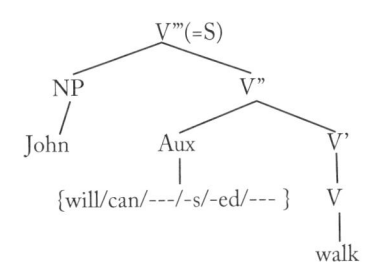

```
              V"'(=S)
             /      \
           NP        V"
           |        /  \
          John    Aux    V'
                   |     |
     {will/can/---/-s/-ed/---}  V
                                |
                              walk
```

12. The implication is that *not* does not block any movement under our framework so long as we do not assume X^0-Movement *from Spec to Spec*. In this connection, though, I do not consider *adverb movement*. For those who assume adverb movement, *not* could possibly block some form of adverb movement or other.

13. This section is mainly based on Nomura (2003a).
    Nomura (2003a) is a revised version of Nomura (2002b), a paper presented at the 20th National Conference of the English Linguistics Society of Japan, held at Aoyama Gakuin University on November 17th, 2002. I have benefited from discussion with the participants, among whom were Go Mizumoto, Madoka Murakami, Masaki Sano, and

Shigeo Tonoike. I am also much indebted to Donald L. Smith and Loretta Church for acting as my informants.

14. As a good review of Potsdam (1997, 1998), see especially Murakami (1998) and Kuwabara (2001).

15. It goes without saying that (47) is a *necessary* condition on deletion, not a *sufficient* condition. For example, deletion of the object DP or the complement AP is not allowed, as shown in (ia, b):

(i) a. *John bought books, and Mary bought ϕ, too.
　 b. *John looked happy, and Mary looked ϕ, too.

Lobeck (1995) expresses these facts as the following licensing condition in (iii) under *strong agreement* in (ii):

(ii) Strong Agreement
　　An X-0 is specified for 'strong' agreement iff X-0, or the phrase or head with which X-0 agrees, morphologically realizes agreement in a productive number of cases.
　　　　　　　　　　　　　　　　　　　　　　　　　　　　　　　　(Lobeck 1995: 51)
(iii) Licensing and Identification of pro
　　An empty, non-arbitrary pronominal must be properly head-governed, and governed by an X-0 specified for strong Agreement.　　　　　(Ibid.: 52)

I will leave the *necessary* and *sufficient* conditions on deletion for future study. (As for interesting attempts to account for (iii) in the Minimalist framework by using the notion Phase (Chomsky (2000, 2001a, b)), see Takahashi (2001, 2002) and Tonoike (2001).)

16. Needless to say, since (54a) is an example of an infinitive, it is not direct evidence for me, but according to D. L. Smith, (53a) can be much improved if *that*, which causes unacceptability, is omitted, as shown in (i):

(i) OK/? We can't count on Josh to be waiting for us at the airport so we request you *be* ϕ instead. (cf. (53a))

This example will be evidence for me without doubt.

17. As for (53c) in Potsdam (1997), note in particular that *come to* is used instead of *arrived* in Potsdam (1998). We may say that the sentence would be even less acceptable when *come to* is used:

   (i) *When the laborers have *come to* a decision, it is important that the leader *have* ϕ as well. (Potsdam 1998: 154)

   D. L. Smith also judged (i) to be unacceptable. On the other hand, note that (53c) (=(54c)) is much better as compared to (i).

18. As for the *main* verb *have* in subjunctive present clauses, VP-deletion cannot apply, just as in the case with the indicative *have*. Consider the following example that I made:

   (i) */* I insist that you *have a driver's license*, but I don't insist that Mary *have* ϕ.

19. As for *PrP*, see Bowers (1993). (See also note 16 in Chapter 5.)
    Incidentally, he assumes PrP in transitive verb constructions as well, but in this book I am assuming that not PrP but *only* vP exists in transitive verb constructions.

20. Though the framework is different, Okuno (1999), which is a review article of Lobeck (1995), gives an alternative account for VP-deletion by assuming PrP.

21. Masaki Sano asked me an important question at the presentation of Nomura (2002b), as shown in (i):

   (i) Do the Spec elements other than *not* license deletion?

   We can easily think of a case of IP-Spec (i.e. the subject of a sentence), but this does not license deletion, as shown in (ii):

   (ii) a. *John likes Mary, and Bill ϕ.
        b. John [vP likes Mary], and [IP *Bill* Pres [vP likes Mary]].

   In this case we could assume that (iia) is ruled out by a general *phonological* principle, as shown in (iii):

(iii) The subject DP and the verbal element (including *not*) must be stressed in the clauses where deletion applies.

I will leave details relating to this problem for future study; but let me just mention that Madoka Murakami pointed out the possibility that *Comparative Deletion* is another case of the Spec elements licensing deletion, though she also said that the nature is a little different. Moreover, Go Mizumoto suggested the case of *Sluicing*. Indeed, sluicing is a good example where a *Spec* element (=*wh*-words) licenses deletion (=IP-deletion). Consider the following example:

(iv) He is writing something, but you can't imagine [CP what [IP φ]].

22. Incidentally, we can further assume the following condition on ModalP-deletion:

(i) When ModalP-deletion applies, the deleted Modal (=trace) must be c-commanded by the moved Modal (=copy).

For example, the following examples are all subject to (i):

(ii) a. Mary wants to go to the fashion show but her husband might *not* φ.

(Potsdam 1997: 534)

b. [IP her husband might$_i$ [NegP not NE [ModalP t$_i$ [VP want to go to the fashion show]]]]

    c-command

(iii) a. Some of the guests tried the appetizers but most did *not* φ. (Ibid.)

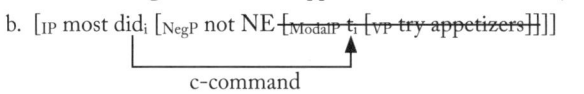

b. [IP most did$_i$ [NegP not NE [ModalP t$_i$ [VP try appetizers]]]]

    c-command

(iv) a. A: Should I attend the meeting?
B: I suggest that you not φ. (Ibid.: 538)

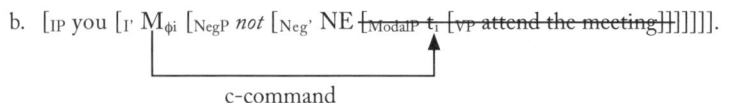

b. [IP you [I' M$_{\phi i}$ [NegP *not* [Neg' NE [ModalP t$_i$ [VP attend the meeting]]]]]].

    c-command

On the other hand, the following example of the infinitive is ungrammatical because of the violation of (i):

(v) a. *John told Mary to leave, but Bill told her *not* ϕ.
        cf. John told Mary to leave, but Bill told her not *to* ϕ.
     b. [IP Bill told her_i [IP PRO_i [I' [I Nonfinite T] [NegP *not* [Neg' NE [ModalP to [VP leave]]]]]].

That is, the deleted *to* (=a type of Modal) cannot be c-commanded by the moved Modal because *to* does not raise to I, as we discussed in Chapter 3.

In conclusion, we can submit the following *descriptive* generalization:

(vi) Only *tensed* Modal can be deleted.

Chapter 12

Have-Be Raising in Subjunctive Present Clauses

12.1 Introduction

In this chapter I discuss the possibility of *have-be* raising in subjunctive present clauses. First, I reconsider the analysis of the word order <have/be + not> as sentential negation seen in subjunctive present clauses. Next, I will briefly discuss a historical overview from the perspective of the negative and word order.

12.2 A Reconsideration of the Analysis of the Word Order <Have/Be + Not> in Subjunctive Present Clauses[1)]

12.2.1 Proposals

So far I have assumed a covert subjunctive modal M_ϕ in subjunctive present clauses throughout this book. Strong evidence for this assumption is that in negative subjunctive present clauses the word order is <not + have/be>, not <have/be + not> (cf. indicative finite sentences). Consider the following examples again:

(1) a. I demand that you *not be* such a fool.
  b. *I demand that you *be not* such a fool. (Culicover 1971: 41)
(2) a. He suggested that he *not have* finished the work before 10 o'clock.
  b. *He suggested that he *have not* finished the work before 10 o'clock.
  (Beukema and Coopmans 1989: 429)

However, other word orders are in fact seen. Observe the following examples:

(3) The student required that his work on Italian *be not* marked by Professor Vincent. (Beukema and Coopmans 1989: 430, fn. 13)
(4) a. I demand that he *not have* left before I return.

b. I demand that he *have not* left before I return.   (Fiengo 1980: 80)

Note, however, that Beukema and Coopmans (1989), Potsdam (1997, 1998) claim that *not* as seen in (3) or (4b) is not *sentential negation* but *constituent negation*. I myself made the same claim in Nomura (2000a). But considering many other examples, I will modify my assumption and make the following assumption instead:

(5) In Present-Day English two types of *have* and *be* exist in subjunctive present clauses; the root forms *have* and *be* (after the covert subjunctive modal M_ϕ) and the subjunctive present forms *have* and *be* (having the [uSubj] feature in itself).

(6) In negative subjunctive present clauses <not + have/be> (=root forms) is an *unmarked* word order, but <have/be + not> (=subjunctive forms) is also allowed as a *marginally marked* word order even in Present-Day's English, so that the latter word order must be supported semantically according to the *semantic condition* (see (32) below).

In the following subsections I discuss the adequacy of these proposals by examining many examples.

12.2.2 Studies Claiming That the <Have/Be + Not> Word Order Is Ungrammatical

Many theoretical linguists have claimed that the <have/be + not> word order is ungrammatical in subjunctive present clauses. Observe the following examples:

(7) a. I demand that you *not be* such a fool.
   b. *I demand that you *be not* such a fool.   (Culicover 1971: 41)
(8) *They demand that John *be not* given special treatment.
   (Emonds 1970: 196)
(9) a. *She requests that they *be not* examined.
   b. *It is of great importance that the children *be not* in the street when he comes.   (Emonds 1976: 214)

(10) a. *I require that he *be not* there by 8.
   b. *I require that he *have not* left before I arrive.   (Roberts 1985: 41, fn.12)
(11) *I demand that the chairman *be not* reinstated.   (Radford 1988: 457)
(12) a. *He suggested that he *be not* arrested by the police.
   b. He suggested that he *not be* arrested by the police.
   c. *He suggested that he *have not* finished the work before 10 o'clock.
   d. He suggested that he *not have* finished the work before 10 o'clock.
                                        (Beukema and Coopmans 1989: 429)
(13) a. It's important that he *not be* foolish.
   b. *It's important that he *be not* foolish.   (Culicover 1999: 153)
(14) a. *I urge that Tom *be not* promoted because of his attitude.
   b. *The association urges that he *be not* examined by that quack.
   c. ?It is imperative that the contestant *have not* seen the answers ahead of time.   (Potsdam 1997: 537)

Here we should pay careful attention to Potsdam's comment concerning (14a-c) which follows:

(15) It is necessary to differentiate sentential negation from constituent negation. The latter, which may also be expressed with *not*, typically serves to contrast a constituent with some alternative and bears contrastive stress. The examples in (11) [=(14a-c) in this chapter] may be grammatical with constituent negation but are not grammatical as instances of sentential negation. This can be seen by applying Iatridou's (1990) *because*-adjunct diagnostic. (i) with sentential negation is ambiguous, having the readings in (iia-b). (iii) with constituent negation has the only the reading in (iia), in which just the verb phrase is within the scope of negation. <u>Crucially, (11a) [=(14a)], if it is grammatical, patterns with the constituent negation example and has only the first reading. This indicates that the examples are ungrammatical with sentential negation, as claimed.</u>
   (i) Tom was not promoted because of his attitude.
   (ii) a. Tom was not promoted and the reason is because of his attitude.
      b. Tom was promoted but not because of his attitude.
   (iii) Tom will be not promoted because of his attitude.

(Potsdam 1997: 536, fn. 2, underlines are mine)

However, D. L. Smith (personal communication, 2003) crucially pointed out that (14a) is grammatical and moreover has both readings in (16a, b):

(16) a. I urge that Tom not be promoted and the reason is because of his attitude.
   b. I urge that Tom be promoted but not because of his attitude.

It follows from this we can clearly conclude that the <have/be + not> word orders as a form of sentential negation exist,[2] but we shall consider additional examples in the next section to demonstrate that the solution to this problem is not attributed to differing intuitions alone.[3]

12.2.3 Counterexamples

In the previous section we reviewed the claim that the <have/be + not> word order is ungrammatical in subjunctive present clauses, but we can easily find many counterexamples; first, as for weak evidence, we can submit examples of *formulaic subjunctives*. Consider the following examples:

(17) a. If it *be/is* ever so humble, there's no place like home.
   b. *Be* it ever so humble, there's no place like home.
   c. **Is* it ever so humble, there's no place like home.

   (Suzuki and Yasui 1994: 309)

It follows that we should consider that this subjunctive *be* has the [uSubj] feature and thus raises to T and further to C, but the indicative *is* does not. (In this case we can consider that I has the feature [Pres] and *C has the feature [Subj]* as a fossilized expression.) Observe the following additional examples:

(18) a. *Be it* noted that this offer was made in good faith.
   b. *Be that* as it may, we have nothing to lose.   (Quirk *et al.* 1985: 157-158)
(19) a. Far *be it* from me to spoil the fun.
   b. So *be it* then.   (Declerck 1991a: 353)

(20) a. Without care from some other human being, *be it* mother, grandmother or nurse, a child is very unlikely to survive. (Anne and Peter Doughty, *Language and Community*)
   b. *Be a life* long or short, its completeness depends on what it was lived for. (David Starr Jordan)
(21) But this is not, *be it* noted, a limitation on quantitative patterns as such. (Halliday (1973), *Explanations in the Functions of Language*, p.117,
quoted from Chiba (2001: 1))

It is possible that these might be *fossilized* expressions and *not productive*. Note that inversion is also seen in other *intransitive* subjunctive verbs as well in this type of formulaic subjunctive use, as shown below:[4]

(22) a. *Come what may*, we will go ahead with our plan.
   b. *Suffice it* to say that we won.   (Quirk *et al.* 1985: 157)
(23) Long *live the King*!   (Declerck 1991a: 353)

On the other hand, the following examples can be seen as *direct* counterexamples to the claim that only one other allows sentential negation:

(24) With all verbs except BE, the verb phrase is made negative by placing *not* before the subjunctive form. In the case of *be, not* may be placed either before or after the verb, whereas with *were* it follows it:
   It is essential that this mission not fail.
   The Senate has decreed that the students { be not / not be } exempted from college dues.
   If I weren't/were not your best friend, you would regret that remark.
(Quirk *et al.* 1985:156, underlines are mine)
(25) a. I demand that he *not have* left before I return.
   b. I demand that he *have not* left before I return.   (Fiengo 1980: 80)
(26) a. We prefer that the men *not be* cutting down redwoods.
   b. We prefer that the men *be not* cutting down redwoods.
(Weeda 1981: 410, fn. 2)

(27) a. It is important that the committee *not have* seen the report.
b. It is important that the committee *have not* seen the report.   (Ibid.)
(28) a. The will requires that the beneficiary *not have been* married at the time of death of the deceased.
b. The will requires that the beneficiary *have not been* married at the time of death of the deceased.
c. The will requires that the beneficiary *have been not* married at the time of death of the deceased.   (Ibid.)
(29) a. It's important that he *not have* finished the work before I get home.
b. It's important that he *have not* finished the work before I get home.
(Culicover 1999: 154)

Furthermore, we can find many attested examples similar to the above as follows:

(30) a. —very little of (Edward Taylor's) verse was published in his day, but he left enough in ms. to fill a large volume, with the request that it *be not* printed. (Kenneth B. Murdock)
b. —provided further, that if any such increased rate *be not* acceptable to the shipper. (cargo contract)   (Quoted from Zandvoort (1954))
c. —it is very helpful, I would say almost necessary, that history *be not* written in one county alone (cf. Carey (1953))
(Quoted from Zandvoort (1954))
(31) a. It is of course reasonable that a set *be not* definable by properties of a subset of its members. (Huddleston (1971), *The Sentence in Written English*, p.224)
b. But all of the assumptions (3)-(5) are moot (to say the least), and if any one of them *be not* accepted, C's argument for the necessary correctness of (1) falls through. (*Lingua* 50 (1980), p.126)
c. In all our communication with people, if it *be not* of an inspirational nature, it is best to remain silent. (Grace Speare, *Everything Talks to Me*, p.138)
d. "To me, now, the most important is that we *be not* disturbed here," Pablo said. (Earnest Hemingway, *For Whom the Bell Tolls*, p.19)
e. It remained merely for the West Chicago Street Railway Company to secure an injunction vacating the first injunction, praying that its rights,

privileges, Liberties, etc., *be not* interfered with, and .... (Theodore Dreiser, *The Titan*, p. 255) (All quoted from Chiba (1987: 50))

Note in particular that we cannot but consider the meanings of these attested examples to be *sentential negation*, not constituent negation. Also we note that these word orders do not come from *dialectal variations* since they are seen both in American English and in British English.

12.2.4 Semantic Condition on the <Have/Be + Not> Word Order in Subjunctive Present Clauses

Now that we have shown that the <have/be + not> word orders as sentential negation do exist in subjunctive present clauses even in Present-Day English, I propose the following semantic condition on the <have/be + not> word order in these clauses:

(32) a. In negative subjunctive present clauses both the word orders of (i) <not + have/be> (=unmarked) and (ii) <have/be + not> (=marginal, marked) are allowed even in Present-Day English.
 b. However, since the <have/be + not> word order in (ii) is a *marginally marked* word order in Presnt-Day English, the predicate in the embedded subjunctive clause must express *Action* as an added meaning implied by the word order of verbal elements and *not*.

Adding (32b), the possibility of a marked word order, to the unmarked word order of <not + have/be>, we can make the following predictions:

(33) (i) The word order <not + have/be> in subjunctive present clause implies *State*.[5), 6)]
 (ii) The word order <have/be + not> in subjunctive present clause implies *Action*.[7)]

Here, turning to (32b), in negative subjunctive present clauses, both the word orders of (i) <not + have/be> and (ii) <have/be + not> are allowed even in Present-

Day English, but since the <have/be + not> word order in (ii) is a *marginally marked* word order in Present-Day English, it must exceptionally express Action based on (33ii) to be supported semantically.[7]

Now we are in the position to consider the unacceptable examples again. Though Potsdam (1997, 1998) claims that all the <be + not> examples in subjunctive present clauses are ungrammatical, we should note that the unacceptability of his examples is caused by the fact that the predicates express State, not Action. Consider the following examples:

(34) *I demand that you *be not* such a fool. (=(7b))
(35) *I demand that you *be not* dishonest.
(36) a. *It is of great importance that the children *be not* in the street when he comes. (=(9b))
  b. *I require that he *be not* there by 8. (=(10a))
(37) a. *Humility requires that one *be not* proud.
  b. *His mother is always urging that he *be not* a cheapskate.
  c. *Hilda requested that the guests *be not* going so soon.
  d. *Professor Zok asks that we *be not* sleeping during his lectures.
  e. *In the interest of matrimonial bliss, the counselor suggests that you *be not* keeping secrets from your wife.   (Potsdam 1998: 147-148)

On the other hand, note that the attested examples shown in Section 12.2.3 express Action:

(38) a. — very little of (Edward Taylor's) verse was published in his day, but he left enough in ms. to fill a large volume, with the request that it *be not* printed. (=(30a))
  b. — it is very helpful, I would say almost necessary, that history *be not* written in one county alone (=(30c))
  c. "To me, now, the most important is that we *be not* disturbed here," Pablo said. (=(31d))

Next, as for the cases of <have + not>, we can consider that the perfective, i.e. the <have + not + P.P (=-*en* form)> word order, will become much more acceptable than the <be + not> word order, since the perfect forms can express Action easily as compared to constructions with the copula *be*, the passive *be*, and the progressive *be*. In fact, Potsdam himself admitted that this word order is not completely ungrammatical, as shown in (39), and thus judges all the examples in (40a-c) to be "?", not "*" (see also the judgments of Johnson (1988) and Culicover (1999)).

(39) Johnson 1988 demonstrates that the behavior of negation with respect to perfective *have* in subjunctives is exceptional and examples like this one with *not* following *have* are sometimes acceptable.　(Potsdam 1998: 96, fn. 20)[8]

(40) a. ?My parents suggested that the baby sitter *have not* <u>left a mess in the kitchen for them to clean when they get back</u>.
　　b. ?I urged that Mary *have not* <u>just skimmed over his critique simply because of his attitude</u>.
　　c. ?Who demanded that we *have not* <u>eaten everything before sitting down to supper</u>.　(Ibid.: 149)

In fact, D. L. Smith judged (40a-c) to be all grammatical. Note that they all express Action.

Furthermore, taking (32b) into consideration, I constructed the following examples in (41-43) and asked informants (two Americans and two Englishmen) whether they are grammatical or not:

(41) COUPULA BE
　　a. I demand that all of you *be not* <u>up</u> when I get back. (Complement =PP)
　　b. John ordered that the children *be not* <u>noisy</u> when he gets home from work. (Complement = AP)
　　c. I demand that you *be not* <u>a person who never turns up to class on time</u>. (Complement = DP)[9]

(42) PROGRESSIVE BE
　　I demand that when I get home you *be not* <u>waiting upstairs</u>.

(43) PASSIVE BE
　　I demand that John *be not* <u>promoted</u> for that reason.

(44) PERFECTIVE HAVE

I demand that you *have not* gone to bed before I return.[10]

The result is that they said some examples in (41-44) sound *archaic*, or that <not + have/be> word order would be better, but agreed that all the examples in (41-44) are grammatical.

Here in order to make clear the differences between Action and State, I will submit some paraphrases by informants, as shown in (45-46), though the interpretations are, needless to say, delicate. Note the *conjunctions* used in the paraphrases in (45a, b):

(45) a. I demand that all of you *be not* up when I get back. (=(41a))
    =*Go to bed* before *I get back.* (Action)
  b. I demand that all of you *not be* up when I get back.
    =*Stay in bed* when *I get back.* (State)
(46) a. John ordered that the children *be not* noisy when he gets home from work. (=(41b))
    =John said to the children, "*Don't be noisy* when I get home from work." (Action)
  b. I demand that you *be not* a person who never turns up to class on time. (=(41c))
    =I want you *not to be a person* who never turns up to class on time. (Action)

So far I have discussed the adequacy of (32b), but it goes without saying that other factors are involved in judgements of unacceptability. For example, we can consider that the following sentence expresses an Action, but it is, nevertheless, unacceptable:

(47) *He* suggested that *he* have not finished the work before 10 o'clock. (=(12c))

In this case informants had difficulty conceiving that the matrix subject *he* and the embedded subject *he* are different persons at the same time. So when two different persons are used as the matrix and embedded subjects, the sentence was judged more acceptable:[11]

(48) *I* order that *you* have not finished the work before 10 o'clock.

Next, it seems that the following examples express Action as well, but they are unacceptable all the same:

(49) a. *They demand that *John* be not given special treatment. (=(8))
  b. *She requests that *they* be not examined. (=(9a))
  c. *He suggested that *he* be not arrested by the police. (=(12a))
  d. *The association urges that *he* be not examined by that quack. (=(14b))
  e. *It is advised that *everyone* be not fooled by his chicanery.
  (Potsdam 1998: 148)
  f. *For his own sake, the association urges that *he* be not examined by that quack. (Ibid.)

In each case, since the power relations between the addressees (=the persons who are given a command by the matrix subject) and the embedded subjects (=the persons who should do the action) are unclear, unacceptability results. Note that in all the examples in (41-44) the addressees (=the persons who are given a command by the matrix subject) and the embedded subjects (=the persons who should do the action) are clearly the same persons.[12]

Last, I would like to mention a *stylistic* factor. We find that the <have/be + not> word is allowed more easily in *legalistic* examples. Consider the following examples:

(50) a. The Senate has decreed that the students *be not* exempted from college dues. (=(24))
  b. The will requires that the beneficiary (i)*have not been* (ii)*have been not* married at the time of death of the deceased. (=(28b, c))
  c. It is important that the committee *have not* seen the report. (=(29b))
  d. The hearing in Court shall be public, unless the Court shall decide otherwise, or unless the parties demand that the public *be not* admitted. (Article 46, League of Nations and United Nations Statutes of the Permanent Court of International Justice)

We can consider that this usage may be because ambiguity must be avoided as much as possible in *legalistic* sentences. For example, (28a) (repeated as (51) here), where the unmarked word order <not + have> is used, is in fact ambiguous, in that it has two interpretations, as shown in (52a, b):

(51) The will requires that the beneficiary *not have been* married at the time of death of the deceased. (=(28a))
(52) a. The will requires that the beneficiary have never been married (=unmarried in the past) at the time of death of the deceased. (=(50b(i)))
    b. The will requires that the beneficiary have been not married at the time of death of the deceased. (The will will be met even if the beneficiary was formerly married in the past.) (=(50b(ii)))

If we used the ambiguous (51) for a will, it would be inappropriate since accuracy should be required. It would be better if we used the marked <have + not> word order rather than the unmarked <not + have> word order in such a case to avoid ambiguity.[13]

In conclusion, in this section I have shown that even in Present-Day English both the word orders of <not + have/be> and <have/be + not> are allowed in subjunctive present clauses as sentential negation. I then claimed that the latter marginal word order must be subject to the semantic condition in (32b) to be supported semantically, and that the unacceptable sentences with the <have/be + not> word order are due to the violation of (32b) or other factors. Last I argued that this word order is allowed more easily in the legalistic styles.

12.3 Historical Overview

Next, in this section I will briefly consider historical perspective of the subjunctive present from the viewpoint of the negative and the <not + V> word order from a historical perspective.

12.3.1 The Development of the Negative and the <Not + V> Word Order in Subjunctive Present Clauses

As I emphasized and discussed at several points in this chapter, the <not + V> word order is one of the most important characteristics in the subjunctive present. Observe the following examples again:

(53) a. His father insisted that John *not smoke* at home.
 b. I demand that you *not be* such a fool.
 c. He suggested that he *not have* finished the work before 10 o'clock.

There are mainly two opinions concerning this word order (cf. Wakatabe (1985: 133)):

(54) a. Kirchner (1970-72: §105.4) regards the word order as one of the preserved Early Modern English usages in American English.
 b. Visser (1966: §871) regards the word order as one of the comparatively newer usages in American English.

To quote them each below:

(55) Voranstellung von '*not*' vor Verbalform war Shakepeare-Zeit noch ganz geläufig, wurde aber selten nach dem 17. Jh. (vgl. Jesp., MEG., V, p. 428). die Voranstellung von '*not*' heute nur gelegentlich und höchstens in der Antithese begegnet, hat AE. diese Konstr. im kojunctivischen Nebensatz durchaus bewahrt.   (Kirchner 1970-72: §105.4, p.520)
 (Placing *not* before the verb was quite common pervasive in Shakespeare's Day, but this usage has become rare since the 17th century (see Jespersen (1909-49, V: 428)). In today's English placing *not* before the verb is occasionally seen in the contrastive expressions at most, but this construction [i.e. the <not + V> word order] is well preserved in the subjunctive subordinate clauses.)
 (Translations are mine)

(56) It [i.e. the <not + V> word order in subjunctive present clauses] seems to have arisen—quite recently, judging from the evidence come to light so far

—in the United States; it is probably not one of the numerous post-colonial survivals of mother-country usage. (Visser 1966: 847)

As for the two opinions, I claim that Visser's one is more appropriate. Here, consider the historical development of the (indicative) negative construction in English. As an illustration of this, consider table (57):

(57) a. Old English   Ic *ne* secge
    b. Early Middle English—15th century   I *ne* seye *not*
    c. Late 14th century—Early Modern English   I say *not*
    c'. 15th century—Early Modern English   I *not* say
    d. 16th century—Late 17th century (Completed)   I *do not* say
    e. 17th century   I *don't* say
    (cf. Jespersen (1924: 115-6), Araki and Ukaji (1984: 508),
        Pollock (1989:367), Nakao and Koma (1990: 159), etc.)

If the word order <not + V> in the present subjunctives in Present-Day English is one of the preserved Early Modern English usages in American English, as Kirchner indicates, then we should conclude that it came from (57c'). To examine this idea, consider further the development of the <V + not> word order both in the indicative (=(57c')) and the subjunctive.

First, as for the word order in (57c'), we can observe not just a few <V + not> examples in the 16th and 17th centuries (for discussion of this topic, see especially Ukaji (1992)). The following examples are from Shakespeare's plays:

(58) a. To chide at your extremes it *not becomes* me: (*The Winter's Tale*, IV. iv. 6)
    b. Robs me of that which *not enriches* him
       And makes me poor indeed. (*Othello*, III. iii. 160-1)
    c. For who *not needs* shall never lack a friend (*Hamlet*, III. ii. 207)[14]

However, this word order was commonly used for only two centuries (i.e. the 16th and 17th centuries), and this use was hardly seen in the 18th century (cf. Araki and Ukaji (1984: 509), Ukaji (1992), and Ukaji (2000: 313-316)), as shown in (61):

(59) a. 15th century   Hoccleve   2
                        Pecock   1
                        Paston Letters 2
                        Malory   0

   b. 16th century   Ascham   1
                        Marlowe   1
                        Nashe   5
                        Shakespeare   12

   c. 17th century   Shakespeare   33
                        Jonson   20
                        D'Avenant   7
                        Dryden   3

   d. 18th century   Defoe   1
                        Lady Mary   1
                        Johnson   1
                        Richardson   1

(Ukaji 1992)

According to the *OED*, the last example which can be found is (60) in 1816 and this use is obsolete:

(60) making a marvel that it *not decays*. (Byron, 1816)

Next, consider the historical development of word order with negative in the present subjunctive. Compared to the indicative case reviewed above, the word order with negative in subjunctives did not change from the 15th century to the 18th century, i.e., the <V + not> word order was regularly used throughout that period. Observe the following examples:

(61) 15th century
   a. take good kepe þat þe nedil *touche not* þe ye (c1410 Duke of York, Master of Grame (ed. Baillie/Groman) 52)

b. Y praie you that ye *be not* the furst to take new shappes and gises of array. (c1450 knight Tour-Landry 29. 31)
   (Quoted from Visser (1966: 837-839))

(62) 16th century
   To prouide that a thing *happen not*, 'precauseo' (1573-80 John Baret, An Alvearie or Triple Dictionarie, P 801)   (Quoted from ibid.)

(63) 17th century
   a. Beware thou that thou *bring not* my son thither again. (1611 Authorized Version, Genesis 24, 6: V 869)   (Quoted from Roberts (1985: 61, fn. 12))
   b. But pray yee that your flight *bee not* in the winter, neither on the Sabbath day. (Ibid., Matthew xxii. 20)
   c. But I say vnto you, that yee *resist not* euill. (Ibid., Matthew v. 39)
   d. But I have prayed for thee, that thy faith *faile not*.   (Ibid., Luke xxii. 32)
   (b-d, quoted from Ukaji (1978: 36))[15), 16)]

(64) 18th century
   a. ... and take heed that he *be not* tempted to do a vile thing....
   b. Let her take care... Let her take care... that she *give* me *not* ground to suspect her....
   c. I wish he *be not* now proud indeed!
   (a-c, examples from periodicals published
         in the early 18th century, quoted from Charleston (1941: 140))
   d. If the spirit *be not* tamed and broken by this happy method, it is stubborn and litigious. (Edmund Burke, *On Conciliation with America*, 1775)
   e. ...let your judment interpose; and take care that it *be not* at the expense of any body. (Chesterfield: 272)   (Quoted from Akimoto (2002: 78))

(65) 19th century
   a. On thy life see that thou *fail* me *not*. (Sir Henry Rider Haggard, *She*, III, 1886)
   b. God grant that he *be not* deceived. (Robert Louis Stevenson, *Dr. Jekyll and Mr. Hyde*, VIII, 1886)
   c. God grant that it *be not* upon Tower Hill. (Charles Kingsley, *Westward Ho!*, I, 1893)
   d. Look that your turn *come not* next. (Ibid., VII, 1893)
   (Quoted from Hosoe (1933: 111, 127), the years when the books

were published were added.)

On the other hand, it was not until the 20th century that the <not + V> word order was seen. Observe the following examples:

(66) a. May I suggest now that this party break up and *not meet* again...? (V. Markham, Deadly Jest (Albatross) 225, 1936)
  b. [it was believed] that the Secretary of State gave orders that the flag *not be* dipped (Christian Science Monitor, 22 Sept. 4, 1948
  [originally cited in Kirchner (1970-72)])
  c. [Gen. Zwicker:] I respectfully request that I not answer that question (New York Herald Tribune, European ed., 23 Febr., 1954
  [originally cited in Zandvoort (1954)])
  (All quoted from Visser (1966: 648))

In sum, we can summarize the relations reviewed above as follows:

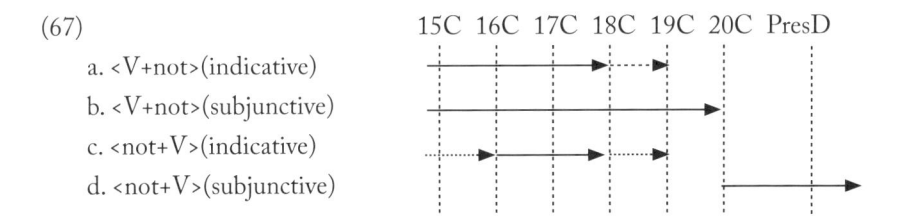

(67) 15C 16C 17C 18C 19C 20C PresD
  a. <V+not>(indicative)
  b. <V+not>(subjunctive)
  c. <not+V>(indicative)
  d. <not+V>(subjunctive)

Considering (67), we can conclude that (i) in subjunctive present clauses, the <V + not> word order (=(67b)=(57c)) was consistently used from the 15th century to the 19th century, (ii) even when the <not + V> word order (=(67c)=(57c')) was characteristically seen in the 16th century and the 17th century, the <V + not> word order (=(67b)) was also used in subjunctive clauses, and (iii) the <not + V> word order (=(67d)) appeared in subjunctive clauses just in the 20th century, and thus this word order did not originate from (67c) but is a new usage, as Visser (1966) asserts.

In conclusion, we should consider Visser's (1966) claim that the <V + not> word order in subjunctives as one of the comparatively newer usages in American English is more appropriate than Kirchner's (1970-72) claim that the <V + not>

12.3.2 The Development of Modals and the Subjunctive Present

As is well known, modal auxiliaries in Present-Day English all originated from main verbs in earlier stage of English. This change seen in the development of English modals is one of the typical examples of *Grammaticalization*,[17] and can be represented as follows in my framework. See the examples in (68a, b), and the representation in (69a, b):

(68) a. ic cann singen. (OE)
→ b. I can sing. (EModE)

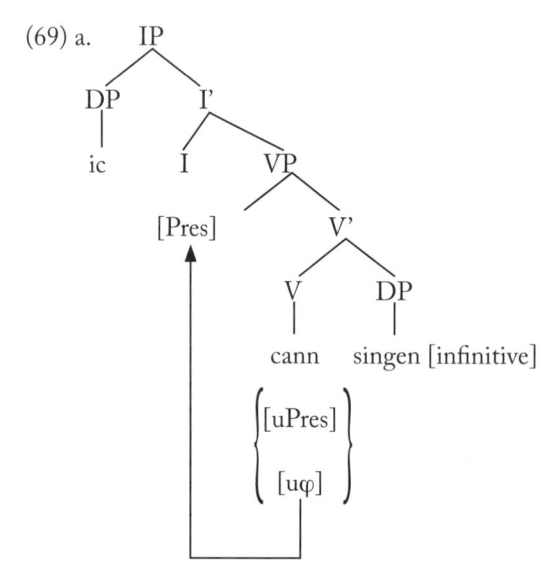

(69) a.

```
           IP
          /  \
        DP    I'
        |    /  \
        ic  I    VP
           [Pres] / \
                 V'
                / \
               V   DP
               |   |
             cann  singen [infinitive]
            {[uPres]}
            { [uφ]  }
```

b.

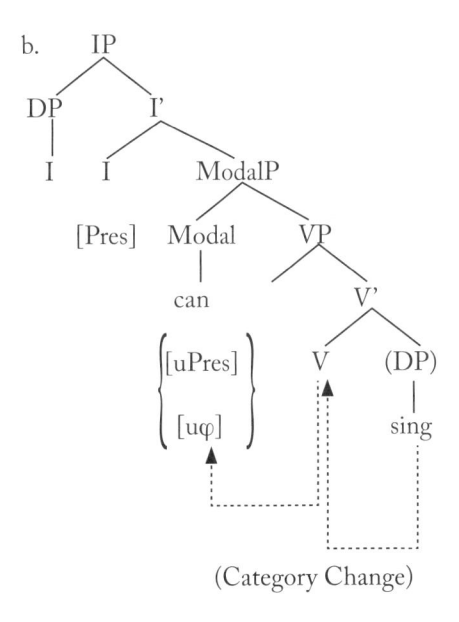

```
        IP
       /  \
      DP   I'
      |   /  \
      I  I   ModalP
         |   /    \
      [Pres] Modal  VP
              |    /  \
             can  V'
                 /  \
                V   (DP)
               /|    |
          [uPres]   sing
           [uφ]
```

(Category Change)

It goes without saying that the development of the English Modals is very complex and thus we should be careful about jumping to conclusions, but we can roughly sketch out the reanalysis model as shown in (70). Here, the important thing is that we can also apply to this model the development of the subjunctive present. Consider the following:

(70) a. I insisted [$_{CP}$ that he *go not* there]. (15C-19C)
→ b. I insisted [$_{CP}$ that he *not go* there]. (20C-Present)

(71) a.

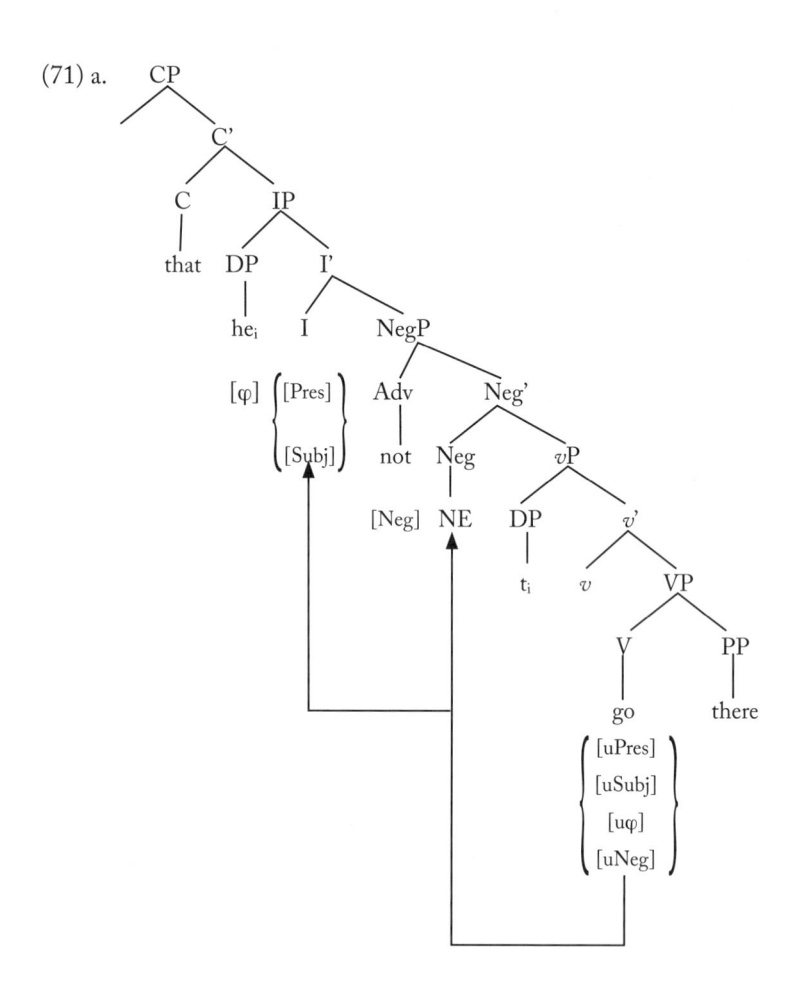

```
            CP
            |
            C'
           / \
          C   IP
          |  / \
       that DP  I'
            |  / \
           heᵢ I   NegP
              [φ]  / \
            [Pres] Adv  Neg'
            [Subj] |   / \
                  not Neg  vP
                      |   / \
                    [Neg] DP  v'
                     NE  |   / \
                        tᵢ  v   VP
                               / \
                              V   PP
                              |   |
                              go there
                            [uPres]
                            [uSubj]
                            [uφ]
                            [uNeg]
```

b.

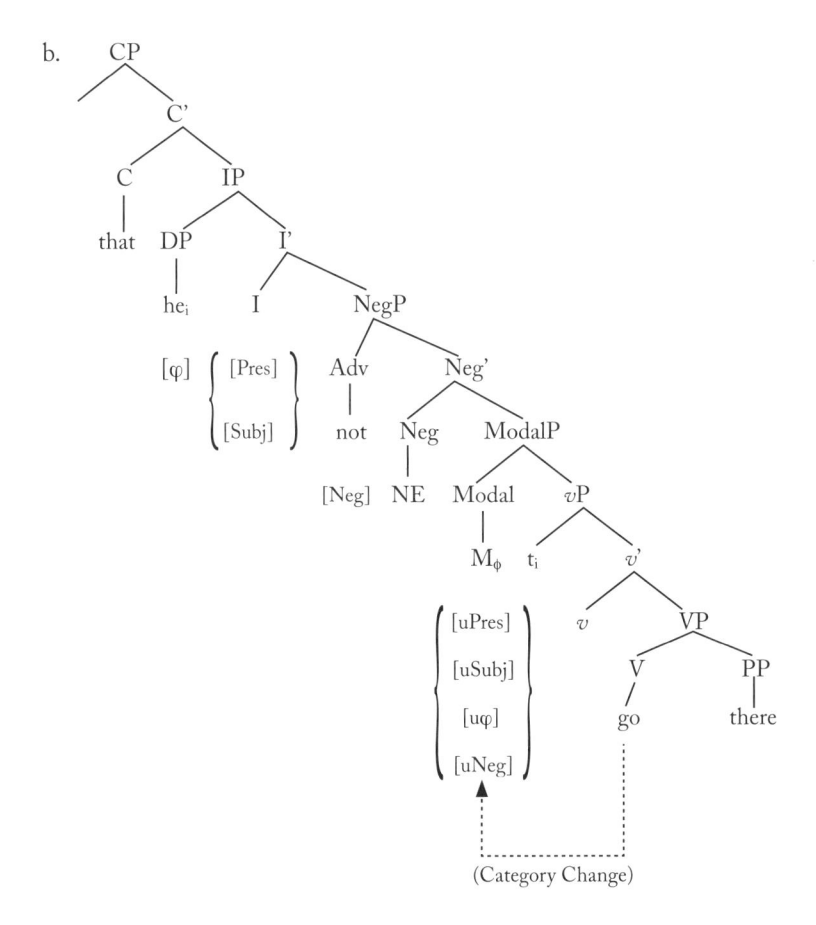

[Tree diagram:
CP
└─ C'
   ├─ C: that
   └─ IP
      ├─ DP: he_i
      └─ I'
         ├─ I: {[φ], [Pres], [Subj]}
         └─ NegP
            ├─ Adv: not
            └─ Neg'
               ├─ Neg: NE [Neg]
               └─ ModalP
                  ├─ Modal: M_φ {[uPres], [uSubj], [uφ], [uNeg]}
                  └─ vP
                     ├─ t_i
                     └─ v'
                        ├─ v
                        └─ VP
                           ├─ V: go
                           └─ PP: there

(Category Change)]

Note that until the 19th century, the subjunctive verbs raised to I *carrying along all the features*, while since the 20th century those features have become separated from the verbs and are raised to Modal⁰ resulting in the *covert* Modal, leaving the verbs in situ.

Then, one question arises. Why didn't the subjunctive covert modal M_φ appear until the 20th century, unlike other the ordinary English Modals?

In the studies of the development of English modals, the Early Modern English period is regarded as important (cf. Traugott (1972), Lightfoot (1979), Steel *et al*. (1981), Roberts (1985), Nakano (1994), etc.); it is in this period that the syntactic characteristics of the Modals used today fully developed. This fact is shown in the following table (72):

(72)　　　　　　　　　EOE　LOE　EME　LME　EModE　LModE　PresE

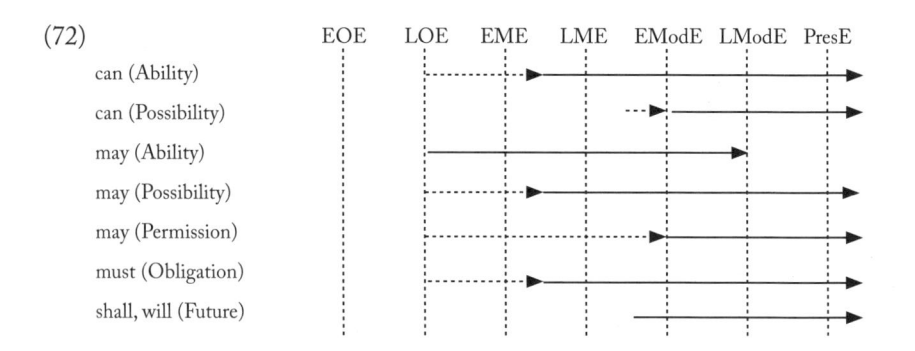

　　can (Ability)

　　can (Possibility)

　　may (Ability)

　　may (Possibility)

　　may (Permission)

　　must (Obligation)

　　shall, will (Future)

(*EOE=700-900, LOE=900-1100, EME=1100-1300, LME=1300-1500,

　　　　EModE=1500-1700, LModE=1700-1900, and PresE=1900-Today.)

(Nakao and Koma 1990: 232)

If the covert modal use of the subjunctive present were also inserted in (72), then it would naturally be as in (73):

(73) the covert modal use of the subjunctive present
　　　　　　　　　　　EOE　LOE　EME　LME　EModE　LModE　PresE
　　the subjunctive M_ϕ

Judging from (72) and (73), there seems to be a time lag in development between the ordinary modals and the covert modal of the subjunctive present. But as for this problem, we can easily think of several reasons why this should be so: First, as I discussed in the previous section, the negative word order of <V + not> was regularly used from the 15th century to the 19th century, as compared to the unstable negative construction in indicative finite sentences, and thus the category change to the covert modal M_ϕ, it seems, would not be permitted. Second, it is quite natural for us to assume that the subjunctive present took much more time in developing into a *covert* modal than did the *overt* modals (e.g. *can*, *may*, *must*, etc.) having concrete meanings. Third, note that table (72) is based mainly on the development of the *semantics* of the Modals. That is, *morphosyntactically* speaking, we may say that modals had not completely developed in EModE: The inflectional morpheme *-(e)st*, corresponding to the 2nd person singular pronoun *thou*, existed still in the paradigms of the modals.[18] Consider the following table:

(74)	Present Form	Past Forms
shall	shalt (since 14C)	schuldest (13C-15C)
		shuldest (15-16C)
		shouldest, shouldst (since 15C)
will	wilt (since 11C)	wouldest, wouldst (since 15C)
		wylt (11C, 14C, 16C)
		wylte (16C)
can	canst (since 11C)	couldest, couldst (since 16C)
may	maiste, mayste (14C-15C)	mightest (since 14C)
	maist (14C-17C)
	maiest (15C-16C)
	mayst (since 14C)
	mayest, may'st (since16C)
dare	darest (since 15C)	------------------------------------
	darste (15C)

(Araki and Ukaji 1984: 214-215)

As is well known, the pronoun *thou* and its inflectional morpheme *-(e)st* were used until the 1750's, so that we can assume that the English modals were not fully developed until the middle of the 18th century.

In sum, we might well conclude that only after the English modal system was established in LModE did the subjunctive present change into the covert modal M_ϕ in the 20th century.

12.4 Concluding Remarks

In this chapter I discussed the various possibilities of *have-be* raising in subjunctive present clauses. First, I reconsidered the analysis of the word order <have/be + not> as sentential negation seen in subjunctive present clauses. I showed that even in Present-Day English both the word orders of <not + have/be> and <have/be + not> are allowed in subjunctive present clauses as sentential negation. Next, I claimed that the latter marginal word order must be supported semantically following specific semantic conditions; since the <have/be

+ not> word order is a marginally marked word order in Present-Day English, the predicate in the embedded subjunctive clause must express *Action* as the meaning implied by the word order of verbal elements and *not*. Then I argued that this word order is allowed more easily in the legalistic styles.

Next, I briefly discussed a historical overview of the <not + V> word order. As for the <not + V> word order in subjunctive present clauses, there are mainly two opinions; (i) Kirchner (1970-72) regards the word order as an Early Modern English usage preserved in American English, while (ii) Visser (1966) regards the word order as one of the comparatively newer usages in American English. After examining the historical development of this word order both in indicative and subjunctive sentences, I concluded that Visser's claim is more appropriate. Then, I argued that until the 19th century the subjunctive verbs raised to I^0 carrying along all the features, but since the 20th century those features become separated from the verbs and raised to $Modal^0$ resulting in the *covert* subjunctive Modal M_ϕ, leaving the verbs in situ. Furthermore, I claimed that this category change is parallel to the development of ordinary modals. Though there seems to be a time lag in development between the ordinary modals and the covert Modal of the subjunctive present, we have good reason to assume that only after the English modal system was established in LModE did the subjunctive present change into the covert modal M_ϕ in the 20th century.

Notes to Chapter 12

1. This section is mainly based on Nomura (2004a). I am deeply indebted to Ken-ichi Takami and Donald L. Smith for their many insightful and helpful comments on earlier versions of Nomura (2004a).

2. Chiba (2001) is equally critical of Potsdam's (1997, 1998) analysis and cast doubt on his judgments.

3. Incidentally, if *because of his attitude* can be topicalized, we can clearly consider the sentence to exhibit sentential negation. For example, (ia) has the interpretation (ib):

(i) a. *Because of his attitude* Tom was not promoted.
 b. Tom was not promoted and the reason is because of his attitude.

However, when *because of his attitude* is topicalized in (14a), ungrammaticality results, as shown in (ii):

(ii) *I urge that *because of his attitude* Tom *be not* promoted.

To all appearances, (ii) shows that the <be + not> word order is not sentential negation, but note here that the following (iii) with the <not + be> word order is ungrammatical just the same:

(iii) *I urge that *because of his attitude* Tom *not be* promoted.

From this fact, we should consider that the ungrammaticality in (ii) and (iii) is not because of the word order but because Topicalization cannot apply in subjunctive present clauses, as is shown in (iv):

(iv) *It's important that the book$_i$ he study t$_i$ carefully.

(Hooper and Thompson 1973: 485)

I tentatively give a functional account for this by making the following assumption:

(v) Topicalization can apply only when the main clause is *semantically transparent* (cf.

Kuno and Takami (1993)).

This will explain not only the subjunctive cases in (ii-iv) above but also the difference in grammaticality in (via, b) below:

(vi) a. I *think* that this book$_i$ you should have read t$_i$.
b. *John *regretted* that Gone With the Wind, we went to see.

(Hooper and Thompson 1973: 479)

In sum, the Topicalization test cannot be used for subjunctive present clauses in order to judge whether the sentence is sentential negation or not.

4. Historically speaking, irrespective of whether the verbs are transitive verbs or intransitive verbs, the same type of overt V-movement to C can also be seen in the uses of the *hortative subjunctive*, exemplified in (i), which expresses command or hortation to a 1st and a 3rd person. Note that *Let's* would be used to express the same meaning in Present-Day English.

(i) a. And then *depart we* to our territories. (Marlowe)
b. *Join we* together. (Shakespeare)

Note also that the same movement is seen in polite imperative sentences in German even today, which is in fact one of the German subjunctive uses (Konjunctiv I):

(ii) a. *Kommen Sie!*
come   you
'Please come.'
b. *Sprechen wir* Deutsch.
speak   we German
'Let's speak German.'

5. D. L. Smith (personal communication, 2003) pointed out that *not* may carry a certain *illocutionary force*, i.e. *volition* in this case. I am grateful to him for pointing out this idea. For example, this idea naturally accounts for the difference in grammaticality in imperative sentences, as shown in (i):

(i) a. *Be angry/afraid.
   b. *Don't* be angry/afraid.

Note also that *not* was assumed to be a verb in deep structure in *generative semantics* (see especially McCawley (1970)), as shown in (iib):

(ii) a. Shin Ichi is not a bachelor.
   b.

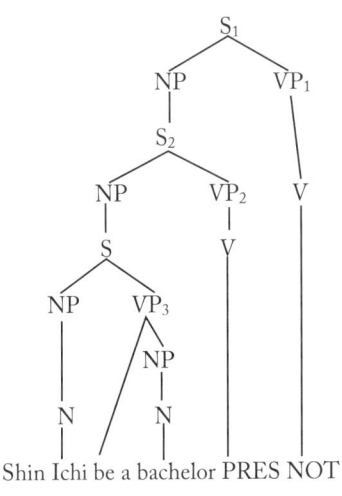

```
                    S₁
                   /  \
                  NP   VP₁
                  |     \
                  S₂     \
                 /  \     \
                NP   VP₂   V
                |    |
                S    V
               / \
              NP  VP₃
              |   /\
              N  /  NP
                /   |
               /    N
              /     |
        Shin Ichi be a bachelor PRES NOT
```
                                            (Imai 1975: 94-95)

6. Here, note that since <not + have/be> is an *unmarked* word order in Present-Day English, it does not necessarily express State *only*, though the *tendency* in (36i) is actually seen. Both Kazuo Nakazawa (personal communication, 2004) and Shigeo Tonoike (personal communication, 2004) asked me if even the <not + have/be> word order cannot also express Action, and this is of course true, as is shown in (i):

(i) I demand that John *not be* promoted. (=Action)

At the same time, however, note that the tendency in (36i) is definitely applicable. D. L. Smith (personal communication, 2004) pointed out that (iia) and (iiia) express Action while (iib) and (iiib) express State, though the interpretations are delicate:

(ii) a. The Senate has decreed that the students *be not* exempted from college dues. (=Action)
   (The Senate has told a university clerk that the students should not be exempted

from college dues.)

b. The Senate has decreed that the students *not be* exempted from college dues. (=State)

(The Senate has issued a decree that there should not be cases where the students are exempted from college dues.)

(iii)a. It is important that the committee *have not* seen the report. (=Action)

(I order the committee not to see the report.)

b. It is important that the committee *not have* seen the report. (=State)

(It is important to keep the report unseen by the committee.)

7. Note incidentally that similar phenomenon are also seen in the following examples of the infinitival marker *to* and *not* in the Modal *be to* constructions:

(i) a. You are *not to* be late. (=Action)

b. *You are *to not* be late. (=State)

(=Don't be late.)

(ii) a. You are *not to* say a word until he has left. (=Action)

(=Don't speak until he has left.)

b. You are *to not* say a word until he has left. (=State)

(=Keep silent until he has left.)

Considering this, we can propose the following generalization:

(iii) The unmarked <not to> word order takes an action predicates (or stative predicates as a syntactic default) while the marked <to not> word order takes only stative predicates.

For further discussion, see Nomura and Smith (2006).

8. Potsdam further comments in the following note:

(i) One interpretation of the data is that *have* is higher than in the structure than *be* in comparable examples. (Potsdam 1998: 96, fn. 20)

However, I am assuming in this chapter that *have* and *be* raising to I is operative even in Present-Day English, and thus do not assume that another functional category only for *have* exists under IP.

9. Incidentally, since the syntactic environments in (34-35) are the same as in (41b, c), it is clear that the ungrammaticality or unacceptability does not come from the complement elements of *be*. Note also that the following (i) is almost acceptable and that the condition in (32b) is met.

(i) I demand that you *be not* <u>so foolish as to marry her</u>. (cf. (35))

10. Incidentally, if the embedded subject *you* in (44) is changed into *the baby*, the pragmatic deviance results, as shown in (ib), unlike (ia):

(i) a.   I demand that *the baby* not have gone to sleep before I return.
   b.   #I demand that *the baby* have not gone to sleep before I return.
                                                                (cf. Nomura (2000a: 157))

I argued in Nomura (2000a) that in the case of (ia), *whatever the reason the baby is in bed asleep may be*, the command is allowed, while in the case of (ib), where *the baby's willingness to go to bed to sleep on its own* would be a precondition, the command is not allowed. Considering the present proposal in (32b), we can consider that (ib) is unacceptable because the <have + not> word order implies Action, i.e. implies that the baby will go to sleep *of its own will*.

11. D. L. Smith (personal communication, 2003) pointed out that from the viewpoint of Action the <have/be + not> word order will be accepted much more easily if the matrix verb is considered to be a *speech act verb* rather than a mere reported subjunctive verb. This means that the most acceptable syntactic environment where the <have/be + not> word order is allowed in subjunctive present clauses is when (i) the matrix subject is the first person pronoun *I*, (ii) the embedded subject is the second person pronoun *you*, and (iii) the matrix verb is the *present* form. I think this to be a very important factor.

12. Note also that in control infinitival clauses the addressee (who is given a command by the matrix subject), i.e. the indirect object, and the embedded subject (who should do the action), i.e. PRO, are clearly the same, as is predicted by *Control Theory*. Consider the following example:

(i) We request you$_i$ [PRO$_i$ not to take a picture]. (cf. (49b))

13. Another reason would be that the legalistic style gives an *archaic* (i.e. more *authoritative*) impression. Note that the <have/be + not> word order was the unmarked order before the 20th century, as we shall discuss in detail in section 12.3.

14. Note that the dominant word order is not (57c') (=<not + V>) but (57c) (=<V + not>) in the Early Modern English period, though both word orders are seen, as shown in the examples from Shakespeare in (i):

    (i) a. I *fear* him *not*. (*Caesar*, I. ii. 128)
        b. I have heard the prince tell him, I *know not* how oft, that that ring was copper! (1 *Henry IV*, III. iii. 96-8)

    And note also that in the cases of modals, and *have* and *be*, the <not + V> word order (=(57c')) was never seen, as was discussed by Ukaji (1992).

15. Note that Ukaji (1978) reports that there is only one example of <not+V> in embedded imperative sentences [i.e. mandative subjunctive clauses in this book] in all the examples that he collected from Early Modern English texts (1585-1625), as shown in (i):

    (i) And that you *not delay* the present, but,
        Filling the air with swords advanced and darts,
        We prove this very hour. (*Coriolanus*, I. vi. 60-62)   (Ukaji 1978: 25)

16. As for the examples of <be + not> in Early Modern English, see Murakami's (2000) examples under (27) in the appendix to Chapter 6.

17. Roughly speaking, the definition of *grammaticalization* is described in (i) and its process is said to be (ii):

    (i) Grammaticalization is generally seen as a process whereby a lexical item, with full referential meaning (i.e. an open-class element), develops grammatical meaning (i.e. it becomes a closed-class element); this is accompanied by a reduction in or a loss of phonetic substance, loss of syntactic independence and of lexical (referential) meaning.   (Fischer and Rosenbach 2000: 2)
    (ii) Content Item > Grammatical Word > Clitic > Inflectional Affix > (Zero)
        (Hopper and Traugott 2003[2]: 7)

For the recent studies and development of *grammaticalization* theory, see Hopper and Traugott (2003^2), Fischer *et al.* eds. (2000), Akimoto ed. (2001), and Akimoto (2002).

18. Needless to say, modals have no inflectional forms for person and number in Present-Day English, which is one of the most important formal characteristics of the English modal auxiliaries, as we observed in reviewing Coates's (1983) Seven Formal Characteristics of Modals under (31) in Chapter 1. Considering this viewpoint, we should pay attention to the inflectional morpheme *-(e)st* in the paradigms of the modals in the Modern English period.

Chapter 13

Conclusion

In this book I have proposed the ModalP Hypothesis and discussed the related phenomena, especially the analysis of infinitival clauses and the subjunctive present based on the ModalP Hypothesis. One of the most important claims of this book is that ModalP is needed both theoretically and descriptively as a minimum for an adequate description of English Syntax.

Chapter 1 constitutes introductory remarks. I presented the aim of this book and our theoretical framework. First, I reviewed Chomsky's (2000, 2001a, b) Case checking systems under the operation Agree and reviewed the status of Head Movement and the EPP feature; he attempts to consider that substantial movement in human language is only XP-movement and thus regards Head Movement as other than a syntactic phenomenon, that is, Head Movement applies in the phonological component. However, I argued that we have good reason to assume that Head Movement applies in narrow syntax. Moreover, Chomsky crucially assumes the EPP feature in explaining movement phenomena, but ideally speaking, we should eliminate the EPP feature in V-movement if possible. Consequently, I submitted a Case checking system that does not involve Agree or the EPP feature and assumed that V-Movement is visible and hence takes place in Syntax; I assumed that NP-movement is driven by the need to satisfy Case assignment, and that Nominative Case is a reflex of the [φ] feature and the Tense feature, based on Feature Dribbling and feature checking under Head-Head relations and Spec-Head relations, and also that Affix Hopping applies as a last resort. As for V-movement I made a hybrid assumption; Functional Verb Elements are inserted into Modal^0 in full forms, carrying along all the features. Since these features are uninterpretable for verbs themselves and thus must be checked off, the functional verbs raise to higher functional heads as a last resort in narrow syntax. On the other hand, Lexical Verb Elements are inserted into V as bare forms, having no features. Since they cannot move by themselves because they have no features, Affix Hopping must apply in phonology so that features in I^0 can be discharged and the lexical verbal elements be pronounced. Additionally, I claimed that, though the syntactic status of the auxiliary *do* has long been debated in the history of generative grammar, from the present perspective it would be most reasonable to assume that the auxiliary *do* is a type of modal.

In Chapter 2 I proposed the ModalP Hypothesis, which is the fundamental framework throughout this book; I claimed that modals constitute their own projections and NegP exists between the IP and the ModalP. Though Ouhalla (1991) and Cinque (1999) use a ModP or argue for the possibility of a ModP, I pointed out differences between the ModalP Hypothesis in this book and their ModP analyses. Then, after reviewing Chomsky's (1995, 2000, 2001a, b) sentence structure, which is generally assumed, I showed that it cannot account for the scope relations of modals and negation properly. That is, Chomsky's assumed sentence structure cannot generate the interpretation of Modal Negation in principle. On the other hand, I argued that the ModalP Hypothesis can provide adequate accounts for the scope interpretations between modals and *not*. Lastly, though the ModalP Hypothesis predicts that modals always have the two interpretations mentioned above, but this is not empirically true. However, I claimed that these apparent exceptions are not counterexamples to the present proposal, but that the gaps can be fully explained under the English modal system itself.

Chapters 3-5 are concerned with infinitival clauses. In Chapter 3 I discussed the structure of infinitival clauses, which has been one of the central issues in generative grammar but for which a decisive conclusion has not yet been reached. I claimed that the infinitival clause is a type of ModalP in syntactic structure; I proposed that contrary to what the generalized assumption implies, the infinitival marker *to* itself does not have features but rather is marked for [Nonfinite Tense] and [Unspecified Person], and thus *to* does not raise at all because it does not check any Tense or Person features. Furthermore, I assumed only one type of *to* and one type of [Nonfinite T], unlike Chomsky and Lasnik (1993), Stowell (1982), Bošković (1995), and Martin (1992, 2001). In this connection, I proposed a framework of Case checking in infinitival clauses, and then discussed especially the Case checking system of *try*-type infinitivals and *want*-type infinitivals, pointing out the problems with Bošković's (1995) analyses. Last, Martin (2001) also claims that two types of the infinitival marker *to* exist based on differences in the deletability of VP after *to*, but I showed that VP-deletion can basically apply to both Control type infinitivals and Raising type infinitivals in syntax. Moreover, I pointed out that VP-deletion applying to Control type infinitivals and Raising type infinitivals is subject to the same functional conditions applying to epistemic modals and root modals as well.

In Chapter 4 I discussed the position of the negative *not* in infinitival clauses. As for the two word orders of <not to V> and <to not V> seen in infinitival clauses, Pollock (1989) assumes that the standard <not to V> order is derived from the marginal <to not V> order, while conversely Hasegawa (2003) assumes that the <to not V> word order is derived from the <not to V> word order. However, after showing that both analyses are empirically problematic, I claimed that the two word orders are not identical constructions and thus only the <not to V> word order is the negation of the whole infinitival clause and the <to not V> word order is verb phrase negation. Last, I argued that assuming that time adverbial phrases can be both IP-adjuncts and VP-adjuncts, our framework can properly account for the differences in scope interpretations that Hasegawa (2003) discusses.

Chapter 5 is concerned with the problems with *ought to* and *be to*. To all appearances, as Sawada (1985, 1995) and Ando (1996, 2003) claim, the assumption that the infinitival marker *to* is a type of modal raises a serious problem; the infinitival marker *to* and *ought* or *be* should not co-occur by the general principle that modals do not co-occur. However, I claimed that we can explain in a non *ad hoc* way the exceptional behavior of *ought to* and *be to* by assuming two or three types of *ought* or *be*.

Chapters 6-12 are concerned with the subjunctive present and constitute the main body of this book. In Chapter 6, I reviewed the terminology of *mood*, *modal*, and *modality*, and the status of the subjunctive mood in Present-Day English. I then discussed the problem as to whether the subjunctive mood still exists or not in Present-Day English, reviewing the argumentations among traditional grammarians. Last, before discussing the syntactic structures of the subjunctive present in the subsequent chapters, I reviewed the uses and the general properties of the subjunctive present, and in particular discussed three important formal characteristics seen in subjunctive present clauses.

In the appendix to Chapter 6 I discussed phonetic *that*-deletion in mandative subjunctive clauses. So far, many linguists have assumed that the subjunctive *that* cannot be deleted, and I also made the same assumption in Nomura (2000b). However, after modifying my assumption on *that*-deletion proposed in Nomura (2000b), I submitted many examples where the subjunctive *that* is deleted. I then proposed that the complementizer *that* can be phonetically deleted in surface structure whether it is the indicative *that* or the subjunctive *that*, though *that*-deletion is subject to two functional conditions on *that*-deletion, i.e. the Parsing Condition and the Semantically Transparent Condition. Last, just as in the cases of infinitival clauses, I posited two types of complementizers in subjunctive present clauses as well: phonetically deleted *that* in surface structure and the null complementizer φ, which is base-generated in the underlying structure.

In Chapter 7 I discussed the syntactic structure of subjunctive present clauses. One of the most important purposes of Chapter 7 was to explain the three formal characteristics of subjunctive present clauses discussed in Chapter 6, which seem to be quite peculiar compared to those of indicative finite sentences, and to account for various phenomenon seen in subjunctive present clauses. I proposed that the subjunctive present in Present-Day English is a type of covert modal, and that movement in subjunctive present clauses is the movement of the covert modal and thus the main verb itself remain in situ. Furthermore, I showed that under the present proposal we can naturally account for various characteristics of subjunctive present clauses, i.e. tense and three formal characteristics of subjunctive clauses, the non-cooccurrence of modals, the position of adverbs, Negative Inversion, contraction phenomena, and the impossibility of VP-Deletion with *do*-support.

In the appendix to Chapter 7 I briefly discussed the subjects of imperative sentences, where root forms are used just as in subjunctive present clauses. Though imperative issues are very complex, I mentioned only the subjects of imperative sentences in connection with a note in Chapter 7. I have left details relating to imperative issues for future study.

In Chapter 8 I discussed the quasi-subjunctive *should* and related topics. After pointing out that the quasi-subjunctive *should* is semantically empty, I proposed that only the quasi-subjunctive modals *should*, *shall*, *may*, and *might* have the [uSubj] feature as a placeholder auxiliary. On the other hand, I assumed that emotional *should* is a modal having the [uInd] feature. Moreover, I claimed that emotional *should* has some emotional meaning and thus the quasi-subjunctive *should* and emotional *should* do not form identical constructions. Last, though many linguists assume *should*-deletion in the derivation of subjunctive present clauses, I concluded from various facts that the subjunctive present cannot be derived by *should*-deletion.

In Chapter 9 I discussed the role of tense in subjunctive present clauses. It is widely accepted in traditional grammar and many previous studies that subjunctive present clauses have no tense in Present-Day English, but I claimed that subjunctive present clauses, in fact, do have *present tense*. As for the three formal characteristics of the subjunctive present, I showed that based on the proposals in Chapter 7, we can adequately explain why subjunctive present clauses behave as if they had no tense. I then showed that there are many additional linguistic facts that force us to conclude that subjunctive present clauses are tensed. Furthermore, I showed that the assumption that Nominative Case checking is based on the presence of Agr rather than Tense is empirically problematic, and thus concluded that the sufficient condition for assigning Nominative Case is the presence of Tense.

In the appendix to Chapter 9 I discussed possibilities and problems with Hasegawa's (2003) Tensed-S Condition (TSC). After reviewing his definition of the TSC and the basic supporting data, I critically discussed several topics; the difference between the TSC and extraction from NP, extraction of *wh*-phrases from Tensed-S and non-Tensed S, reflexive pronouns as the subject in Tensed-S, reflexive pronoun interpretations in picture nouns, and language universals. We will leave it for future study whether this interesting condition is really needed as an independent condition in grammar.

In Chapter 10 I discussed the complex question as to what lexical items can select subjunctive present clauses. After reviewing Chiba (1991) and Konno (2001), I argued that Konno's Condition of an Underlying Appeal is insufficient. Instead, I proposed that both syntactic conditions and semantic conditions are necessary. First, I assumed three types of subjunctive complementizers: (i) the optative null complementizer ɸ, and (ii) the complementizers expressing *condition*, *concession*, and *purpose*, which can select a subjunctive present clause without any semantic support, and (iii) the mandative subjunctive complementizer *that*, which is semantically empty, must be semantically supported as well. As for the semantic condition, I assumed that when the subjunctive *that* is introduced in the sentence, it must express an unspecified desirable future by linguistic elements or contextual meanings. Last, concerning the important problem as to what lexical items can select subjunctive present clauses, I proposed that deontic verbs can potentially select subjunctive present clauses but epistemic verbs cannot select subjunctive present clauses syntactically.

In Chapter 11 I discussed the problem of the presence of NegP and the controversial problem as to which position *not* occupies, the Spec position or the Head position. I claimed that we have good reason to assume a NegP and furthermore that *not* is the Spec of NegP, rather than the Head of NegP. Then, in connection with this problem, I discussed the licensing condition on VP-deletion in subjunctive present clauses. As for this problem, Potsdam (1997, 1998) claims that the negative *not* alone licenses VP-deletion in subjunctive present clauses and therefore concludes that *not* is the Head of the NegP. However, after examining his discussions and examples, I submitted three conclusions: (i) not only the sentential negative *not* but also the auxiliary *have* and *be* and the copula *be* can license VP-deletion in subjunctive present clauses. (ii) The licensing conditions on VP-deletion in subjunctive present clauses are basically the same as those in indicative sentences. The differences between indicatives and subjunctives come from the presence of the covert subjunctive modal M_ϕ in subjunctive present clauses. (iii) VP-deletion using sentential *not* is not decisive evidence for Potsdam's conclusion that *not* is the head of NegP.

In Chapter 12 I discussed the possibilities of *have-be* raising in subjunctive present clauses from various viewpoints. First of all, I reconsidered the analysis of the word order <have/be + not> as exhibiting sentential negation seen in subjunctive present clauses. I argued that even in Present-Day English both the word orders of <not + have/be> and <have/be + not> are allowed in subjunctive present clauses as sentential negation, but that the latter marginal word order must be supported semantically following specific semantic conditions; since the <have/be + not> word order is a marginally marked word order in Present-DayEnglish, the predicate in the embedded subjunctive clause must express Action as the meaning implied by the word order of verbal elements and *not*. Additionally, I argued that this word order is used more easily in the legalistic registers. Next, I discussed the historical overview from the perspective of the word order of the negative and verbs. As for the <not + V> word order in subjunctive present clauses, Kirchner (1970-72) regards the word order as one of the preserved Early Modern English usages in American English, while Visser (1966) regards the word order as one of the comparatively newer usages in American English. But I concluded that Visser's claim is more appropriate by examining the historical development of this word order both in indicative and subjunctive sentences. Last, I discussed the development of the subjunctive present into the covert modal M_ϕ. I argued that until the 19th century the subjunctive verbs raised to I carrying along all the features, but since the 20th century those features were separated from the verbs and raised to $Modal^0$ resulting in the covert subjunctive Modal M_ϕ, leaving the verbs in situ. Furthermore, I claimed that this category change is parallel to the development of ordinary modals. Indeed, there seems to be a time lag in development between the ordinary modals and the covert Modal M_ϕ of the subjunctive present, but we have good reason to assume that only after the English modal system was established in Late Modern English did the subjunctive present change into the covert modal M_ϕ in the 20th century.

Chapter 13 constitutes these concluding remarks.

It goes without saying that new functional categories should not be assumed easily only for the theory internal reasons, but I consider that in this book I have shown that the ModalP Hypothesis is *empirically* needed as a minimum in English Syntax. As for residual problems, we should consider the problems as to what categorial status modals carry in a deeper sense and how universal ModalP might be, considering other languages. I will leave these problems for future study.

Finally, it is hoped that this book will contribute to linguistic studies of modals and subjunctives in some way or other. And I hope that this book will be a good prelude to my future studies.

References

Abbot, Edwin A. (1870^2) *A Shakespearian Grammar*. New York: Haskel House Publishers. (A revised version published by Senjo, Tokyo, 1972.)

Abney, Stephen P. (1987) The English Noun Phrases in Its Sentential Aspect. Doctoral Dissertation, MIT.

Aijmer, Karin (1972) *Some Aspects of Psychological Predicates in English*. Stockholm: Almqvist and Wiksell International.

Akimoto, Minoji (1986) *Eego Idiomu no Kenkyuu* [A Study of English Idioms]. Tokyo: Shinozaki Shorin.

——— (2002) *Bunpooka to Idiomuka* [Grammaticalization and Idiomatization]. Tokyo: Hituzi Syobo.

——— ed. (2001) *Bunpooka—Kadai to Kenkyuu* [Grammaticalization— Problems and Studies]. Tokyo: Eichosha.

Akmajian, Adrian and Thomas Wasow (1975) "The Constituent Structure of VP and AUX and the Position of the Verb BE." *Linguistic Analysis* 1: 205-245.

———, Susan M. Steel, and Thomas Wasow (1979) "The Category AUX in Universal Grammar." *Linguistic Inquiry* 10: 1-64.

Amano, Masachiyo (1999) *Gengo-yooso no Ninka—Dooshi, Meeshiku, Fukushi* [The Licensing of Linguistic Elements—Verbs, Noun Phrases, and Adverbs]. Tokyo: Kenkyusha.

Amanuma, Minoru (1987) "Daifuteeshi no Yohoo [Usages of Pro-infinitives]." *Eego Kyooiku* [The English Teachers' Magazine] 36(9): 76-78.

——— (1988) "Dooshiku no Sakujo—Dooteki · Kinooteki Bunseki— [VP-Deletion: Dynamic and Functional Analyses] (1)–(2)" *Eego Kyooiku* [The English Teachers' Magazine] 36(10): 74-76, 36(11): 66-68.

Anderson, Stephen R. and Paul Kiparsky eds. (1973) *A Festschrift for Morris Halle*. New York: Holt, Rinehart and Winston.

Ando, Sadao (1996) *Eegogaku no Shiten* (The Viewpoint of English Linguistics).

Tokyo: Kaitakusha.

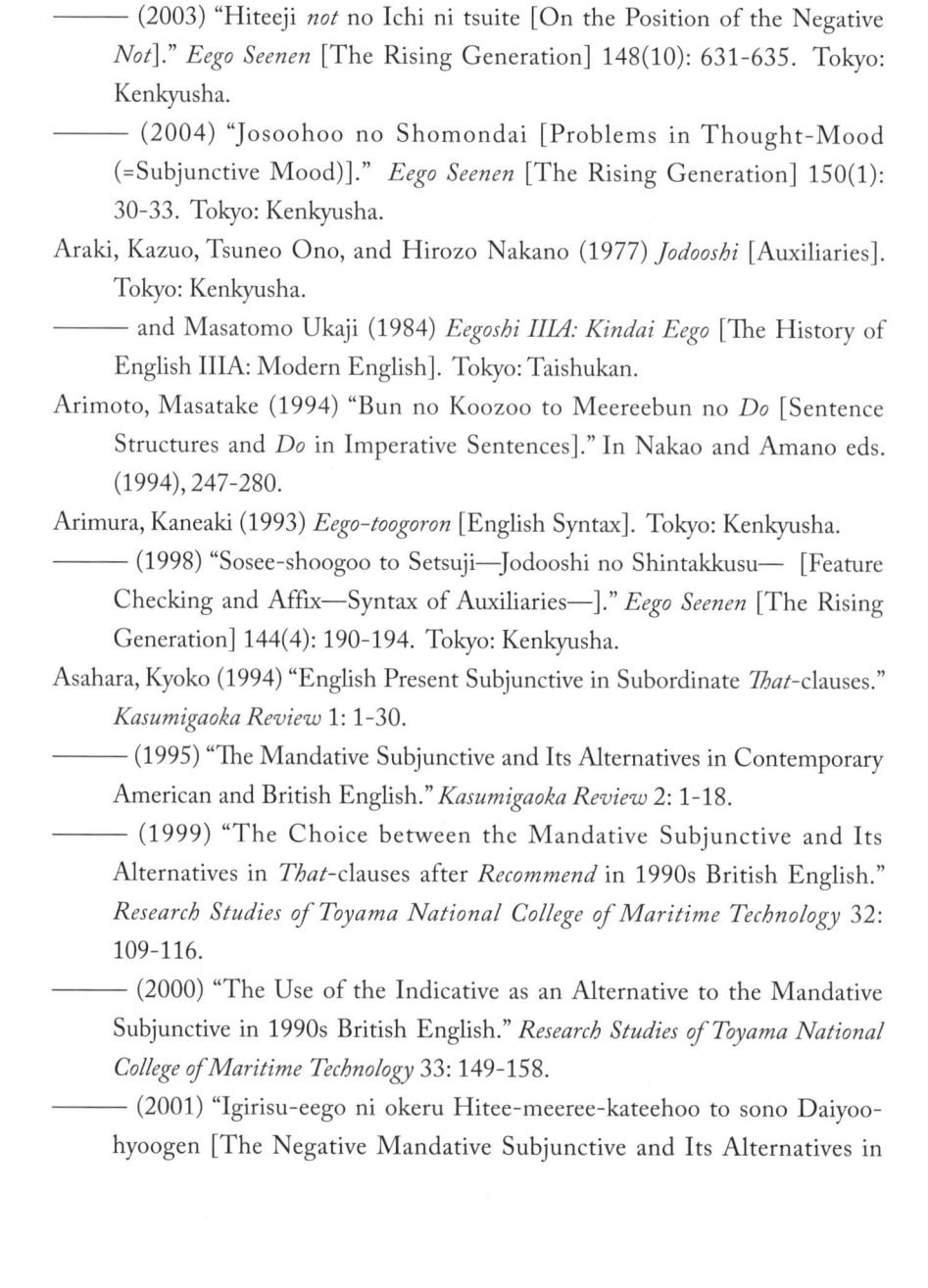

────── (1999) "Subjunctive wa "Setsuzokuhoo" ka [Is the Japanese Translation of Subjunctive "Setsuzokuhoo"]?" *Eego Seenen* [The Rising Generation] 145(6): 378-379. Tokyo: Kenkyusha.

────── (2003) "Hiteeji *not* no Ichi ni tsuite [On the Position of the Negative *Not*]." *Eego Seenen* [The Rising Generation] 148(10): 631-635. Tokyo: Kenkyusha.

────── (2004) "Josoohoo no Shomondai [Problems in Thought-Mood (=Subjunctive Mood)]." *Eego Seenen* [The Rising Generation] 150(1): 30-33. Tokyo: Kenkyusha.

Araki, Kazuo, Tsuneo Ono, and Hirozo Nakano (1977) *Jodooshi* [Auxiliaries]. Tokyo: Kenkyusha.

────── and Masatomo Ukaji (1984) *Eegoshi IIIA: Kindai Eego* [The History of English IIIA: Modern English]. Tokyo: Taishukan.

Arimoto, Masatake (1994) "Bun no Koozoo to Meereebun no *Do* [Sentence Structures and *Do* in Imperative Sentences]." In Nakao and Amano eds. (1994), 247-280.

Arimura, Kaneaki (1993) *Eego-toogoron* [English Syntax]. Tokyo: Kenkyusha.

────── (1998) "Sosee-shoogoo to Setsuji—Jodooshi no Shintakkusu— [Feature Checking and Affix—Syntax of Auxiliaries—]." *Eego Seenen* [The Rising Generation] 144(4): 190-194. Tokyo: Kenkyusha.

Asahara, Kyoko (1994) "English Present Subjunctive in Subordinate *That*-clauses." *Kasumigaoka Review* 1: 1-30.

────── (1995) "The Mandative Subjunctive and Its Alternatives in Contemporary American and British English." *Kasumigaoka Review* 2: 1-18.

────── (1999) "The Choice between the Mandative Subjunctive and Its Alternatives in *That*-clauses after *Recommend* in 1990s British English." *Research Studies of Toyama National College of Maritime Technology* 32: 109-116.

────── (2000) "The Use of the Indicative as an Alternative to the Mandative Subjunctive in 1990s British English." *Research Studies of Toyama National College of Maritime Technology* 33: 149-158.

────── (2001) "Igirisu-eego ni okeru Hitee-meeree-kateehoo to sono Daiyoo-hyoogen [The Negative Mandative Subjunctive and Its Alternatives in

British English]." *Kyushu Eebungaku Kenkyu* [Studies in English Literature in Kyushu] 18: 87-103.

Asakawa, Teruo and Seizaburo Kamata (1986) *Jodooshi* [Auxiliaries]. Tokyo: Taishukan.

Aoun, Joseph and Yen-hui Audrey Li (1993) *Syntax of Scope*. Cambridge, MA.: MIT Press.

Baker, Carl L. (1989) *English Syntax*. Cambridge, MA.: MIT Press.

────── (1991) "The Syntax of English *Not*: The Limits of Core Grammar." *Linguistic Inquiry* 22: 387-429.

Baker, Mark (1988) *Incorporation: A Theory of Grammtical Function Changing*. Chicago: Chicago University Press.

Baugh, Albert C. and Thomas Cable (1994[4]) *A History of the Emglish Language*. London: Routledge.

Behre, Frank (1955) "Meditative-Polemic SHOULD in Modern English THAT-clauses." Stockholm: Almqvist and Wiksell.

Belletti, Adriana (1990) *Generalized Verb Movement: Aspects of Verb Syntax*. Turin: Rosenberg and Sellier.

Beukema, Frits and Peter Coopmans (1989) "A Government-Binding Perspective on the Imperative in English." *Journal of Linguistics* 25: 417-436.

Bloomfield, Leonard (1933) *Language*. New York: Holt, Rinehart and Winston.

Bošković, Željko (1996) "Selection and the Categorial Status of Infinitival Complements." *Natural Language and Linguistic Theory* 14: 269-304.

────── (1997) *The Syntax of Nonfinite Complementation: An Economy Approach*. Cambridge, MA.: MIT Press.

Bobaljik, Jonathan D. (2001) "The Implications of Rich Agreement: Why Morphology Doesn't Drive Syntax." *Proceedings of the 20th West Coast Conference on Formal Linguistics*, 82-95.

Bolinger, Dwight L. (1972) *That's That*. The Hague: Mouton.

────── (1977) *Meaning and Form*. London: Longman.

Bouchard, Denis (1982) On the Content of Empty Categories. Doctoral Dissertation, MIT.

Bowers, John (1993) "The Syntax of Predication." *Linguistic Inquiry* 24: 591-656.

Bradley, Henry (1904) *The Making of English*. London: Macmillan. (Revised by Simeon Potter, Macmillan, 1968[2].)

Brame, Michael (1981) "Trace Theory with Filters vs. Lexically Based Syntax Without." *Linguistic Inquiry* 12: 275-293.

Bresnan, Joan (1970) "On Complementizers: Towards a Syntactic Theory of Complementizer Types." *Foundations of Language* 6: 297: 321.

——— (1976) "On the Form and Functioning of Transformations." *Linguistic Inquiry* 7: 3-40.

——— (1979) *Theory of Complementation in English Syntax*. New York: Garland.

——— (1982) "Control and Complementation." *Linguistic Inquiry* 13: 343-434.

Carey, Gordon V. (1953) *American into English: A Handbook for Translator*. London: William Heinemann.

Celce-Murcia, Marianne and Diane Larsen-Freeman (1983) *The Grammar Book —An ESL/EFL Teachers Course*. Rowley, Mass.: Newbury House.

Charleston, Britta (1941) *Studies on the Syntax of the English Verb*. Bern: Verlag A. Franke Ag.

Chiba, Shuji (1984a) "On Present Subjunctives and Transitive Verb Phrase Complementation in English." *English Linguistics* 2: 81-102.

——— (1984b) " "Kateehoosetsu" ni Arawareru Fukushi no Ichi [The Position of Adverbs in Subjunctive Clauses]." *Eego Seenen* [The Rising Generation] 130(5): 217. Tokyo: Kenkyusha.

——— (1987) *Present Subjunctives in Present-Day English*. Tokyo: Shinozaki Shorin.

——— (1991) "Non-localizable Contextual Features: Present Subjunctive in English." In Nakajima ed. (1991), 19-43.

——— (1994) "Tensed or Not Tensed: INFL in Present Subjunctives." In Shuji Chiba *et al* ed., *Synchronic and Diachronic Approaches to Language: A Festschrift for Toshio Nakao on the Occasion of His Sixtieth Birthday*, 327-343. Tokyo: Liber Press.

——— (1995) "Hobunhyooshiki *that* no Shookyo—*That* Shookyo no Kijutsu o Chuushin ni—[Deletion of the Complementizer *That*—Centering on the Description of the *That*-Deletion]." *Tsudajuku Daigaku Kiyoo* [Journal of Tsuda College], 1-44. Tokyo: Tsuda College.

——— (2000) "Eego no Kateehoo ni tsuite [On the Subjunctive Mood in English]." *Grant-in-Aid for COE Research Report* (4) (No. 08CE1001), *Researching and Verifying an Advanced Theory of Human Language*, 147-172.

Chiba: Graduate School of Language Sciences of Kanda University of International Studies.

—— (2001) "Dooshi-kuriage to Kateehoo-genzai. [Verb Raising and the Subjunctive Present]." *Grant-in-Aid for COE Research Report* (5) (No. 08CE1001), *Researching and Verifying an Advanced Theory of Human Language*, 1-19. Chiba: Graduate School of Language Sciences of Kanda University of International Studies.

Chomsky, Noam (1957) *Syntactic Structures*. The Hague: Mouton.

—— (1964) *Current Issues in Linguistic Theory*. The Hague: Mouton.

—— (1965) *Aspects of the Theory of Syntax*. Cambridge, MA.: MIT Press.

—— (1970) "Remarks on Nominalization." In Roderick A. Jacobs and Peter S. Greenbaum eds., *Readings in English Transformational Grammar*, 184-221. Waltham: Ginn and Company.

—— (1973) "Conditions on Transformations." In Anderson and Kiparsky eds. (1973), 232-286. Also in Chomsky (1977), 81-160.

—— (1975) "Questions of Form and Interpretation." *Linguistic Analysis* 1: 75-107. Also in Chomsky (1977), 23-59.

—— (1977) *Essays on Form and Interpretation*. New York: Elsevier North-Holland.

—— (1980) "On Binding." *Linguistic Inquiry* 11: 1-46.

—— (1981) *Lectures on Government and Binding Theory*. Dordrecht: Foris.

—— (1986a) *Knowledge of Language: Its Nature, Origin, and Use*. New York: Praeger.

—— (1986b) *Barriers*. Cambridge, MA.: MIT Press.

—— (1995) *The Minimalist Program*. Cambridge, MA.: MIT Press.

—— (1998) "Some Observations on Economy in Generative Grammar." In Pilar Barbosa, Danny Fox, Paul Hagstrom, Martha McGinnis, and David Pesetsky eds., *Is the Best Good Enough?: Optimality and Competition in Syntax*, 115-127. Cambridge, MA.: MIT Press.

—— (2000) "Minimalist Inquiries: The Framework." In Roger Martin, David Michaels, and Juan Uriagereka eds., *Step by Step: Essays on Minimalist Syntax in Honor of Howard Lasnik*, 89-155. Cambridge, MA.: MIT Press.

—— (2001a) "Derivation by Phase." In Kenstowicz ed. (2001), 1-52.

—— (2001b) "Beyond Explanatory Adequacy." *MIT Occasional Papers in*

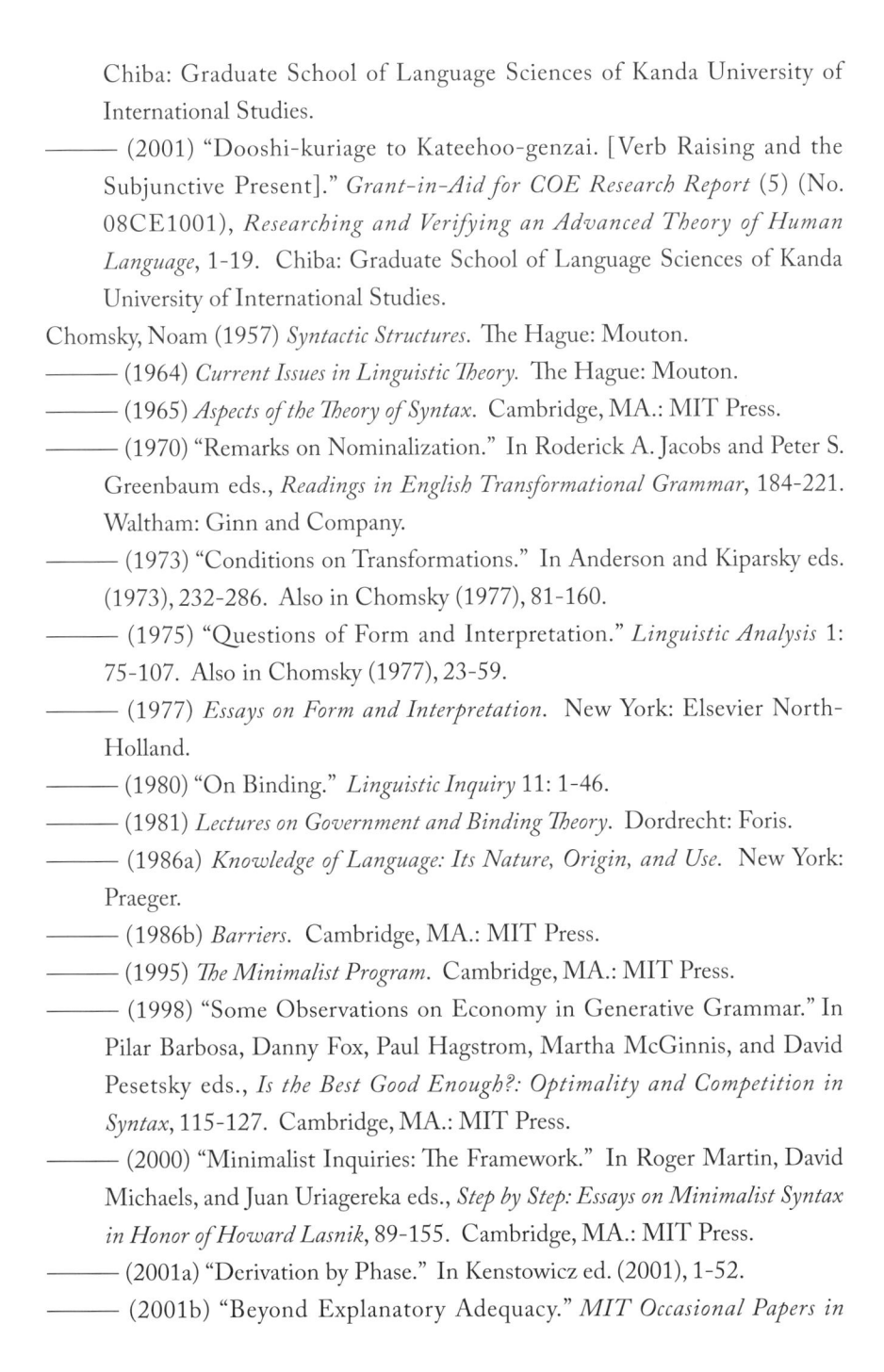

Linguistics 20: 1-28.

——— and Howard Lasnik (1977) "Filters and Control." *Linguistic Inquiry* 8: 425-504.

——— and Howard Lasnik (1993) "The Theory of Principles and Parameters." In Joachim Jacobs, Arnim von Stechow, Wolfgang Sternefeld, and Theo Vennenmann eds., *Syntax: An International Handbook of Contemporary Research*, 506-569. Also in Chomsky (1995), 13-127.

Cinque, Guglielmo (1999) *Adverbs and Functional Heads: A Cross-Linguistic Perspective.* Oxford: Oxford University Press.

Coates, Jennifer (1983) *The Semantics of the Modal Auxiliaries.* London: Croom Helm.

Comrie, Bernard (1985) *Tense.* Cambridge: Cambridge University Press.

Culicover, Peter (1971) Syntactic and Semantic Investigations. Doctoral Dissertation, MIT.

——— (1976) *Syntax.* New York: Academic Press.

——— (1991) "Topicalization, Inversion, and Complementizers in English." In Denis Delfitto, Martin Everaert, Arnold Evers, and Frits Stuurman eds., *Going Romance, and Beyond, Fifth Symposium*, 1-43. Utrecht: University of Utrecht.

——— (1997) *Principles and Parameters: An Introduction to Syntactic Theory.* Oxford: Oxford University Press.

——— (1999) *Syntactic Nuts.* Oxford: Oxford University Press.

——— and Kenneth Wexler (1977) "Some Syntactic Implications of Language Learnability." In Peter Culicover, Thomas Wasow, and Andrew Akmajian eds., *Formal Syntax*, 7-60. New York: Academic Press.

Curme, George O. (1931) *Syntax.* Boston: Heath

Davies, Eirlys (1986) *The English Imperative.* London: Croom Helm.

De Haan, Ferdinand (1997) *The Interaction of Modality and Negation: A Typological Study.* New York: Garland.

Declerck, Renaat (1982) "The Triple Origin of Participial Perception Complements." *Linguistics Analysis* 10: 1-26.

——— (1991a) *A Comprehensive Descriptive Grammar of English.* Tokyo: Kaitakusha.

——— (1991b) *Tense in English: Its Structure and Use in Discourse.* London:

Routledge.

Denison, David (2000) "Combining English Auxiliaries." In Fischer *et al.* eds. (2000), 111-147.

Doherty, Cathal (1997) "Clauses without Complementizer: Finite IP-Complementation in English." *The Linguistic Review* 14: 197-220.

Dubinsky, Stanley and Kemp Williams (1995) "Recategorization of Prepositions as Complementizers: The Case of Temporal Prepositions in English." *Linguistic Inquiry* 26: 125-137.

Embick, David and Rolf Noyer (2001) "Movement Operation after Syntax." *Linguistic Inquiry* 32: 555-595.

Emonds, Joseph (1970) Root and Structure-Preserving Transformations. Doctoral Dissertation, MIT.

—— (1976) *A Transformational Approach to English Syntax*. San Diego: Academic Press.

—— (1985) *A Unified Theory of Syntactic Categories*. Dordrecht: Foris.

Enç, Mürvet (1987) "Anchoring Conditions for Tense." *Linguistic Inquiry* 18: 633-657.

Ernst, Thomas (1992) "The Phrase Structure of English Negation." *The Linguistic Review* 9: 109-144.

Erteschick-Shir, Nomi (1973) On the Nature of island Constraints. Doctoral Dissertation, MIT.

Evans, Bergen and Cornelia Evans (1957) *A Dictionary of Contemporary American Usage*. New York: Random House.

Farkas, Don (1992) "On Obviation." In Ivan A. Sag and Anna Szabolcsi eds., *Lexical Matters*, 85-109. Stanford: CSLI.

Fauconnier, Gilles (1997) *Mapping in Thought and Language*. Cambridge: Cambridge University Press.

Felser, Claudia (1998) "Perception and Control: A Minimalist Analysis of English Direct Perception Complements." *Journal of Linguistics* 34: 351-385.

Fiengo, Robert (1980) *Surface Structure*. Cambridge, MA.: Harvard University Press.

Finer, Daniel L. (1985) "The Syntax of Switch Reference." *Linguistic Inquiry* 16: 35-55.

Fischer, Olga, and Anette Rosenbach (2000) "Introduction." In Fischer *et al.* eds.

(2000), 1-37.

———, Anette Rosenbach, and Dieter Stein eds. (2000) *Pathways of Change: Grammaticalization in English*. Amsterdam and Philadelphia: John Benjamins.

Fitzmaurice, Susan (2000) "Remarks on the De-grammaticalisation of Infinitival *to* in Present-Day American English." In Fischer *et al.* eds. (2000), 171-186.

Foster, Brian (1968) *The Changing English Language*. London: Macmillan.

Fowler, Henry W. (1965^2) *A Dictionary of Modern English Usage*. Oxford: Clarendon Press.

Franz, Wilhelm (1934^4) *Die Sprache Shakespeares in Vers und Prosa*. Halle: Niemeyer.

Gazdar, Gerald, Geoffrey K. Pullum, and Ivan A. Sag (1982) "Auxiliaries and Related Phenomena in a Restrictive Theory of Grammar." *Language* 58: 591-638.

Givón, Talmy (1994) "Irrealis and the Subjunctive." *Studies in Language* 18: 265-337.

Groefsema, Marjolein (1995) "*Can, may, must* and *should*: A Relevance Theoretic Account." *Journal of Linguistics* 31: 53-79.

Grousu, Alexander and Jukia Horvath (1984) "The GB Theory and Raising in Rumanian." *Linguistic Inquiry* 15: 348-353.

Haegeman, Liliane (1986) "The Present Subjunctive in Contemporary British English." *Studia Anglica Posnaniensia* 19: 61-74.

——— (1994^2) *Introduction to Government and Binding Theory*. Oxford: Blackwell.

——— ed. (1997) *Elements of Grammar*. Dordrecht: Kluwer Academic Press.

——— and Jacqueline Guéron (1999) *English Grammar: A Generative Perspective*. Oxford: Blackwell.

Halle, Morris and Alec Marantz (1993) "Distributed Morphology and the Pieces of Inflection." In Kenneth Hale and Samuel J. Keyser eds., *The View from Building 20*, 111-176. Cambridge, MA.: MIT Press.

Halliday, M. A. K. (1970) "Functional Diversity in Language as Seen from a Consideration of Modality and Mood in English." *Foundations of Language* 6: 322-361.

Harsh, Wayne (1968) *The Subjunctive in English*. Alabama: University of Alabama

Press.

Hasegawa, Hiroshi (1998) "English Infinitival Relatives as Prepositional Phrases." *English Linguistics* 15: 1-27.

Hasegawa, Kinsuke (1963) "Subjunctive no Hitee [The Negation of Subjunctive]." *Eego Seenen* [The Rising Generation] 109(10): 609. Tokyo: Kenkyusha.

——— (1965) "English Imperatives." *Nakajima Fumio Kyooju Kanreki Kinen Ronbunshuu* [Festschrift for Professor Fumio Nakajima on the Occasion of His Sixtieth Birthday], 20-28. Tokyo: Kenkyusha.

——— (1974) "Generalized A-over-A Principle (1)-(2)." *Eego Seenen* [The Rising Generation] 119(11): 736-737, (12): 808-810. Tokyo: Kenkyusha.

——— (1981) "Henkee no Seeshitsu to Chomusukii no Bunpoo-taikee [Properties of Transformations and Chomsky's System of Grammar]." In Yoshio Terasawa ed., *Eego no Rekishi to Koozoo—Miyabe Kikuo Kyooju Kanreki Kinen Ronbunshuu* [The History and Structure of the English Language Presented to Professor Kikuo Miyabe in Honor of His Sixtieth Birthday], 331-350. Tokyo: Kenkyusha.

——— (1983) "Bunpoo no Wakugumi—Toogo-riron no Shomondai [The Framework of Grammar: The Problems in Syntactic Theory] (2)" *Gengo* [Language] 12(6): 100-108. Tokyo: Taishukan.

——— (1993-1994) "*That*-konseki-genshoo to Kiseekuusho-koobun [*That*-trace Phenomena and Parasitic Gap Constructions]. *Eego Seenen* [The Rising Generation] 139(8): 393-395, (9): 452-454, (10): 497-99, (11): 560-562, (12): 606-609. Tokyo: Kenkyusha. Also in Hasegawa (2003), 235-272.

——— (2001) "Feature Checking and *Wh*-Movement." Paper Presented at Workshop, Phase and Cyclicity, 19th National Conference of the English Linguistic Society of Japan.

——— (2002) "Sosee-idoo to *Wh*-ku-idoo. [Feature Movement and *Wh*-phrase Movement]." *Eego Seenen* [The Rising Generation] 148(5): 283-287. Tokyo: Kenkyusha. Also in Hasegawa (2003), 273-283.

——— (2003) *Seeseebunpoo no Hoohoo—Eego-toogoron no Shikumi* [Approaches to Generative Grammar: The Fundamentals of English Syntax]. Tokyo: Kenkyusha.

———, Ryoji Kasai, Sachie Kajita, Hiroshi Hasegawa, and Noriko Imanishi (2000) *Bun* (I) [Sentence Structure (I)]. Tokyo: Kenkyusha.

Haumann, Dagmar (1997) *The Syntax of Subordination.* Tübingen: Niemeyer.

Hayashi, Ryujiro (1988) "A Note on *NOT.*" *English Linguistics* 5: 197-203.

Henry, Alison (1995) *Belfast English and Standard English: Dialect Variation and Parameter Setting.* Oxford: Oxford University Press.

Hiroe, Akira (1999) "Mood and Complementizer Deletion." *English Linguistics* 16: 55-77.

Hojo, Kazuaki (1971) "The Present Subjunctive in English NP Complements." *Ronshuu* [The Review of Inquiry and Research] 17: 93-112. Osaka: Kansai Gaidai University.

Hooper, Joan B. (1975) "On Assertive Predicates." In John P. Kimball ed., *Syntax and Semantics,* vol. 4, 91-124. New York: Academic Press.

―――― and Sandra A. Thompson (1973) "On the Applicability of Root Transformations." *Linguistics Inquiry* 4 : 465-497.

Hopper, Paul J. and Elizabeth C. Traugott (2003^2) *Grammaticalization.* Cambridge: Cambridge University Press.

Hornby, A. S. (1975^2) *Guide to Patterns and Usage in English.* Oxford: Oxford University Press.

Hornstein, Norbert (1990) *As Time Goes By: Tense and Universal Grammar.* Cambridge, MA.: MIT Press.

―――― (1999) "Minimalism and Quantifier Raising." In Samuel D. Epstein and Norbert Hornstein eds., *Working Minimalism,* 45-75. Cambridge, MA.: MIT Press.

Hosoe, Itsuki (1933) *Dooshi Johoo no Kenkyuu* [Studies in the Mood of the English Verb]. Tokyo: Taibundo.

Huddleston, Rodney D. (1976) "Some Theoretical Issues in the Description of the English Verb." *Lingua* 40: 331-383.

Iatridou, Sabine (1990) "About Agr(P)." *Linguistic Inquiry* 21: 766-772.

Imai, Kunihiko (1975) *Henkee-bunpoo no Hanashi* [Topics in Transformational Grammar]. Tokyo: Taishukan.

―――― and Heizo Nakajima (1978) *Bun* (II) [Sentence Structure (II)]. Tokyo: Kenkyusha.

――――, Heizo Nakajima, Shigeo Tonoike, Hajime Fukuchi, and Kimiya Adachi (1989) *Ippo Susunda Eebunpoo* [One-Step Advanced English Grammar]. Tokyo: Taishukan.

———, Heizo Nakajima, Shigeo Tonoike, and Christopher D. Tancredi (1995) *Essentials of Modern English Grammar*. Tokyo: Kenkyusha.

Imanishi, Noriko and Ichiro Asano (1990) *Shoooo to Sakujo* [Anaphora and Deletion]. Tokyo: Taishukan.

Ishihara, Yuki (1998) "Eego no Genkee-futeeshi no Seeki ni tsuite [On the Occurrences of Root Infinitives in English]." *JELS* 15: 61-70. The English Linguistic Society of Japan.

Ishikawa, Kazuhisa (1995) "A History of *NOT*: The Change from a Phrase to a Head." *English Linguistics* 12: 197-221.

Jackendoff, Ray (1973) "The Base Rule for Prepositional Phrases." In Anderson and Kiparsky eds. (1973), 345-356.

——— (1977) *X'-Syntax: A Study of Phrase Structure*. Cambridge, MA.: MIT Press.

Jacobson, Pauline (1992) "The Lexical Entailment Theory of Control and the *Tough*-Construction." In Ivan A. Sag and Anna Szabolcsi eds., *Lexical Matters*, 269-299. Stanford: CSLI Publications.

James, Francis (1986) *Semantics of the English Subjunctive*. Vancouver: University of Columbia Press.

Jespersen, Otto (1909-49) *A Modern English Grammar on Historical Principles*. 7 vols. Heidelberg: C. Winter, London: George Allen and Unwin, Copenhagen: Munksgaard. (Part I, 1909; Part II, 1913; Part III, 1927; Part IV, 1931; Part V, 1940; Part VI, 1942; Part VII, 1949.)

——— (1924) *The Philosophy of Grammar*. London: George Allen and Unwin.

——— (1933) *Essentials of English Grammar*. London: George Allen and Unwin.

Johnson, Kyle (1984) "Some Notes on Subjunctive Clauses and Binding in Icelandic." *MIT Working Papers in Linguistics* 6: 102-137.

——— (1988) "Verb Raising and *Have*." *McGill Working Papers in Linguistics: Special Issues on Comparative German Syntax*, 156-167. Montreal: McGill University.

Kajita, Masaru (1968) *A Generative-Transformational Study of Semi-Auxiliaries in Present-Day American English*. Tokyo: Sanseido.

——— (1976) *Henkeebunpooriron no Kiseki* [The Trace of Transformational Theory]. Tokyo: Taishukan.

——— (1977) "Towards a Dynamic Model of Syntax." *Studies in English*

Linguistics 5: 44-76.

Kaneko, Yoshiaki (1999) "Eego-hoojodooshi no Imi-kaishaku: Goi-tokusee, Goyooron, Jojutsu-yooshiki no Intaafeesu [Semantic Interpretations of English Modal Auxiliaries: Interface among Lexical Properties, Pragmatics, and the Types of Predication]." In Shige-Yuki Kuroda and Masaru Nakamura eds., *Kotoba no Shuuhen to Kaku: Nihongo to Eego no Aida* [The Core and Periphery of Language: Comparisons between Japanese and English], 321-355. Tokyo: Kurosio Publishers.

Kasai, Ryoji (2000) "Hitee [Negation]." In Hasegawa *et al.* (2000), 227-299.

Kashino, Kenji (2002) *Eego-jodooshi no Gohoo* [Usages of English Auxiliaries]. Tokyo: Kenkyusha.

Katz, Jerrold J. and Paul M. Postal (1964) *An Integrated Theory of Linguistic Descriptions.* Cambridge, MA.: MIT Press.

Kayne, Richard (1980) "Extensions of Binding and Case Marking." *Lingusitic Inquiry* 11: 75-96.

—— (1994) *The Antysymmetry of Syntax.* Cambridge, MA.: MIT Press.

—— (1998) "Overt vs. Covert Movement." *Syntax* 1: 128-191.

Kempchinsky, Paula (1986) Romance Subjunctive Clauses and Logical Form. Doctoral Dissertation, UCLA.

Kenstowicz, Michael ed. (2001) *Ken Hale: A Life in Language.* Cambridge, MA.: MIT Press.

Kiparsky, Paul and Carol Kiparsky (1970) "Fact." In Manfred Bierwisch and Karl E. Heidolph eds., *Programs in Lingusitics: A collection of Papers*, 143-173. The Hague: Mouton.

Kirchner, Gustav (1970-72) *Die Syntaktischen Engentümlichkeiten des Amerikanischen Englisch*, 2 Bde. Halle (Saale): Max Niemeyer.

Koizumi, Masatoshi (1999) *Phrase Structure in Minimalist Syntax.* Tokyo: Hituzi Syobo.

—— (2002) "The Split VP Hypothesis: Evidence from Language Acquisition." In Mengistu Ambeber and Peter Collins eds., *Language Universals and Variation*, 61-81. Westport: Praeger.

Konno, Hiroaki (2002) "Gendai-eego ni okeru Kateehoo-genzai no Imi・Goyooron-teki Ninka-jooken [Semantic and Pragmatic Conditions on the Subjunctive Present in Present-Day English]." *JELS* 19: 41-49. The

English Linguistic Society of Japan.

Kono, Tsuguyo (2002) "Jiree-kenkyuu: Dooshiku-sakujo-genshoo [A Case Study: VP-Deletion]." In Yukio Otsu, Masayuki Ikeuchi, Noriko Imanishi, and Masanori Suiko eds., *Gengo-kenkyuu Nyuumon—Seesee-bunpoo o Manabu Hito no tameni* [An Introduction to Linguistic Studies—For Those Who Want to Study Generative Grammar: Festschrift for Shuji Chiba on the Occasion of His Sixtieth Birthday], 276-288. Tokyo: Kenkyusha.

Kozu, Harushige (1954) *In-oogo Hikaku-bunpoo* [Comparative Grammar in Indo-European Languages]. Tokyo: Iwanami Shoten.

Kruisinga, Etsuko (1932^6) *A Handbook of Present-Day English*, 4 vols. Groningen: Noordhoff

Kuno, Susumu (1987) *Functional Syntax: Anaphora, Discourse, and Empathy*. Chicago: University of Chicago Press.

—— and Ken-ichi Takami (1993) *Grammar and Discourse Principles: Functional Syntax and GB Theory*. Chicago: University of Chicago Press.

—— and Ken-ichi Takami (1997) "Remarks on Negative Islands." *Linguistic Inquiry* 28: 553-576.

Kuwabara, Kazuki (2001) "Kateehoosetsu [Subjunctive Clauses]." In Kuwabara and Matsuyama (2001), 167-191.

—— and Tetsuya Matsuyama (2001) *Hobun-koozoo* [The Structure of Complement Clauses]. Tokyo: Kenkyusha.

Lightfoot, David (1979) *Principle of Diachronic Syntax*. Cambridge: Cambridge University Press.

Langacker, Ronald W. (1987) "Nouns and Verbs." *Language* 63: 53-94.

Laka, Itziar M. (1990) Negation in Syntax; On the Nature of Functional Categories and Projections. Doctoral Dissertation, MIT.

Lasnik, Howard (1995) "Verbal Morphology: *Syntactic Structures* Meets the Minimalist Program." In Héctor Campos and Paula Kempchinsky eds., *Evolution and Revolution in Linguistic Theory: Essays in Honor of Carlos Otero*, 251-275. Washington, D. C.: Georgetown University Press. Also in Lasnik (1999), 97-119.

—— (1999) *Minimalist Analysis*. Oxford: Blackwell.

—— (2000) Syntactic Structures *Revisited*. Cambridge, MA.: MIT Press.

—— and Mamoru Saito (1991) "On the Subject of Infinitives." *CLS* 27:

324-343. Also in Lasnik (1999), 7-24.

——— and Mamoru Saito (1992) *Move α: Conditions on Its Application and Output*. Cambridge, MA.: MIT Press.

Leech, Geoffrey N. (1971) *Meaning and the English Verb*. London: Longman.

——— (1987^2) *Meaning and the English Verb*. London: Longman.

——— and Jan Svartvik (1994^2) *A Communicative Grammar of English*. London: Longman.

Lees, Robert B. (1964) "On Passives and Imperatives in English." *Gengo Kenkyu* [Journal of the Linguistic Society of Japan] 46: 28-41.

Lobeck, Anne (1995) *Ellipsis: Functional Heads, Licensing, and Identification*. New York: Oxford University Press.

Lyons, John (1977) *Semantics*, vol. 2. Cambridge: Cambridge University Press.

Mailing, Joan (1984) "Non-clause-bounded Reflexives in Modern Icelandic." *Linguistics and Philosophy* 7: 211-241.

Martin, Roger (1992) "On the Distribution and Case Features of PRO." MS., University of Connecticut.

——— (2001) "Null Case and the Distribution of PRO." *Linguistic Inquiry* 32: 141-166.

Matsubara, Fuminori (1997a) Studies in Argument Structure. Doctoral Dissertation, Yasuda Women University.

——— (1997b) "Bunri I Kasetsu to NegP [Split-I Hypothesis and NegP]." *Eego Seenen* [The Rising Generation] 143(4): 200-204. Tokyo: Kenkyusha.

Matsui, Chie (1981) "The Present Subjunctive in Embedded *That* Clauses." *Insight* 13: 45-59. Kyoto: Kyoto Notre Dame University.

Matsuyama, Tetsuya (2001) "Futeeshi-hobun [Infinitival Complement Clauses]." In Kuwabara and Matsuyama (2001), 65-142.

May, Robert (1985) *Logical Form: Its Structure and Derivation*. Cambridge, MA.: MIT Press.

McCawley, James D. (1970) "On the Deep Structure of Negative Clauses." In Shin-Ichi Harada and Donald L. Smith eds., *Selected Papers in Generative Semantics*, 3-13. Papers for the Fifth International Seminar in Linguistic Theory from August 24 to September 3 in 1970.

——— (1971) "Tense and Time Reference in English." In Charles Fillmore and D. Terence Langendoen eds., *Studies in Semantics*, 97-114. New York: Holt.

Also in McCawley (1973), 257-272.

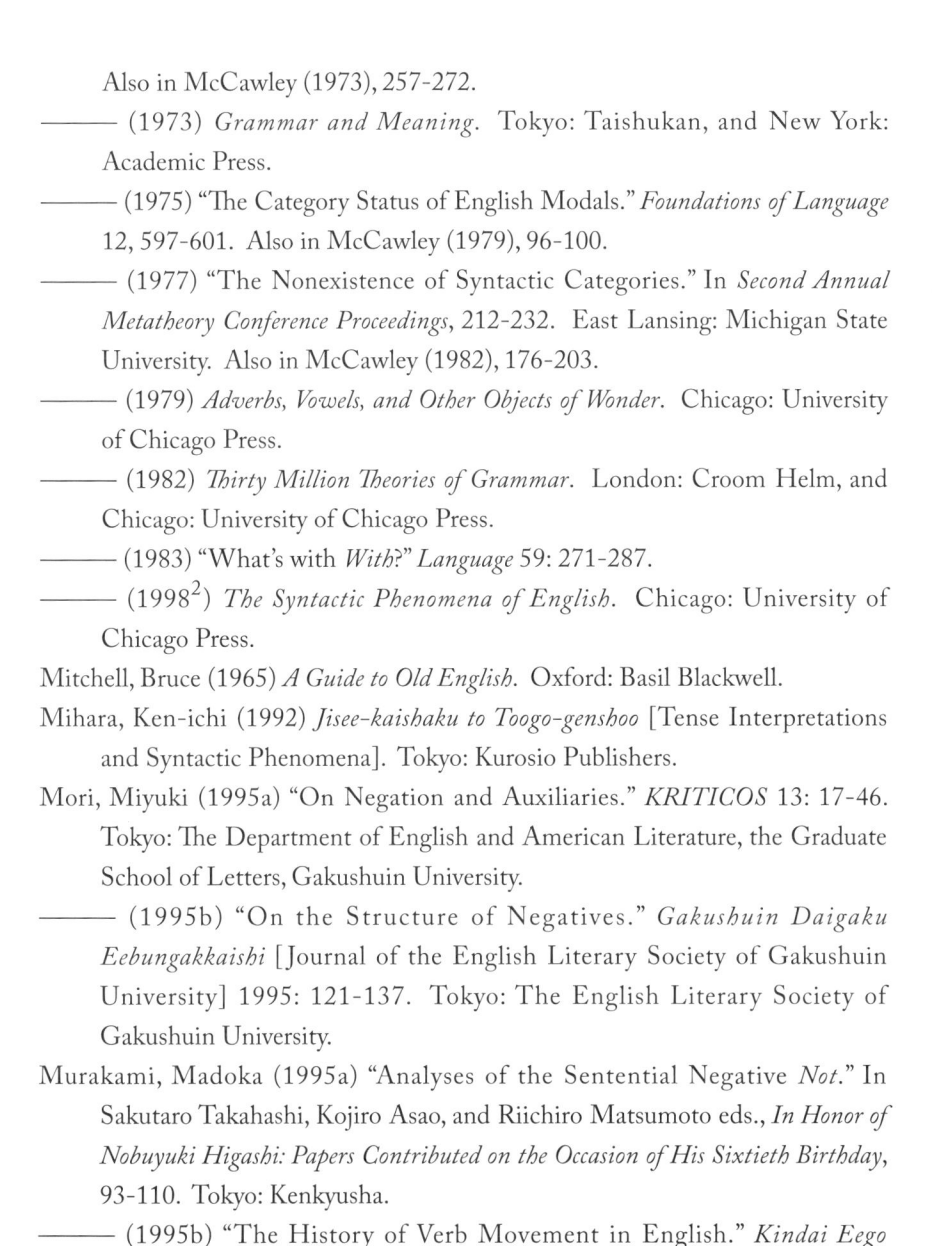

―――― (1973) *Grammar and Meaning*. Tokyo: Taishukan, and New York: Academic Press.

―――― (1975) "The Category Status of English Modals." *Foundations of Language* 12, 597-601. Also in McCawley (1979), 96-100.

―――― (1977) "The Nonexistence of Syntactic Categories." In *Second Annual Metatheory Conference Proceedings*, 212-232. East Lansing: Michigan State University. Also in McCawley (1982), 176-203.

―――― (1979) *Adverbs, Vowels, and Other Objects of Wonder*. Chicago: University of Chicago Press.

―――― (1982) *Thirty Million Theories of Grammar*. London: Croom Helm, and Chicago: University of Chicago Press.

―――― (1983) "What's with *With*?" *Language* 59: 271-287.

―――― (1998^2) *The Syntactic Phenomena of English*. Chicago: University of Chicago Press.

Mitchell, Bruce (1965) *A Guide to Old English*. Oxford: Basil Blackwell.

Mihara, Ken-ichi (1992) *Jisee-kaishaku to Toogo-genshoo* [Tense Interpretations and Syntactic Phenomena]. Tokyo: Kurosio Publishers.

Mori, Miyuki (1995a) "On Negation and Auxiliaries." *KRITICOS* 13: 17-46. Tokyo: The Department of English and American Literature, the Graduate School of Letters, Gakushuin University.

―――― (1995b) "On the Structure of Negatives." *Gakushuin Daigaku Eebungakkaishi* [Journal of the English Literary Society of Gakushuin University] 1995: 121-137. Tokyo: The English Literary Society of Gakushuin University.

Murakami, Madoka (1995a) "Analyses of the Sentential Negative *Not*." In Sakutaro Takahashi, Kojiro Asao, and Riichiro Matsumoto eds., *In Honor of Nobuyuki Higashi: Papers Contributed on the Occasion of His Sixtieth Birthday*, 93-110. Tokyo: Kenkyusha.

―――― (1995b) "The History of Verb Movement in English." *Kindai Eego Kenkyuu* [Studies in Modern English] 11: 11-45. The Modern English Association.

―――― (1998) "*Not* in Subjunctive Clauses: A Review of Potsdam (1997)." *Kumamoto Kenritsu Daigaku Bungakubu Kiyoo* [Journal of the Faculty of

Letters of Prefectural University of Kumamoto] 5(1): 37-49. Kumamoto: The Faculty of Letters of Prefectural University of Kumamoto

―――― (1999) "*That*-less Subjunctives in Earlier English." Paper Presented at the 12th World Congress of Applied Linguistics.

―――― (2000) "*That*-less Subjunctives in Earlier English." *Kindai Eego Kenkyuu* [Studies in Modern English] 16: 85-97. The Modern English Association.

―――― (2002) "Whether Agr or Mood: V Movement across European Languages." *JELS* 19: 166-175. The English Linguistic Society of Japan.

―――― (2003) "Bun-hiteeji *not* no Bunseki to Rekishi [Analyses and History of the Sentential Negative *not*]." Paper Presented at the 20th General Meeting of the Modern English Association.

Nakajima, Heizo (1989) "Heejobun [Declarative Sentences]." In Imai *et al.* (1989), 13-39.

―――― (1996) "Complementizer Selection." *The Linguistic Review* 13: 143-164.

―――― ed. (1991) *Current English Linguistics in Japan*. Berlin: Mouton de Gruyter.

Nakamura, Masaru (2003) *Imiron—Dooteki-imiron* [Semantics—Dynamic Semantics]. Tokyo: Kaitakusha.

Nakano, Hirozo (1994) *Eego-hoojodooshi no Imiron* [The Semantics of the English Modal Auxiliaries]. Tokyo: Eichosha.

Nakao, Toshio and Osamu Koma eds. (1990) *Rekishiteki ni Saguru Gendai no Eebunpoo* [Present-Day English Grammar from the View of the History of the English Language]. Tokyo: Taishukan.

Nakao, Yuji and Masachiyo Amano eds. (1994) *Jodooshi* Do—*Kigen, Hattatsu, Kinoo* [The Auxiliary *Do*—Origin, Development, and Function]. Tokyo: Eichosha.

Nakau, Minoru (1994) *Ninchi-imiron no Genri* [Principles of Cognitive Semantics]. Tokyo: Taishukan.

Nawata, Hiroyuki (2003) "The Rich Agreement Hypothesis and the Loss of Verb Second in English." *Kindai Eego Kenkyuu* [Studies in Modern English] 19: 55-62. The Modern English Association.

Newmeyer, Frederick J. (1969) English Aspectual Verbs. Doctoral Dissertation, University of Illinois.

Nomura, Tadao (1999a) "Meereeteki-setsuzokuhoo-setsu no naka ni Arawareru *should* ni tsuite [On *Should* in Mandative Subjunctive Clauses]." *Eego Gohoo Bunpoo Kenkyuu* [Studies in English Grammar and Usage] 6: 215-229. The Society of English Grammar and Usage.

――― (1999b) "Tense in Mandative Subjunctive Clauses." *Metropolitan Linguistics* 19: 41-58. Tokyo: The Linguistic Circle of Tokyo Metropolitan University.

――― (2000a) "Meereeteki-setsuzokuhoo-setsu ni okeru *not* to *have · be* tono Ichikankee ni tsuite [On the Ordering Relations between *Not* and *Have/Be* in Mandative Subjunctive Clauses]." *Eego Gohoo Bunpoo Kenkyuu* [Studies in English Grammar and Usage] 7: 151-165. The Society of English Grammar and Usage.

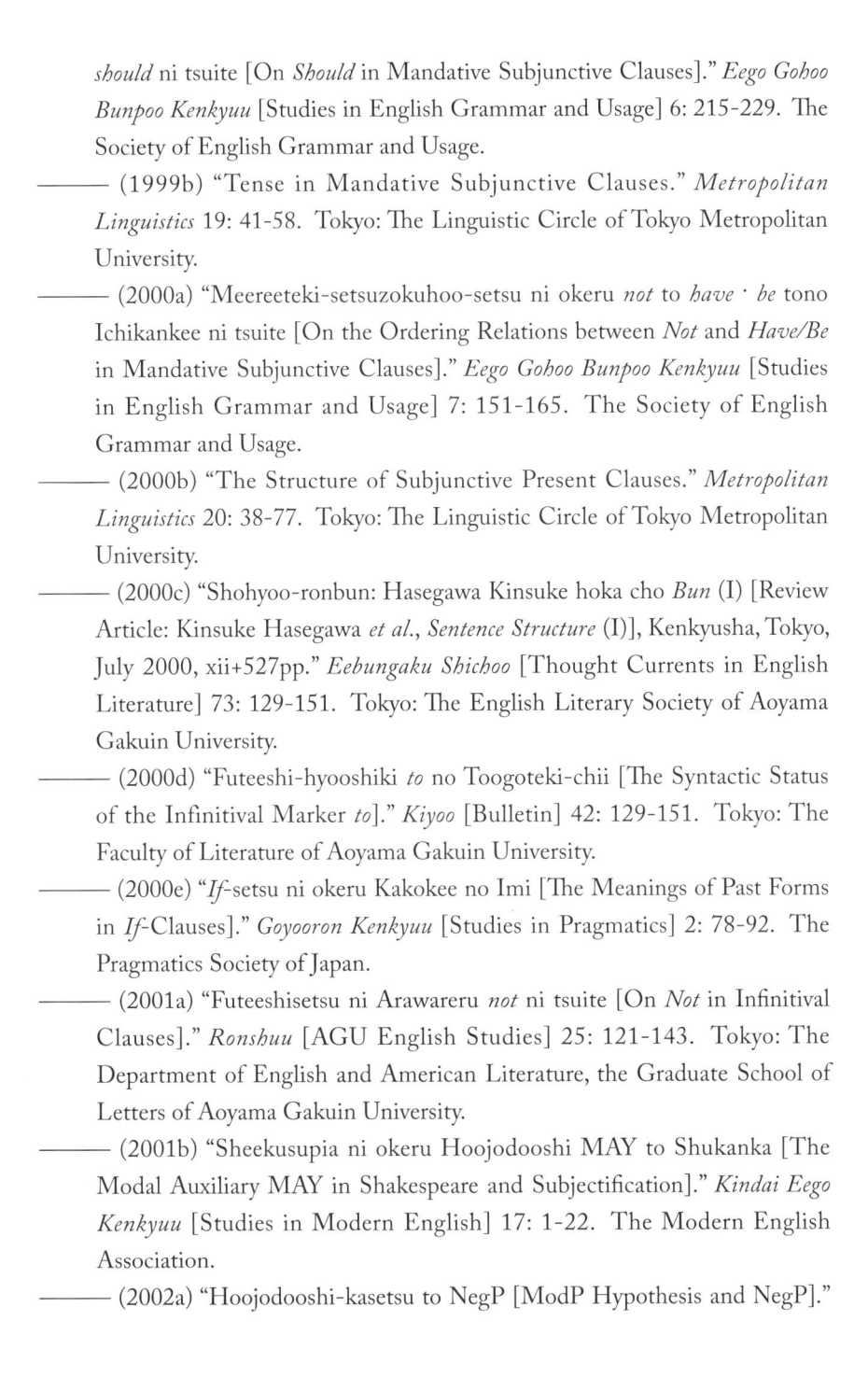

――― (2000b) "The Structure of Subjunctive Present Clauses." *Metropolitan Linguistics* 20: 38-77. Tokyo: The Linguistic Circle of Tokyo Metropolitan University.

――― (2000c) "Shohyoo-ronbun: Hasegawa Kinsuke hoka cho *Bun* (I) [Review Article: Kinsuke Hasegawa *et al.*, *Sentence Structure* (I)], Kenkyusha, Tokyo, July 2000, xii+527pp." *Eebungaku Shichoo* [Thought Currents in English Literature] 73: 129-151. Tokyo: The English Literary Society of Aoyama Gakuin University.

――― (2000d) "Futeeshi-hyooshiki *to* no Toogoteki-chii [The Syntactic Status of the Infinitival Marker *to*]." *Kiyoo* [Bulletin] 42: 129-151. Tokyo: The Faculty of Literature of Aoyama Gakuin University.

――― (2000e) "*If*-setsu ni okeru Kakokee no Imi [The Meanings of Past Forms in *If*-Clauses]." *Goyooron Kenkyuu* [Studies in Pragmatics] 2: 78-92. The Pragmatics Society of Japan.

――― (2001a) "Futeeshisetsu ni Arawareru *not* ni tsuite [On *Not* in Infinitival Clauses]." *Ronshuu* [AGU English Studies] 25: 121-143. Tokyo: The Department of English and American Literature, the Graduate School of Letters of Aoyama Gakuin University.

――― (2001b) "Sheekusupia ni okeru Hoojodooshi MAY to Shukanka [The Modal Auxiliary MAY in Shakespeare and Subjectification]." *Kindai Eego Kenkyuu* [Studies in Modern English] 17: 1-22. The Modern English Association.

――― (2002a) "Hoojodooshi-kasetsu to NegP [ModP Hypothesis and NegP]."

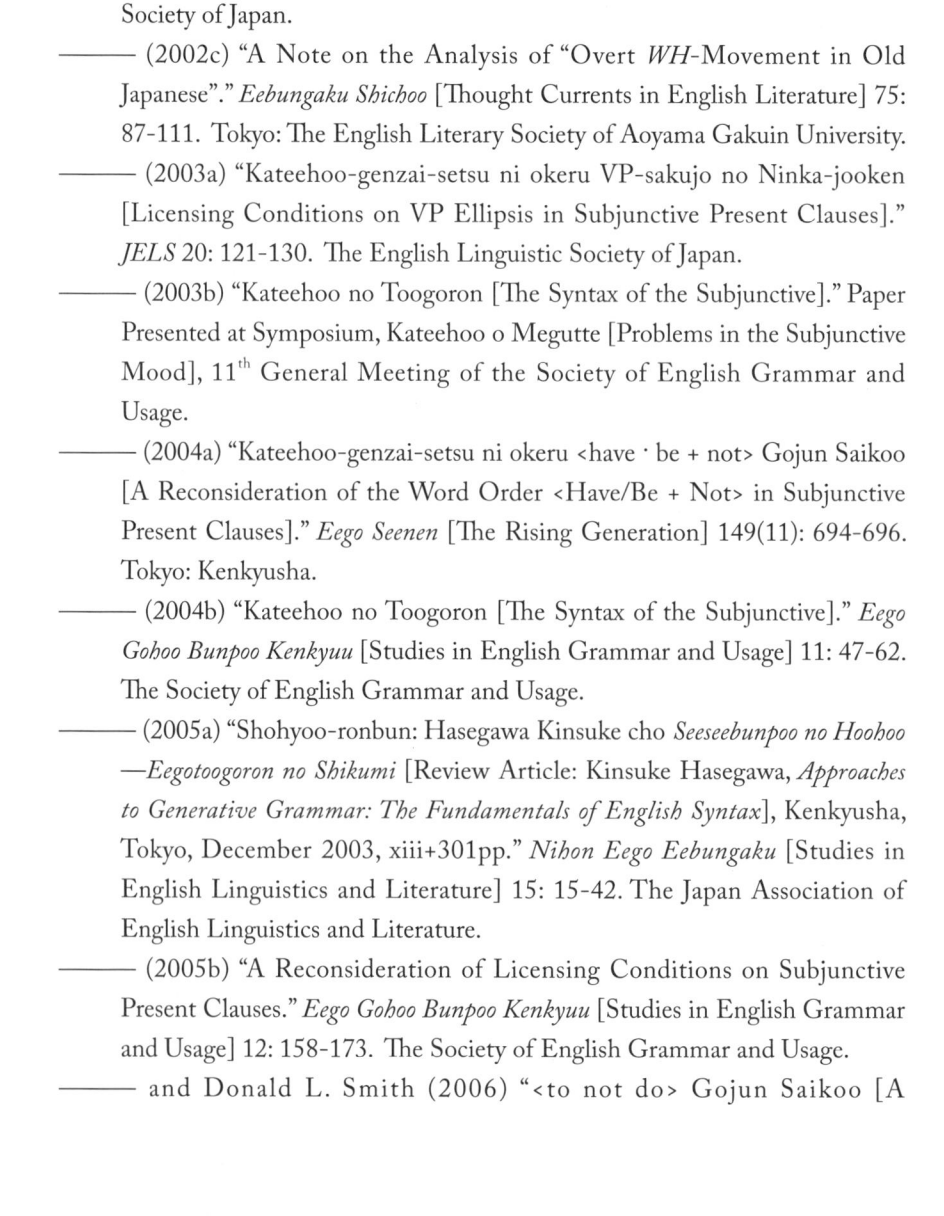

Ronshuu [AGU English Studies] 26: 83-108. Tokyo: the Department of English and American Literature, the Graduate School of Letters of Aoyama Gakuin University.

―――― (2002b) "Kateehoo-genzai-setsu ni okeru VP-sakujo no Ninka-jooken [Licensing Conditions on VP Ellipsis in Subjunctive Present Clauses]." Paper Presented at the 20th National Conference of the English Linguistic Society of Japan.

―――― (2002c) "A Note on the Analysis of "Overt *WH*-Movement in Old Japanese"." *Eebungaku Shichoo* [Thought Currents in English Literature] 75: 87-111. Tokyo: The English Literary Society of Aoyama Gakuin University.

―――― (2003a) "Kateehoo-genzai-setsu ni okeru VP-sakujo no Ninka-jooken [Licensing Conditions on VP Ellipsis in Subjunctive Present Clauses]." *JELS* 20: 121-130. The English Linguistic Society of Japan.

―――― (2003b) "Kateehoo no Toogoron [The Syntax of the Subjunctive]." Paper Presented at Symposium, Kateehoo o Megutte [Problems in the Subjunctive Mood], 11th General Meeting of the Society of English Grammar and Usage.

―――― (2004a) "Kateehoo-genzai-setsu ni okeru <have · be + not> Gojun Saikoo [A Reconsideration of the Word Order <Have/Be + Not> in Subjunctive Present Clauses]." *Eego Seenen* [The Rising Generation] 149(11): 694-696. Tokyo: Kenkyusha.

―――― (2004b) "Kateehoo no Toogoron [The Syntax of the Subjunctive]." *Eego Gohoo Bunpoo Kenkyuu* [Studies in English Grammar and Usage] 11: 47-62. The Society of English Grammar and Usage.

―――― (2005a) "Shohyoo-ronbun: Hasegawa Kinsuke cho *Seeseebunpoo no Hoohoo —Eegotoogoron no Shikumi* [Review Article: Kinsuke Hasegawa, *Approaches to Generative Grammar: The Fundamentals of English Syntax*], Kenkyusha, Tokyo, December 2003, xiii+301pp." *Nihon Eego Eebungaku* [Studies in English Linguistics and Literature] 15: 15-42. The Japan Association of English Linguistics and Literature.

―――― (2005b) "A Reconsideration of Licensing Conditions on Subjunctive Present Clauses." *Eego Gohoo Bunpoo Kenkyuu* [Studies in English Grammar and Usage] 12: 158-173. The Society of English Grammar and Usage.

―――― and Donald L. Smith (2006) "<to not do> Gojun Saikoo [A

Reconsideration of the Word Order <To Not Do>]." MS., Wako University and Notre Dame Seishin University.

Nomura, Takashi (1995) "*Ka* ni yoru Kakarimusubi Shiron [A Note on *Kakarimusubi* from the View of *Ka*]." *Kokugo Kokubun* [Studies in Traditional Japanese Linguistics and Japanese Literature] 64(9): 1-27.

Obunsha Dictionary Editorial Office eds. (1999) PLANET BOARD Question Box for English Teachers. In *Argument Forum* 1999(1). http://www.obunsha.co.jp/argu/html/5argu6.html.

Ogawa, Akira (1988) "Shohyoo [Review]: Chiba (1987)." *Eebungaku Kenkyuu* [Studies in English Literature] 65(1): 144-149.

Ogawa, Hiroshi (1989) *Old English Modal Verbs: A Syntactical Study*. Copenhagen: Rosenkilde.

Okuno, Tadanori (1999) "Review Article: Lobeck (1995)." *English Linguistics* 16: 152-183.

Onions, Charles T. (1932^6) *An Advanced English Syntax*. London: Kegan Paul

Ono, Hayashi and Hiroyuki Ito (1993) *Kindai-eego no Hattatsu* [A History of the Development of Modern English]. Tokyo: Eichosha.

Ono, Shigeru (1969) *Eego-hoojodooshi no Hattatsu* [The Development of the English Modal Auxiliaries]. Tokyo: Kenkyusha.

―――― (1989) *On Early English Syntax and Vocabulary*. Tokyo: Nan'undo.

Onoe, Keisuke (2001) *Bunpoo to Imi* (I) [Grammar and Meaning (I)]. Tokyo: Kurosio Publishers.

Ota, Akira (1980) *Hitee no Imi: Imiron-josetsu* [The Meanings of Negation: An Introduction to Semantics]. Tokyo: Taishukan.

Ouhalla, Jamal (1990) "Sentential Negation, Relativized Minimality, and the Aspectual Status of Auxiliaries." *The Linguistic Review* 7: 183-231.

―――― (1991) *Functional Categories and Parametric Variation*. London: Routledge.

Övergaard, Gerd (1995) *The Mandative Subjunctive in American and British English in the 20th Century*. Stockholm: Almqvist and Wiksell.

Palmer, Frank F. (1974) *The English Verb*. London: Longman.

―――― (1987^2) *The English Verb*. London: Longman.

―――― (1990^2) *Modality and the English Modals*. London: Longman.

―――― (2001^2) *Mood and Modality*. London: Cambridge University Press.

Papafragou, Anna (1998) "Inference and Word Meaning: The Case of

Modal Auxiliaries." *Lingua* 105: 1-47.

—— (2000) *Modality: Issues in the Semantics—Pragmatics Interface*. Amsterdam: Elsevier.

Pesetsky, David M. (1982) Paths and Categories. Doctoral Dissertation, MIT.

—— (1995) *Zero Syntax: Experiencers and Cascades*. Cambridge, MA.: MIT Press.

—— and Esther Torrego (2001) "T-to-C Movement: Causes and Consequences." In Kenstowicz ed. (2001), 355-426.

Picallo, Carme (1985) Opaque Domains. Doctoral Dissertation, City University of New York.

Pollock, Jean-Yves (1989) "Verb Movement, Universal Grammar, and the Structure of IP." *Linguistic Inquiry* 20: 365-424.

—— (1997) "Notes on Clause Structure." In Haegeman ed. (1997), 237-279.

Postal, Paul M. (1974) *On Raising: One Rule of English Grammar and Its Theoretical Implications*. Cambridge, MA.: MIT Press.

Potsdam, Eric (1997) "NegP and Subjunctive." *Linguistic Inquiry* 28: 533-541.

—— (1998) *Syntactic Issues in the English Imperative*. New York: Garland.

Poutsma, Hendrik (1904-29) *A Grammar of Late Modern English*, 5 vols. Groningen: Noordhoff.

Prince, Ellen F. (1978) "A Comparison of WH-Clefts and IT-Clefts in Discourse." *Language* 54: 833-906.

Progovac, Ljiljana (1993) "Long-Distance Reflexives: Movement-to-Infl versus Relativized SUBJECT." *Linguistic Inquiry* 24: 755-772.

Quirk, Randolph, Sidney Greenbaum, Geoffrey Leech, and Jan Svartvik (1985) *A Comprehensive Grammar of the English Language*. London: Longman.

Radford, Andrew (1988) *Transformational Grammar: A First Course*. London: Cambridge University Press.

—— (1997) *Syntactic Theory and the Structure of English: A Minimalist Approach*. London: Cambridge University Press.

—— (2004) *Minimalist Syntax: Exploring the Structure of English*. London: Cambridge University Press.

Raposo, Eduardo (1987) "Case Theory and Infl-to-Comp: The Inflected Infinitive in European Portuguese." *Linguistic Inquiry* 18: 85-109.

Reichenbach, Hans (1947) *Elements of Symbolic Logic*. New York: The Free Press, and London: Collier-Macmillan.

Rizzi, Luigi (1990) *Relativized Minimality*. Cambridge, MA.: MIT Press.

Reuland, Eric (1983) "Governing *–ing*." *Linguistic Inquiry* 14: 101-136.

Roberts, Ian G. (1985) "Agreement Parameters and the Development of English Modal Auxiliaries." *Natural Language and Linguistic Theory* 3: 21-58.

―――― (1992) *Verb and Diachronic Syntax: A Comparative History of English and French*. Dordrecht: Kluwer.

―――― (1994) "Two Types of Head Movement in Romance." In David Lightfoot and Norbert Hornstein eds., *Verb Movement*, 207-242. Cambridge: Cambridge University Press.

―――― (1998) "*Have/Be* Raising, Move F and Procrastinate." *Linguistic Inquiry* 29: 113-125.

Rohrbacher, Bernard (1999) *Morphology-Driven Syntax: A Theory of V to I Raising and Pro-drop*. Amsterdam: John Benjamins.

Rosenbaum, Peter (1967) *The Grammar of English Predicate Complement Construction*. Cambridge, MA.: MIT Press.

Ross, John R. (1967) Constrains on Variables in Syntax. Doctoral Dissertation, MIT. Published as Ross (1986).

―――― (1969) "Auxiliaries as Main Verbs." *Journal of Philosophical Linguistics* 1-1: 77-102.

―――― (1972) "The Category Squish: Endstation Hauptwort." *CLS* 8: 316-328.

―――― (1973) "Nouniness." In Yasushi Fujimura ed., *Three Dimensions of Linguistic Theory*, 137-257. Tokyo: TEC.

―――― (1984) "Inner Islands." *Proceeding of the Tenth Annual Meeting of the Berkeley Linguistic Society*, 258-265. Berkeley: Berkeley Linguistic Society, University of California.

―――― (1986) *Infinite Syntax!* Norwood, N.J.: Ablex Publishing Corporation.

Rupp, Laura (2003) *The Syntax of Imperatives in English and Germanic: Word Order Variation in the Minimalist Framework*. New York: Palgrave Macmillan.

Safir, Ken (1982) "Inflection-Government and Inversion." *The Linguistic Review* 1: 417-467.

Sag, Ivan A. (1980) *Deletion and Logical Form*. New York: Garland.

Saito, Mamoru and Keiko Murasugi (1990) "N'-deletion in Japanese." *Uconn Working Papers in Linguistics* 3: 87-107.

Sawada, Harumi (1983) "Eego Meereebun no Koozooteki Tokusee: Tokuni Hanchuu AUX to COMP no Fuzai o Chuushin toshite [Structural Properties of English Imperatives: Centering on the Absence of the Category AUX and COMP]." *Gengo Kenkyu* [Journal of the Linguistic Society of Japan] 83: 15-40.

―――― (1985) "The Infinitival Marker *to* and AUX System in English." *English Linguistics* 2: 184-201.

―――― (1993) *Shiten to Shukansee* [Viewpoint and Subjectivity]. Tokyo: Hituzi Syobo.

―――― (1995) *Studies in English and Japanese Auxiliaries: A Multi-stratal Approach.* Tokyo: Hituzi Syobo.

―――― (1998) "*Should* (=Kanjoo) no Imiron—Hyookatekina Shinteki-taido o Megutte [The Semantics of *Should* (=Emotion)—On Evaluative Modality]." *Konishi Tomoshichi Sensee Sanju Kinen Ronbunshuu—Gendai Eego no Gohoo to Bunpoo* [Festschrift for Professor Tomoshichi Konishi on the Occasion of His Eightieth Birthday—Usage and Grammar in Present-Day English], 160-168. Tokyo: Taishukan.

―――― (2001) "Hoojodooshi no Imi o Saguru [Considering the Meanings of Modal Auxiliaries]." *Gengo* [Language] 30(2): 65-72. Tokyo: Taishukan.

Schachter, Paul (1978) "English Propredicates." *Linguistic Analysis* 4: 187-224.

Scheurweghs, Gustaaf (1959) *Present-Day English Syntax.* London: Longman

Selkirk, Elizabeth (1980) *The Phrase Phonology of English and French.* New York: Garland.

Shumaker, Linda and Susumu Kuno (1980) "VP Deletion in Verb Phrases Headed by *Be.*" *Harvard Studies in Syntax and Semantics* 3: 317-67. Cambridge, MA.: Harvard University Press.

Sigurðsson, Halldór Á. (1990) "Long-distance Reflexives and Moods in Icelandic." In Joan Mailing and A. Zaenen eds., *Modern Icelandic Semantics*, 309-346. San Diego: Academic Press.

Smith, Donald L. (1978) "Mirror Images in Japanese and English." *Language* 54: 78-122.

―――― (1981) "Attributes of English Reflexive Pronouns." *Tohoku* 16: 6-30. Sendai: The Department of English, the Graduate School of Tohoku Gakuin University.

Sonnenschein, Edward A. (1916) *A New English Grammar.* London: Oxford University Press.
——— (1927) *The Soul of Grammar.* London: Cambridge University Press.
Steele, Susan, Adrian Akmajian, Richard Demers, Eloise Jelinek, Chisato Kitagawa, Richard Oehrle, and Thomas Wasow (1981) *An Encyclopedia of AUX.* Cambridge, MA.: MIT Press.
Stowell, Tim (1981) Origins of Phrase Structure. Doctoral Dissertation, MIT.
——— (1982) "The Tense of Infinitives." *Linguistic Inquiry* 13: 561-570.
Suzuki, Hidekazu and Izumi Yasui (1994) *Dooshi* [Verbs]. Tokyo: Kenkyusha.
Swan, Michael (1995^2) *Practical English Usage.* Oxford: Oxford University Press.
Sweet, Henry (1892-98) *A New English Grammar: Logical and Historical*, 2 vols. Oxford: Clarendon Press.
Takahashi, Daiko (1994) "Sluicing in Japanese." *Journal of East Asian Linguistics* 3: 265-300.
——— (2001) "Phase Recycling." Paper Presented at Workshop, Phase and Cyclicity, 19th National Conference of the English Linguistic Society of Japan.
——— (2002) "Feezu no Risaikuru [Phase Recycling]." *Eego Seenen* [The Rising Generation] 148(5): 270-273. Tokyo: Kenkyusha.
Takami, Ken-ichi (1992) *Preposition Stranding: From Syntactic to Functional Analyses.* Berlin: Mouton de Gruyter.
Terazu, Noriko (1980) "Eego no Jodooshi-koozoo ni kansuru Hitotsu no Oboegaki [A Note on the Structure of English Auxiliaries]." *Toyama Daigaku Jinbungakubu Kiyoo* [Bulletin of the Faculty of Humanities of Toyama University] 4: 195-210.
Terzi, Arhont (1992) PRO in Finite Clauses: A Study of the Inflectional Heads of the Balkan Languages. Doctoral Dissertation, City University of New York.
——— (1997) "PRO and Null Case in Finite Clauses." *The Linguistic Review* 14: 335-360
Tokieda, Motoki (1941) *Kokugogaku Genron* [An Introduction to (Traditional) Japanese Linguistics]. Tokyo: Iwanami Shoten.
Tonoike, Shigeo (1989a) "Meeshiku [Noun Phrases]." In Imai *et al.* (1989), 79-105.
——— (1989b) "Bunshi Koobun [Participle Constructions]." In Imai *et al.*

(1989), 106-118.

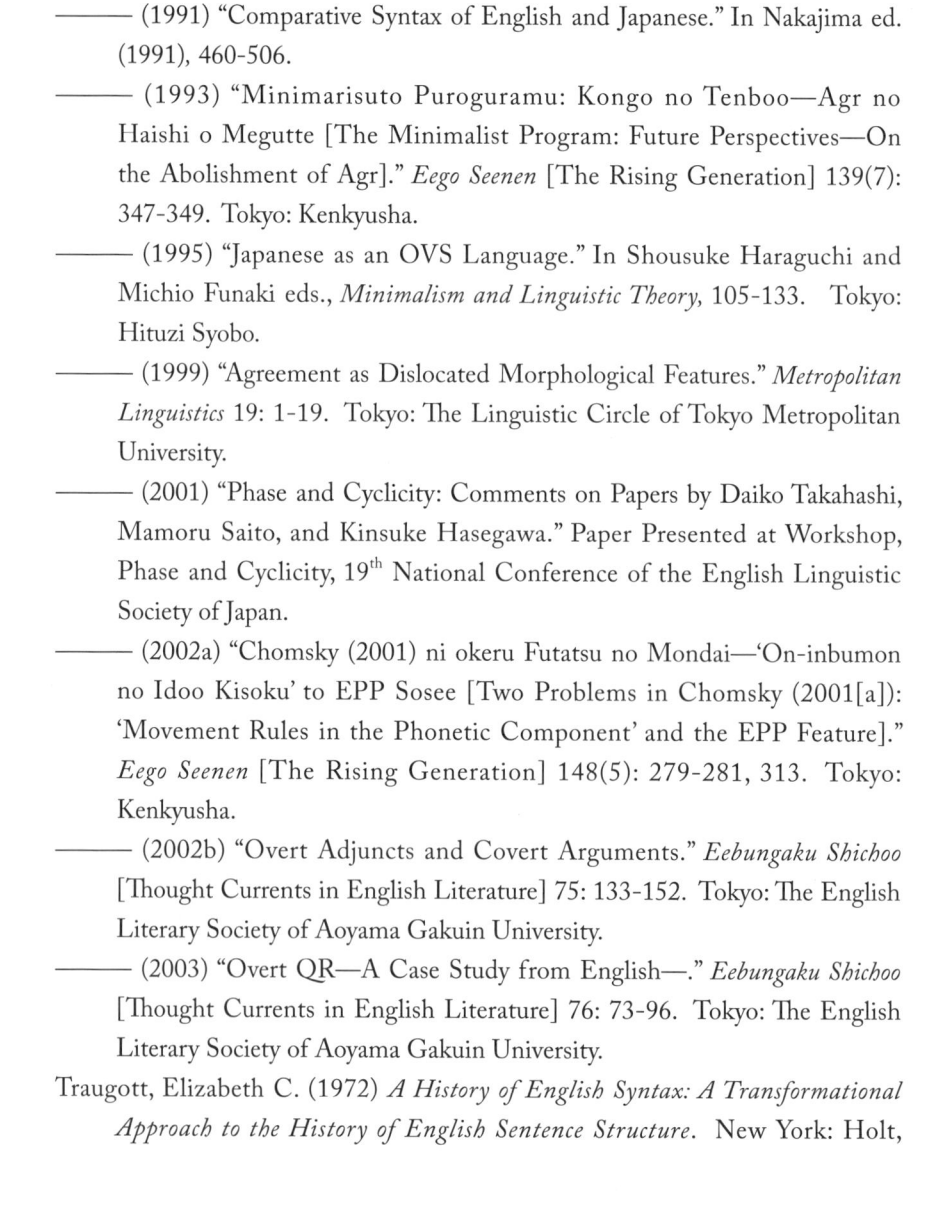

——— (1989c) "Meereebun [Imperative Sentences]." In Imai *et al.* (1989), 119-128.

——— (1989d) "Zero Daiyookee [Zero Pro-forms]." In Imai *et al.* (1989), 223-234.

——— (1991) "Comparative Syntax of English and Japanese." In Nakajima ed. (1991), 460-506.

——— (1993) "Minimarisuto Puroguramu: Kongo no Tenboo—Agr no Haishi o Megutte [The Minimalist Program: Future Perspectives—On the Abolishment of Agr]." *Eego Seenen* [The Rising Generation] 139(7): 347-349. Tokyo: Kenkyusha.

——— (1995) "Japanese as an OVS Language." In Shousuke Haraguchi and Michio Funaki eds., *Minimalism and Linguistic Theory*, 105-133. Tokyo: Hituzi Syobo.

——— (1999) "Agreement as Dislocated Morphological Features." *Metropolitan Linguistics* 19: 1-19. Tokyo: The Linguistic Circle of Tokyo Metropolitan University.

——— (2001) "Phase and Cyclicity: Comments on Papers by Daiko Takahashi, Mamoru Saito, and Kinsuke Hasegawa." Paper Presented at Workshop, Phase and Cyclicity, 19th National Conference of the English Linguistic Society of Japan.

——— (2002a) "Chomsky (2001) ni okeru Futatsu no Mondai—'On-inbumon no Idoo Kisoku' to EPP Sosee [Two Problems in Chomsky (2001[a]): 'Movement Rules in the Phonetic Component' and the EPP Feature]." *Eego Seenen* [The Rising Generation] 148(5): 279-281, 313. Tokyo: Kenkyusha.

——— (2002b) "Overt Adjuncts and Covert Arguments." *Eebungaku Shichoo* [Thought Currents in English Literature] 75: 133-152. Tokyo: The English Literary Society of Aoyama Gakuin University.

——— (2003) "Overt QR—A Case Study from English—." *Eebungaku Shichoo* [Thought Currents in English Literature] 76: 73-96. Tokyo: The English Literary Society of Aoyama Gakuin University.

Traugott, Elizabeth C. (1972) *A History of English Syntax: A Transformational Approach to the History of English Sentence Structure.* New York: Holt,

Reinhart and Winston.
Travis, Lisa (1988) Parameters and Effects of Word Order Variation. Doctoral Dissertation, MIT.
Tsuchiya, Hiroki (2003) *Eego no Imi to Keeshiki* [Meanings and Forms in English]. Tokyo: Eihosha.
Uchibori, Asako (1997) "Opacity and Subjunctive Complements in Japanese." *Japanese Korean Linguistics* 6: 399-414.
―――― (2000) The Syntax of Subjunctive Complements: Evidence from Japanese. Doctoral Dissertation, University of Connecticut.
Ukaji, Masatomo (1978) *Imperative Sentences in Early Modern English*. Tokyo: Kaitakusha.
―――― (1992) ""I not say": Bridge Phenomenon in Syntactic Change." In Matti Rissannen, Terttu Nevalainen, and Irma Taavitisainen eds., *History of Englishes: New Methods and Interpretations in Historical Linguistics*, 453-462. Berlin: Mouton de Gruyter.
―――― (2000) *Eegoshi* [History of English]. Tokyo: Kaitakusha.
Vikner, Sten (1997) "V^0-to-I^0 Movement and Inflection for Person in All Tenses." In Haegeman ed. (1997), 189-213.
Visser, Frederik Theodoor (1966) *A Historical Syntax of the English Language* II. Leiden: E. J. Brill.
Wada, Naoki (2001) *Interpreting English Tenses: A Compositional Approach*. Tokyo: Kaitakusha.
Wakatabe, Hiroya (1985) *Eegoshi IIIB: Beegoshi* [The History of English IIIB: American English]. Tokyo: Taishukan.
Watanabe, Akira (1993a) "The Notion of Finite Clauses in AGR-based Case Theory." *MIT Working Papers in Linguistics* 18: 281-296.
―――― (1993b) Agr-based Case Theory and Its Interaction with A-bar System. Doctoral Dissertation, MIT.
―――― (1996a) *Case Absorption and Wh-agreement*. Dordrecht: Kluwer.
―――― (1996b) "Switch Reference in Control: Toward a Minimal Theory of Control." *Gengo Kyooiku Kenkyu* [Studies in Linguistics and Teaching] 7: 89-160. Chiba: Kanda University of International Studies.
―――― (2000) "Feature Copying and Binding: Evidence from Complementizer Agreement and Switch Reference." *Syntax* 3: 159-181.

―――― (2001) "Theoretical and Empirical Investigations under the Minimalist Program." Paper Presented at Workshop, Minimalist Program and Linguistics Studies, 16th Annual Meeting of Sophia University Linguistics Society.

Weeda, Don (1981) "Tenseless *That*-clauses in Generalized Phrase Structure Grammar." *CLS* 17: 404-410.

Wilkins, Wendy (1977) The Variable Interpretation Covention: A Condition on Variables in Syntactic Transformation. Doctoral Dissertaiton, UCLA.

Yagi, Katsumasa (1996) *Neitibu no Chokkan ni Semaru Eebunpoo―Gendai-eego e no Kijutsuteki Apuroochi* [English Grammar Approaching Native Intuitions―Descriptive Approaches to Present-Day English]. Tokyo: Kenkyusha.

―――― (2002) "Dooshi to *that*-hobun―Sono Musubitsuki no "Igaisee" ni tsuite [Verbs and *that*-complement Clauses―On Their "Unexpected" Relations]." Paper presented at the 11th General Meeting of the Society of English Grammar and Usage.

Yasui, Minoru (2004) "Hitee no Modaritii to Modaritii no Hitee [Negative Modality and the Negation of Modality]." *Eego Seenen* [The Rising Generation] 149(12): 759-761. Tokyo: Kenkyusha.

Zandvoort, Reinard W. (1954) *English Studies*, vol. 35.

―――― (1966^4) *A Handbook of English Grammar*. London: Longman.

Zanuttini, Raffaella (1991) Syntactic Properties of Sentential Negation: A Comparative Study of Romance Languages. Doctoral Dissertation, University of Pennsylvania.

Zhang, Shi (1990) The Status of Imperatives in Theories of Grammar. Doctoral Dissertation, University of Arizona.

Zwart, C. Jan-Wouter (1993) "Verb Movement and Complementizer Agreement." *MIT Working Papers in Linguistics* 18: 281-296.

―――― (1997) *Morphosyntax of Verb Movement: A Minimalist Approach to the Syntax of Dutch*. Dordrecht: Kluwer.

―――― (2001) "Syntactic and Phonological Verb Movement." *Syntax* 4: 34-62.

Zwicky, Arnold M. (1982) "Stranded *to* and Phonological Phrasing in English." *Linguistics* 20: 3-57.

Index

Author Index

A

Abbot, Edwin A. 61
Abney, Stephen P. 77
Aijmer, Karin 168, 207
Akimoto, Minoji 93, 175, 193, 218, 318, 333
Akmajian, Adrian 82, 84, 94
Amano, Masachiyo 32, 36, 296
Amanuma, Minoru 81, 83, 85
Ando, Sadao 53, 55, 123, 128, 130–132, 137, 141, 144, 146, 151, 164, 169, 175, 193, 224, 226, 227, 233, 270, 276, 293, 295, 337
Aoun, Joseph 107
Araki, Kazuo 217, 221, 255, 316, 325
Arimoto, Masatake 196
Arimura, Kaneaki 27, 221
Asahara, Kyoko 160, 166, 167, 193, 206
Asakawa, Teruo 67, 82, 134, 138, 147, 191, 290
Asano, Ichiro 85

B

Baker, Carl L. 102, 269, 276, 295,
Baker, Mark 4, 295
Baugh, Albert E. 152
Belletti, Adriana 269, 275, 296
Beukema, Firts 162, 303–305
Bloomfield, Leonard 293
Bobaljik, Jonathan D. 27
Bolinger, Dwight L. 80, 166, 170, 171, 173, 175, 196, 216, 260, 261
Bošković, Željko 63, 74, 75, 77, 78, 85, 88, 145, 336
Bouchard, Denis 231
Bowers, John 36, 89, 147, 299
Bradley, Henry 164, 165
Brame, Michael 190
Bresnan, Joan 88, 93, 145, 224, 247, 282, 294

C

Cable, Thomas 152
Carey, G. V. 308
Celce-Murcia, Marianne 295
Charleston, Britta 166, 318
Chiba, Shuji 1, 23, 25, 27, 80, 88, 156,

158, 159, 160, 165–167, 170, 172,
175, 186, 187, 189, 194, 209, 210,
211, 217, 218, 222, 224, 227, 229,
230, 235, 249, 250, 252, 254, 257,
259, 260–262, 266, 307, 309, 327,
339
Chomsky, Naom 1–7, 10, 16, 17, 19, 21, 25
–31, 33, 34, 35, 37, 38, 52–54, 58,
59, 62, 63, 65, 75, 77, 85, 87, 91, 92,
98, 100, 113, 119, 123, 143, 169,
171–173, 195, 223, 224, 227–229,
233, 241, 243–245, 258, 269, 275–
277, 294, 296, 298, 335, 336
Church, Loretta 287, 289
Cinque, Guglielmo 35, 36, 94, 336
Coates, Jennifer 15, 47, 54, 59, 60, 64, 126,
146, 200, 201, 215, 333
Comrie, Bernard 96
Coopmans, Peter 162, 303–305
Culicover, Peter 161, 162, 166, 167, 171,
186, 188, 191, 194–196, 220, 221,
229, 231, 235, 245, 246, 286, 303–
305, 308, 311
Curme 153, 155, 166, 168

D

Davies, Eirlys 196, 295
De Haan, Ferdinand 54
Declerck, Renaart 48, 49, 52, 54, 96, 97,
125, 131, 138, 144, 156–158, 203,
205, 208, 216, 235, 260, 306, 307
Denison, David 87
Doherty, Cathal 172, 175
Dubinsky, Stanley 89

E

Embick, David 5
Emonds, Joseph 88, 186, 296, 304
Enç, Mürvet 96
Ernst, Thomas 55, 103, 269, 276, 295
Erteschick-Shir, Nomi 175
Evans, Bergen 205
Evans, Cornelia 205

F

Farkas, Don 26
Fauconnier, Gilles 227
Felser, Claudia 131
Fiengo, Robert 190, 304, 307
Finer, Daniel L. 30
Fischer, Dlga 332, 333
Fitzmaurice, Susan 97, 118, 119
Foster, Brian 206
Fowler, Henry W. 206
Fox, Danny 58
Franz, Wilhelm 61

G

Gazdar, Gerald 125, 144, 282
Givón, Talmy 258
Groefsema, Marjolein 59
Grous, Alexander 26, 248
Guéron, Jacqeline 170, 172, 193

H

Haegeman, Liliane 170, 172, 193, 206,
224, 227, 269
Halle, Morris 17, 29, 34
Halliday, M. A. K. 61

Harsh, Wayne 156
Hasegawa, Hiroshi 88, 93
Hasegawa, Kinsuke 7, 21, 22, 33, 53, 74, 87, 88, 97, 98, 100, 101, 103, 106, 112, 113, 115–119, 161, 174, 193, 196, 217–220, 233, 235, 241–244, 246–248, 270, 276, 293, 294, 296, 337, 339
Hasegawa, Nobuko 26
Haumann, Dagmar 89
Hayashi, Ryujiro 221
Henry, Alison 197
Higuchi, Masayuki 193
Hiroe, Akira 170, 172
Horn, Lawrence 55
Hojo, Kazuaki 210, 211
Hooper, Joan 258, 327, 328
Hopper, Paul J. 332
Hornby, A. S. 60
Hornstein, Nobert 96
Horvath, Jukia 248
Hosoe, Ttsuki 151, 156, 164, 207, 215, 258, 318
Huddleston, Rodney D. 31

I

Iatridou, Sabine 53, 101, 116, 269, 274, 305
Imai, Kunihiko 95, 157, 196, 221, 255, 329
Imanishi, Noriko 85
Ishihara, Yuki 146
Ishikawa, Kazuhisa 296
Ito, Hiroyuki 137, 138

J

Jackendoff, Ray 88, 296

Jacobson, Pauline 252
James, Francis 26, 156, 162, 258
Jespersen, Otto 88, 99, 147, 151, 153–156, 163, 164, 165, 207, 258, 259, 280, 315, 316
Johnson, Kyle 26, 311

K

Kajita, Masaru 83, 94, 251, 266
Kamata, Seizaburo 67, 82, 134, 138, 147, 191, 290
Kaneko, Yoshiaki 146
Kasai, Ryoji 56
Kashino, Kenji 60–62, 193
Katz, Jerrold J. 196
Kayne, Richard 27, 91, 171
Kempchinsky, Paul 26
Kiparsky, Carol 209
Kiparsky, Paula 209
Kirchner, Gustav 171, 315, 316, 319, 326, 341
Koizumi, Masatoshi 53
Koma, Osamu 279, 316, 324
Konno, Hiroaki 23, 251–255, 258, 262, 265, 266, 339
Kono, Tsuguyo 82–85
Kozu, Harushige 151
Kruisinga, Etsuko 153, 155
Kuno, Susumu 2, 67, 76, 88, 173, 247, 281, 328
Kuwabara, Kazuki 222, 223, 298

L

Laka, Itziar M. 269, 274
Langacker, Ronald W. 32
Larsen-Freeman, Diane 295

Lasnik, Howard 7, 17–20, 63, 75, 78, 85, 94, 113, 169, 172, 196, 245, 295, 336
Leech, Geoffrey N. 48, 54, 134, 157, 199–201, 203, 207, 208, 215
Lees, Robert B. 196
Li, Yen-hui Audrey 107
Lightfoot, David 323
Lobeck, Anne 85, 282, 283, 285, 298, 299
Lyons, John 258

M

Mailing, Joan 25, 248
Marantz, Alec 17, 29, 34
Martin, Roger 63, 75, 78, 80, 81, 85, 87, 88, 93, 94, 96, 336
Matsubara, Fuminori 53, 99, 113, 118, 193, 224, 225, 233, 270–273, 276, 295
Matsui, Chie 210, 211
Matsuyama, Tetsuya 92, 131, 132
May, Robert 107
McCawley, James D. 7, 32, 82, 88, 89, 96, 125, 126, 144, 172, 329
Mihara, Ken-ichi 96
Mitchell, Bruce 152
Mizumoto, Go 297, 300
Mori, Miyuki 55, 273
Murakami, Madoka 25, 27, 170, 172, 174, 175, 203, 224, 229, 236, 253, 269, 270, 273, 276, 280, 291, 295–298, 300, 332
Murasugi, Keiko 80
Murata, Yuzaburo 165, 193

N

Nakajima, Heizo 76, 87, 113, 114, 170, 175, 193, 194, 196, 221
Nakamura, Masaru 88
Nakano, Hirozo 54, 83, 95, 323
Nakao, Toshio 32, 279, 316, 324
Nakau, Minoru 83, 95
Nakazawa, Kazuo 218, 329
Nawata, Hiroyuki 27
Newmeyer, Frederick J. 87
Nomura, Tadao 14, 22, 25, 26, 29, 32, 38, 53, 61, 87, 106, 113, 121, 132, 143, 156, 160, 164, 165, 169, 172, 176, 177, 193, 215, 216, 224, 233, 241, 245, 265, 266, 280, 297, 299, 304, 327, 330, 331, 338
Nomura, Takashi 216
Noyer, Rolf 5

O

Ogawa, Akira 218, 267
Okuno, Tadanori 289, 299
Onions, C. T. 153, 155, 164, 258
Ono, Hayashi 137
Ono, Shigeru 137, 138
Onoe, Keisuke 163, 217
Ota, Akira 54
Ouhalla, Jamal 35, 36, 39, 55, 269, 273, 336
Övergaard, Gerd 160, 206

P

Palmer, Frank F. 31, 60, 151, 164, 207
Papafragou, Anna 59
Pesetsky, David M. 113, 175, 231, 236, 237, 258
Picallo, Carme 26
Pollock, Jean-Yves 5, 6, 10, 21, 25, 27, 38,

53, 55, 87, 97–101, 111, 113, 114, 143, 196, 269, 273, 280, 316, 337
Postal, Paul M. 78, 171, 196
Potsdam, Eric 23, 186–188, 191, 196, 222, 224, 269, 281– 287, 291, 292, 298 –300, 304–306, 310, 311, 313, 327, 330, 340
Poutsma, Hendrik 153–155
Prince, Ellen 77
Progovac, Ljiljana 248

Q

Quirk, Randolph 135, 138, 146, 155–162, 164, 171, 199, 205–208, 215, 230, 235, 253, 306, 307

R

Radford, Andrew 7, 57, 66, 76, 87, 147, 170, 187, 190, 197, 198, 228, 231, 270, 271, 276, 294, 295, 305
Raposo, Eduardo 229
Reichenbach, Hans 96
Reinhart, Tanya 58
Rizzi, Luigi 31, 38, 67, 113, 188, 189, 224, 269, 275, 281, 294–296
Roberts, Ian G. 27, 224, 269, 276, 295, 296, 305, 318, 323
Rohrbacher, Bernard 27
Rosenbach, Anette 332
Rosenbaum, Peter 169
Ross, John R. 32, 77, 93, 231, 281, 294
Rupp, Laura 196, 198

S

Safir, Ken 186

Sag, Ivan A. 82, 85
Saito, Mamoru 78, 80, 94, 113
Sano, Masaki 297, 299
Sawada, Harumi 54, 56, 57, 59–61, 78, 83, 95, 99, 100, 113, 123, 125–131, 141, 144, 145, 147, 151, 193, 196, 207, 217, 220, 233, 270, 276, 295, 337
Schachter, Paul 81
Scheurweghs, Gustaaf 153, 155
Selkrik, Elizabeth 189
Shumaker, Linda 67, 88
Sigurðsson, Halldór Á. 26
Smith, Donald L. 29, 32, 54, 56, 120, 121, 194, 246, 247, 265, 287, 289, 298, 299, 306, 311, 327, 328, 329– 331
Sonnenschein, E. A. 153, 154
Steele, Susan 82, 94, 323
Stowell, Tim 63, 75, 76, 85, 88, 96, 175, 336
Suzuki, Hidekazu 306
Svartvik, Jan 134, 208
Swan, Michael 48, 54, 60, 84, 97, 124, 125, 140, 141, 144, 146, 147, 162, 199, 208, 260
Sweet, Henry 151, 153, 155

T

Takahashi, Daiko 30, 34, 80, 298
Takami, Ken-ichi 2, 76, 173, 193, 247, 281, 327, 328
Terazu, Noriko 82
Terzi, Arhont 233
Thompson, Sandra A. 327, 328
Tokieda, Motoki 60
Tonoike, Shigeo 29, 30, 34, 53–59, 66, 77, 87, 89, 91, 113, 119, 147, 162, 193,

196, 197, 203, 221, 222, 231, 235, 238, 244, 298, 329
Torrego, Esther 113, 231, 236, 237
Traugott, Elizabeth C. 209, 323, 332
Travis, Lisa 36, 99, 276, 294
Tsuchiya, Hiroki 165, 193, 216

U

Uchibori, Asako 26
Ukaji, Masatomo 196, 221, 316, 317, 318, 325, 332

V

Vikner, Sten 27
Visser, F. Th. 165, 166, 209, 315, 316, 318, 319, 326, 341

W

Wada, Shiro 32, 96, 193
Wakatabe, Hiroya 206, 315
Wasow, Thomas 82, 84, 94
Watanabe, Akira 26, 30, 33, 88, 194, 215, 216, 233, 248
Weeda, Don 186, 191, 290, 307
Wexler, Kenneth 171, 229
Wilkins, Wenndy 169, 235
Williams, Edwin 17
Williams, Kemp 89

Y

Yagi, Katsumasa 140, 259, 261
Yasui, Izumi 306
Yasui, Minoru 61

Z

Zandvoort, Reinard W. 155, 308, 319
Zanuttini, Raffaela 38, 220, 269, 274
Zhang, Shi 196
Zwart, C. Jan-Wouter 5, 30
Zwicky, Arnold M. 81

Subject Index

A

A-Movement 4, 57, 58, 281
A'-Movement 4
Absolute Nominative 235
accidental gap 47, 50, 260
Accusative Case 8, 73, 89–92, 228
Accusative Gerund 231
AdvP-in-Spec-Hypothesis 35
Affix Hopping 7, 12–14, 17, 19, 20, 30, 33, 114, 117, 119, 335, 336
AGR 25, 227
Agr 10, 22, 37, 53, 115, 185, 193, 229, 230, 232, 233, 235, 236, 339
AGRoP 37, 38, 100
AGRP 37
AgrP 9, 37, 38, 100, 113, 225
AGRsP 37, 38, 100
ambiguity 80, 173, 314
ambiguous 119–121

B

backshifting of tense 161, 238, 239
bare form 18, 30, 31, 34, 136, 335
Binding Condition 62
Binding Principle 242
Binding Theory 227, 241, 245
blocking 62

C

Case checking 2, 4, 7, 21, 22, 63, 68, 78, 85, 91, 223, 229, 230, 232, 233, 248, 335, 336, 339,
CFC (=Complete Functional Complex) 245
complementizer 10, 30, 68, 72–79, 88, 89, 92, 93, 96, 145, 172, 173, 175 –177, 184, 194, 230, 233, 234, 236–238, 245, 253, 256, 258, 262, 265, 266, 338, 339
Condition of an Underlying Appeal 23, 252, 253, 258, 262, 339
constituent negation 293, 304, 305
contraction 41, 189, 190, 192, 195, 338
control verbs 262

D

disguised subjunctive 207, 215
DC (=Degree of Complexity) 87, 243, 244
default 198, 257, 330
Defective Intervention Constraint (DIC) 31, 294
Deletion 144, 271, 272, 294, 300
deontic verbs 259–261, 263, 340
Displacement 27–29
Distributed Morphology 17, 29, 34
do-support 12, 14, 20, 31, 32, 117, 147, 161, 167, 185, 191, 192, 195, 204, 225, 229, 270, 286, 338
Doubly-filled COMP Filter 176

E

ECP (=Empty Category Principle) 113, 245

emotional *should* 22, 207, 208, 212, 338, 339
epistemic verbs 259, 261–263, 266, 340
EPP 3, 4, 6, 7, 19, 21, 27, 29, 53, 335
equidistance 53, 91
expletive *there* 133

F

Feature Dribbling 8, 11, 13, 20, 29, 69, 71, 73, 180, 182, 183, 335
feature transfer 251, 252
finiteness 87, 88
force 238, 328
formulaic subjunctive 156, 158, 164, 306, 307
Fronting 271, 272
full form 7, 8, 70, 134, 139, 180
functional approach 2, 76, 173
functional conditions 337, 338
Functional Head Constraint 294
Functional Verb Elements 7, 11, 20, 30, 34, 335

G

GB Theory 2, 89, 113, 128, 245
Generalized A-over-A Principle (GAoA) 244, 294
generative semantics 32, 145, 329
Genitive Case 228
Gerund 235
governing category 245
grammaticalization 175, 320, 332, 333

H

harmonic system of the English modals 50

have-be raising 5, 23, 223, 303, 325, 330, 340
Head-Head 9, 20, 230, 335
Head Movement 4, 5, 6, 19–21, 58, 277, 335
Head Movement Constraint (HMC) 31, 99, 276–278
hortative subjunctive 328
hybrid 7, 15, 18, 335

I

imperative 151, 153, 182, 193, 195–198, 204, 221, 222, 229, 328, 338
Inclusiveness Condition 31
indicative 151, 153–155, 162–165, 167, 169, 173, 174, 177, 181, 183, 187–189, 194, 195, 203, 204, 206, 208, 222, 228, 229, 239, 256–258, 266, 269, 283, 291, 303, 316, 317, 324, 326, 338, 340, 341

L

lexicalist 15–17, 33, 34
lexical redundancy rule 93, 119
Lexical Verb Elements 7, 10, 11, 20, 30, 34, 335
LF 4, 33, 241, 245
licensing condition on VP-deletion 269, 291, 292
Licensing Conditions on Deletion 285
Long Distance Binding 248

M

manner-of-speaking verbs 92
marginally marked word order 309, 314,

325, 326
Minimalist Program 1, 2, 16, 26, 27, 29, 37, 75, 113, 195, 218, 234, 245, 298
Minimal Link Condition (MLC) 31, 294
mirror image 56
Modal-derived structure 44, 45
Modal-underlying structure 44
Modal Criteria 31
modality 22, 83, 149, 151, 162–164, 337
modally marked forms 165, 166
Modal Negation 1, 21, 35, 40, 42–52, 58, 59, 61, 62, 225, 336
ModalP Hypothesis 1, 21, 35, 38, 39, 43, 45, 52, 62, 179, 225, 236, 237, 335, 336, 341
mood 10, 22, 25, 27, 35, 149, 150, 151, 153 –156, 160, 162–165, 181, 193, 204, 217, 218, 229, 236–238, 258, 337
morphologically identifiable head 285, 290
morphologically realized Head 285, 286, 290
morphologically realized Spec 285, 286, 290
Move 19

N

narrow syntax 5, 17, 19–21, 32, 335
Negative Inversion (NI) 188, 189, 192, 194, 338
Negative Islands 281
Negative Polarity Item (NPI) 5
NEGP 37
NegP 23, 35, 37, 38, 39, 42, 52, 53, 55, 269 –271, 273, 275, 278, 280, 290, 292– 294, 336, 340
NICE properties 31

Nominative Case 2, 3, 8, 9, 11, 19, 20, 22, 92, 181, 182, 197, 198, 223, 228– 233, 236, 245, 248, 335, 339
non-bridge verbs 173, 174
non-cooccurrence of modals 338
non-localizable 251, 253
Nonfinite Tense 63, 68, 74, 85, 336, 238
not 5, 13, 21, 23, 33, 39, 40, 42–44, 54, 65, 81, 97, 116, 117, 123, 191, 269 – 271, 273, 276–278, 280–284, 290 –295, 297, 299, 300, 305, 309, 326, 328–330, 336, 337, 340
nouniness 77, 93
NP-Movement 2, 4, 6, 7, 19, 20, 77, 92, 248, 335
Null Case 8, 68, 72, 74, 75, 88, 262, 261

O

Objective-Subjective Transfer Model 60
Oblique Case 8, 68, 70
optative 151, 156, 164, 184, 230, 253, 256, 257, 265, 339

P

putative *should* 207
Parsing Condition 80, 173, 177, 338
Participle Construction 231
perceptual 76, 79
PF 7, 8, 12–14, 16, 18–20, 29, 134, 139
phonetically deleted 79, 172, 173, 175, 177, 256, 338
phonetic *that*-deletion 169, 337
phonological component (PF) 4, 5, 335
phrasal constituency 271
phrasal constituent 272
picture nouns 242, 246, 247, 339

place-holder modals 204
placeholder auxiliary 212, 216, 338
Positive Polarity Items (PPI) 59
pragmatically unacceptable examples 287
presumed finiteness 244
preterite-present verb 146
Principle of the Inviolability of Epistemic Modality 47, 59
Principles and Parameters (P & P) Theory 1, 26, 28, 220, 223
Propositional Negation 35, 40, 42, 44–52, 55, 58, 61, 62, 225, 270, 271,
PrP (=Predication Phrase) 139, 147, 290, 299
pseudo-cleft sentences 129
putative *should* 215

Q

quasi-subjunctive 22, 160, 161, 186, 194, 199–203, 205, 207, 208, 212, 215, 223, 226, 338, 339,

R

raising verbs 262
reflex 3, 8, 19, 70, 181, 182, 237, 238, 335
reflexive pronouns 198, 242, 245, 248, 339
Relativized Minimality 31, 294, 295
Rich Agreement Hypothesis 27
root form 16, 30, 136, 161, 166, 185, 190, 196, 205, 225, 226, 238, 304, 338

S

Sc (=Small Clause) 147, 231
scope 21, 44, 35, 55, 56, 106, 336, 337
self-controllable 67, 68, 88

semantically empty 22, 204, 212, 217, 257, 262, 338, 339
semantically more important information 173, 174
Semantically Transparent Condition 173, 177, 327, 338
semantic condition 23, 36, 121, 251, 253, 255, 257, 260, 262, 266, 304, 309, 314, 325, 339, 340,
sentential negation 23, 40, 55, 101, 303–307, 309, 314, 325, 327, 328, 340,
sequencing of tenses 238, 239
Seven Formal Characteristics of Modals 15, 126, 146, 333
should-deletion 22, 209, 210, 212, 213, 217, 218, 339
sister relation 29, 91
Sluicing 300
Spec-Head 19, 20, 39, 89, 335
speech act verb 331
Split-I Hypothesis 37, 100, 143, 269
split infinitives 118
Split VP Hypothesis 37, 53
Subject-Aux Inversion (SAI) 5, 188, 189
substitute modals for mood 204
substitution theory 218
successive cyclic 26, 92, 243
Superiority Condition 294
syntactic conditions 23, 251, 256, 262, 266, 339

T

tag question 41, 48, 55
temporal semantics 96
Tensed-S Condition (TSC) 22, 87, 228, 229, 234, 235, 241–243, 245, 247,

339
that-deletion 169, 173–175, 177, 338
that-trace effect 113, 234
three formal characteristics of the subjunctive present 161, 162, 185, 192, 225, 231, 337–339
Topicalization 188, 194, 327, 328
transformationalist 16, 34

U

uniformity of syntactic structures 172, 222, 270
uninterpretable 3, 7, 9, 19, 28, 27, 30, 134, 139, 182, 236–238, 335,
unmarked word order 309, 314
unspecified desirable future event 23, 258, 262, 266, 340
Unspecified Person 63, 69, 71, 85, 336

V

V-movement 6, 7, 15, 19–21, 328, 335
verb phrase negation 21, 40, 49, 50, 101, 337
VP-deletion 18, 20, 21, 23, 33, 63, 66, 67, 80, 81, 83, 85, 88, 94, 100, 113, 191, 192, 195, 204, 269, 282, 283, 285–287, 289–292, 299, 337, 338, 340
VP-preposing 96
VP Internal Subject Hypothesis 56
V raising 236

W

were-subjunctive 156, 234
wh-island constraint 31, 87, 244
wh-movement 4, 19, 26, 53, 243, 244, 281

X

XP-Movement 4, 7, 20, 281, 335

【著者紹介】

野村 忠央 (のむら ただお)

和光大学表現学部文学科専任講師・博士（文学）.
　1972 年 北海道生まれ.
　1996 年 学習院大学文学部英米文学科卒業.
　1998 年 青山学院大学大学院文学研究科英米文学専攻博士
　　　　前期課程修了.
　2005 年 青山学院大学大学院文学研究科英米文学専攻博士
　　　　後期課程修了. 博士（文学）（博英甲第 1 号）
　2003 年より現職.

【主要論文】「命令的接続法節に現れる should について」（『英語語法文法研究』第 6 号），「シェイクスピアにおける法助動詞 MAY と主観化」（『近代英語研究』第 17 号），「仮定法現在節における＜ have・be ＋ not ＞語順再考」（『英語青年』2004 年 2 月号）.

Hituzi Linguistics in English No. 3

ModalP and Subjunctive Present

発行	2006 年 2 月 28 日　初版 1 刷
定価	15000 円＋税
著者	ⓒ 野村 忠央
発行者	松本　功
装丁	向井裕一（glyph）
印刷所	三美印刷株式会社
製本所	田中製本印刷株式会社
発行所	株式会社 ひつじ書房
	〒 112-0002 東京都文京区小石川 5-21-5
	Tel.03-5684-6871　Fax.03-5684-6872
	郵便振替 00120-8-142852
	toiawase@hituzi.co.jp　http://www.hituzi.co.jp/

ISBN4-89476-267-6　C3082

造本には充分注意しておりますが，落丁・乱丁などがございましたら，小社かお買上げ書店にておとりかえいたします．ご意見，ご感想など，小社までお寄せ下されば幸いです．

Hituzi Linguistics in English

No. 1　Lexical Borrowing and its Impact on English
　　　　Makimi Kimura-Kano　8400YEN

No. 2　From a Subordinate Clause to an Independent Clause
　　　　Yuko Higashiizumi　13440YEN

No. 3　ModalP and Subjunctive Present
　　　　Tadao Nomura 15750YEN